THE DEFENCE OF 'OBEDIENCE TO SUPERIOR ORDERS'

THE DEFENCE OF 'OBEDIENCE TO SUPERIOR ORDERS' IN INTERNATIONAL LAW

by

YORAM DINSTEIN

A reprinted edition with a new Postscript Preface

OXFORD
UNIVERSITY PRESS

OXFORD
UNIVERSITY PRESS

Great Clarendon Street, Oxford, OX2 6DP,
United Kingdom

Oxford University Press is a department of the University of Oxford.
It furthers the University's objective of excellence in research, scholarship,
and education by publishing worldwide. Oxford is a registered trade mark of
Oxford University Press in the UK and in certain other countries

Reprinted Edition published in 2012

Published in the United States of America by Oxford University Press
198 Madison Avenue, New York, NY 10016, United States of America

British Library Cataloguing in Publication Data
Data available

ISBN 978–0–19–967081–9

TABLE OF CONTENTS

PART IV: THE CASES

PART V: INTERNATIONAL LEGISLATION SINCE 1946

TABLE OF CASES

NEW CASES CITED IN POSTSCRIPT PREFACE

LIST OF ABBREVIATIONS

A.B.A.J. – American Bar Association Journal.
A.D. – Annual Digest and Reports of Public International Law Cases.
A.J.I.L. – American Journal of International Law.
A.P.S.R. – American Political Science Review.
A.S.I.L. – Proceedings of the American Society of International Law.
Bellot, 'Punishment' – Bellot, 'War Crimes: Their Prevention and Punishment', *T.G.S.*, vol. 2 (1917), pp. 31–55.
Bellot, 'War Criminals' – Bellot, 'War Crimes and War Criminals', *C.L.T.*, vols. 36 (1916), pp. 754–768, 876–886; 37 (1917), pp. 9–22.
B.Y.B.I.L. – British Year Book of International Law.
C.L.R. – California Law Review.
C.L.T. – Canadian Law Times.
Clunet – Journal du Droit International.
C.M.A.I. – Cursos Monograficos, Academia Interamericana de Derecho Comparado e Internacional.
Cmd. – Command Papers.
Colby, 'War Crimes' – Colby, 'War Crimes', *Mich. L.R.*, vol. 23 (1924–1925), pp. 482–511, 606–634.
C.R. Report – Commission on the Responsibilities of the Authors of the War and on Enforcement of Penalties – Report, 29 March 1919 – *A.J.I.L.*, vol. 14 (1920), pp. 95–154.
C.Y.B.I.L. – Czechoslovak Yearbook of International Law.
Dalloz – Recueil Dalloz (Analytique et Critique) de Doctrine de Jurisprudence et de Législation.
Donnedieu de Vabres, 'Nuremberg' – Donnedieu de Vabres, 'Le Procès de Nuremberg devant les Principes Modernes du Droit Pénal International', *R.A.D.I.*, vol. 70 (1947), pp. 477–582.
ECOSOC – Economic and Social Council.
Eustathiades, 'Ordres' – Eustathiades, 'Quelques Aspects de la Jurisprudence concernants les Criminels de Guerre: l'Exception des Ordres Reçus et Autres Moyens de Défense Similaires', *Gegenwartsprobleme des Internationalen Rechtes und der Rechtsphilosophie* (1953), pp. 395–421.
Finch, 'Superior Orders' – Finch, 'Superior Orders and War Crimes', *A.J.I.L.*, vol. 15 (1921), pp. 440–445.
For. Aff. – Foreign Affairs.
G.A. – General Assembly.
Garner, 'Articles' – Garner, 'Recent Important Articles from Scientific Journals', *A.P.S.R.*, vol. 14 (1920), pp. 137–143.
Garner, *International Law* – Garner, *International Law and the World War* (1920).
Garner, 'Punishment' – Garner, 'Punishment of Offenders against the Laws and Customs of War', *A.J.I.L.*, vol. 14 (1920), pp. 70–94.
German Views – *Nuremberg, German Views of the War Trials* (ed. by Benton and Grimm, 1955).
Glaser, *Introduction* – Glaser, *Introduction à l'Etude du Droit International Pénal* (1954).
Glaser, 'L'Ordre' – Glaser, 'L'Ordre Hiérarchique en Droit Pénal International', *R.D.P.C.*, vol. 33 (1952–1953), pp. 283–330.

Glaser, 'Nuremberg' – Glaser, 'La Charte du Tribunal de Nuremberg et les Nouveaux Principes du Droit International', *R.P.S.*, vol. 63 (1948), pp. 13–38.
G.L.J. – Georgetown Law Journal.
Glueck, *War Criminals* – Glueck, *War Criminals, their Prosecution and Punishment* (1944).
Graven, 'Code' – Graven, 'Principes Fondamentaux d'un Code Répressif des Crimes contre la Paix et la Sécurité de l'Humanité', *I.L.R.*, vol. 28 (1950), pp. 173–204, 361–392.
Graven, 'Crimes' – Graven, 'Les Crimes contre l'Humanité', *R.A.D.I.*, vol. 76 (1950), pp. 433–607.
Gros, *Symposium* – Gros, Address in a Symposium on the subject of 'The Responsibility of Governments and their Agencies in International Law', *Mishpat Vekalkala*, vol. 1 (1955), pp. 130–151.
Higgins – Hall, *International Law* – Hall, *A Treatise on International Law* (8th ed., by Higgins, 1924).
History of U.N.W.C.C. – *History of the United Nations War Crimes Commission and the Development of the Laws of War* (1948).
H.L.R. – Harvard Law Review.
I.C.L.Q. – International and Comparative Law Quarterly.
I.L.A. – Reports of the Conferences of the International Law Association.
I.L.C. – International Law Commission.
I.L.R. – International Law Review (Revue de Droit International, de Sciences Diplomatiques et Politiques).
I.L.Q. – International Law Quarterly.
I.M.T. – *Trial of the Major War Criminals before the International Military Tribunal.*
Int. Aff. – International Affairs.
Int. Con. – International Conciliation.
International Conference – *International Conference on Military Trials, London, 1945* (ed. by Jackson, 1949).
J.C.L.C. – Journal of Criminal Law and Criminology.
J. Rev. – Juridical Review.
J.S.C.L.I.L. – Journal of the Society of Comparative Legislation and International Law.
J.Y.B.I.L. – Jewish Yearbook of International Law.
Kelsen, 'Acts of State' – Kelsen, 'Collective and Individual Responsibility for Acts of State in International Law', *J.Y.B.I.L.*, 1948, pp. 226–239.
Kelsen, *Peace* – Kelsen, *Peace through Law* (1944).
Kelsen, *Principles* – Kelsen, *Principles of International Law* (1952).
Kelsen, 'Responsibility' – Kelsen, 'Collective and Individual Responsibility in International Law with Particular Regard to the Punishment of War Criminals', *C.L.R.*, vol. 31 (1942–1943), pp. 530–571.
Kelsen, *Theory* – Kelsen, *General Theory of Law and State* (3rd printing, 1949).
Lauterpacht, 'War Crimes' – Lauterpacht, 'The Law of Nations and the Punishment of War Crimes', *B.Y.B.I.L.*, vol. 21 (1944), pp. 58–95.
Lauterpacht – Oppenheim, *International Law* – Oppenheim, *International Law, a Treatise* (5th ed. *et seq.* by Lauterpacht).
L.G.R. – Lawyers Guild Review.
Liang, 'Notes' – Liang, 'Notes on Legal Questions concerning the United Nations: The Second Session of the International Law Commission: Review of its Work by the General Assembly', *A.J.I.L.*, vol. 45 (1951), pp. 509–525.
L.Q.R. – Law Quarterly Review.
L.R.U.N.W.C.C. – *Law Reports of Trials of War Criminals, Selected and Prepared by the United Nations War Crimes Commission* (1947–1949).

Mérignhac, 'Sanction' – Mérignhac, 'De la Sanction des Infractions au Droit des Gens Commises, au Cours de la Guerre Européenne, par les Empires du Centre', *R.G.D.I.P.*, vol. 24 (1917), pp. 5–56.

Mich. L.R. – Michigan Law Review.

Minn. L.R. – Minnesota Law Review.

Mod. L.R. – Modern Law Review.

Morgan, *Assize* – Morgan, *The Great Assize, an Examination of the Law of the Nuremberg Trials* (1948).

Morgan, 'Nuremberg' – Morgan, 'Nuremberg and After', *Q. Rev.*, vol. 285 (1947), pp. 318–336, 605–625.

N.L.G. Report – National Lawyers Guild – Report Adopted by the National Executive Board on the Punishment of War Criminals, 16 December 1944 – *L.G.R.*, vol. 4 (1944), pp. 18–23.

N.M.T. – *Trials of War Criminals before the Nuernberg Military Tribunals under Control Council Law No. 10, 1946–1949* (1950).

O.R. – Official Records.

People's Verdict – *The People's Verdict, a Full Report of the Proceedings at the Krasnodar and Kharkov German Atrocity Trials.*

Phillipson – Wheaton, *International Law* – Wheaton, *Elements of International Law* (5th English ed., rev. enl. and rewritten by Phillipson, 1916).

P.S.Q. – Political Science Quarterly.

Q. Rev. – Quarterly Review.

R.A.D.I. – Recueil des Cours de l'Académie de Droit International.

R.D.I.L.C. – Revue de Droit International et de Législation Comparée.

R.D.P.C. – Revue de Droit Pénal et de Criminologie.

Red Cross Commentary – *Commentary on the Geneva Conventions of 12 August 1949* (ed. by Pictet, 1952).

R.G.D.I.P. – Revue Générale de Droit International Public.

R.I.D.P. – Revue Internationale de Droit Pénal.

R.P.D.P. – Revue Pénitentiaire et de Droit Pénal (Bulletin de la Société Générale des Prisons).

R.P.S. – Revue Pénale Suisse (Schweizerische Zeitschrift für Strafrecht).

R.S.C.D.P.C. – Revue de Science Criminelle et de Droit Pénal Comparé.

Sack, 'Punishment' – Sack, 'Punishment of War Criminals and the Defence of Superior Order', *L.Q.R.*, vol. 60 (1944), pp. 63–68.

Sack, 'Superior Order' – Sack, 'War Criminals and the Defense of Superior Order in International Law', *L.G.R.*, vol. 5 (1945), pp. 11–17.

Schick, 'Nuremberg' – Schick, 'The Nuremberg Trial and the Development of an International Criminal Law', *J. Rev.*, vol. 59 (1947), pp. 192–207.

Schick, 'War Criminals' – Schick, 'War Criminals and the Law of the United Nations', *T.L.J.*, vol. 7 (1947–1948), pp. 27–67.

Schwarzenberger, 'Inductive Approach' – Schwarzenberger, 'The Inductive Approach to International Law', *H.L.R.*, vol. 60 (1946–1947), pp. 539–570.

Schwarzenberger, *Lawlessness* – Schwarzenberger, *International Law and Totalitarian Lawlessness* (1943).

Schwarzenberger, 'War Crimes' – Schwarzenberger, 'War Crimes and the Problem of an International Criminal Court', *C.Y.B.I.L.*, 1942, pp. 67–88.

S.G. Memorandum – Memorandum Submitted by the Secretary General of the United Nations on the Charter and Judgment of the Nürnberg Tribunal, History and Analysis, 3 March 1949 (A/CN.4/5).

S.J.L.R. – St. John's Law Review.

H. Smith, 'Nuremberg' – H. Smith, 'The Nuremberg Trials', *Free Europe*, vol. 13 (1946), pp. 201–204.

Spiropoulos, 'Code (1st Report)' – Spiropoulos, '(First) Report on a Draft Code of Offences against the Peace and Security of Mankind', 26 April 1950 (A/CN.4/25) – *I.L.C. Yearbook*, 1950, vol. 2, pp. 253–278.

Spiropoulos, 'Code (2nd Report)' – Spiropoulos, 'Second Report on a Draft Code of Offences against the Peace and Security of Mankind', 12 April 1951 (A/CN.4/44) – *I.L.C. Yearbook*, 1951, vol. 2, pp. 43–69.

Spiropoulos, 'Code (3rd Report)' – Spiropoulos, 'Third Report relating to a Draft Code of Offences against the Peace and Security of Mankind', 30 April 1954 (A/CN.4/85) (mimeographed).

Spiropoulos, 'Principles' – Spiropoulos, 'Report on the Formulation of the Nürnberg Principles', 12 April 1950 (A/CN.4/22) – *I.L.C. Yearbook*, 1950, vol. 2, pp. 181–195.

Tex. L.R. – Texas Law Review.

T.G.S. – (Transactions of) Grotius Society.

T.L.J. – University of Toronto Law Journal.

T.L.R. – Tulane Law Review.

V.L.R. – Virginia Law Review.

W.C.T.S. – War Crimes Trials Series (ed. by Maxwell-Fyfe, 1948–1951).

Winfield – Lawrence, *International Law* – Lawrence, *The Principles of International Law* (7th ed., rev. by Winfield, 1931).

Y.B.W.A. – Year Book of World Affairs.

UNITED NATIONS DOCUMENT SYMBOLS

A – General Assembly.
AC – Ad Hoc Committee.
BUR – General Committee of the General Assembly.
C – Committee.
CN – Commission.
E – Economic and Social Council.

POSTSCRIPT PREFACE FOR REPRINTED EDITION

I. PROLEGOMENA

A.

The book reprinted here is based on a doctoral thesis submitted to the Hebrew University in Jerusalem and approved in 1964. In 1965, the dissertation was published in Hebrew (by Magnes Press) and later in English (by A.W. Sijthoff in Leiden). The English version drew quite a few positive reviews worldwide in diverse languages. Over the years, it has been cited and quoted extensively in scholarly literature and also in judgments delivered by courts (notably, the Supreme Court of Canada).[1]

I must confess that not every citation of the book has uniformly elated me. On various occasions, I discovered to my consternation that my message did not get across. I felt that I needed an opportunity to recapitulate in a more limpid fashion my views on sundry thorny issues. The notion of producing some sort of a postscript, highlighting the gist of my thesis and adding a terse update, therefore attracted me long ago.

The trouble was that by the time I came to entertain these thoughts, Sijthoff had virtually disappeared from the international legal scene. Thus matters stood for almost half a century. Then, in 2011, an exceedingly complimentary review essay appeared in the *Journal of International Criminal Justice* by Professor Robert Cryer of the University of Birmingham[2] (whom I had not even met at that stage). The review ends with a strong recommendation for reissuing the book. There was a ripple effect, and John Louth, Editor-in-Chief of Academic Law Books at Oxford University Press, took up the challenge. Here is the result.

B.

The genesis of my interest in the plea of obedience to superior orders was a Master's thesis that I wrote at the Hebrew University in 1958.

1. *R v. Finta* (1994) 112 *Dominion Law Reports* (4th Series) 513.
2. R. Cryer, 'Superior Scholarship on Superior Orders', (2011) 9 *Journal of International Criminal Justice*, pp. 959–72.

My chosen theme was the historical Judgment rendered by the International Military Tribunal at Nuremberg in 1946. I graduated *summa cum laude* and was much encouraged by my supervisor, Professor Nathan Feinberg, to continue with the research on Nuremberg and its legal repercussions. When (a year later) I enrolled as a candidate for the doctoral degree, I knew that I wanted to examine more closely the defence pleas raised by counsel for the accused at Nuremberg and rejected by the International Military Tribunal. What I was less confident about was which aspect of the defence strategy I wanted most to tackle: initially I toyed with the idea of concentrating on the 'act of State' doctrine. In any event, I did not advance too far with the project right away. I was otherwise engaged: as a law clerk at the Israel Supreme Court, and later a cadet at the Ministry of Foreign Affairs, serving simultaneously as an Assistant at the Hebrew University (not even in international law).

I got into my stride only in New York. In 1960, I accepted a generous offer of a scholarship enabling me to study full-time for the LL.M. degree in international law at the New York University School of Law. I graduated in 1961 and lingered in New York for another year under the aegis of the Israel Mission to the United Nations. Throughout the two-year period of my stay in the city, I tapped the rich lode of the NYU Law Library (complementing it, when a gap occurred, with the resources of other institutions nearby), delving into books and journals not then readily available in Israel. It must be kept in mind that in those days there were no digital data bases: even the Xerox photocopying technique was a recent invention. Ergo, everything had to be done manually. I filled dozens of hefty notebooks with longhand verbatim quotations from an abundance of sources—on both obedience to superior orders and the 'act of State' doctrine—plus ruminative (not always coherent) scrawls of my own on the back of almost every page.

Fortunately, the NYU Law School allowed me some independent research as part of my LL.M. requirements. I accordingly submitted an embryonic paper on obedience to superior orders to Professor Albert Garretson. The paper met with resounding success: Garretson even shared it with several colleagues and urged me to publish a properly edited modification as a law review article. I eventually declined on the ground that such a move would be premature, inasmuch as I still had to wrestle with a slew of difficulties with which the subject was fraught. But the positive response served to stoke my interest in forging ahead with this particular motif, discarding 'act of State'. When I returned to Israel in 1962, the Eichmann trial had just come to an end. If in 1959 obedience to superior orders had only a tepid appeal to me, in 1962 I found it irresistible. Now that I was moderately familiar with the legal landscape, I felt that I could contribute to improving its architecture.

My old-new mentor at the Hebrew University, Feinberg (who had earlier tried to dampen my enthusiasm for 'act of State'), warmly welcomed this development. We met regularly, and he was quite pleased with my progress reports about the wrinkles that I was in the process of ironing out in 1962/3. Feinberg's sole, mildly phrased admonition was that I was gradually growing more iconoclastic in my dissection of treatises carrying the names of pre-eminent figures in the field of international law. It is true that doctoral students are supposed to demonstrate original thinking, he said, but perhaps I was overdoing it. I had to assure Feinberg of my genuine veneration (which has not abated to this day) for such revered names as Lassa Oppenheim and Hans Kelsen. Regrettably and with sincere due respect, after prolonged exploration of both theory and practice, I could not avoid disagreeing with their points of view regarding pivotal questions underlying my study. Feinberg did not persist, and I was given a free hand. Yet, when I submitted my final draft, the same issue was brought up *de novo* (with even greater emphasis) by one of the external examiners. I was not privy to the confidential exchange of views, but I have been reliably informed that it was only thanks to Feinberg that the dissertation was approved without alterations.

It was Feinberg who immediately thereafter submitted my disquisition to Magnes Press for publication in Hebrew. He also commenced to exert moral pressure on me—now that I had obtained my prerequisite doctoral degree—to forsake the foreign service and join the groves of Academe. After some meanderings on my part, I opted for the career realignment that he had set his mind on. I cherish his memory as my principal academic tutor.

As soon as the Hebrew manuscript was in the hands of the printers, I began recasting my thesis in English. Here I was lucky: at the Foreign Ministry I got to know Ambassador Max Nurock, then the *arbiter elegantiae* in charge of English recension of all the Ministry's communiqués. He kindly took me under his wing, going through my *oeuvre* and showering on me indispensable guidance concerning the intricacies of English usage and style. Ever since, when I write in English, I have his didactic image vividly engraved on my mind.

Upon completion of the English redaction, I turned to Ambassador Shabtai Rosenne who had been for a while my superior in the Foreign Ministry and who became another life-long mentor (I subsequently had the privilege of editing a *Festschrift* in his honour).[3] Rosenne liked what he saw, took the initiative, and got the book accepted for publication by Sijthoff. He even volunteered to add a short introduction by way of endorsement.

I only wish that Feinberg, Rosenne, Garretson, and Nurock could have seen this handsome new edition.

II. THE *MENS REA* PRINCIPLE

The main thrust of the present study was to propose a new outlook on the age-old problem of obedience to superior orders, which has served as an excuse for countless subordinates (whether military or civilian) accused of war crimes.[4] I advocated my innovative approach as a substitute for two diametrically opposed precepts that had dominated the scene heretofore. The older school of thought, associated with the name of Oppenheim, was *respondeat superior*, whereby obedience to superior orders constitutes a full defence in war crimes trials, bringing about an automatic transference of accountability from the subordinate to his commanders (see pp. 38–48)[5]. At the other end of the spectrum stood the more contemporary postulate of absolute liability, according to which obedience to superior orders should play no role at all in appraising the guilt of the defendant in the dock, regardless of any defence plea put forward (see pp. 68–75). The latter doctrine gained the upper hand in the formulation of Article 8 of the 1945 London Charter of the International Military Tribunal, the linchpin of the proceedings at Nuremberg (see pp. 117–18). Contrary to what many scholars seem to believe, when the Tribunal delivered its Judgment the following year, it sustained *in toto* this stern posture (see p. 156).

After protracted inner struggles, I felt compelled to brandish a new banner. This was not a neutral, a-plague-on-both-your-houses, stance. I utterly sympathized with the desire of the proponents of absolute liability to make short shrift of *respondeat superior.* The insight that my research provided was that obedience to superior orders

3. Y. Dinstein (ed.), *International Law at a Time of Perplexity: Essays in Honour of Shabtai Rosenne* (1989).

4. The plea of obedience to superior orders can be (and has been) invoked with respect to other international crimes, not only war crimes (see p. 1). For reasons of simplicity, I shall refer generically to war crimes in this Postscript Preface.

5. Citations of Arabic numbered pages are linked to the pages of the reprinted edition. Roman numbers interconnect with the sections of the Postscript Preface.

could not qualify as an admissible defence relieving the perpetrator of a crime from personal accountability. But I was unable to come to terms with the rigidity of absolute liability, notwithstanding the imprimatur stamped on it by the International Military Tribunal. I arrived at the conclusion that, when later jurisprudence is probed in depth, many of the judgments may be construed in a manner conducive to a more nuanced perspective which I called 'the *mens rea* principle'. I crafted this principle in the following way:

> 'the fact of obedience to orders constitutes not a defence *per se* but only a factual element that may be taken into account in conjunction with the other circumstances of the given case within the compass of a defence based on lack of *mens rea*, that is, mistake of law or fact or compulsion' (see p. 88).

Obviously, in 1965, the *mens rea* principle could merely be advanced as a novel conception, striving to finesse the post-World War II legal developments by pushing the boundaries of absolute liability. I could not contend that this construct had already entrenched itself in the existing jurisprudence. All that I submitted was that the principle was reconcilable with critical segments of both theory and practice (see pp. 88, 214).

After publication of the book, the *mens rea* principle found favour with a fairly large number of scholars, but there was no resonant approbation of my way of thinking in the case law. Then, in 1997, in *Erdemović*, the Joint Separate Opinion of Judges McDonald and Vohrah—speaking for the majority of the Appeals Chamber of the International Criminal Tribunal for the former Yugoslavia (ICTY)—stated unequivocally:

> 'We subscribe to the view that obedience to superior orders does not amount to a defence *per se* but is a factual element which may be taken into consideration in conjunction with other circumstances of the case in assessing whether the defences of duress or mistake of fact are made out.'[6]

Surprisingly, although the present book was referred to in another context by another judge in *Erdemović* (see section VI below), no direct credit was given where credit was due.[7] All the same, there is such a

6. *Prosecutor v. Erdemović* (Sentencing Appeal) (ICTY, Appeals Chamber, 1997), 111 *International Law Reports* 298, 333.

7. Let it be recorded, however, that a month before the *Erdemović* judgment was rendered, Judge McDonald had invited me to contribute the chapter on defences ('specifically superior orders, duress and official position') to a multi-volume tome that she was going to publish on international criminal law, alerting me to the forthcoming *Erdemović* decision and promising to send me the judges' opinions as soon as they were made public. In that chapter, I overtly drew attention to the origin of the *Erdemović* locution on obedience to superior orders. See Y. Dinstein, 'Defences', in G.K. McDonald and O. Swaak-Goldman (eds), *Substantive and Procedural Aspects of*

degree of correspondence between the language in which the passage as quoted is couched and my own turn of phrase that no room for doubt is left about the provenance of the view to which the majority subscribed.

The quintessence of *mens rea* in international criminal law is irrefutable. Its centre-stage place as a *sine qua non* condition of every penal prosecution is enshrined in Article 30 of the Rome Statute of the International Criminal Court concluded in 1998: this provision (entitled '[m]ental element') rests on the two classical pillars of intent and knowledge.[8]

III. ARTICLE 33(1) OF THE ROME STATUTE

Following the general prescription of Article 30, the Rome Statute goes on to enumerate specific grounds for excluding criminal responsibility. Appropriately, Articles 31 and 32 (analysed in sections IV to VI below) dwell, inter alia, upon mistake of fact, mistake of law, and duress. However, then comes Article 33(1), which promulgates:

> '1. The fact that a crime within the jurisdiction of the Court has been committed by a person pursuant to an order of a government or of a superior, whether military or civilian, shall not relieve that person of responsibility unless:
> (a) The person was under a legal obligation to obey orders of the government or the superior in question;
> (b) The person did not know that the order was unlawful; and
> (c) The order was not manifestly unlawful.'[9]

What this clause implies is that, although, as a rule, obedience to superior orders does not qualify as a defence *per se*, an exceptional situation arises when three cumulative conditions are fulfilled. These are the existence of a legal obligation to obey orders, the lack of knowledge of the illegality of the order, and the fact that the order is not manifestly unlawful. Criminal accountability is then quashed on the ground of obedience to superior orders as such.

Suffice it to juxtapose the Rome text with the Nuremberg Principles, outlined by the International Law Commission in 1950 (see p. 237), to realize that Article 33(1) represents a complete break with

International Criminal Law: The Experience of International and National Courts, vol.1, pp. 371, 379 (2000).

8. Rome Statute of the International Criminal Court, 1998, [1998] *United Nations Juridical Yearbook* 294, 310.
9. *Ibid.*, 311.

the Nuremberg legacy of absolute liability. As may be expected, there have been adaptations of the law governing obedience to superior orders over the decades since Nuremberg. But, when these are stitched together, the dissonant note struck by Article 33(1) becomes even more grating. In 1996, the International Law Commission presented the final version of the Draft Code of Crimes against the Peace and Security of Mankind, where it basically reiterated the language of Article 8 of the London Charter.[10] More poignantly, the Security Council set forth in 1993–4 the Statutes of two ad hoc international criminal tribunals, one for the former Yugoslavia (ICTY) and the other for Rwanda (ICTR). In both Statutes there are lucid parallel stipulations on obedience to superior orders (Article 7(4) of the ICTY Statute[11] and Article 6(4) of the ICTR)[12] following in the same footsteps. If that is not enough, Article 2 of the 1984 United Nations Convention against Torture lays down *tout court* that '[a]n order from a superior officer or a public authority may not be invoked as a justification of torture'.[13]

When all the pre-1998 paraphrases are adumbrated as a backdrop for Article 33(1), it is not easy to figure out where this bolt from the blue came from.[14] But, curiously, similar constituent elements (looked at from an inverse baseline angle) appear in the following instructions given by the military judge in the American court-martial proceedings in the Vietnam War (My Lai) *Calley* case of 1971:

> 'The acts of a subordinate done in compliance with an unlawful order given him by his superior are excused and impose no criminal liability upon him unless the superior's order is one which a man of ordinary sense and understanding would, under the circumstances, know to be unlawful, or if the order in question is actually known to the accused to be unlawful.'[15]

10. Draft Code of Crimes against the Peace and Security of Mankind, Report of the International Law Commission, 48th Session, [1996] II (2) *Yearbook of the International Law Commission* 17, 23(Article 5).
11. Report of the Secretary-General Pursuant to Paragraph 2 of Security Council Resolution 808, (1993) 32 *International Legal Materials* 1163, 1175.
12. United Nations Security Council Resolution 955 Establishing the International Tribunal for Rwanda, (1994) 33 *International Legal Materials* 1598, 1605.
13. Convention against Torture and Other Cruel, Inhuman or Degrading Treatment or Punishment, 1984, [1984] *United Nations Juridical Yearbook* 135, 136.
14. Technically, it came from the Preparatory Committee on the Establishment of the International Criminal Court. See O. Triffterer, 'Superior Orders and Prescription of Law', in O. Triffterer (ed.), *Commentary on the Rome Statute of the International Criminal Court*, 2nd edn, pp. 915, 919 (2008).
15. 'Court-Martial of William L. Calley, Jr., 1971', in L. Friedmann (ed.), *The Law of War: A Documentary History*, vol. 2, pp. 1703, 1722 (1972).

Article 33(1) of the Rome Statute is incompatible with the doctrine of absolute liability—and, by the same token, with the *mens rea* principle—in contemplating obedience to superior orders (albeit in exceptional circumstances) as a defence *per se*. What we are confronted with is an inexplicable (if only partial) recrudescence of *respondeat superior*. Indisputably, Article 33(1) 'departs from customary international law without any well-grounded motivation'.[16]

Intriguingly, Article 33(1) is by no means the last word in the textual evolution of the treatment of obedience to superior orders. Article 6(4) of the Statute of the Special Court for Sierra Leone—a hybrid court set up by agreement between the United Nations and Sierra Leone in 2002 (namely, after the conclusion of the Rome Statute)—goes back to the language of Articles 7(4) and 6(4) of the Statutes of the ICTY and ICTR.[17] This 'may be taken as providing some evidence that Article 33 was not considered customary by those drafting the Special Court's Statute.'[18] The practice of the ICTY, which has unswervingly posited obedience to superior orders to be a plea solely in mitigation of punishment (section VIII below), corroborates this train of thought. It remains to be seen how Article 33(1) will be interpreted in the future adjudication of the International Criminal Court.

The inadequacy of Article 33(1) of the Rome Statute transcends the question of the status of obedience to superior orders as a defence *per se*. There are two additional queries that crop up. First, it is not clear why—if the wrongdoer genuinely does not know that the order he obeys is illegal under international law (the order not being manifestly unlawful)—it matters whether or not he was actually under a legal obligation to obey the order. Either way, the illicit act ought to come under the mantle of the defence of mistake of law (as laid down in Article 32(2), quoted below in section V).

Secondly, while there is nothing wrong with observing obedience to superior orders through the prism of the defence of mistake of law (within the framework of knowledge of the law and manifest illegality), it is wrong to focus on it in this exclusive fashion. The framers of Article 33(1) disregarded other possible combinations between

16. P. Gaeta, 'The Defence of Superior Orders: The Statute of the International Criminal Court versus Customary International Law', (1999) 10 *European Journal of International Law*, pp. 172, 190.
17. Statute of the Special Court for Sierra Leone, attached to Agreement between the United Nations and the Government of Sierra Leone on the Establishment of a Special Court for Sierra Leone, 2002 (UN doc. S/2002/246), p. 32.
18. See R. Cryer, *Prosecuting International Crimes: Selectivity and the International Criminal Law Regime*, p. 301 (2005).

obedience to superior orders and the defence of mistake of fact (Article 32(1)) or duress (Article 31). More on this in section VI below.

IV. THE DEFENCE OF MISTAKE OF FACT

Mistake of fact as a defence (based on the maxim *ignorantia facti excusat*) has never been much contested. Admittedly, it was formally acknowledged for the first time only in Article 32(1) of the Rome Statute, which reads:

> '1. A mistake of fact shall be a ground for excluding criminal responsibility only if it negates the mental element required by the crime.'[19]

Differently put, an act which otherwise would be a war crime may be excused should the court be satisfied that the accused committed it under an honest but mistaken belief in the existence of a constellation of facts that, if true, would have made his conduct lawful.

When I dealt in the book with the issue of obedience to superior orders embedded in the defence of mistake of fact, I was hard put to flesh out the empirical contours of mistake of fact as a defence. There was a paucity of either scholarly discussion (see pp. 83–4) or, for that matter, judicial landmarks (see pp. 202–4). Yet, in reality, mistake of fact recurs quite frequently in armed conflict and is almost taken for granted as a viable defence. Possibly, that is the very reason why it has not elicited more heat (or light). Prosecutors simply avoid instituting criminal proceedings once they reckon that they are liable to be blocked by the barrier of a credible mistake of fact.

By way of illustration, targeting in wartime is often based on flawed information, which is hard to verify given the 'fog of war'. In consequence, excessive civilian casualties may be inflicted in the wrong belief—both by the command echelon, planning the action, and by those executing the order to attack—that the strike is aimed at immaculate military objectives.[20] Surely, assuming that any excessive harm to civilians is due to a reasonable mistake of fact, *mens rea* cannot be ascribed to those in the loop. Criminal accountability is then vitiated on the ground of mistake of fact.[21]

19. Rome Statute, n. 8 above, at 311.
20. See Y. Dinstein, *The Conduct of Hostilities under the Law of International Armed Conflict*, 2nd edn, p. 127 (2010).
21. The most recent UK Manual gives the following example for the application of the defence of mistake of fact: 'if an artillery commander is ordered to fire at an enemy command post in a particular building and he does so believing that it is a command post but it later turns out that, unbeknown to him, it was a school, he would not be guilty of a war crime because he did not intend to attack a school': UK Ministry of Defence, *The Manual of the Law of Armed Conflict*, p. 442 (2004).

V. THE DEFENCE OF MISTAKE OF LAW

Mistake of law is profoundly more problematic than the cognate category of mistake of fact. Indeed, it took me quite a while to resign myself to the admissibility of mistake of law as a defence, bearing in mind the maxim *ignorantia juris non excusat* that is widely accepted within a host of domestic legal systems. I finally harnessed the rationale that an axiomatic presupposition of knowledge of the law (whatever its reputed merits in domestic legal systems) cannot be seriously taken as applicable to members of the armed forces where the *jus in bello* is concerned (see pp. 31–2). The same rationale had already struck a chord in several of the post-World War II war crimes trials (see especially *Peleus* (1945), pp. 199–200).

If I harboured any doubts in the matter, they have now been removed by Article 32(2) of the Rome Statute, which proclaims:

> '2. A mistake of law as to whether a particular type of conduct is a crime within the jurisdiction of the Court shall not be a ground for excluding criminal responsibility. A mistake of law may, however, be a ground for excluding criminal responsibility if it negates the mental element required by such a crime, or as provided for in article 33.'[22]

The second sentence leads to the ineluctable conclusion that mistake of law is an admissible defence in certain settings that include obedience to superior orders (hence the allusion to Article 33). This has apparently not been wholly perceived even by those entrusted with the formulation of the Elements of Crimes under the Rome Statute.[23]

Naturally, the scope of the defence of mistake of law—pursuant to the Rome Statute and otherwise—is 'relatively limited', as enunciated by a Pre-Trial Chamber of the International Criminal Court, in 2007, in *Lubanga Dyilo*.[24] The Chamber pronounced that there was nothing in the evidence to show that the accused had actually been unaware of the criminality of the acts of conscripting or using child-soldiers (under the age of 15) to participate actively in hostilities.[25]

Awareness or knowledge of the illegality of the act charged is the acid test here. In the book, I endeavoured to develop the 'principle of personal knowledge', meaning that an accused should be relieved of responsibility only if he committed an act without being aware of its illegality (see p. 30). The principle ties in with the key issue of

22. Rome Statute, n. 8 above, at 311.
23. See K. Dörmann (ed.), *Elements of War Crimes under the Rome Statute of the International Criminal Court: Sources and Commentary*, p. 250 (2003).
24. *Prosecutor v. Lubanga Dyilo* (Decision on the Confirmation of Charges) (International Criminal Court, Pre-Trial Chamber, 2007), para. 305.
25. *Ibid.*, paras 304, 316.

'manifest illegality', which has gained much popularity and is now grafted on to Article 33(1) of the Rome Statute jointly with personal knowledge (see quotation above in section III). Knowledge of the illegality of an order—like all knowledge—is a subjective matter, and it may not be easily fathomed by a court of law. Consequently, international criminal law relies on an objective criterion of manifest illegality, creating a presumption of knowledge when any reasonable person would have been aware of the unlawfulness of the order, *viz.* when a 'black flag' is displayed over it (to use the famous idiom of the Israeli court in *Kafr Kassem*; see p. 9). The epitome would be carrying out an order to open fire on an enemy ambulance palpably marked with a Red Cross emblem (a war crime under Article 8(2)(b)(xxiv) of the Rome Statute).[26]

The way I see it, manifest illegality—as an operative presumption—is no more than an auxiliary device of the law of evidence (p. 29). As such, it should not be viewed as conclusive. On the one hand, if manifest illegality does not exist (objectively), yet the personal knowledge of unlawfulness can be proved (subjectively), the individual concerned ought to be caught in the criminal net. On the other hand, where (objectively) manifest illegality is not contested, but (subjectively) the person charged with a war crime—afflicted, perhaps, with some cognitive disability—failed to grasp the unlawfulness of the act, he is entitled to be absolved of criminal accountability (unless we are faced with an irrebuttable *praesumptio juris et de jure*) (see p. 30).

One more remark on mistake of law is triggered by the modern practice of assigning legal advisers at an appropriate level of command of the armed forces.[27] Such presence is most beneficial to harassed commanders called upon to follow orders entailing death and devastation in ambiguous situations. In the final analysis, the decision-making process culminates in the commander. However, the expression of an opinion at headquarters by a competent legal adviser (albeit non-binding) may increase the chances of an eventual invocation by the commander of a plea of mistake of law. If the legal adviser wrongly assures the commander that the order may be safely executed by virtue of its lawfulness, any bona fide action predicated on that advice will plausibly come within the ambit of an admissible defence of mistake of law.

26. Rome Statute, n. 8 above, at 300.
27. See Article 82 of Protocol Additional to the Geneva Conventions of 12 August 1949, and Relating to the Protection of Victims of International Armed Conflicts (Protocol I), 1977, [1977] *United Nations Juridical Yearbook* 95, 128.

In principle, the defence of duress is time-honoured, and so is its interlacing with obedience to superior orders. Duress is affirmed as a defence in Article 31(1)(d) of the Rome Statute:

> '1. In addition to other grounds for excluding criminal responsibility provided for in this Statute, a person shall not be criminally responsible if, at the time of that person's conduct:
>
> . . .
>
> (d) The conduct which is alleged to constitute a crime within the jurisdiction of the Court has been caused by duress resulting from a threat of imminent death or of continuing or imminent serious bodily harm against that person or another person, and the person acts necessarily and reasonably to avoid this threat, provided that the person does not intend to cause a greater harm than the one sought to be avoided. Such a threat may either be:
>
> (i) Made by other persons; or
>
> (ii) Constituted by other circumstances beyond that person's control.'[28]

As the last words denote, a distinction is drawn between duress by threat and duress by circumstances.[29] In the former scenario (frequently labelled 'coercion'), the dire consequences that the accused is trying to avert are presented as a threat by another human being. The latter setting (best described as 'necessity') unfolds when the accused tries to avoid fatal results generated by circumstances beyond anybody's control (for instance, a raging fire). This is entirely in line with tradition as set out in the book (see p. 77).

Precisely because the framers of the Rome Statute were sensitive to the potential impact of the defence of duress in war crimes trials, one cannot but be puzzled by the fact that they abstained from linking it with the issue of obedience to superior orders in Article 33(1). As a matter of fact, Article 33(1) compounds the injury: not only does it improperly recognize obedience to superior orders as a defence *per se* (see section III), but it wrongly looks at the *materia* through the single lens of mistake of law. By focusing on mistake of law alone, the framers of Article 33(1) came up with a fragmented solution to a wider-ranging problem, disregarding the well-established amalgamation of obedience to superior orders with duress.[30]

28. Rome Statute, n. 8 above, at 300.

29. See K. Ambos, 'Other Grounds for Excluding Criminal Responsibility', in A. Cassese, P. Gaeta, and J.R.W.D. Jones (eds), *The Rome Statute of the International Criminal Court: A Commentary*, vol. 1, pp. 1003, 1038 (2002).

30. Fragmentation in this area may cut both ways. In 1954, the International Law Commission—in drafting the provision on obedience to superior orders in the Draft Code of Offences against the Peace and Security of Mankind (as it was then designated)—did exactly the opposite, turning its back on mistake of law and setting its sights on duress (see pp. 248–51).

The real underpinning of the defence of duress is that the accused acted in the absence of 'moral choice'. That is to say, the choice available to him is morally nullified by the dire straits looming. Moral choice, as the 'true test' of criminal responsibility, was highlighted in the Nuremberg Judgment of the International Military Tribunal (although, oddly, the Tribunal associated moral choice with obedience to superior orders rather than with duress; see pp. 147–54). Absence of moral choice means that a war crime was committed only because the malefactor had reasonable grounds to expect imminent disaster (to befall either him or another person close to him) if he refrained from acting as he was told.

Notwithstanding the unassailable presence of the defence of duress in the firmament of international criminal law, one must be mindful of built-in limitations affecting its efficacy. Most significantly, there is an imperative need to weigh the actual harm caused against the potential harm sought to be avoided. The requisite balancing act is explicitly mandated by Article 31(1)(d) of the Rome Statute (see quotation at the beginning of this section), and I deem it to be incontrovertible (see p. 180).

The crucial question is whether the defence of duress can ever be accepted in a case of murder. In *Einsatzgruppen* (1948) it was enunciated, in connection with the mass killings of Jews by Nazi extermination squads:

> 'there is no law which requires that an innocent man must forfeit his life or suffer serious harm in order to avoid committing a crime which he condemns' (see p. 79).

This is an *obiter dictum* in a Judgment that ultimately dismissed the defence of duress on factual grounds. Still, the assertion has induced severe criticism, which is echoed in the book (p. 80). I am implacably opposed to the view that duress can ever exculpate mega-extermination. I object to the hypothesis that the life of the perpetrator may be regarded as more valuable than that of another human being, let alone thousands of human beings.

In the 1997 Judgment in appeal in *Erdemović*, the Joint Separate Opinion of Judges McDonald and Vohrah (speaking for the majority of the Appeals Chamber of the ICTY) had this to say:

> 'duress cannot afford a complete defence to a soldier charged with crimes against humanity or war crimes in international law involving the taking of innocent lives'.[31]

31. *Prosecutor v. Erdemović*, n. 6 above, at 373.

The Joint Separate Opinion found that 'the *Einsatzgruppen* decision is in discord with the preponderant view of international authorities'.[32]

Judges McDonald and Vohrah did not allude to my comments on this issue. However, Judge Stephen—in his dissenting opinion in *Erdemović*—quoted at length my reflections on moral choice (as articulated on pp. 152–3).[33] He then opined:

> 'It is noteworthy that even this passage, while conceding that in some cases of duress moral choice is eliminated, confines itself to the choice between the victim's life or the life of the actor who is subjected to duress. It does not go to the necessarily stronger case where the victim's fate is sealed and all that remains for the actor is whether or not to join the victim in death.'[34]

All that I can say in response is that the question whether the fate of the victim is really 'sealed', and what in all probability would have happened to the accused had he resisted the threats levelled at him, can only be speculated at the time of action. To my mind, the accused is not allowed to play God at that crucial moment.

Interestingly, in 1976, the Privy Council (by a majority of three to two) held, in *Abbot v. The Queen*, that duress is not available as a defence to anyone charged with murder as a principal in the first degree.[35] Although the case did not relate to an international offence, the Privy Council expressly said (*per* Lord Salmon):

> 'In the trials of those responsible for wartime atrocities such as mass killings of men, women or children, inhuman experiments on human beings, often resulting in death, and like crimes, it was invariably argued for the defence that these atrocities should be excused on the ground that they resulted from superior orders and duress: if the accused had refused to do these dreadful things, they would have been shot and therefore they should be acquitted and allowed to go free. This argument has always been universally rejected. Their Lordships would be sorry indeed to see it accepted by the common law of England.'[36]

VII. INTERPLAY OF DEFENCES

The orbits of the three independent defences based on lack of *mens rea*—mistake of fact, mistake of law, and duress—may intersect in circumstances of obedience to superior orders. At times, two (or even all three) of the defences would be set as alternative strategies, with one poised to take over should the other fold. A paradigmatic

32. *Ibid.*, 338.
33. *Ibid.*, 454–5.
34. *Ibid.*, 455.
35. *Abbott v. The Queen* [1976] 3 All E.R. 140.
36. *Ibid.*, 146.

scenario would be that of obedience to an order to open fire on a Red Cross ambulance. A defence of mistake of law will in all likelihood be disallowed in such circumstances as a corollary of the manifest illegality of the action taken (section V above). However, a defence of mistake of fact may be crowned with success if it is established that—for instance, due to poor visibility—the ambulance was erroneously identified as a military vehicle.[37]

Furthermore, when orders are obeyed, the defences of mistake of fact and mistake of law may have distinct patterns of convergence. In the book, I pointed at such convergence in the context of belligerent reprisals (see pp. 86–7), as well as in the factual setting of *Scuttled U-Boats* (pp. 193, 202–3). In subsequent jurisprudence, the combination of obedience to superior orders, mistake of fact, and mistake of law has been conjured up in relation to Hitler's notorious 'euthanasia order': the mistake of fact blended with mistake of law by dint of the lawful status of the order under the German domestic system during the Nazi period).[38] It is easy to dispose of this claim on grounds of manifest illegality. But not all cases are so clear-cut. Ordinarily, it may be reasonable for a soldier to mistakenly assume that there is no mismatch between domestic and international law.

As a graphic example of the interaction between mistake of fact and mistake of law—superimposed on a layer of obedience to superior orders—one may take the act of conscripting child-soldiers (under the age of 15) to participate actively in hostilities (section V above). No doubt, this is a war crime, both under the Rome Statute[39] and present-day customary international law.[40] Still, when orders are issued to conscript youngsters for service in combat units, mistake of fact may amount to a potent defence, since the defendant may be able to maintain credibly that a 14-year-old conscript appeared to him to be older than 15.[41]

Moreover, mistake of fact may be interwoven in this case with mistake of law. It is true that, in its 2008 Judgment in *Brim* et al., the Appeals Chamber of the Special Court for Sierra Leone expressly

37. See G. Werle, *Principles of International Criminal Law*, 2nd edn, p. 211 (2009).
38. See S. Mehring, 'Medical War Crimes', (2011) 15 *Max Planck Yearbook of United Nations Law*, pp. 229, 272.
39. See Article 8(2)(b)(xxvi) of the Rome Statute, n. 8 above, at 300.
40. In 2004, the Appeals Chamber of the Special Court for Sierra Leone held that by 1996 (the critical date for the proceedings) the injunction against child recruitment had 'crystallized as customary international law': *Prosecutor v. Norman* (Special Court for Sierra Leone, Appeals Chamber, 2004), (2004) 43 *International Legal Materials* 1129, 1136–7.
41. See W.A. Schabas, *An Introduction to the International Criminal Court*, 4th edn, p. 242 (2011).

rejected a mistake of law defence concerning the crime of conscription of child-soldiers.[42] But is it not possible for a defendant to press the argument that he had been led to believe that conscription of child-soldiers is unlawful only up to the age of, say, 12 or 13?[43] If so, mistake of fact may well be leavened by mistake of law.

VIII. MITIGATION OF PUNISHMENT

Whereas obedience to superior orders is inadmissible as a defence *per se*, it may lead to the lessening of a sentence imposed on a person convicted of war crimes. The possibility of mitigation of punishment owing to obedience to superior orders is forthrightly acknowledged in Article 8 of the London Charter (see p. 117) and replicated in Article 7(4) of the ICTY Statute (cited above in section III).

Reduction of the sentence on the ground of extenuating circumstances is left entirely to the discretion of the relevant court. In other words, although alleviation of punishment is permissible under Article 8 (and similar texts), it is not mandatory. This is a point of singular importance, missed by the defence in *Barbie* in 1987, in its appeal to the French *Cour de Cassation*.[44] As the Nuremberg Judgment amply attests, the enormity of the crimes perpetrated by the accused may negate any proclivity for leniency (see p. 154).

Not all war crimes are of equal gravity. In a raft of judgments in the post-World War II trials, obedience to superior orders was actually factored in when meting out punishment for crimes that were less egregious (see pp. 188, 205–6). The tension between extenuating and aggravating circumstances affecting obedience to superior orders re-emerged in the jurisprudence of the ICTY in light of Article 7(4) of the Statute. In *Mrđa* (2002), a Trial Chamber held:

> 'With respect to adherence to superior orders, a discretionary mitigating factor provided for in Article 7(4) of the Statute of the Tribunal, we consider that the orders Mrđa acted on were so manifestly unlawful that he must have been well aware that they violated the most elementary laws of war and the basic dictates

42. *Prosecutor v. Brima* et al. (Special Court for Sierra Leone, Appeals Chamber, 2008), paras 293–7 .
43. This is not to suggest that ratcheting down the age bar of prohibited conscription of child-soldiers is on the international agenda. On the contrary, the legal pendulum is swinging the other way. In an Optional Protocol of 2000, the age bar of prohibited compulsory recruitment of children has been raised from 15 to 18 years: Optional Protocol to the Convention on the Rights of the Child on the Involvement of Children in Armed Conflict, (2000) 39 *International Legal Materials* 1286, 1287 (Article 2).
44. See N. R. Doman, 'Aftermath of Nuremberg: The Trial of Klaus Barbie', (1989) 60 *Colorado Law Review* 449, 467.

of humanity. The fact that Mrđa obeyed such orders, as opposed to acting on his own initiative, does not merit mitigation of punishment.'[45]

In *Erdemović*, in 1996, the Trial Chamber recorded that:

> 'tribunals have tended to show more leniency in cases where the accused arguing a defence of superior orders held a low rank in the military or civilian hierarchy.'[46]

Yet, when standing by itself, low rank is not a mitigating factor. In *Delalić* et al. of 2001, the Appeals Chamber denied the validity of the proposition that 'if the accused's place was by comparison low, a low sentence should automatically be imposed'.[47] In *Boškoski* et al. (2010), the Appeals Chamber was even more emphatic: 'the subordinate role of an accused is legally irrelevant in determining his individual criminal responsibility'.[48] Earlier, in *Banović* (2003), the Trial Chamber cast aside the allegation that low rank—supposedly indicating inability to resist the power of superiors—has to be considered in mitigation, unless there is downright evidence that duress had taken place.[49]

In *Erdemović*, the Trial Chamber rightly added that obedience to superior orders may serve in mitigation of punishment only when the orders had an influence on the behaviour of the accused, and not when he was anyhow inclined to carry out the criminal act.[50] In *Blaškić* in 2000, the Trial Chamber stressed:

> 'Duress, where established, does mitigate the criminal responsibility of the accused when he had no choice or moral freedom in committing the crime. This must consequently entail the passing of a lighter sentence if he cannot be completely exonerated of responsibility.'[51]

Still, the Chamber proceeded to rule that no duress had taken place in the case at hand, and that therefore the accused did not deserve mitigation of punishment.[52] The evidence as adduced (and evaluated) in *Češič* in 2004 similarly led the Trial Chamber to a repudiation of submissions in mitigation based on both obedience to superior orders and duress.[53]

45. *Prosecutor v. Mrđa* (Judgment) (ICTY, Trial Chamber, 2004), para. 22.
46. *Prosecutor v. Erdemović* (Sentencing Judgment) (ICTY, Trial Chamber, 1996), (1996) 108 *International Law Reports* 180, 199.
47. *Prosecutor v. Delalić* et al. (Judgment) (ICTY, Appeals Chamber, 2001), para. 847.
48. *Prosecutor v. Boškoski* et al. (Judgment) (ICTY, Appeals Chamber, 2010), para. 52.
49. *Prosecutor v. Banović* (Sentencing Judgment) (ICTY, Trial Chamber, 2003), paras 17, 63.
50. *Prosecutor v. Erdemović* (Sentencing Judgment), n. 46 above, at 200.
51. *Prosecutor v. Blaškić* (Judgment) (ICTY, Trial Chamber, 2000), (2000) 122 *International Law Reports* 2, 230.
52. *Ibid.*
53. *Prosecutor v. Češič* (Sentencing Judgment) (ICTY, Trial Chamber, 2004), para. 97.

In *Bralo*, in 2005, another Trial Chamber of the ICTY pronounced that '[d]uress and superior orders are separate, but related, concepts and either may count in mitigation of sentence'.[54] Nevertheless, the Chamber found that the defendant had not been exposed to 'any form of duress emanating from his superiors such that he was compelled to commit the crimes of which he has been convicted' (adding that he had not 'specifically pleaded superior orders as a factor in mitigation of sentence').[55] On appeal, in 2007, the Appeals Chamber confirmed that the pressures brought to bear upon the accused failed to 'demonstrate that he was under "duress" to obey illegal orders'.[56]

While the ICTY did not address directly the issue of calibration of punishment in cases of obedience to superior orders coupled with mistake (of law or of fact), it is worth mentioning that, in *Delalić* et al., the Trial Chamber—having rejected the contention that one of the accused had acted in obedience to superior orders—took into account that he 'had no proper military training or instruction in how to comport himself in relation to detainees'.[57] In 2001, the Appeals Chamber confirmed the disavowal of obedience to superior orders as a mitigating factor in these proceedings.[58]

IX. THE 'ACT OF STATE' DOCTRINE

As mentioned above (section I), when I commenced my study, I was of two minds whether to proceed with the theme of obedience to superior orders or 'act of State' (the exponent of which was Kelsen). Once I selected the former topic, I assumed that I was done with the latter. But I soon found out that there was no way to ignore it completely. Since both Kelsen and Oppenheim were of the opinion that the defendant in the dock should be relieved of accountability for war crimes, the two trains of thought were often blurred. I was unhappy to discover such confusion even in the *Eichmann* pleadings (see pp. 66–7). I found it imperative to draw a line in the sand between *respondeat superior* and 'act of State'. As I showed, Kelsen was not concerned with obedience to superior orders. He thought, however, that all authorized acts (including war crimes) were imputed by international law to the belligerent party, and—as a result of that

54. *Prosecutor v. Bralo* (Sentencing Judgment) (ICTY, Trial Chamber, 2005), para. 53.
55. *Ibid.*, para. 54.
56. *Prosecutor v. Bralo* (Judgment on Sentencing Appeal) (ICTY, Appeals Chamber, 2007), para. 24.
57. *Prosecutor v. Delalić* et al. (Judgment) (ICTY, Trial Chamber, 1998), paras 1281, 1283.
58. *Prosecutor v. Delalić* et al., n. 47 above, at paras 835–8.

attribution—no criminal accountability could be attached to individuals acting in their capacity as organs of the State (see pp. 57–60).

The London Charter and the Nuremberg Judgment collided head-on with the 'act of State' doctrine. There was a lot more that I could say on the topic in the book, but I was constantly on my guard against a temptation to open the floodgates for an outpouring of information on a sphere from which I had consciously withdrawn after near-completion of the basic research. I probably bent over backwards in not tracing in print all the manifestations of the dismissal of the 'act of State' doctrine in the post-World War II literature and case law, as inscribed minutely in my longhand notebooks. In order not to compound the omission, let me advert to Article 27(1) of the Rome Statute,[59] where this trend has reached its climax. Patently, as an overarching rule today, the attribution of an act to a State—albeit engendering State responsibility—does not displace the criminal liability of the individuals acting as organs on behalf of that State.[60]

X. CONCLUSION

The axiomatic premise on which the book hinges is the existence of international criminal law as an established branch of both customary international law and treaty law. Some of the general precepts of international criminal law (such as the fundamental construct of *mens rea*) are derived from domestic criminal legal systems. But there can be no denial that the international and domestic attitudes *vis-à-vis* identical problems of penal law may be disparate and even contradictory (the issue of mistake of law is a prime example).

Interest in international criminal law today—compared to what it was in 1965—has grown exponentially. The creation of the two ad hoc international tribunals (ICTY and ICTR) and, later, the International Criminal Court, is proof positive of that. The *problématique* of obedience to superior orders is only one modest dimension of international criminal law, but its import (especially in the context of war crimes trials) is not likely to recede in the years ahead.

Yoram Dinstein

59. Rome Statute, n. 8 above, at 309.
60. See Article 58 and Commentary, Draft Articles on Responsibility of States for Internationally Wrongful Acts, (2001) *Report of the International Law Commission, 53rd Session* 43, 363–5.

FOREWORD

THE purpose of this study is to examine and elucidate the problem whether, and when, the perpetrator of an international offence, acting in obedience to superior orders, is to be relieved of responsibility under international criminal law. It should be made abundantly clear from the outset that the study is based upon several major premises, regarded by the writer as axiomatic. The first and foremost premise is that international criminal law is really in force, and that the transgressor of its provisions is ordinarily liable to incur international responsibility and account for his actions before a national court or an international tribunal. Were it not for this major premise, had we not contemplated, in principle, the possibility that an individual may be held criminally responsible under international law, there would have been no sense in the ensuing discussion, for there is no reason to consider relief from responsibility when no responsibility is existent in the first place.

The problem of committing an offence pursuant to superior orders may materialize whenever a hierarchical relationship of superiors and subordinates is in being, and on whatever occasion the subordinate, within the ambit of that relationship, is in duty bound to comply with the instructions of his superior. The problem is not confined within military bounds or restricted to the category of war crimes, so that there is no justification for circumscribing the scope of our discussion exclusively to the pale of the subject-matter of obedience to superior orders in armed forces in time of war. Just the same, the special practical significance of the plea of obedience to superior orders is self-evident in the context of punishment of war criminals;[1] and in fact as well as in theory the problem presents itself in all its acuteness and pungency when the military are concerned.[2] In

1. This was noted by Boissier, *L'Epée et la Balance* (1953), p. 39; Daniel, *Le Problème du Châtiment des Crimes de Guerre* (1946), p. 152; Dunbar, 'Some Aspects of the Problem of Superior Orders in the Law of War', *J. Rev.*, vol. 63 (1951), pp. 234–261 at p. 234; Lauterpacht, 'War Crimes', p. 69; Maunoir, *La Répression des Crimes de Guerre devant les Tribunaux Français et Alliés* (1956), p. 203; Morgan, *Assize*, p. 11; Morgan, 'Nuremberg', p. 328; Mullins, *The Leipzig Trials* (1921), p. 218; *N.L.G. Report*, pp. 20–21; Schwarzenberger, *Lawlessness*, p. 62; Schwarzenberger, 'War Crimes', p. 71; Schwelb, 'The United Nations War Crimes Commission', *B.Y.B.I.L.*, vol. 23 (1946), pp. 363–376 at p. 373; H. Smith, 'Nuremberg', p. 203.

2. Dunbar summed it up as follows: 'While in principle the question of superior orders is raised whenever an act is performed by a subordinate owing some recognized duty of obedience to a duly constituted superior authority, in practice the problem assumes its

consequence, it is customary to scrutinize the general problem of obedience to superior orders through the lens of the specific case of soldiers committing war crimes, and to apply the emergent rules by inference, *mutatis mutandis*,[3] to civilians violating the provisions of international law while subject to orders: policemen, civil servants in an authoritarian-dictatorial régime,[4] and so forth.

We shall endeavour to analyze the phenomenon of obedience to superior orders as a shelter against criminal prosecution under international law from the varying viewpoints of theory and practice. First, we shall attempt to discover trends and appraise prevailing doctrines in the theory of international law, tracing their rationale and penetrating their verbal disguises, trying to become aware—and to beware—of inconsistencies. Then we shall seek to detect how far ideas, conceived by scholars and jurists in the seclusion of their chambers, are substantiated by the pronouncements of courts and by international legislation. But, to lay a proper foundation for the discussion and see things in perspective, we shall start with a cursory glance at national law.[5]

greatest significance in connection with the relationship of disciplinary subordination which exists between various ranks of the armed forces' (Dunbar, *op. cit.*, p. 234). See also Eustathiades, 'Ordres', p. 404 n. 28. Cf. Knieriem, *The Nuremberg Trials* (1959), p. 254; Sibert, *Traité de Droit International Public* (1951), vol. 1, p. 441; *L.R.U.N.W.C.C.*, vol. 15 (Digest), p. 158.

3. Of course it is sometimes feasible, and even necessary, to distinguish between soldiers and others. See Donnedieu de Vabres, 'Nuremberg', pp. 569–571; Greenspan, *The Modern Law of Land Warfare* (1959), p. 492; Farben case, Closing Statement for the Prosecution, *N.M.T.*, vol. 8, p. 1045. See also Daniel, *op. cit.*, p. 173; Maunoir, *op. cit.*, p. 248.

4. Donnedieu de Vabres said very aptly that when criminal responsibility is assessed one should liken the position of officials in a dictatorial régime to that of the military in a free country (Donnedieu de Vabres, 'Nuremberg', p. 571). And cf. Knieriem, *op. cit.*, p. 255.

5. I have preferred using throughout this study the term 'national law', rather than 'municipal law', for the sake of the symmetrical parallelism with the expression 'international law'.

PART I: NATIONAL LAW

CHAPTER I

THE DILEMMA AND ITS SOLUTIONS

THE question whether obedience to superior orders creates an aegis for the offender, a shield under which he can hide himself from the arm of the law, has long disturbed juristic thinking within different systems of national law. In the main, it is a product of the national need to keep and maintain an efficient army. Any army by its very nature is founded on the basis of discipline. Discipline means that every subordinate must needs obey the orders of his superiors. And, when we deal with an army, ordinary discipline is not enough. Military discipline is designed, ultimately, to conduct men to battle, to lead them under fire to victory, and, if and when necessary, to impel them to sacrifice their lives for their country.[6] In this aspect, military discipline entails a total revaluation in the soul of the soldier: he must overcome his natural instinct to save his skin.[7] The success of the military objective, to wit, victory in battle, as well as the lives of many soldiers, and, above all, the security of the nation seem, therefore, to compel 'total and unqualified obedience without any hesitation or doubt'[8] to orders in time of war and emergency, and complementary training and instruction in time of peace.[9] In the heat of battle, disciplined soldiers are expected to act in accordance with the poet's behest:

6. See particularly Boissier, *op. cit.*, pp. 45, 61–62.
7. See particularly *ibid.*, pp. 45–46, and a quotation from a statement by Field-Marshal Montgomery—*ibid.*, p. 61 n. 4.
8. As stated by the Israel Military Court in the Kafr Kassem case (first instance) (Military Court, Central District 3/57, Military Prosecutor v. Melinki), *Pesakim* (D.), vol. 17, p. 90 at p. 213.
9. See on this subject-matter Boissier, *op. cit.*, pp. 47, 61–62; Montgomery quoted by Defendant Naumann, Einsatzgruppen case, *N.M.T.*, vol. 4, p. 394; Poljokan, *La Responsabilité pour les Crimes et Délits de Guerre* (1923), p. 162; Kafr Kassem case (first instance), *op. cit.*, p. 213; Kafr Kassem case (second instance), (Ap. 279–283/58, Ofer v. Chief Military Prosecutor), *Pesakim* (S.), vol. 44, p. 362 at p. 408. Cf. Bower, 'The Laws of War: Prisoners of War and Reprisals', *T.G.S.*, vol. 1 (1916), pp. 23–37 at p. 31; Colby, 'War Crimes and their Punishment', *Minn. L.R.*, vol. 8 (1923–1924), pp. 40–46 at p. 43; Dunbar, *op. cit.*, p. 259; Glueck, *War Criminals*, p. 148; Kilmuir (Maxwell-Fyfe), *Nuremberg in Retrospect* (1956), p. 14; Maunoir, *op. cit.*, p. 203.

'Theirs not to make reply,
Theirs not to reason why,
Theirs but to do and die'.[10]

For the sake of the maintenance of discipline within the national army, the national legal system, through the decrees of military law, imposes upon soldiers a legal duty to obey orders, and threatens them with the direst of sanctions in case of insubordination, especially in time of war and in the presence of the enemy.[11]

The problem is that, when a soldier is confronted with an (illegal) order to perform an act constituting a criminal offence, the demands of military discipline, as expressed in the duty of obedience to superior orders, come into conflict with the imperative need to preserve the supremacy of the law as manifested in the prescriptions of criminal law: military discipline requires unflinching compliance with orders; the supremacy of the law proscribes the commission of criminal acts.

Stephen has already noted 'the double necessity of preserving on the one hand the supremacy of the law and on the other the discipline of the army'.[12] The judgment of the Israel District Military Court, in the Kafr Kassem case, did, indeed, seek to make the extremes meet, pronouncing that

> 'These two basic values—the discipline of the army and the supremacy of the law—balance each other and also complement one another. There is no contradiction between them, and each has to be kept intact without detracting from the other'.[13]

But, as was rightly pointed out by the Military Court of Appeal in the same case, this conception is 'too simplified', and there is no escape from the conclusion that the values of military discipline and the supremacy of the law 'conflict with each other when the soldier is required to comply with an illegal order'.[14] This head-on collision creates a difficult dilemma, from the practical as well as the theoretical angle.[15]

The practical dilemma, upon whose horns the recipient of superior orders is driven, is one of exceptional severity: if the soldier submits

10. Tennyson, 'The Charge of the Light Brigade'.
11. See particularly Boissier, *op. cit.*, pp. 39, 60; Knieriem, *op. cit.*, p. 242; Maunoir, *op. cit.*, pp. 203, 277; Kafr Kassem case (second instance), *op. cit.*, p. 408.
12. Stephen, *A History of the Criminal Law of England* (1883), vol. 1, p. 206. Cf. Bellot, 'War Criminals', vol. 36, p. 766; Finch, 'Superior Orders', p. 444; Eichmann trial (second instance) (Criminal Appeal 336/61, Eichmann v. Attorney General), Judgment (mimeographed, English), p. I31. Cf. also Dunbar, *op. cit.*, p. 234.
13. Kafr Kassem case (first instance), *op. cit.*, p. 212.
14. Kafr Kassem case (second instance), *op. cit.*, p. 408.
15. See *ibid.*

to an illegal order, and commits a crime, he is violating the prescriptions of criminal law and will consequently be liable to the penalties it lays down; if he defies the order, and abstains from commission of the crime, he may be infringing the dictates of military law and as a consequence be liable to the penalties which that provides. Dicey describes this choice of evils in famous words:

> 'The position of a soldier is in theory and may be in practice a difficult one. He may, as it has been well said, be liable to be shot by a court-martial if he disobeys an order, and to be hanged by a judge and jury if he obeys it'.[16]

Indeed, the soldier may be caught in an insufferable plight, 'between the devil and the deep sea'.[17]

And the horns of the dilemma are sharp and strong enough to mangle the entire legal system insofar as its theory is concerned: if a soldier commits an offence in obedience to superior orders, and is, therefore, criminally indicted, or, alternatively, if he refuses to comply with an order to perform an act constituting an offence and is consequently charged before a court-martial—will he be convicted or acquitted? If he is convicted anyhow, whether he commits the criminal act as ordered or refrains from doing so, the legal system seems to be tainted by an iniquitous inconsistency that is all but incredible. And if the soldier is to incur criminal responsibility for his act only in one of the two cases and not in the other, certain difficulties emerge. On the one hand, if the soldier risks his life in disobeying superior orders and refusing to carry out the criminal act, whereas he is exculpated when the offence is committed by him in compliance with the orders—this solution may incite the commission of crimes and bring about a public outcry that a soldier

> 'could get away with things that nobody else could get away with—a modern form of benefit of clergy, substituting the right to wear a uniform for the ability to recite a psalm'.[18]

On the other hand, if the soldier is penalized for committing the offence pursuant to orders, whereas he can defy the orders with impunity—this solution may encourage insubordination and undermine military discipline.[19] To use the words of dyed-in-the-wool disciplinarians, such a solution is 'inimical to service discipline',[20] and 'it is just placing a premium on cowardice and escapism in the

16. Dicey, *Introduction to the Study of the Law of the Constitution* (10th ed., 1959), p. 303. See also Stephen, *op. cit.*, vol. 1, p. 205. Cf. Bellot, 'War Criminals', vol. 36, p. 766; Kafr Kassem case (second instance), *op. cit.*, p. 409.
17. Bellot, 'Punishment', p. 47.
18. Calvocoressi, *Nuremberg, the Facts, the Law and the Consequences* (1947), p. 100.
19. See Maunoir, *op. cit.*, p. 204; Kafr Kassem case (second instance), *op. cit.*, p. 409.
20. Cf. below, note 138.

proper carrying out of orders'.[21] In time of war, public opinion will usually share this harsh view.

For generations, systems of national law have endeavoured to repel the two-pronged attack of this difficult dilemma and scholars have ventured to tackle it, but not always with great success. Thus the following, diametrically opposed, doctrines have been advocated, and sometimes gained acceptance:[22]

(a) The doctrine of *respondeat superior*,[23] or, as the French term it, *l'obéissance passive*, according to which a soldier committing an offence in obedience to superior orders is relieved of responsibility automatically, without any condition or qualification. Let the superior issuing the order be criminally answerable, not the subordinate complying with his command!

(b) The doctrine of absolute liability, or, as the French term it rather derisively, *les baïonnettes intelligentes*, in accordance with which a soldier must examine and weigh every superior order that is given to him. If it is an order to perform a criminal act, he must refuse to carry it out, and it is impossible to punish him for the refusal. If he obeys the order, he does so at his own risk. The fact of obedience to orders will not save him from criminal conviction.

As a matter of fact, neither solution overcomes the dilemma which we have just discussed. On the contrary, each actually succumbs, in its own way, to one of the two menacing horns. The first doctrine is incompatible with the interests of criminal law, the second is inconsistent with the demands of military discipline. The quest of jurists, legislators and judges for a better solution, which might enable the legal system to lop off both horns instead of being impaled upon one of them, has produced, *inter alia*, the following doctrine:[24] the general rule is that a soldier committing an offence in obedience to superior orders is relieved of responsibility for his wrongdoing. If, however, the illegality of the order is clear on the face of it, that is, manifestly and palpably, the soldier must refuse to obey it or else pay the

21. Hankey, *Politics, Trials and Errors* (1950), p. 60.
22. See particularly Coste-Floret, 'La Répression des Crimes de Guerre et le Fait Justificatif Tiré de l'Ordre Supérieur', *Dalloz*, 1945, Chronique IV, pp. 21–22 at p. 21; Maunoir, *op. cit.*, pp. 203–204; Kafr Kassem case (second instance), *op. cit.*, pp. 409–410.
23. It should be understood that the familiar use of the term *respondeat superior* is, in this context, meant to point out not so much the responsibility of the superior as the lack of responsibility on the part of the subordinate committing an offence in pursuance of superior orders. Appleman defined it well by stating: '*respondeat superior*—or, let the master answer rather than the servant' (Appleman, *Military Tribunals and International Crimes* (1954), p. 54. Cf. Woetzel, *The Nuremberg Trials in International Law* (1960), p. 68 n. 31).
24. See particularly Coste-Floret, *op. cit.*, p. 21; Kafr Kassem case (second instance), *op. cit.*, p. 410.

penalty. Hereinafter we shall call this solution, which is aimed at adjusting the concurrent, conflicting demands of military discipline and the supremacy of the law, 'the manifest illegality principle'.

The manifest illegality principle has the imprimatur of the legislation in force in Israel, which provides in Section 19(b) of the Criminal Code Ordinance, 1936:

> 'A person is not criminally responsible for an act or omission if he does or omits to do the act under any of the following circumstances, that is to say:
>
> '. . .
>
> '(b) in obedience to the order of a competent authority which he is bound by law to obey, unless the order is manifestly unlawful'.[25]

The concept of manifest illegality was explained in a passage from the judgment rendered by the District Military Court in the Kafr Kassem case:

> 'The distinguishing mark of a "manifestly unlawful" order should be displayed like a black flag over the order given, as a warning reading "Prohibited!" Not formal unlawfulness, hidden or half-hidden, not unlawfulness which is discernible only to the eyes of legal experts is important here, but a conspicuous and flagrant breach of the law, a certain and imperative unlawfulness appearing on the face of the order itself, a clearly criminal character of the order or of the acts ordered, an unlawfulness which pierces the eye and revolts the heart, if the eye is not blind and the heart not obtuse or corrupted—that is the extent of "manifest" unlawfulness required to override the duty of obedience of a soldier, and to charge him with criminal responsibility for his acts'.[26]

The Military Court of Appeal referred to these words as 'striking' and 'deserving to be heeded and remembered';[27] and it added that the manifest illegality principle is 'something like a golden mean', as well as 'the best attainable'.[28]

The manifest illegality principle was also applied, in a very significant and well-known way, in the course of the trials of the German war criminals of the First World War, which took place at Leipzig in 1921. And it is befitting that, at this juncture, we give a full and particular account of these important trials.

25. Criminal Code Ordinance, No. 74 of 1936, Section 19(b). This Section is discussed in the Eichmann trial (first instance) (Criminal Case 40/61, Attorney General v. Eichmann), Judgment (mimeographed, English), ss. 218–219, 221.
26. Kafr Kassem case (first instance), *op. cit.*, pp. 213–214. The translation given here is partly based on the one rendered in the Eichmann trial (first instance), Judgment, *op. cit.*, s. 219.
27. Kafr Kassem case (second instance), *op. cit.*, p. 410. Cf. Eichmann trial (first instance), Judgment, *op. cit.*, s. 219.
28. Kafr Kassem case (second instance), *op. cit.*, pp. 410–411. Cf. Eichmann trial (first instance), Judgment, *op. cit.*, s. 219; Eichmann trial (second instance), Judgment, *op. cit.*, p. 132.

CHAPTER 2

THE LEIPZIG TRIALS

A. *Historical Background*[29]

Article 228 of the Treaty of Versailles, dated 28 June 1919, recognized the right of the Allied Powers to commit to trial the German war criminals of the First World War and put the German

29. The above-mentioned book by Mullins (*The Leipzig Trials* (1921)) should be consulted on any question pertaining to the trials. See also, with respect to their historical background, Bellot, 'A Permanent International Criminal Court', *I.L.A.*, 1922, vol. 1, pp. 63–81 at p. 72; Birkenhead, *International Law* (6th ed., by Moelwyn-Hughes, 1927), p. 301 ; Birkett, 'International Legal Theories Evolved at Nuremberg', *Int. Aff.*, vol. 23 (1947), pp. 317–325 at p. 321 ; Bishop, *International Law, Cases and Materials* (1953), p. 632; Calvocoressi, *op. cit.*, pp. 20–21; Cave, 'War Crimes and their Punishment', *T.G.S.*, vol. 8 (1923), pp. xix–xxxi at pp. xxvii–xxix; Colby, 'War Crimes', p. 615; Corbett, *Law and Society in the Relations of States* (1951), p. 229; Daniel, *op. cit.*, pp. 31–32; Descheemaeker, 'Le Tribunal Militaire International des Grands Criminels de Guerre', *R.G.D.I.P.*, vol. 50 (1946), pp. 210–289 at p. 213; Fenwick, *International Law* (3rd ed., rev. enl., 1948), pp. 668–669; Finch, 'Retribution for War Crimes', *A.J.I.L.*, vol. 37 (1943), pp. 81–88 at p. 83; Garner, *International Law*, vol. 2, pp. 477–478; Garner, 'Punishment', p. 77; Glueck, 'By What Tribunal Shall War Offenders be Tried?', *H.L.R.*, vol. 56 (1942–1943), pp. 1059–1089 at p. 1059; Glueck, 'The Nuernberg Trial and Aggressive War', *H.L.R.*, vol. 59 (1945–1946), pp. 396–456 at p. 427 n. 91; Glueck, *The Nuremberg Trial and Aggressive War* (1946), p. 55; Glueck, *War Criminals*, pp. 23–33; Hackworth, *Digest of International Law* (1940–1944), vol. 6, p. 279; Hankey, *op. cit.*, pp. 5–6; Higgins – Hall, *International Law*, p. 499; *History of U.N.W.C.C.*, pp. 44, 46, 286; Janeczek, *Nuremberg Judgment in the Light of International Law* (1949), pp. 49–52; Lachs, *War Crimes* (1945), p. 79; Lauer, 'The International War Criminal Trials and the Common Law of War', *S.J.L.R.*, vol. 20 (1945–1946), pp. 18–24 at p. 20; Lauterpacht, 'War Crimes', p. 84; Levy, 'The Law and Procedure of War Crime Trials', *A.P.S.R.*, vol. 37 (1943), pp. 1052–1081 at p. 1062; L'Huillier, *Eléments de Droit International Public* (1950), p. 313; Marin, 'The Evolution and Present Status of the Laws of War', *R.A.D.I.*, vol. 92 (1957), pp. 629–751 at p. 685; Maxwell-Fyfe, 'Foreword' to *W.C.T.S.*, vol. 1 (Peleus trial), p. xvii; Mérignhac, 'De la Responsabilité Pénale des Actes Criminels Commis au Cours de la Guerre de 1914–1918', *R.D.I.L.C.*, 3rd series, vol. 1 (1920), pp. 34–70 at pp. 61–68; Mérignhac and Lémonon, *Le Droit des Gens et la Guerre de 1914–1918* (1921), vol. 2, pp. 591–604; Merle, *Le Procès de Nuremberg et le Châtiment des Criminels de Guerre* (1949), pp. 27–28; Myerson, *Germany's War Crimes and Punishment* (1944), pp. 129–130; Pella, 'Towards an International Criminal Court', *A.J.I.L.*, vol. 44 (1950), pp. 37–68 at p. 38 n. 4; E. Pollock, 'Introduction' to Mullins, *op. cit., passim*; Rochette, *L'Individu devant le Droit International* (1956), p. 148; Rousseau, *Droit International Public* (1953), p. 576;

Government under an obligation to surrender the culprits.[30] But when the Allies tried to enforce the Treaty, submitting long lists of war criminals whose extradition was sought, the German Government refused to comply with the demand. It was claimed that the surrender of these people, among whom were civilian leaders and high-ranking military commanders regarded by German public opinion as national heroes, would stir up such a stormy reaction against the new régime in Germany that the consequences could hardly be foreseen. The Allied Powers conceded that internal conditions in Germany were parlous, and they assented, therefore,[31] to the proposal that the war criminals be brought to trial before the German Supreme Court (*Reichsgericht*) in Leipzig. Ultimately, only a handful of secondary offenders were tried and sentenced by this Court, and the whole episode of Leipzig has become synonymous, for many, with a judicial farce. In this study, however, we do not have to occupy ourselves with an exploration of the general aspects of the Leipzig trials. Our interest in them boils down to a concern with the solution given by the German Court to the problem of obedience to superior orders, because that solution has in the course of time become famous far and wide.

We shall now separately discuss each of the trials in which the Court tackled the question of obedience to orders.

B. *Robert Neumann's Case*[32]

The accused was charged with ill-treatment of British prisoners-of-war. The prosecution was able to prove several instances of this

Rox-burgh, 'Submarines at the Washington Conference', *B.Y.B.I.L.*, vol. 3 (1922–1923), pp. 150–158 at pp. 155–156; Scelle, *Manuel de Droit International Public* (1948), p. 982; Scott, 'The Trial of the Kaiser', *What Really Happened at Paris* (ed. by House and Seymour, 1921), pp. 251–256; Svarlien, *An Introduction to the Law of Nations* (1955), p. 400 n. 19; Trainin, *Hitlerite Responsibility under Criminal Law* (1945), pp. 22–23; Winfield – Lawrence, *International Law*, p. 546; Woetzel, *op. cit.*, pp. 31–34; Q. Wright, 'The Outlawry of War', *A.J.I.L.*, vol. 19 (1925), pp. 76–103 at p. 79.

30. *A.J.I.L.*, vol. 13 (1919), Supp., p. 151 at pp. 250–251.
31. Fenwick claims that one of the reasons why the Allied Powers relinquished the exercise of their right to try the war criminals in their own courts was 'the obvious legal difficulty that many of the accused persons had acted in obedience to higher authority' (Fenwick, *op. cit.*, p. 669. Cf. Hostage case, Opening Statement for Defendant List (by Laternser), *N.M.T.*, vol. 11, p. 860). But nowhere have I found support for this claim. If there is a grain of substance in it, it can be detected in the fact that the Allies failed to apprehend the greatest war criminal of them all—Kaiser Wilhelm II, who had found political asylum in the Netherlands—and hence tended, perhaps, not to press too strongly for the extradition of the lesser criminals. See Hankey, *op. cit.*, p. 6.
32. Robert Neumann's case, *A.J.I.L.*, vol. 16 (1922), p. 696. See also Mullins, *op. cit.*, pp. 87–98. Cf. Colby, 'War Crimes', p. 611.

ill-treatment; but it was established that on one occasion, when Neumann had struck a prisoner for his refusal to go to work, the act had been performed in obedience to a superior order. The Court convicted the defendant on the basis of his other acts, but exculpated him from all guilt in respect of that specific striking of a prisoner. The Court ruled as follows:

> 'The accused cannot . . . be held responsible for these events. He was covered by the order of his superior which he was bound to obey. According to § 47 of the Military Penal Code a subordinate can only be criminally responsible under such circumstances when he knows that his orders involve an act which is a civil or military crime. This was not the case here'.[33]

In other words, the Court pronounced here that by virtue of the German national law, Section 47 of the Military Penal Code, to be more precise, it is possible to convict a defendant who had committed a crime pursuant to a superior order only if he knew that the order called upon him to perform a criminal act.

C. *The Dover Castle Case*[34]

The accused here, Karl Neumann, had been in command of a German submarine, and was charged with torpedoing the British hospital-ship Dover Castle. The defendant admitted sinking the ship, but pleaded that he had merely done what he had done in pursuance of the instructions of the German Admiralty.

33. Robert Neumann's case, *A.J.I.L.*, vol. 16 (1922), p. 699.
34. Dover Castle case, *A.J.I.L.*, vol. 16 (1922), p. 704. See also Mullins, *op. cit.*, pp. 99–107, 198, 221–222. Cf. Bellot, 'A Permanent International Criminal Court', *op. cit.*, pp. 73, 78; Birkenhead, *op. cit.*, p. 301; Cameron, 'Introduction' to *W.C.T.S.*, vol. 1 (Peleus trial), p. xliii; Cave, *op. cit.*, p. xxviii; Colby, 'War Crimes', pp. 611–612; Colby, 'War Crimes and their Punishment', *op. cit.*, p. 43; Daniel, *op. cit.*, p. 163; Dunbar, *op. cit.*, p. 256; Eustathiades, 'Ordres', pp. 402 n. 22, 405 n. 31; Finch, 'Superior Orders', p. 440; Glaser, *Introduction*, p. 115 n. 2; Glaser, 'L'Ordre', p. 305; Glaser, 'Nuremberg', p. 30; Glueck, *War Criminals*, p. 233 n. 15; Greenspan, *op. cit.*, p. 441; Guggenheim, *Traité de Droit International Public* (1953–1954), vol. 2, p. 48 n. 1; Hackworth, *op. cit.*, vol. 6, pp. 462–463; Higgins, 'Book Review (on Oppenheim)', *L.Q.R.*, vol. 38 (1922), pp. 104–105; Higgins – Hall, *International Law*, p. 499; *History of U.N.W.C.C.*, p. 287; Janeczek, *op. cit.*, p. 74; Kelsen, 'Responsibility', p. 558 n. 30; Lauterpacht, 'War Crimes', p. 77; Lauterpacht – Oppenheim, *International Law*, vol. 2 (5th ed., 1935), p. 454 n. 1, (7th ed., 1952), p. 569 n. 1; Levie, 'Penal Sanctions for Maltreatment of Prisoners of War', *A.J.I.L.*, vol. 56 (1962), pp. 433–468 at p. 463 n. 122; Maunoir, *op. cit.*, pp. 218, 269; Myerson, *op. cit.*, pp. 154–155, 157–158; Roxburgh, *op. cit.*, pp. 155–156; Sack, 'Punishment', p. 67; Sack, 'Superior Order', p. 15 n. 28; Schick, 'War Criminals', p. 47; Schwarzenberger, *Lawlessness*, p. 64 n. 1; Schwarzenberger, 'War Crimes', p. 72 n. 6; Starke, *An Introduction to International Law* (4th ed., 1958), p. 370 n. 4; Winfield – Lawrence, *International Law*, p. 546; Woetzel, *op. cit.*, p. 33; *L.R.U.N.W.C.C.*, Notes, Dostler trial, vol. 1, p. 31; Peleus trial, Closing Speech for Defendants Hoffmann *et al.* (by Pabst), *W.C.T.S.*, vol. 1, pp. 110–111.

The defence made out its case as follows: in 1917, the German Government declared that, as the Allied Powers had been utilizing hospital-ships for military purposes in violation of the provisions of the Hague Convention No. X of 1907, thenceforth any enemy hospital-ship sailing in the Mediterranean without fulfilling certain prerequisites set forth in the declaration would be regarded as a man-of-war and constitute a target for attack. The Allies refuted the allegation of misuse of hospital-ships, and declined to abide by arbitrary preconditions not sanctioned by the Hague Convention, as required by Germany. The Dover Castle was attacked and torpedoed in the Mediterranean, on the strength of, and following, the declaration, which had been transmitted by the German Admiralty to the German Fleet as an order.

The Court acquitted Karl Neumann, holding:

> 'It is a military principle that the subordinate is bound to obey the orders of his superiors. This duty of obedience is of considerable importance from the point of view of the criminal law. Its consequence is that, when the execution of a service order involves an offence against the criminal law, the superior giving the order is alone responsible.
>
> 'This is in accordance with the terms of the German law, § 47, para. 1 of the Military Penal Code. It also accords with the legal principles of all other civilized states...
>
> 'According to § 47 of the Military Penal Code, No. 2, a subordinate who acts in conformity with orders is... liable to punishment as an accomplice, when he knows that his superiors have ordered him to do acts which involve a civil or military crime or misdemeanor. There has been no case of this here. The memoranda of the German Government about the misuse of enemy hospital ships were known to the accused. The facts set out in them he held to be conclusive... He was therefore of the opinion that the measures taken by the German Admiralty against enemy hospital ships were not contrary to international law, but were legitimate reprisals...
>
> 'The accused... cannot, therefore, be punished for his conduct'.[35]

Clearly the Court reiterated here the *ratio* of its decision in Robert Neumann's case, but added an elaborate exposition of its reasoning. The general rule, again according to Section 47 of the Military Penal Code, that is, German national law, is that a subordinate, committing an offence in obedience to superior orders, does not incur criminal responsibility. This rule is inapplicable only when the subordinate knows, while committing the offence, that the act which he was ordered to carry out constitutes a crime or a misdemeanour. In this particular case the accused believed, when he sank the British ship in compliance with the German Admiralty's order, that he was executing a legitimate act of reprisal. Consequently, the Court did not find any reason which might preclude the application of the

35. Dover Castle case, *A.J.I.L.*, vol. 16 (1922), pp. 707–708.

general rule, as enunciated above, and pronounced Karl Neumann to be not-guilty.

D. *The Llandovery Castle Case*[36]

The Llandovery Castle was also a British hospital-ship, torpedoed by a German submarine, but, unlike the Dover Castle, it fell victim when sailing in the Atlantic Ocean, beyond the region referred to by the German declaration of 1917. The commander of the German submarine, a man named Patzig, attacked the Llandovery Castle despite the fact that he had identified it as a hospital-ship, and even though he knew that he was deviating from the instructions of his superiors. When most of the crew of the Llandovery Castle managed, before it foundered, to launch the lifeboats, three in number, Patzig decided to obliterate all traces of the crime and send the witnesses of it to the bottom. His submarine, therefore, opened fire on the lifeboats and sank two of them with all hands. After the war, all attempts by the German authorities to apprehend Patzig proved

36. Llandovery Castle case, *A.J.I.L.*, vol. 16 (1922), p. 708. See also Mullins, *op. cit.*, pp. 107–133, 221. Cf. Benton, 'Introduction' to *German Views*, p. 23; Bishop, *op. cit.*, p. 632; Cameron, *op. cit.*, pp. xlii–xliii; Colby, 'War Crimes', pp. 612–613; Coste-Floret, *op. cit.*, p. 22; Daniel, *op. cit.*, p. 163; Dunbar, *op. cit.*, p. 245; Eustathiades, 'Ordres', pp. 402 n. 22, 405 n. 33, 413; Fenwick, *op. cit.*, p. 669 n. 56; Glaser, *Introduction*, p. 115; Glaser, 'L'Ordre', pp. 304–305; Glaser, 'Nuremberg', p. 30; Glueck, *War Criminals*, pp. 151–152; Green, 'Book Review (on *L.R.U.N.W.C.C.*, vol. 1)', *Mod.L.R.*, vol. 11 (1948), pp. 106–108 at p. 106; Green, 'Book Review (on *L.R.U.N.W.C.C.*, vol. 2)', *Mod.L.R.*, vol. 11 (1948), pp. 358–360 at p. 359; Greenspan, *op. cit.*, p. 441; Guggenheim, *op. cit.*, vol. 2, p. 47; *History of U.N.W.C.C.*, pp. 286–287; Janeczek, *op. cit.*, pp. 74–75; Keenan and Brown, *Crimes against International Law* (1950), p. 133; Kelsen, *Peace*, p. 106; Kelsen, *Principles*, pp. 136–137 n. 27; Kelsen, 'Responsibility', pp. 558–559 n. 30; Lauterpacht, 'War Crimes', p. 73 n. 2; Lauterpacht – Oppenheim, *International Law*, vol. 2 (7th ed., 1952), p. 569 n. 2; Levie, *op. cit.*, p. 463 n. 122; Maunoir, *op. cit.*, p. 217; Kilmuir (Maxwell-Fyfe), *op. cit.*, p. 15; Maxwell-Fyfe, 'Foreword' to *W.C.T.S.*, *op. cit.*, p. xx; Myerson, *op. cit.*, pp. 159–162; Paston, *Superior Orders as Affecting Responsibility for War Crimes* (1946), p. 5; Sack, 'Punishment', p. 67; Sack, 'Superior Order', pp. 14–15; Schwarzenberger, *Lawlessness*, p. 64 n. 1; Schwarzenberger, 'War Crimes', p. 72 n. 6; Simon, 'Foreword' to *W.C.T.S.*, vol. 8 (Double Tenth trial), p. xiv; Starke, *op. cit.*, p. 370; Trainin, *op. cit.*, p. 90; Woetzel, *op. cit.*, p. 33; Double Tenth trial, Closing Speech for the Prosecution, *W.C.T.S.*, vol. 8, p. 258; Eichmann trial (second instance), Judgment, *op. cit.*, p. I 33; Einsatzgruppen case, Closing Statement of the Prosecution, *N.M.T.*, vol. 4, p. 376; Einsatzgruppen case, Judgment, *N.M.T.*, vol. 4, pp. 483–484; Golkel trial, *L.R.U.N.W.C.C.*, vol. 5, pp. 50–51; Holzer trial—Notes, Sawada trial, *L.R.U.N.W.C.C.*, vol. 5, p. 15; Hostage case, Judgment, *N.M.T.*, vol. 11, p. 1236; Kharkov trial, Prosecution, *People's Verdict*, p. 114; Peleus trial, Closing Speech for Defendants Hoffmann *et al.* (by Pabst), *W.C.T.S.*, vol. 1, p. 111; Peleus trial, Closing Speech for the Prosecution, *W.C.T.S.*, vol. 1, pp. 118–119; *L.R.U.N.W.C.C.*, Notes, Peleus trial, vol. 1, pp. 19–20; *L.R.U.N.W.C.C.*, Notes, Stalag Luft III case, vol. 11, pp. 47–49.

unavailing, so they brought to trial in his stead two officers—Dithmar and Boldt—who had served in the same submarine and had helped Patzig to massacre the survivors of the Llandovery Castle. In their trial, the defendants sought to rely on Patzig's orders,[37] but the Court rejected this defence, analyzing the legal situation in the following way:

> 'The firing on the boats was an offence against the law of nations...
>
> 'The rule of international law, which is here involved, is simple and is universally known...
>
> 'Patzig's order does not free the accused from guilt. It is true that according to para. 47 of the Military Penal Code, if the execution of an order in the ordinary course of duty involves such a violation of the law as is punishable, the superior officer issuing such an order is alone responsible. According to No. 2, however, the subordinate obeying such an order is liable to punishment, if it was known to him that the order of the superior involved the infringement of civil or military law. This applies in the case of the accused. It is certainly to be urged in favor of the military subordinates, that they are under no obligation to question the order of their superior officer, and they can count upon its legality. But no such confidence can be held to exist, if such an order is universally known to everybody, including also the accused, to be without any doubt whatever against the law'.[38]

Nevertheless, the Court acknowledged that obedience to superior orders is a factor that ought to be taken into account for mitigation of punishment, and consequently sentenced the accused to imprisonment for a period of only four years.[39]

This important decision represents the other side of the coin which was minted in the Dover Castle case:[40] it was here affirmed that

37. In the *History of U.N.W.C.C.*, p. 287, it is stated that Dithmar and Boldt tried to rely on the German Admiralty's orders; but this is an error. The orders were issued by Patzig, who acted on his part in defiance of the instructions of the Admiralty.
38. Llandovery Castle case, *A.J.I.L.*, vol. 16 (1922), pp. 721–722.
39. *Ibid.*, p. 723.
40. An attempt is sometimes made to distinguish between the two judgments rendered in the Dover Castle and in the Llandovery Castle cases, as if the former admitted the defence of obedience to superior orders whereas the latter excluded it (i.e., when manifestly illegal acts are committed). An ambiguity on this point is discernible—for instance—in a footnote, appended by Lauterpacht to the fifth edition of Oppenheim's treatise on International Law (deleted, however, from the subsequent editions of the same book, although the editor had not changed): Lauterpacht – Oppenheim, *International Law*, vol. 2 (5th ed., 1935), p. 454 n. 1. Schwarzenberger refers to Lauterpacht's words, saying: 'As is admitted in the footnote, the judgments of the German Supreme Court cancel each other out' (Schwarzenberger, 'Inductive Approach', p. 546). And see also Eustathiades, 'Ordres', p. 402 n. 22. But a comparison of the two judgments demonstrates that, far from cancelling each other out, they are actually complementary: both confirm the rule that obedience to superior orders relieves defendants of criminal responsibility, and both except from this rule the particular defendant who acted with full knowledge of the illegality of his act. If there is a difference between the two

the general rule of German national law, in accordance with which a subordinate committing an offence pursuant to superior orders is not criminally responsible, does not apply to defendants who knew full well the illicit character of the act which they had been ordered to perform. The act committed by Dithmar and Boldt constituted an offence against international law, but their responsibility was established by the German Court in conformity with criteria of German law, as expressed in the statutory provision of Section 47 of the Military Penal Code, regarding obedience to orders.

Special consideration should be given to the last two sentences in the citation from the judgment. Here the Court loosened the bonds of statutory law a trifle, and tried to make a contribution of its own to clarification of the questions raised in the context of obedience to superior orders. The Court, in those sentences, pronounced the general rule to be that a subordinate may count on the legality of the orders received by him; but when it is known to one and all, the subordinate himself not excluded, that the order is unlawful, we encounter an exception to the rule, and the subordinate can rely no longer on the alleged legality of the order. Let us now compare this dual ruling of the Court with the statutory concept of Section 47, as applied in the Dover Castle case. The general rule that a subordinate can count on the legality of orders is parallel to the statutory provision reflected in the Dover Castle case that obedience to orders ordinarily frees from responsibility. We have before us, however, not a mere parallelism but also an explanation and an interpretation: apparently the Court founded discharge from responsibility on the subordinate's right to count on the legality of the orders issued to him. So much for the general rule. But the Court also laid down that this rule is subject to exception. In the judgment rendered in the Llandovery Castle case, the formulation of the exception is that the subordinate cannot count on the legality of the order when it is universally known to everybody, including the subordinate himself, that the order is indubitably unlawful. This exception corresponds to the statutory proviso expounded in the decision in the Dover Castle case that obedience to orders does not relieve a subordinate of responsibility if he acted while being aware of the illegality of the orders. But a perusal of the language used by the Court in the Llandovery Castle case shows that two new elements were added in the judgment to the statutory exposition of the exception: first, the Court spoke about an order which is 'without any doubt whatever' illegal; and secondly, it supplemented the personal knowledge of the accused

judgments, it is in the concrete outcome which is based on different sets of factual circumstances, but there is no distinction between them.

relating to the illegality of the order with universal knowledge on the same subject. These two additional points denote that, when formulating the exception, the Court had a manifestly illegal order in mind.

Even though the Court broke away slightly from the moorings of the statutory law, there is no indication that it wished to form a criterion of its own for establishing criminal responsibility in contradistinction to the one existing under Section 47, as applied in the Dover Castle case. An illustration will make this clearer. Suppose that a certain defendant knew right well that a particular order, received and executed by him, was not lawful, although it cannot be regarded as manifestly illegal. According to the precepts of German statutory law, such a defendant should be convicted on account of his personal knowledge, which is of paramount importance. In my opinion, it emerges plainly from the Court's enunciation, cited above, that the judgment in the Llandovery Castle case did not seek to contest that. What, then, is the relevance of the manifest illegality factor? One must say that it is only intended to constitute an auxiliary test for the purpose of establishing the personal knowledge of the defendant with regard to the illegality of the order. It is difficult to search a person's mind and ascertain what he knew during some past event; but, when an order is manifestly illegal, it can be said with a great deal of certitude that every defendant, including John Doe or Richard Roe who are in the dock in an actual trial, is presumed to have been aware of the unlawfulness of the order, and that consequently he should be held responsible. To put it in Glueck's words:

> 'Evidently the German rule does not protect the soldier if he actually knows the order to be illegal; and an inference of such knowledge is used against him when the order is one which "is universally known to everybody... to be without any doubt whatever against the law"'.[41]

By the same token, it may happen, in rare cases of course, that a particular defendant successfully proves that he was not aware of the unlawfulness of the order, despite its being manifestly illegal. What will the verdict then be? As far as the German statutory rule is concerned, the personal knowledge element is the overriding consideration, and the Court in the Llandovery Castle case did not wish to refute this: the judgment expressly declared that the universal knowledge of the unlawfulness of the act does not suffice; the particular defendant must share this knowledge with the rest of

41. Glueck, *War Criminals*, p. 152.

the world.[42] Again it is clear that the Court used the manifest illegality circumstance as an auxiliary test only.

E. *Stenger and Crusius Case*[43]

General Stenger was charged with issuing an order to execute French prisoners-of-war, and Major Crusius was accused of killing wounded prisoners while carrying out that order. As for Stenger, the Court ruled that the charge was groundless: he had never given the alleged order. With regard to Crusius, the Court found that he had committed the act, but that he had been under an intense mental strain at the time, so as to believe mistakenly that the General had actually issued the order in question. Furthermore, the Court reached the conclusion that Crusius had not been aware of the illegality of the non-existent order when he acted in compliance with it.[44] Yet Crusius was found guilty of manslaughter by negligence and sentenced to two years imprisonment. Why was he convicted? Assuming—and the judgment is not sufficiently clear to quit assumption for certainty—that the Court was ready and willing to consider the erroneous state of facts existing only in the mind of the accused owing to illusion of the senses, and to decide the case accordingly, then the conviction must hinge on the following statement of the Court:

> 'the indiscriminate killing of all wounded was a monstrous war measure, in no way to be justified'.[45]

This description of the act done by Crusius portrays its heinous character in such a way that it was probably regarded by the Court as manifestly illegal. Yet the Court declined to take into consideration its own finding, expressly made, that the accused had been personally unaware of the unlawfulness of the act. Thus the Court departed, in effect, from the criterion set in the judgment which it had delivered in the Llandovery Castle case, and turned the manifest illegality factor from an auxiliary test into the principal touchstone of criminal responsibility. It is doubtful, however, whether this transformation

42. Emphasis should be laid here upon the words 'including also the accused' in the citation from the judgment. Glueck is of opinion, for one reason or another, that, according to the judgment rendered in the Llandovery Castle case, a defendant is estopped from pleading that he was unaware of the unlawfulness of a manifestly illegal order (Glueck, *War Criminals*, pp. 152–153); but one is at a loss to discover how such a contention can possibly be substantiated in the judgment.
43. Stenger and Crusius case, Mullins, *op. cit.*, pp. 151–167. Cf. Glaser, 'L'Ordre', p. 305; *History of U.N.W.C.C.*, p. 50; Maunoir, *op. cit.*, p. 218.
44. The actual words used by the Court are as follows: 'He was not conscious of the illegality of such an order' (Stenger and Crusius case, Mullins, *op. cit.*, p. 160).
45. Stenger and Crusius case, Mullins, *op. cit.*, p. 161.

was accomplished by the judges intentionally; possibly, they simply recoiled subconsciously from the conclusion which ought to have flowed from their peculiar, 'never-never-land', factual findings. The offence of which Crusius was found guilty—manslaughter by negligence, of all things—and the lenient punishment meted out to him perhaps reflect the perplexity of the Court.

F. *Summary*

The Leipzig trials, excluding the Stenger and Crusius case, demonstrate a clear-cut and unified approach to the question of obedience to superior orders, which can be epitomized as follows:

(1) As a general rule, a subordinate committing a criminal act pursuant to an order should not incur responsibility for it.

(2) This rule is inapplicable if the subordinate knew that the order entailed the commission of a crime, and obeyed it nonetheless.

(3) To determine whether the subordinate was aware of the fact that he had been ordered to perform a criminal act, the Court may use the auxiliary test of manifest illegality.

Clearly the *Reichsgericht* in Leipzig applied and interpreted principles of German national law, and not of international law, in dealing with the problem of obedience to orders.[46] But the Court gave expression to a certain way of solving the problem, and the question that we ought to ask ourselves now is whether the same way may also serve the needs of international law.[47]

46. It might not have been necessary to underscore this fact, which stands out distinctly when one reads the citations from the judgments that are given *in extenso* above, had I not noticed that at least one important jurist refers to the *Reichsgericht*'s decision on the subject of obedience to superior orders, in the Llandovery Castle case, thus: 'This judgment purported to and did express existing international law' (Kilmuir (Maxwell-Fyfe), *op. cit.*, p. 15). Without going, at this juncture, into the question whether the judgment did in point of fact express the rules of positive international law, along with those of German national law, on that subject, it is important for us to note that the Court had no intention of entering the international field; hence, the words 'purported to'—at any rate—are inaccurate. As for the national character of the rule pronounced in Leipzig in regard to obedience to orders, see particularly Cave, *op. cit.*, p. xxviii; Coste-Floret, *op. cit.*, p. 22; Daniel, *op. cit.*, pp. 162–163; Eusthatiades, 'Ordres', p. 413; Glueck, *War Criminals*, pp. 151–152; Higgins – Hall, *International Law*, p. 499; Kelsen, *Peace*, p. 106; Kelsen, *Principles*, p. 136 n. 27; Kelsen, 'Responsibility', pp. 558–559 n. 30; Mullins, *op. cit.*, pp. 218, 220–221; Winfield – Lawrence, *International Law*, p. 546 n. 1; Hostage case, Opening Statement for Defendant List (by Laternser), *N.M.T.*, vol. 11, p. 863; *L.R.U.N.W.C.C.*, Notes, Stalag Luft III case, vol. 11, pp. 48–49.

47. It is noteworthy that in the Peleus trial one of the defence counsel contended that 'the case of the *Llandovery Castle*... has no effect and can have no effect upon this Court which is administering International Law, because the case of the *Llandovery Castle* was a case decided under Municipal Law by the Municipal

Court' (Peleus trial, Closing Speech for Defendant Lenz (by Lermon), *W.C.T.S.*, vol. 1, p. 114. Cf. Peleus trial, *L.R.U.N.W.C.C.*, vol. 1, p. 20). Cameron comments on this statement in the following words: 'That distinction was obviously bad, as there is no necessary difference between Municipal and International Law applicable to the same given circumstances' (Cameron, *op. cit.*, p. xxxiii). This comment is justified inasmuch as it draws attention to the fact that the provisions of international law do not necessarily differ from those of that national law which is applicable to the same state of facts. But one should beware of going to extremes in this approach, and to that extent credit should be given to counsel for the defence in the Peleus trial: the provisions of international law also do not necessarily have to be similar to those of national law. If national law solves the problem of obedience to orders in a certain given way, it does not follow, as a matter of course, that international law espouses the same solution.

PART II: INTERNATIONAL THEORY

INTRODUCTORY NOTE

At the outset of our discussion of the theory of international law on the subject of obedience to superior orders, it is desirable to note that the supposition that the preservation of discipline in the national army is exceedingly important, a supposition which is at the very root of the dilemma created by the execution of a crime pursuant to orders, seems to rest on a quicksand insofar as international law is concerned. Why should international law take an interest in the maintenance of discipline in national armies? There appears to be an inherent fallacy in an argument which equates the relative positions of national law *vis-à-vis* national army and of international law as against a plethora of national armies in the four corners of the earth. If and when the international community does one day form an army of its own, then, and only then, will international law have to face problems corresponding to those that national law is ridden with as a result of the national need to maintain a national army. Until that happens, international law does not have to concern itself with the preservation of military discipline, for the security of the international community is not dependent upon the existence of efficient and disciplined national armies. Should it be claimed otherwise, one may well ask if international law has to take heed of the interests of discipline in all national armies, including aggressive ones. After all, we live within an international legal régime based on the unlawfulness of aggressive wars, and the efficiency of an army employed in the service of an aggressor constitutes perhaps the greatest possible threat to the existence of the modern international legal system. In short, as long as no international army, in the real sense of the word, is in being, it seems that the problem of preserving military discipline ought to be restricted to the national sphere.

If international law does not have to mind the interests of discipline in the national army, it does not have to place its seal upon the duty of obedience to orders either. Consequently, when a soldier gets an order to carry out an act constituting a crime from the standpoint of international law, the one and only international duty to which he is bound is not, in any circumstances, to commit international crimes. In any circumstances, that is to say, not even in obedience to superior orders. No international obligation to obey orders competes, under our assumption, with the duty to abstain from criminal conduct, and that duty, therefore, prevails within the international realm. The upshot of all this is that international law, from a theoretical point of view, is not confronted with any dilemma when it enjoins upon soldiers not to commit international crimes, superior orders notwithstanding. As far as the pure theory of international law goes, a soldier faced with an order to commit a criminal act ought to be penalized if he complies with it, and, on the other hand, there is no reason to convict him of insubordination. The trouble is that prosecution for insubordination, if instituted against a soldier who acted counter to an internationally illegal order, will proceed by virtue of national military law, and not on the basis of international law. Military law, which regards military discipline as the mainstay of the army whose interests it is designed to protect, may compel unqualified and unhesitating obedience to orders, irrespective of their legality under international law. Hence, whether international law is, or is not, confronted, as a legal system, with a theoretical dilemma, the soldier who receives an order to commit an offence is driven, in the international as in the national arena, on to the painful horns of a most acute practical dilemma. To restate the words used by Dicey and quoted above,[48] the soldier finds himself in an intolerable position: if he obeys the order and infringes the provisions of international criminal law, he might be sentenced to the gallows by an international tribunal or a national court of the enemy; if he disobeys it, and refrains from committing the crime, he is liable, in many cases, to face a firing-squad by decree of a court-martial of his own State.

This practical dilemma of the soldier, tossed between Scylla and Charybdis in the international sphere, has gained almost universal cognizance,[49] and one writer even comments that occasionally it is a 'tragic dilemma'.[50] It is self-evident that the international legal system, being a legal system, must take the predicament of the hard-pressed soldier into consideration, and rescue him from between the upper and the nether millstone; and this, in the main, is the origin

48. See *supra*, p. 7.
49. See e.g. Appleman, *op. cit.*, p. 55; Eagleton, *International Government* (rev. ed., 1948), p. 103; Eagleton, 'The Responsibility of the State for the Protection of Foreign Officials', *A.J.I.L.*, vol. 19 (1925), pp. 293–314 at p. 301; Fenwick, *op. cit.*, p. 669 n. 56; Glueck, *War Criminals*, pp. 142–143, 155; Hankey, *op. cit.*, pp. 59–60; Maunoir, *op. cit.*, p. 277; Paston, *op. cit.*, p. 4; Sack, 'Punishment', p. 68; Sack, 'Superior Order', p. 15 n. 29; Winfield – Lawrence, *International Law*, p. 547. Cf. *L.R.U.N.W.C.C.*, Notes, Bury and Hafner trial, vol. 3, p. 64; *L.R.U.N.W.C.C.* Notes, Sawada trial, vol. 5, p. 15.
50. Graven, 'Code', p. 375; Graven, 'Crimes', p. 572.

of the problem of obedience to superior orders in the international sphere. But the solution of the problem is not easy. If there is general agreement in respect of one point in this field, particularly when war crimes are concerned, it relates to the fact that the subject bristles with difficulties[51] and that it is a controversial matter.[52] There is no binding rule in general international law that determines the question without much ado and sets it at rest. It is, therefore, important, when we turn to scrutinize the several doctrines of scholars and writers, to note that we do not have to bow to any of them and accept it as final and conclusive, even if it reflects a principle which has won statutory standing within the compass of one national law or another.

We had better make it clear, at once, that we intend to deal solely with the theory that has been evolved in modern times, for the question of obedience to superior orders has been profoundly considered and discussed only in the context, and on the bedrock, of modern international law. And it is no wonder that orthodox international theory skipped this subject: as pointed out above,[53] no discussion on it is feasible save in the light of an antecedent presupposition that the individual may be held criminally responsible under international law. The sages of traditional international law, who only admitted the international responsibility of the State, did not have to subject the international responsibility of the individual to exceptions and exemptions, as they denied the existence of such responsibility in any case; hence they were not troubled by the

51. See Garner, 'Articles', p. 138; Garner, *International Law*, vol. 2, p. 483; Garner, 'Punishment', pp. 82–83; Glaser, 'L'Ordre', p. 283; Glueck, *War Criminals*, p. 140; Graven, 'Code', p. 177; Graven, 'Crimes', p. 575; Higgins, *op. cit.*, p. 105; *History of U.N.W.C.C.*, p. 274; Lauterpacht, 'War Crimes', p. 70; Maunoir, *op. cit.*, p. 203; Mullins, *op. cit.*, p. 218; Pella, *op. cit.*, p. 53; Roxburgh, *op. cit.*, p. 155; Spaight, *Air Power and War Rights* (3rd ed., 1947), p. 56.
52. See Berger, 'The Legal Nature of War Crimes and the Problem of Superior Command', *A.P.S.R.*, vol. 38 (1944), pp. 1203–1208 at p. 1203; Dunbar, *op. cit.*, p. 234; Glaser, *Introduction*, pp. 111–112; Glaser, 'L'Ordre', p. 283; Glaser, 'Nuremberg', p. 29; Graven, 'Code', p. 177; Janeczek, *op. cit.*, p. 68; Lauer, *op. cit.*, p. 22; Mérignhac and Lémonon, *op. cit.*, vol. 2, p. 567. At a certain stage Lauterpacht asserted that a controversy on the question of obedience to superior orders is 'somewhat unreal' nowadays (Lauterpacht, *International Law and Human Rights* (1950), p. 10; Lauterpacht, 'The Subjects of the Law of Nations', *L.Q.R.*, vols. 63 (1947), pp. 438–460, and 64 (1948), pp. 97–119, in vol. 63, p. 442). But subsequently he laid stress on the need for an 'authoritative clarification of the law relating to the punishment of war crimes, in particular with regard to the plea of superior orders' (Lauterpacht, 'The Problem of the Revision of the Law of War', *B.Y.B.I.L.*, vol. 29 (1952), pp. 360–382 at p. 381). Kunz voiced the opinion that this subject, like other subjects pertaining to the laws of war, is 'in a chaotic status' (Kunz, 'The Chaotic Status of the Laws of War and the Urgent Necessity for their Revision', *A.J.I.L.*, vol. 45 (1951), pp. 37–61 at p. 50. See also *ibid.* at p. 53; Kunz, 'The Laws of War', *A.J.I.L.*, vol. 50 (1956), pp. 313–337 at p. 336).
53. See *supra*, p. 1.

problem of obedience to superior orders as a defence.[54] It is true that the fathers of international law disputed with one another on the question whether a person is bound, and entitled, to fight in a war that is, or appears or may turn out to be, 'unjust' (*'bellum injustum'*), when he is ordered to do so by the prince, or whether he is committing an offence upon obeying such an order.[55] In the progress of the disputation, the first sprigs began to sprout of what we have termed the manifest illegality principle, but it is important to lay stress upon the fact that, when the fathers of international law spoke about a duty binding the individual or an offence that he might commit, they had in mind a duty invested with a religious halo and an offence against conscience. They invariably relied, in the course of their arguments, on the pillars of the Catholic Church, the theologians and the canonists; and, when they debated with these venerated authorities, and among themselves, it was more an ecclesiastical, heaven-pointed polemic than a secular, legal controversy. In this study we shall not get into the thick of this disputation, for it springs from the roots of Catholic theology,[56] and the author lacks the necessary qualification to wrestle with the subtleties of ecclesiastical homiletics with any hope of orientation. Furthermore, we ought to emphasize that

(a) the discussion in the writings of the fathers of international law generally concentrated upon a unique order, namely, an order to fight in an 'unjust' or doubtfully 'just' war, and it is hard to tell whether by induction we can infer principles of general applicability from the rules governing this particular order;[57]

(b) the centre of gravity of the discussion is a unique commander, to wit, the prince (or sovereign), who is in sole charge of all matters

54. See Eustathiades, 'Ordres', p. 396.

55. See Ayala, *De Jure et Officiis Bellicis et Disciplina Militari* (Classics of International Law, 1912), vol. 2 (translation), pp. 21–22; Belli, *A Treatise on Military Matters and Warfare* (Classics of International Law, 1936), vol. 2 (translation), pp. 63–66; Grotius, *De Jure Belli ac Pacis* (Classics of International Law, 1925), vol. 2 (translation), pp. 587, 590–593; Pufendorf, *De Jure Naturae et Gentium* (Classics of International Law, 1934), vol. 2 (translation), pp. 1145–1146; Suarez, *Selections from Three Works* (Classics of International Law, 1944), vol. 2 (translation), pp. 831–836; Vattel, *The Law of Nations* (Classics of International Law, 1916), vol. 3 (translation), p. 303; Victoria, *De Indis et de Jure Belli* (Classics of International Law, 1917), pp. 173–177.

56. In this regard, see particularly Vanderpol, *La Doctrine Scolastique du Droit de Guerre* (1925), pp. 103–105, 131–141.

57. Excepted from this rule are Pufendorf and Vattel, who deal with the specific question of obedience to the prince's order to go to war, within the compass of a general discussion on the subject of compliance with the orders of the prince. See Pufendorf, *op. cit.*, pp. 1140–1145; Vattel, *op. cit.*, p. 25. Cf. Vattel, *ibid.*, pp. 237, 240–241.

relative to the subject of declaration of war. An inductive inference from the sovereign war-lord to the ordinary commander, officer or non-commissioned officer is not well-founded.

We must, therefore, resign ourselves to the fact that the subject of obedience to superior orders, as a shield against criminal prosecution under international law, is a modern phenomenon, and there is no sense in a minute dissection of obsolete doctrines to lend support to newborn theories of the international law of the present day.

CHAPTER I

THE MANIFEST ILLEGALITY PRINCIPLE AND THE PERSONAL KNOWLEDGE PRINCIPLE

We shall start our discussion of the problem of obedience to superior orders, from the standpoint of international legal theory, with the principle which was adopted by Israeli statutory law as well as by the Leipzig trials, and gained itself in Israeli jurisprudence the reputation of 'a golden mean',[58] namely, the manifest illegality principle. A substantial number of jurists uphold it as valid, exclusively or among other rules, within the field of obedience to superior orders under international law.[59] Maugham expresses this conception in the following words:

> 'A superior order should not be a defence if the act constituting the alleged crime was clearly and obviously one of a criminal kind'.[60]

Cave says, from an inverted angle, that this principle

> 'limits the impunity of the soldier to cases where the orders are not so manifestly illegal that he must or ought to have known that they were unlawful'.[61]

The long and the short of the principle is that a subordinate should incur responsibility for his act if he commits a crime pursuant to a

58. See *supra*, p. 9.
59. See Calvocoressi, *op. cit.*, p. 73; Cave, *op. cit.*, p. xxiii; Daniel, *op. cit.*, p. 167; Graven, 'Code', p. 374; Graven, 'Crimes', p. 581; Greenspan, *op. cit.*, pp. 490, 495; Higgins, *op. cit.*, pp. 104–105; Higgins – Hall, *International Law*, p. 499; Knieriem, *op. cit.*, p. 244; Lauterpacht, 'War Crimes', pp. 73–74; Lauterpacht – Oppenheim, *International Law*, vol. 2 (7th ed., 1952), p. 569; Maugham, *U.N.O. and War Crimes* (1951), p. 48; Maunoir, *op. cit.*, pp. 243–248, 274, 311; Kilmuir (Maxwell-Fyfe), *op. cit.*, pp. 15–16; Maxwell-Fyfe, 'Foreword' to *W.C.T.S.*, *op. cit.*, p. xx; Myerson, *op. cit.*, p. 165; *N.L.G. Report*, p. 21; F. Pollock, 'The Work of the League of Nations', *L.Q.R.*, vol. 35 (1919), pp. 193–198 at pp. 197–198; Sleeman, 'Introduction' to *W.C.T.S.*, vol. 3 (Gozawa trial), p. liv; Starke, *op. cit.*, p. 370; Trainin, *op. cit.*, p. 90; Q. Wright, 'War Criminals', *A.J.I.L.*, vol. 39 (1945), pp. 257–285 at p. 278 (re: offences against the law of war); Q. Wright, *A Study of War* (1942), vol. 2, Appendix 30, p. 1396 n. 6 (*ditto*). In one of his articles, Bellot apparently subscribed also to the manifest illegality principle (see Bellot, 'War Criminals', vol. 36, p. 765), but in his later writings he relinquished that principle and shifted ground to a support of the doctrine of absolute liability (see below, note 205).
60. Maugham, *op. cit.*, p. 48.
61. Cave, *op. cit.*, p. xxiii.

manifestly illegal order, whereas he ought to be absolved of guilt if he commits an offence in compliance with an order whose illegality is not palpable. Clearly the manifest illegality test is objective in character, and based on the intelligence of the reasonable man. To stand this test, the illegality must, to use Lauterpacht's definition, be 'obvious to any person of ordinary understanding'.[62]

To get to the bottom of the manifest illegality principle in the theory of international law, to grasp its meaning and discern its full import, we have to uncover its rationale. For that purpose, we must try to apply it to the following two sets of facts, already touched upon during the discussion of the Leipzig trials:[63]

(1) Suppose that the soldier John Doe commits an international offence pursuant to an order which is not manifestly illegal from the viewpoint of the reasonable man. Suppose, further, that John Doe is well versed in the intricacies of international law, being, for instance, a Professor in international law, drafted to the army in time of war, and that, when committing the offence, he is well aware of the criminal nature of his act. Will he be held responsible for the offence in accordance with the manifest illegality principle?

(2) Let us take another case, diametrically opposed to the preceding one: the soldier Richard Roe commits an international offence in compliance with an order that is manifestly illegal from the outlook of the reasonable man. Richard Roe has a subnormal IQ, so that he does not necessarily comprehend things which are transparent to a man of ordinary understanding, and, when committing the offence, he is not aware of the criminal character of his act. Will he be found guilty of the offence in accordance with the manifest illegality principle?

The common denominator of these two opposite cases is that, in both, the objective perception of the reasonable man relating to the illegality of the situation does not tally with the subjective cognition of the particular delinquent on account of his peculiar faculties, for better or for worse. The question is whether, in accordance with the manifest illegality principle, which is anchored, as stated, to the

62. Lauterpacht, 'War Crimes', p. 73. See also Sack, 'Punishment', p. 64; Sack, 'Superior Order', p. 12. Incidentally, it is interesting to note that Section 19(b) of the Israel Criminal Code Ordinance, 1936—which, as indicated above, adopts the manifest illegality principle—provides that 'whether an order is or is not manifestly unlawful is a question of law'. In the judgment of the District Court in the Eichmann trial it is stated that this question is 'left to be decided by the Court according to objective criteria' (Eichmann trial (first instance), Judgment, *op. cit.*, s. 221). That was also emphasized by the Military Court of Appeal in the Kafr Kassem case (Kafr Kassem case (second instance), *op. cit.*, p. 413).

63. See *supra*, p. 17.

objective criterion, we have to disregard the subjective state of mind or may pay full attention to it.

First, we ought to note that many of the writers who analyze the manifest illegality principle in the international sphere cite the judgment rendered at Leipzig in the Llandovery Castle case as an example of the practical application of the principle.[64] It will be recalled that,[65] in this judgment, the criterion of manifest illegality was used not as an independent touchstone for establishing the criminal responsibility of a subordinate committing an offence in pursuance of orders, but only as an auxiliary test for the purpose of ascertaining the personal knowledge of the subordinate as to the unlawfulness of the order. On the one hand, the rule laid down in the Llandovery Castle case has to be understood in such a way that, when an offender is aware of the unlawfulness of the order executed by him, he ought to be held criminally responsible for his act even though the order does not reach the degree of manifest illegality. That, therefore, is the answer to the question raised by John Doe's case. On the other hand, it is expressly prescribed in the judgment that the universal knowledge of the unlawfulness of the act does not suffice, meaning that it is not enough for an order to be manifestly illegal: it is necessary that the particular defendant in the dock be aware of the unlawfulness.[66] This is the answer to the question raised by Richard Roe's case. In both cases, the objective factor of manifest illegality serves only as a device to appraise the subjective knowledge of the defendant.

As a matter of fact, one may already deduce the rationale of the manifest illegality principle from the very way in which the principle is defined by Cave, as quoted above. After all, Cave speaks about orders being so manifestly illegal that the person carrying them out must or ought to have been aware of their unlawfulness.[67] From this alone, one can draw the conclusion that, if the executant of the order actually knows of its unlawfulness, he ought to be convicted, no matter whether the order is or, as in John Doe's case, is not manifestly illegal. The subjective knowledge of the subordinate as to the illicit nature of the order consequently constitutes the overrid-ing

64. See Cameron, *op. cit.*, p. xliii; Fenwick, *op. cit.*, p. 669 n. 56; Greenspan, *op. cit.*, pp. 441, 494; Kilmuir (Maxwell-Fyfe), *op. cit.*, p. 15; Lauterpacht, 'War Crimes', p. 73 n. 2; Lauterpacht – Oppenheim, *International Law*, vol. 2 (7th ed., 1952), p. 569 n. 2; Myerson, *op. cit.*, p. 165; Starke, *op. cit.*, p. 370; Trainin, *op. cit.*, p. 90; Q. Wright, *A Study of War* (1942), vol. 2, Appendix 30, p. 1396 n. 6; *L.R.U.N.W.C.C.*, Notes, Stalag Luft III case, vol. 11, p. 49.

65. See *supra*, pp. 17, 19.

66. See *supra*, note 42.

67. A similar phrasing of the principle may be found in Higgins – Hall, *International Law*, p. 499.

consideration. What, then, is the role of the objective criterion of manifest illegality? Our answer will be that this criterion operates only as an auxiliary, technical contrivance of the law of evidence, designed to ease the burden of proof lying on the prosecution, insofar as the subjective knowledge of the accused is concerned. As it is very difficult to fathom the innermost recesses of the defendant's soul and examine whether or not he was really aware of the illegality of the order obeyed by him, the law contrives an objective test which will facilitate the task of ascertaining his subjective knowledge. Nevertheless, this evidentiary technique does not exclude the possibility of a direct inquiry into the subjective knowledge of the defendant, without making use of objective criteria. That is to say, the prosecution is under the *onus probandi* that the specific defendant, being charged with having committed a crime pursuant to an illegal order, knew, subjectively speaking, that he was ordered to carry out an unlawful act. If the prosecution is willing and able to prove that in a direct way, that is entirely acceptable—and this is the answer to the question posed by John Doe's case. But if the prosecution is unable to do so, the law of evidence comes to its rescue, empowering it to take a short-cut and prove merely that the order was manifestly illegal, namely, illegal from the objective standpoint of the reasonable man. Once the prosecution's effort in carrying this lesser burden is crowned with success, a presumption is created against the defendant that he himself was personally aware, like the rest of the world, of the illegality of the order. This presumption stems from the notion that the defendant, to use Cave's words, 'must or ought to have known' in such a case that the order was unlawful. If he had to know it, he is presumed to have known it.

Another question which arises now is how to reconcile this analysis with the opinion, occasionally heard, that, if a defendant obeyed a manifestly illegal order, his subjective knowledge or, actually, lack of knowledge relative to the subject of illegality is entirely irrelevant. Starke expresses such an opinion, saying:

> 'if he believed that the order was lawful, this belief might be a defence, but not if the order was obviously illegal'.[68]

This view, to the effect that the accused may not benefit from his subjective unawareness of the unlawfulness of the order when this unlawfulness, objectively speaking, is manifest, is opposed to the position taken by the Leipzig Court. But, even if it is right, there is no need to revise in their essence the conclusions that we have just reached. The only new element introduced by this view is that, once

68. Starke, *op. cit.*, p. 370. Cf. also Glueck, *War Criminals*, pp. 152–153; Glueck quoted by Paston, *op. cit.*, p. 18; Maunoir, *op. cit.*, pp. 247, 256.

the prosecution proves that the defendant obeyed a manifestly illegal order, it does not really matter whether he is able, factually speaking, to rebut the presumption of his personal awareness of the legal situation—as in the case of Richard Roe—for, legally speaking, he is incapacitated from rebutting it. In other words, the presumption cannot be refuted; it is not an ordinary *praesumptio juris*, but rather a *praesumptio juris et de jure*. Nevertheless, it is still a presumption, and the manifest illegality principle still constitutes an auxiliary test of the law of evidence. It is important to recall that, even if a certain defendant, like Richard Roe, is precluded from submitting evidence that he was unaware of the unlawfulness of an order which was manifestly illegal, the prosecution is not precluded from submitting evidence that another defendant, like John Doe, was aware of the unlawfulness of an order which was not manifestly illegal. Hence, we must emphatically reiterate that the manifest illegality principle constitutes a mere auxiliary device, an important and, in certain cases, perhaps even a decisive one, but nothing more.

Many writers, who endorse the manifest illegality principle as applicable to the subject of obedience to superior orders in the realm of international law, admit expressly or by implication that the ultimate object of the principle is to ascertain the subjective knowledge of the defendant regarding the illegality of the order.[69] But, if we approbate this approach, and to my mind there are no two ways about it, it is not desirable merely to propound that under international law the responsibility of the subordinate committing an offence in pursuance of orders is contingent on the manifest illegality of the orders. Those adherents of the manifest illegality principle who perceive its entire spectrum and realize its full import must strive to find a more appropriate phrasing for the principle whose banner they carry. Tentatively, we would suggest the following formulation: an accused should not be held responsible, under international law, for a criminal act executed in obedience to a superior order if he committed the act without being aware of its illegality. This is the substantive principle, to be termed hereinafter 'the personal knowledge principle'; and we can append subsidiary rules to it, including a rule of evidence to provide that, if the order was manifestly illegal, the defendant is presumed to have been aware of this illegality, and perhaps will not even be allowed to present proof in rebuttal of the presumption.

In one phrasing or another, the personal knowledge principle, with or without the appendage relating to manifest illegality, or any

69. See Daniel, *op. cit.*, pp. 166–167; Greenspan, *op. cit.*, pp. 490, 495; Knieriem, *op. cit.*, p. 244; Lauterpacht, 'War Crimes', p. 73; Maunoir, *op. cit.*, pp. 274–275; F. Pollock, *op. cit.*, p. 197.

other appendage, is indeed regarded by many writers as obtaining, exclusively or in conjunction with other rules, in the field of obedience to superior orders under international law.[70]

If this is the rule in force, then it most certainly constitutes a departure from the generally accepted legal tenet that ignorance of the law, or mistake of law, does not free from responsibility, in accordance with the well-known maxims: *ignorantia juris non excusat* and *error juris nocet*.[71] Castrén, in dealing with the problem of obedience to orders in international law, reminds us that

> 'ignorance of legal rules and failure to discover their content does not... relieve a person of responsibility'.[72]

And other jurists are also of opinion that the maxim *ignorantia juris non excusat* is applicable within the international just as it is within the national legal system.[73] How, then, can we explain away the principle that a subordinate is not responsible for an offence committed in compliance with an order when he is not aware of the illegality of his act? Some writers try to do it by saying that in actuality this principle is not predicated upon mistake of law but rather upon a mistake in the facts that turn the act done pursuant to the

70. See Appleman, *op. cit.*, pp. 55, 312; Berger, *op. cit.*, pp. 1203–1204, 1208; Daniel, *op. cit.*, p. 166; Dunbar, *op. cit.*, p. 253; Eustathiades, *Ordres*, pp. 404–405, 407, 411–413; Glaser, *Introduction*, pp. 123–124; Glaser, 'L'Ordre', pp. 285, 318–319, 325; Glaser, 'Nuremberg', p. 30; Glueck, *War Criminals*, pp. 142, 155–156, 183, 236 n. 14; T. Gregory, 'Murder is Murder and the Guilty Can be Punished', *A.B.A.J.*, vol. 32 (1946), pp. 544–549 at p. 548; Keenan and Brown, *op. cit.*, pp. 132–133; Lande, *The Legal Basis of the Nuremberg Trial* (1945, mimeographed), p. XI ; Lauterpacht, 'War Crimes', p. 73; Maunoir, *op. cit.*, p. 274; Paston, *op. cit.*, pp. 4, 6; Sack, 'Punishment', pp. 64, 68; Sack, 'Superior Order', pp. 12, 15; Simon, *op. cit.*, p. xiii; Starke, *op. cit.*, p. 370.

71. See particularly Maunoir, *op. cit.*, p. 275. It is well worth noting that the Military Court of Appeal in the Kafr Kassem case stated in its judgment that in the manifest illegality principle—being, as indicated, a constituent part of Israel statutory law—the legislator 'relinquishes the application of the general principle that "ignorance of the law does not afford any excuse for any act or omission which would otherwise constitute an offence" (see Section 8, Criminal Code Ordinance). Owing to the special circumstances affecting a person who is subject to the duty of obeying orders issued to him by a superior authority, the legislator forgoes his ignorance of the law, namely, his ignorance that the order is illegal, provided only that the unlawfulness does not reach the degree of "manifestly illegal". For that purpose the legislator equated mistake of law with the general rule that an honest and reasonable mistake of fact relieves the mistaken person of criminal responsibility (Section 12, Criminal Code Ordinance)' (Kafr Kassem case (second instance), *op. cit.*, p. 410). Cf. also Glueck, *War Criminals*, p. 236 n. 14; Maunoir, *op. cit.*, pp. 240–241.

72. Castrén, *The Present Law of War and Neutrality* (1954), p. 88.

73. See e.g. Kranzbühler, 'Nuremberg as a Legal Problem', *German Views*, pp. 106–126 at p. 122; F. Pollock, *op. cit.*, p. 197; *L.R.U.N.W.C.C.*, Notes, Stalag Luft III case, vol. 11, p. 50.

order into a crime.[74] Such an approach, however, entails either a drastic curtailment of the scope of application of the personal knowledge principle or an artificial inflation of the purview of the plea of mistake of fact. The subject of mistake of fact will be dwelt upon at another stage in this study.[75] Here it will suffice to observe that the natural, simple and accepted course of solving the problem under discussion is by way not of partial admission but of flat denial: denial of the applicability of the maxim *ignorantia juris non excusat* in the province of international criminal law or at least in important segments of that law, on account of the relative uncertainty of its injunctions—particularly when the laws of war are concerned—as compared to the prohibitions of national law.[76] A mild expression is given to this view by the editors of the Law Reports of the United Nations War Crimes Commission, who point out that in the sphere of international law there is an

> 'apparent reluctance of legal authorities to apply to the full the maxim *ignorantia juris non excusat*'.[77]

They suggest the following explanation of this reluctance:

> 'It would seem that an accused is not expected to be as well acquainted with rules of international law as with his own municipal law, which touches more frequently or closely upon his own everyday experience'.[78]

Kelsen, proceeding along the same line of thought, states:

> 'Everybody knows, or is in a position to know, what the general criminal law of his country forbids. But can it reasonably be assumed that every soldier knows what international law forbids?'[79]

And many writers lay stress upon the need to take the relative uncertainty of the laws of war into consideration when the plea of obedience to superior orders is raised.[80] Dunbar voices a widespread opinion when he says:

74. See F. Pollock, *op. cit.*, p. 197. Cf. Keenan and Brown, *op. cit.*, pp. 132–133. Cf. also Stephen, *A Digest of the Criminal Law* (1877), pp. 142–143.
75. See below, Chapter 4, Section 2.
76. See particularly Glaser, *Introduction*, pp. 122–123; Glaser, 'L'Ordre', pp. 317–318.
77. *L.R.U.N.W.C.C.*, Notes, Milch case, vol. 7, p. 64. Cf. *L.R.U.N.W.C.C.*, Notes, Buck trial, vol. 5, p. 44.
78. *L.R.U.N.W.C.C.*, Notes, Milch case, vol. 7, p. 64. Cf. *L.R.U.N.W.C.C.*, vol. 15 (Digest), p. 182.
79. Kelsen, *Peace*, p. 107. Cf. Kelsen, 'Responsibility', p. 558.
80. See Boissier, *op. cit.*, pp. 48–50, 52; Dunbar, *op. cit.*, p. 261; Glaser, *Introduction*, p. 123; Glaser, 'L'Ordre', p. 318; Lauterpacht, 'War Crimes', pp. 74–75; Lauterpacht – Oppenheim, *International Law*, vol. 2 (7th ed., 1952), p. 569; Maunoir, *op. cit.*, pp. 243–247, 256, 259, 268, 275, 311; Schick, 'Nuremberg', p. 198; Schick. 'War Criminals', pp. 46–47.

'there are numerous practices of modern warfare in respect of which no rule of law has been established or, at any rate, the law is disputed. A soldier cannot be expected to carry in his knapsack not only a Field Marshal's baton but also a treatise on international law'.[81]

We ought to note here, in passing, that, once the contention relating to the uncertainty of the provisions of international criminal law is stretched beyond a legitimate extent and its significance is exaggerated, we reach a point of no return which in effect compels denial of the possibility that manifestly illegal orders may often occur in this field. Manifestly illegal orders and an indistinct law, enveloped in mist, are mutually contradictory. Indeed, Kelsen, who, as just shown, is of opinion that the injunctions of international law are not within common knowledge, draws the following conclusion—referring to the terms used in the judgment rendered in the Llandovery Castle case:

'If the illegality of the command consists in a violation of international law, it is almost impossible to suppose that the command is "universally known" to be "without any doubt" against the law'.[82]

Other jurists, on the other hand, tend to hold the converse view, claiming that manifestly illegal orders are most recurrent within the bounds of international law; they maintain that such orders are involved in a majority of cases when soldiers are ordered to carry out acts constituting war crimes.[83] But writers belonging to this school of thought are estopped from attaching too great importance to the uncertainty of the laws of war, for, if the laws are vague, how can there be any certitude concerning the illegality of orders? This problem is noticed by Maunoir, who resolves it in the following way:

'En dépit des incertitudes qui peuvent régner dans plusieurs domaines importants du droit de la guerre, il existe sans aucun doute des règles universellement reconnues dont la force obligatoire s'impose à tous'.[84]

The question whether, in principle, one should take into consideration the relative uncertainty of the laws of war and other branches of international law, to the extent of repudiating the validity of the maxim *ignorantia juris non excusat* in international law, raises a complicated problem, which can be argued both ways, but its solution is not essential for the scope of this study. Clearly it is a problem of a general nature, and not particularly related to the subject of obedience to superior orders. Ignorance of the law and

81. Dunbar, *op. cit.*, p. 261.
82. Kelsen, *Peace*, p. 106. Schick follows in Kelsen's footsteps in this regard (Schick, 'Nuremberg', p. 198; Schick, 'War Criminals', pp. 46 n. 63, 47).
83. See particularly Coste-Floret, *op. cit.*, pp. 21–22; Daniel, *op. cit.*, p. 167.
84. Maunoir, *op. cit.*, p. 275.

obedience to orders are not linked together by divine right, and there is no indissoluble bond between them. Superior orders do not automatically cover international law with a mantle of obscurity and render its provisions less visible or intelligible, nor is mistake of law, in the nature of things, a derivative of every superior order. A soldier may be entirely ignorant of the provisions of international law when acting on his own, just as he may be fully aware of their content when acting pursuant to orders.

It may be contended that one ought to distinguish between the general problem of mistake of law and the particular subject of obedience to superior orders, because the mistake of law which occurs in the case of obedience to orders cannot be equated with an ordinary mistake and is *sui generis*. The starting-point of such an argument may be predicated on the right of the subordinate, underscored by the German *Reichsgericht* at Leipzig in the Llandovery Castle case,[85] to count as a general rule upon the legality of the order that he receives. And, indeed, several writers hold that the subordinate is entitled to assume that the order issued to him by his superior is lawful, and that he does not have punctiliously to scrutinize its legal implications.[86] The ultimate meaning of such an approach is that the subordinate is entitled to rely on his superior's knowledge of the law. But in that case the superior is in effect conceded the clairvoyance of a Mr. Know-all and invested with the sceptre of proficiency not only in military strategy and tactics but also in international law. On what foundation are the clairvoyance and proficiency based? In point of fact, they turn on the sweeping assumption that any addition of a stripe on the sleeve, or some sort of insignia on the epaulette, increases the knowledgeability of the soldier in matters of international law. This is entirely fallacious. Why should the corporal necessarily be regarded as a greater expert in the laws of war than the private, and why must the lieutenant treat the captain as a legal oracle? Especially nowadays, when the bulk of the armed forces in time of war consists of conscript soldiers drawn from all walks of life, it is by no means certain that the commander can judge the legality of his orders more adeptly than the subordinate who is called upon to comply with them. Even in peacetime, differences in rank are not conclusive, for, after all, military promotion is not precisely based on scholastic attainment or on erudition in international law. This is particularly conspicuous

85. See *supra*, pp. 15–16.
86. See e.g. Greenspan, *op. cit.*, p. 495; Knieriem, *op. cit.*, pp. 242–244; Lauterpacht, 'War Crimes', p. 73; Lauterpacht – Oppenheim, *International Law*, vol. 2 (7th ed., 1952), p. 569; Maunoir, *op. cit.*, pp. 248–249, 252, 256–257, 273–274; F. Pollock, *op. cit.*, p. 197.

where reserve units are concerned, as the subordinates in such units may be, for instance, lawyers or experts on international relations in civilian life, and consequently their erudition in international law may far transcend that of their superiors. But even in the conditions of service prevailing in the regular army, the relative proficiency in law of the person issuing an order is, in many cases, a fiction. To cite a self-explanatory case, by way of illustration, a junior officer in the Judge Advocate's office in the army may be a much greater expert on international law than the commanding general of an armoured corps. The superior is not a walking encyclopaedia, and the subordinate cannot be absolved from personally contemplating and examining the character and the substance of the orders that he receives.[87] This contemplation and examination may, of course, lead the subordinate to mistaken conclusions in regard to the legality of the act ordered, and, insofar as the mistake is *bona fide* in the light of the perceptive capacity of the subordinate, his intelligence and education, and the other circumstances of the case, it might save him from criminal conviction. But the mistake must be his own, and not that of another person.

Yet it is possible that a soldier, faced with a superior order, will examine and re-examine its meaning, and still will not be able to make up his mind whether the act ordered is, or is not, lawful. Is the soldier entitled, in such circumstances, to rely on his superior? If the answer to this question is affirmative, it should next be asked whether there is a distinction between the case of a subordinate being ordered by his commander to commit a criminal act and the case of a subordinate committing such an act on his own initiative, but after having received an encouraging opinion, as distinct from an order, from his commander concerning the legal situation? If the subordinate is allowed to count on his superior, why should he be permitted to do so only when the utterance of the superior can be labelled as an order, but not in the event that it can only be regarded as an ordinary opinion? And, if it be argued that it is permissible for a soldier to rely on his commander not merely when an order is involved, one may pose the question why the soldier should not be empowered to rely on other people as well, particularly on those who specialize in the field of international law? Suppose that a soldier suspects that a certain act which he intends to carry out is unlawful, and, proceeding with caution, consults someone who is not his commander but is considered an authority on international law, such as a lawyer or even a well-known professor, and gets an erroneous opinion to the effect that the act, subsequently to be determined a

87. As we shall see below (p. 53), even the interests of military discipline require the soldier to obey orders intelligently and judiciously.

war crime, is perfectly legal. Is it possible that mistake of law will avail the soldier as a defence when he gets an erroneous advice from a person whose expertness is due to legal fiction, that is, from his commander, but will not be able to stand him in good stead when the counsel is proffered by a real expert?

It emerges from all that has been said above that there is no sense in drawing a distinction between the state of facts of obedience to superior orders and other factual situations involving the commission of international offences under mistake of law. And there are divers possible ways to commit an international offence: the delinquent may act both in obedience to superior orders and under mistake of law, just as he may act under mistake of law but without obeying orders, or in obedience to orders but without any mistake of law, or even without either of these two factors being present. The personal knowledge principle relates to the first possibility amidst this variety, to the exclusion of the others. But it is impossible to regard the principle as the acid test in the sphere of obedience to superior orders, unless it is considered as a part of a broader concept that recognizes mistake of law as a legitimate defence under international criminal law. The logic underlying the personal knowledge principle is that of *ignorantia juris excusat*; and, bearing in mind what was termed by Cardozo as

> 'the tendency of a principle to expand itself to the limit of its logic',[88]

we must break down the barriers of this principle, so that of the several possible ways to commit international offences, as enumerated, it will apply not only to the first but also to the second. Both possibilities deal with offences committed under mistake of law, and this mistake ought to protect the offender, if at all, whether he acted pursuant to orders or not.

I believe that we have reached a point in our discussion where we may conclude, with some degree of sureness, that the cloak of obedience to superior orders, under which the personal knowledge principle and the subsidiary principle in respect of manifest illegality are supposed to be applicable, is simply misleading. When the husk is removed, we get to the kernel of the principle, namely, that mistake of law is a valid defence under international law. If the legitimacy of such a defence is admitted, the Court ought also to relieve of responsibility an accused who complied with an illegal order under mistake of law. On the other hand, if the legitimacy of the defence of mistake of law is denied within the scope of international law, as it is within the scope of most national legal systems, then its applicability should also be denied *eo ipso* in the case of obedience to superior orders;

88. Cardozo, *The Nature of the Judicial Process* (1921), p. 51.

consequently the personal knowledge principle, in conjunction with the manifest illegality principle, their lifeblood thereby cut off, must be doomed. Whichever way it is, the defence of mistake of law is the prime factor, the fact of obedience to superior orders is of secondary importance.

So far we have dealt with the twin principles of manifest illegality and personal knowledge. We shall proceed now to analyze other propositions which have been put forward as possible solutions of the problem of obedience to superior orders under international law. In this context, we shall closely examine the two diametrically opposed doctrines which we have already mentioned cursorily, and confuted casually, during our discussion of national law, namely, the doctrine of *respondeat superior* and the doctrine of absolute liability.

CHAPTER 2

THE DOCTRINE OF *RESPONDEAT SUPERIOR*

1. OPPENHEIM'S PROPOSITION

The main authority in international legal theory for the doctrine of *respondeat superior*, in accordance with which the fact of obedience to superior orders constitutes in itself, automatically and *a priori*, a complete and absolute defence against a criminal prosecution, is to be found in the first five editions of the second volume of Oppenheim's *Treatise on International Law*.[89] The first edition, published in 1906, contained the following noted passage:

> 'violations of rules regarding warfare are war crimes only when committed without an order of the belligerent Government concerned. If members of the armed forces commit violations *by order* of their Government, they are not war criminals and cannot be punished by the enemy; the latter can, however, resort to reprisals. In case members of forces commit violations ordered by their commanders, the members may not be punished, for the commanders are alone responsible, and the latter may, therefore, be punished as war criminals on their capture by the enemy'.[90]

And save for a very slight stylistic alteration the passage is reproduced verbatim in the four subsequent editions:[91] the second edition (of 1912), revised by the author himself;[92] the third edition (of 1921), prepared by Roxburgh;[93] the fourth edition (of 1926), undertaken by McNair;[94] and the fifth edition (of 1935), published by Lauterpacht.[95] As for newer editions, also with Lauterpacht as editor, we shall see below that he changed his mind and renounced the ideas expressed in the passage.

It is obvious that Oppenheim drew a distinction here between

89. In the first three editions, the second volume was entitled: 'War and Neutrality'. Since the fourth edition, it has borne the title: 'Disputes, War and Neutrality'.
90. Oppenheim, *International Law*, vol. 2 (1st ed., 1906), pp. 264–265.
91. The stylistic alteration consisted of replacing the words: 'cannot' and 'can' in the second sentence by the words: 'may not' and 'may'.
92. Oppenheim, *International Law*, vol. 2 (2nd ed., 1912), p. 310.
93. Oppenheim, *International Law*, vol. 2 (3rd ed., by Roxburgh, 1921), pp. 342–343.
94. Oppenheim, *International Law*, vol. 2 (4th ed., by McNair, 1926), pp. 410–411.
95. Lauterpacht – Oppenheim, *International Law*, vol. 2 (5th ed., 1935), pp. 453–454.

obedience to orders emanating from the Government, on the one hand, and obedience to the orders of ordinary commanders in the hierarchical system, on the other. In the first case, relating to the violation of the laws of war in obedience to the Government's orders, he held the view that it was out of place to talk about any war crime being committed. Conversely, in the other case, regarding the violation of the laws of war pursuant to ordinary orders, he was of opinion that a war crime was actually committed, but that exclusive responsibility for it lay on the shoulders of the commander, and the subordinate ought to be absolved of guilt. In another section of this study we shall investigate this distinction in detail, and examine to what extent the first case falls beyond the compass of the discussion concerning obedience to superior orders.[96] At the present point, it is important to note that, whatever may be the interpretation of the first part of the passage cited, the second part clearly and definitely established the rule that a subordinate committing a war crime in submission to orders should not incur responsibility for his act. Indeed, the passage is regarded in the literature on the subject as 'the' expression given to the doctrine of *respondeat superior*, its backbone and cornerstone.[97] Some of the professed opponents of the doctrine go so far as to assert that it was originally conceived and formed by Oppenheim.[98]

In the first two editions of the second volume of his treatise, Oppenheim failed to adduce any authority for the support of his proposition on the subject of obedience to orders,[99] nor did he find it necessary to expound his view. Actually, his theory was not in contestation up to some time after the publication of the second edition (of 1912). Those were days of peace, and the problems pertaining to the laws of war were not pressing or urgent; apprehension of war crimes being committed on a vast scale, in compliance with superior orders, certainly did not prey on anyone's mind.[100] But not

96. See below, Section 3.
97. See Bellot, 'Punishment', p. 46 n. 27; Bellot, 'War Criminals', vol. 36, p. 763; Berger, *op. cit.*, p. 1203; Dunbar, *op. cit.*, pp. 241–242; Finch, 'Superior Orders', pp. 441–442; Garner, 'Articles', p. 139; Garner, *International Law*, vol. 2, p. 486; Garner, 'Punishment', p. 86; Knieriem, *op. cit.*, pp. 247–248; Levy, *op. cit.*, p. 1080 n. 77; Maunoir, *op. cit.*, p. 214; Roxburgh, *op. cit.*, p. 155; Sack, 'Punishment', pp. 65–66; Sack, 'Superior Order', p. 13; Schick, 'War Criminals', pp. 50–51; Schwarzenberger, *Lawlessness*, pp. 62–63; Schwarzenberger, 'War Crimes', pp. 71–72.
98. See Dunbar, *op. cit.*, p. 241; Sack, 'Punishment', pp. 65–66; Sack, 'Superior Order', p. 13.
99. This fact is especially emphasized by Morgan, *Assize*, pp. 12–13; Morgan, 'Nuremberg', pp. 329–330; Schwarzenberger, 'Inductive Approach', p. 546.
100. In this regard, see particularly Dunbar, *op. cit.*, p. 242; Sack, 'Punishment', p. 66; Sack, 'Superior Order', p. 13.

long after the second edition had been issued, the world was overtaken by a *guerre à outrance* that scorched almost every nation with its flame. The question of granting impunity to war criminals acting in pursuance of orders suddenly materialized with all its gravity and became a burning topic of the day. The soldier, the statesman and the man in the street began to knock on the door of legal pundits and demand a real solution for this all too practical problem. Many jurists, who belatedly realized the full import of Oppenheim's proposition, abandoned their attitude of unconcern, girded up their loins and went all-out against it. Among those who openly challenged the doctrine of *respondeat superior* during the First World War, we should particularly note Phillipson,[101] Bellot[102] and Mérignhac.[103]

The torrent of remonstrations and denunciations did not induce Oppenheim to shift his ground in the slightest.[104] On the contrary, he composed a footnote to be subjoined in substantiation of the above passage in his treatise, and this was incorporated after his death (in 1919) in the third edition of the book, issued in 1921 by Roxburgh.[105] Here Oppenheim conceded that 'the contrary is sometimes asserted', and cited Bellot and Mérignhac as illustrating this iconoclastic school.[106] On the other hand, he found support for his view in the writings of Dumas[107] and Renault,[108] published during

101. Phillipson, *International Law and the Great War* (1915), pp. 260–261; Phillipson – Wheaton, *International Law*, pp. 478–479.
102. Bellot, 'Punishment', p. 46; Bellot, 'War Criminals', vol. 36, p. 763.
103. Mérignhac, 'Sanction', pp. 50–51.
104. At a certain stage Bellot apparently believed that Oppenheim had changed his mind (see Bellot, 'War Criminals', vol. 36, p. 764). But if he really thought so, it was wishful thinking.
105. Oppenheim, *International Law*, vol. 2 (3rd ed., by Roxburgh, 1921), pp. 342–343 n. 3.
106. *Ibid.*
107. Dumas, *Les Sanctions Pénales des Crimes Allemands* (1916), pp. 28–30.
108. Renault's important contribution to the subject was part of an address delivered in 1915 during the proceedings of the Société Générale des Prisons and entitled: 'Dans Quelle Mesure le Droit Pénal Peut-il s'Appliquer à des Faits de Guerre contraires au Droit des Gens?'. The address was published, in the same year, in the journal of the Society (*R.P.D.P.*, vol. 39 (1915), pp. 405–429), and also—with some modifications—in *Clunet*, as an article entitled: 'De l'Application du Droit Pénal aux Faits de Guerre' (*Clunet*, vol. 42 (1915), pp. 313–344). In 1918 the article was reprinted in *R.G.D.I.P.* (vol. 25 (1918), pp. 5–29). Oppenheim referred to *Clunet*, and so will I below.

Despite the fact that, in the address as well as in the article, Renault voiced unqualified support for the doctrine of *respondeat superior*—as noticed by Oppenheim and by several other writers (see e.g. Glaser, *Introduction*, p. 115 n. 3; Glaser, 'L'Ordre', p. 306), and as we shall presently see for ourselves—Garner curiously found it appropriate to state, referring to the article in *R.G.D.I.P.*, that 'Renault, however, expressed no positive opinion on the question and he appears to have been in doubt as to whether the individual soldier should be held responsible for

the war (that is to say, after Oppenheim had disseminated his doctrine in two earlier editions of his treatise; authorities antecedent to the first edition were still nowhere to be found) in France.[109]

Possibly because Oppenheim was not content with the contradictory authorities, he determined to found his proposition on a logical explanation. This was accomplished by the insertion of the following statement into the footnote:

> 'The law cannot require an individual to be punished for an act which he was compelled by law to commit'.[110]

This laconic exposition is riddled with ambiguity. Presumably, the term 'law', appearing twice in the sentence, has one and the same meaning in both instances, namely, that of international law.[111] That being so, Oppenheim must have meant that international law compels the military to carry out orders, and hence it cannot penalize any individual soldier who discharges his obligation and obeys orders. Oppenheim did not disclose the legal basis, or the logical reason, for the contention that international law really compels soldiers to obey the orders of their superiors in the national army. But he probably held the view that international law ought to care, and does in fact care, about the maintenance of discipline and good order in the national army.[112] We have already observed that international law need not concern itself with the preservation of discipline in such an army.[113] But even if we suppose, for the sake of argument, that international law in fact takes an interest in the discipline of the national army and consequently imposes the duty of obedience to

criminal acts committed under orders' (Garner, *International Law*, vol. 2, p. 487 n. 3).

109. Oppenheim, *International Law*, vol. 2 (3rd ed., by Roxburgh, 1921), p. 343 n. 3.
110. *Ibid.*
111. Had Oppenheim referred in both cases to national law, his statement would have ceased to be of any consequence in the realm of international law.
112. Indeed, several of Oppenheim's supporters gave expression to this conception, contending that the imposition of sanctions upon a subordinate submitting to a superior order is likely to undermine the foundations of military discipline. See Boissier, *op. cit.*, pp. 45–46; Bower, *op. cit.*, p. 32; H. Smith, 'Nuremberg', pp. 203–204; Q. Wright, 'The Outlawry of War', *op. cit.*, p. 79. Cf. Dunbar, *op. cit.*, p. 259; Garner, 'Articles', p. 138; Kelsen, *Peace*, p. 105; Kelsen, 'Responsibility', pp. 556–557. Daube made a very interesting statement, as follows: 'there was... a slightly anarchic element in the doctrine that the war criminals might be punished even where they had acted under orders... In Shakespeare's *Winter's Tale* the minister bravely tries to dissuade the king from venting his fury on his baby daughter but in the end carries out the order to expose her. A bear pursues him to tear him to pieces. That bear is a *sans culotte*' (Daube, 'The Defence of Superior Orders in Roman Law', *L.Q.R.*, vol. 72 (1956), pp. 494–515 at p. 497).
113. See *supra*, p. 21.

orders within its hierarchical structure, the question ought to be asked whether the duty of obedience pertains to any kind of order, no matter how illegal it may turn out to be and irrespective of the circumstances. Is it not odd that a law should compel obedience to any order whatever, even if it entails the most flagrant violation of that very law?[114] To that we should add that, anyway, Oppenheim's statement is clearly defective insofar as it ignores the fact that international law also compels obedience to the laws of war. If, to the extent that it exists, the duty of obedience to orders demands immunity from sanctions, the duty of obedience to the laws of war, undoubtedly in force, emphatically requires a high-handed imposition of sanctions. It is of the essence of things that these two duties conflict with each other when they coexist under the roof of one legal system, and thence the above-mentioned dilemma.[115] Consequently, Oppenheim's explanatory statement does not so much render support to the doctrine of *respondeat superior* as it exposes the Achilles' heel of the doctrine: a total disregard of the interests of the supremacy of international criminal law, a transfixing on one of the horns of the dilemma.

It may be argued that Oppenheim used the term 'law', appearing twice in his explanatory statement, in two different meanings: once, having in mind international law, and the second time referring to national law. If that is the case, he must have wished to say that national law compels soldiers to obey orders, and, therefore, international law cannot inflict punishment on them if they perform that duty. If this is the correct interpretation of his statement, then Oppenheim sinned not only against style but also against legal logic. Why is it incumbent upon international law to take into account duties laid down by virtue of national law? International law alone determines when a certain act constitutes an international offence, irrespective of whether the same act does, or does not, constitute an offence against national law, and by the same token international law is fully competent to decide when the international offender is entitled to impunity.[116] When international offences are concerned, international law, and not national law, is the lamp to guide our footsteps, the light to brighten our path. If it so desires, international law may take into consideration the hardship of the soldier

114. In the judgment rendered in the Hostage case, the American Military Tribunal at Nuremberg quoted Oppenheim's explanatory statement under discussion, and pronounced: 'The statement completely overlooks the fact that an illegal order is in no sense of the word a valid law which one is obliged to obey' (Hostage case, Judgment, *N.M.T.*, vol. 11, p. 1237).
115. See *supra*, p. 6.
116. See and cf. Sack, 'Punishment', p. 67; Sack, 'Superior Order', p. 14; *L.R.U.N.W.C.C.*, vol. 15 (Digest), p. 157.

confronted with an order which is unlawful under international law though legal under national law, and resolve to relieve him of responsibility for the international offence committed by him. International law may do that, but it is not obliged to.

Whichever way you look into Oppenheim's explanatory statement, it is not persuasive in its reasoning. No wonder, therefore, that adverse criticism of the doctrine propounded by him did not abate after the disclosure of its grounds, but went on incessantly. Yet the editors of the fourth and fifth editions of the treatise—McNair and Lauterpacht—left Oppenheim's text intact, and only in the references that they listed in the appended footnotes did they mention the increasing criticism of it.[117] Whereas Roxburgh, in charge of the third edition, did not express his own view regarding the question of obedience to superior orders,[118] McNair added his personal weight to the support of Oppenheim's proposition, noting that, despite the remonstrances against the text, recent developments had not disproved its correctness.[119] Lauterpacht reiterated McNair's statement in the fifth edition,[120] but, when he was about to issue the sixth edition (in 1940), he reversed his position altogether. Not only the content of the footnotes was completely altered, but the body of the text itself underwent what is very aptly described by Schwarzenberger as 'a remarkable *volte-face*'.[121] Thus we read in the sixth edition of the treatise, in lieu of the original passage quoted above:

> 'The fact that a rule of warfare has been violated in pursuance of an order of the belligerent Government or of an individual belligerent commander does not deprive the act in question of its character as a war crime; neither does it, in principle, confer upon the perpetrator immunity from punishment

117. Oppenheim, *International Law*, vol. 2 (4th ed., by McNair, 1926), p. 410 n. 2; Lauterpacht – Oppenheim, *International Law*, vol. 2 (5th ed., 1935), p. 454 n. 1. As for the references to the criticism of Oppenheim's proposition, Dunbar remarks: 'it is only fair to say that the relevant footnotes in succeeding editions cast increasing doubt upon the validity of the rule as expounded in the body of the text' (Dunbar, *op. cit.*, p. 242).
118. In an article that he wrote a short while after the publication of the third edition of Oppenheim's treatise, Roxburgh did not go beyond stating that the subject of obedience to superior orders poses a difficult problem, and that Oppenheim persisted in his view 'until the end of his life and in spite of strong criticism' (Roxburgh, *op. cit.*, p. 155).
119. This remark was annexed to the footnote written by Oppenheim. See Oppenheim, *International Law*, vol. 2 (4th ed., by McNair, 1926), p. 410 n. 2.
120. Lauterpacht – Oppenheim, *International Law*, vol. 2 (5th ed., 1935), p. 454 n. 1.
121. Schwarzenberger, 'Inductive Approach', p. 547. Morgan refers to Lauterpacht and says: 'It was not till 1940 that the latter, in the sixth edition of the book, suddenly, like Saul on the road to Damascus, saw the light' (Morgan, *Assize*, p. 14; Morgan, 'Nuremberg', p. 331).

by the injured belligerent. A different view has occasionally been adopted ... by writers, but it is difficult to regard it as expressing a sound legal principle'.[122]

So that he should not be suspected of being arbitrarily and demonstrably oblivious to the theory propounded by Oppenheim, whose name still appears on the cover of the book containing this statement, Lauterpacht, when mentioning those writers who had 'occasionally' held a different view, referred in a footnote to the previous editions of the treatise.[123] But, save for this vague reference in an obscure note, Lauterpacht did not pay much heed to Oppenheim's doctrine, erstwhile subscribed to by himself. An illustrative expression of the revolution which occurred in Lauterpacht's way of thinking may be found in an article that he published in 1944,[124] where he completely repudiated the doctrine of *respondeat superior*, and pronounced:

'writers on international law have almost universally rejected the doctrine of superior orders as an absolute justification of war crimes'.[125]

Lauterpacht repeated his new opinion in subsequent editions of the second volume of Oppenheim's treatise: the sixth revised edition (of 1944),[126] and the seventh and last edition (of 1952).[127] Thus the doctrine of *respondeat superior* was finally and conclusively spilt from its cradle.

The great majority of writers, indeed, do not espouse Oppenheim's proposition. One must list among the opponents of the doctrine of *respondeat superior* all who profess any solution of the problem of obedience to superior orders which does not imply that submission to orders is a reason for automatic exemption from criminal responsibility. First and foremost among them are, of course, the adherents of the antipodal doctrine of absolute liability.[128] Then one has to count all those jurists who support the manifest illegality principle,[129]

122. Lauterpacht – Oppenheim, *International Law*, vol. 2 (6th ed., 1940), pp. 453–454.
123. *Ibid.*, p. 454 n. 2.
124. As to this article, see below, note 336.
125. Lauterpacht, 'War Crimes', p. 73. Cf. Morgan, *Assize*, p. 14, note; Morgan, 'Nuremberg', p. 331, note.
126. Lauterpacht – Oppenheim, *International Law*, vol. 2 (6th rev. ed., 1944), p. 452.
127. Lauterpacht – Oppenheim, *International Law*, vol. 2 (7th ed., 1952), p. 568.
128. See below, note 205.
129. See *supra*, note 59. In one case, at least, I find that a writer, endorsing the manifest illegality principle (Knieriem, *op. cit.*, p. 244), feels himself nevertheless free to state that Oppenheim's proposition constitutes the 'correct view of international law' (*ibid.*, p. 247). This, however, is blowing hot and cold. There is a logical gap between the conception that every defendant who obeyed superior orders ought to be automatically relieved of responsibility and the theory that

or the personal knowledge principle.[130] Last, but not least, there is a long line of scholars, whose opinions in this regard defy classification within the compass of any one of these clear-cut categories, but—and this is the crux of the matter—who are, at any rate, antagonistic to the conception underlying the doctrine of *respondeat superior.*[131]

Opposition to Oppenheim is so predominant that some of his severe critics frequently tend to create the impression of his being completely isolated in his advocacy of the doctrine of *respondeat superior.*[132] Yet, though his proposition may have been cut adrift

only certain defendants (be they even the decisive majority) who obeyed orders—namely, those acting pursuant to orders not manifestly illegal—ought to be exonerated. By disregarding this gap, or making light of it, one does not bridge it.

130. See *supra*, note 70.
131. See Biddle, 'Le Procès de Nuremberg', *R.I.D.P.*, vol. 19 (1948), pp. 1–19 at pp. 11–12; Castrén, *op. cit.*, pp. 87–88; Descheemaeker, *op. cit.*, pp. 235–236; Donnedieu de Vabres, 'Le Procès de Nuremberg', *R.S.C.D.P.C.*, 1947, pp. 171–183 at p. 181; Donnedieu de Vabres, 'Nuremberg', pp. 569–571; Eisenstadt, 'The Responsibility of Governments for International Criminality' (Hebrew), *Iyunim Benleumiyim* (International Studies), No. 25 (1957), pp. 14–16 at p. 15; Fenwick, *op. cit.*, p. 672 (re: grave crimes); Finch, 'Superior Orders', pp. 441–445; Finch, 'The Nuremberg Trial and International Law', *A.J.I.L.*, vol. 41 (1947), pp. 20–37 at p. 21; Finch, 'Three Problems of International Law', *C.M.A.I.*, vol. 4 (1954), pp. 1–42 at p. 13; Franklin, 'Sources of International Law Relating to Sanctions against War Criminals', *J.C.L.C.*, vol. 36 (1945–1946), pp. 153–179 at pp. 160–161; Garçon, Speech, *R.P.D.P.*, vol. 39 (1915), p. 478; Guggenheim, *op. cit.*, vol. 2, pp. 47–48; Harris, *Tyranny on Trial* (1954), p. 557; Jessup, 'The Crime of Aggression and the Future of International Law', *P.S.Q.*, vol. 62 (1947), pp. 1–10 at p. 10; Lauer, *op. cit.*, p. 22; Lawrence (Oaksey), 'The Nuremberg Trial', *Int. Aff.*, vol. 23 (1947), pp. 151–159 at pp. 156–157; Levie; *op. cit.*, p. 465; Levy, *op. cit.*, p. 1080; Mérignhac, 'Sanction', pp. 50–51; Mérignhac and Lémonon, *op. cit.*, vol. 2, p. 568; Muszkat, 'Problems of International Criminal Law' (Hebrew), *Hapraklit*, vol. 14 (1958), pp. 333–350 at p. 335; Muszkat, *Theory and Realities in International Law* (1959) (Hebrew), vol. 1, p. 325; Scelle, *op. cit.*, pp. 984 n. 2, 997; Schafer, *Crimes against Peace* (1952), pp. 140–141, 143–144; F. Smith (Birkenhead) quoted by Garner ('Articles', p. 139; *International Law*, vol. 2, p. 486; 'Punishment', p. 86); Svarlien, *op. cit.*, p. 409. See also Dickinson, Speech, *A.S.I.L.*, 1943, p. 49; S. Gregory, 'Criminal Responsibility of Sovereigns for Willful Violations of the Laws of War', *V.L.R.*, vol. 6 (1919–1920), pp. 400–421 at pp. 419–420; Gros, *Symposium*, p. 145; Herzog, 'Les Principes Juridiques de la Répression des Crimes de Guerre', *R.P.S.*, vol. 60 (1946), pp. 277–304 at p. 287; Hyde, Speech, *A.S.I.L.*, 1943, p. 42; W. E. Jackson, 'Putting the Nuremberg Law to Work', *For. Aff.*, vol. 25 (1946–1947), pp. 550–565 at pp. 557–558; Lachs, *op. cit.*, p. 84; Politis, *The New Aspects of International Law* (1928), p. 41; Pompe, *Aggressive War an International Crime* (1953), pp. 176–177; Potter, 'Offences against the Peace and Security of Mankind', *A.J.I.L.*, vol. 46 (1952), pp. 101–102 at p. 101; Rochette, *op. cit.*, p. 135; Stone, *Legal Controls of International Conflict* (1954), pp. 362–363. Cf. Garner, 'Articles', pp. 138–139; Garner, *International Law*, vol. 2, pp. 486–487; Garner, 'Punishment', pp. 86–87.
132. See Bellot, 'Punishment', p. 46; Bellot, 'War Criminals', vol. 36, pp. 763–764; Finch, 'Superior Orders', p. 441; Levy, *op. cit.*, p. 1080 n. 77; Maunoir, *op. cit.*, p. 214; Morgan, *Assize*, p. 12; Morgan, 'Nuremberg', p. 329.

from the main stream of juristic thinking on the subject of obedience to orders under international law, he never had to navigate alone. First, we should recall Dumas and Renault, in whose writings Oppenheim himself found support for his view. But, even aside from them, quite a number of jurists, some of them of very high standing, have endorsed in the past, and still uphold, the doctrine of *respondeat superior* as reflective of positive international law in the field of obedience to superior orders.[133] Hence we cannot dismiss the doctrine with a perfunctory examination, and must probe its foundations carefully.

But before we do that, it is necessary to put on record that we are not of opinion that the doctrine may rely upon the authority of Article 443 (Chapter XIV) of the British Manual of Military Law, as it was in force during the three decades between 1914 and 1944, or of the corresponding, contemporaneous provision of the American Rules of Land Warfare. The stipulation of Article 443, prescribing that whoever violates the laws of war in obedience to superior orders

133. See Belgion, *Victors' Justice* (1949), p. 143; Berthélemy, Speech, *R.P.D.P.*, vol. 39 (1915), p. 444; Birkenhead, *International Law* (6th ed., by Moelwyn-Hughes, 1927), pp. 301–302; Bower, *op. cit.*, p. 31; Eagleton, 'Punishment of War Criminals by the United Nations', *A.J.I.L.*, vol. 37 (1943), pp. 495–499 at p. 497; Erickson, 'A Judicial Reckoning for William Hohenzollern', *Law Notes*, vol. 22 (1918–1919), pp. 184–189 at p. 187; Jones, Speech, *T.G.S.*, p. xl; Jullien, Speech, *R.P.D.P.*, vol. 39 (1915), p. 446; Manner, 'The Legal Nature and Punishment of Criminal Acts of Violence contrary to the Laws of War', *A.J.I.L.*, vol. 37 (1943), pp. 407–435 at pp. 416–418, 433; Rivière, Speech, *R.P.D.P.*, vol. 39 (1915), p. 491; Schick, 'Nuremberg', pp. 195, 197–198; Schick, 'War Criminals', pp. 45, 49, 51; H. Smith, 'Nuremberg', pp. 203–204; Winfield – Lawrence, *International Law*, pp. 544, 546–547. See also Boissier, *op. cit.*, pp. 40, 45–47, 59–62; Borchard, 'International Law and International Organization', *A.J.I.L.*, vol. 41 (1947), pp. 106–108 at p. 107 n. 1; Colby, 'War Crimes', pp. 606–607; Colby, 'War Crimes and their Punishment', *op. cit.*, p. 43; Hankey, *op. cit.*, pp. 59–60; Hankey, 'Postscript' to Maugham, *op. cit.*, p. 111; Fenwick, *op. cit.*, p. 669 (re: ordinary offences); Genet, 'The Charge of Piracy in the Spanish Civil War', *A.J.I.L.*, vol. 32 (1938), pp. 253–263 at p. 256; Poljokan, *op. cit.*, pp. 159–160, 162–164; H. Smith, *The Law and Custom of the Sea* (3rd ed., 1959), pp. 213–217.

In the 'twenties, Q. Wright also expressed support for the doctrine of *respondeat superior* insofar as war criminals are concerned (see Q. Wright, 'The Effect of the War on International Law', *Minn.L.R.*, vol. 5 (1920–1921), pp. 436–458, 515–539 at p. 539; Q. Wright, 'The Outlawry of War', *op. cit.*, pp. 79–80). But Wright has changed his mind since then, and now subscribes to the manifest illegality principle within the pale of the laws of war (see *supra*, note 59). In other fields he even tends to accept the doctrine of absolute liability (see below, note 205).

Kelsen, who is admittedly of opinion (as we shall see below, in Section 3) that the whole problem relating to obedience to superior orders belongs of right to the sphere of national—and not international—law, states that 'The idea of justice . . . is certainly not favorable to the prosecution of individuals who commit war crimes in response to a superior command' (Kelsen, *Peace*, p. 107; Kelsen, 'Responsibility', p. 558).

is not a war criminal and cannot be punished,[134] first appeared in the British Manual in 1914 and was phrased by Oppenheim himself in conjunction with Edmonds;[135] whereas the American rule was drafted later in the same year after the British example.[136] The two provisions did not have any counterpart in previous editions of the British Manual and the American Rules, respectively;[137] and, subsequent to Lauterpacht's revision of the relevant passage in Oppenheim's treatise dealing with the question of obedience to superior orders, the parallel clauses of the Manual and the Rules were amended and redrafted (in 1944) in line with the new statement of the law.[138] But even while the original provisions were still in force, they could not be admitted as evidence bearing upon the application of Oppenheim's theory in positive international law. To begin with, it is obvious that, even if the armed forces of Britain and the United States found it advisable to regulate conduct within their own units in conformity with this doctrine, it does not necessarily follow that this is a legal tenet binding on the whole international community. As the American Military Tribunal stated in the Hostage case, referring to Oppenheim's proposition:

> 'The fact that the British and American Armies may have adopted it for the regulation of its [*sic*] own armies as a matter of policy does not have the effect of enthroning it as a rule of international law'.[139]

Whoever wants to derive the rule of international law, regarding the question of obedience to superior orders, from the source of 'the

134. See *L.R.U.N.W.C.C.*, vol. 1, p. 18.
135. See Bellot, 'Punishment', p. 46; Bellot, 'War Criminals', vol. 36, p. 764; Colby, 'War Crimes', p. 491; Dunbar, *op. cit.*, p. 242; Hankey, Speech, *Hansard* (Parliamentary Debates), House of Lords, vol. 168 (1950), pp. 467–469; Janeczek, *op. cit.*, p. 72; Morgan, *Assize*, p. 12; Morgan, 'Nuremberg', p. 329; Schwarzenberger, 'Inductive Approach', p. 546; Schwarzenberger, *Lawlessness*, p. 62; Schwarzenberger, 'War Crimes', p. 71; Hostage case, Judgment, *N.M.T.*, vol. 11, p. 1237.
136. See Dunbar, *op. cit.*, p. 242; Finch, 'Superior Orders', p. 441; Janeczek, *op. cit.*, p. 71; Schwarzenberger, 'Inductive Approach', p. 546; Schwarzenberger, *Lawlessness*, pp. 62–63; Schwarzenberger, 'War Crimes', pp. 71–72; Hostage case, Judgment, *N.M.T.*, vol. 11, p. 1237.
137. See Bellot, 'Punishment', p. 47; Finch, 'Superior Orders', p. 441; Janeczek, *op. cit.*, p. 71; Morgan, *Assize*, p. 12; Morgan, 'Nuremberg', p. 329.
138. See Lauterpacht – Oppenheim, *International Law*, vol. 2 (7th ed., 1952), p. 568 n. 1; *L.R.U.N.W.C.C.*, vol. 1, pp. 18, 32. It is noteworthy that in 1950 a motion was proposed in the British House of Lords to the effect that the amendment of 1944 to the Manual of Military Law was 'inimical to military discipline', but it was not accepted (see *Hansard* (Parliamentary Debates), House of Lords, vol. 168 (1950), pp. 446, 503–504). The discussion in the House was most enlightening (see *ibid.*, pp. 437–504).
139. Hostage case, Judgment, *N.M.T.*, vol. 11, p. 1237. Cf. Kranzbühler, *op. cit.*, p. 122.

general principles of law recognized by civilized nations', to use the words of Article 38(1)(c) of the Statute of the International Court of Justice, must make a comparative study of principles common to a considerable number of national legal systems, and it is not enough to direct the limelight at an isolated provision in one or two military manuals. Furthermore, the British Manual's clause, as drafted by Oppenheim, was never in conformity with the rules of the general criminal law, either in Britain or in the United States, in respect of obedience to orders.[140] Garner indeed states categorically that

> 'it is an axiom of English and American law that the plea of superior command is no defense for the commission of an illegal act'.[141]

The British Manual and the American Rules, as the editors of the Law Reports of the United Nations War Crimes Commission point out, are not legislative instruments, formally binding, and their publication is designed for informative purposes only.[142] To use the language of the British Lord Chancellor, Jowitt:

> 'The function of the Manual of Military Law is to reproduce correctly the relevant law: it does not itself make the law, but merely records what the law is'.[143]

Considering the fact that it was Oppenheim who in this instance recorded what the law was, every reliance upon the provision of the British Manual as an authority in the sphere of international law ultimately constitutes a reliance upon Oppenheim as an authority on this law. Inasmuch as Oppenheim himself found support for his proposition in that stipulation,[144] this, as indicated by Schwarzenberger, was, to a certain extent, 'an oblique self-quotation'.[145]

140. See and cf. Anonymous ('Correspondent'), 'War Crimes', *J.S.C.L.I.L.*, vol. 18 (1918), pp. 153–154 at p. 154; Bellot, 'Punishment', p. 47; Bellot, 'War Criminals', vol. 36, p. 764; Cave, *op. cit.*, p. xxiii; Dunbar, *op. cit.*, pp. 235–240; Garner, 'Articles', p. 138; Garner, *International Law*, vol. 2, p. 485; Garner, 'Punishment', p. 85; Glueck, *War Criminals*, pp. 144–149; Janeczek, *op. cit.*, p. 71; Myerson, *op. cit.*, p. 155; *N.L.G. Report*, p. 21; Paston, *op. cit.*, p. 5; Schwarzenberger, 'Inductive Approach', p. 546; Schwarzenberger, *Lawlessness*, p. 63; Schwarzenberger, 'War Crimes', p. 72; Eichmann trial (second instance), Judgment, *op. cit.*, pp. I32–I33.
141. Garner, 'Articles', p. 138. See also Garner, *International Law*, vol. 2, p. 485; Garner, 'Punishment', p. 85. Cf. Schick, 'War Criminals', p. 49.
142. *L.R.U.N.W.C.C.*, Notes, Dostler trial, vol. 1, p. 32; *L.R.U.N.W.C.C.*, Notes, Peleus trial, vol. 1, p. 19.
143. Jowitt (Lord Chancellor), Speech, *Hansard* (Parliamentary Debates), House of Lords, vol. 168 (1950), p. 447.
144. See reference in the same footnote, composed by Oppenheim, which has already been discussed at length—Oppenheim, *International Law*, vol. 2 (3rd ed., by Roxburgh, 1921), p. 343 n. 3.
145. Schwarzenberger, 'Inductive Approach', p. 546.

2. MISTAKE OF LAW AND COMPULSION AS THE BASIS OF THE DOCTRINE OF *RESPONDEAT SUPERIOR*

It is to the credit of the proponents of Oppenheim's theory that they do not usually cling to the explanatory statement which their mentor chose to put forward as the rationale underlying the doctrine of *respondeat superior.* Most of them prefer to ground the doctrine on different arguments, accenting less the theoretical aspects and more the practical problem emanating from the straits to which the soldier, confronted with superior orders, is reduced.

Especially significant in this regard are the arguments submitted by Renault, who, we may recall, was regarded by Oppenheim himself as a strong supporter of his proposition. Renault is of opinion that two important factors ought to be taken into account when the subject of obedience to orders is brought up for consideration.[146] Referring to the first factor, he states:

> 'La première, c'est que la discipline militaire est une chose absolument indispensable, que l'on ne peut pas admettre que des soldats, des sous-officiers, même des officiers, discutent les ordres qui leur sont donnés, parce qu'ils ne peuvent pas toujours se rendre compte de l'illégalité de ces ordres'.[147]

Up to this point, the reasoning looks like a mere echo of the familiar contention originating from the standpoint of the demands of military discipline. All that can be said at first blush is that Renault puts this idea into new shape but leaves its essence intact. In its new shape, the argument is proceeding along the line that soldiers are not capable of determining whether an order is legal or not, and, therefore, the interests of military discipline require immediate obedience without much fuss or hesitation. Garner recapitulates this argument, without personally concurring with it, as follows:

> 'Obedience to orders is the first duty of a soldier, and it is absolutely necessary to military discipline. He cannot discuss or question the commands that are given him, he is not the judge of their legality or illegality; and if he were, his ignorance of the laws of war would in many cases make him an incompetent judge'.[148]

Ignorance of the law (of war) is advanced here only in order to point out the indispensability of unqualified obedience to orders, and to explain that the policy of penalizing subordinates acting pursuant to illegal orders is fraught with danger. The conclusion, in keeping with Oppenheim's outlook, is that every solution beyond the confines of the doctrine of *respondeat superior* will be detrimental

146. Renault, *op. cit.*, (*Clunet*), p. 341.
147. *Ibid.* Cf. Mérignhac, 'Sanction', p. 50.
148. Garner, *International Law*, vol. 2, p. 484; Garner, 'Punishment', p. 84.

to military discipline, whose interests are held in high esteem by international law.[149]

Renault does not, however, restrict himself to the statement just quoted. Once he touches the vulnerable spot of soldiers' ignorance of the law, he is bent upon pursuing that subject. In the sequence of his argumentation he in fact substitutes the pragmatic viewpoint of the soldier for the theoretical one of military discipline: he notes that knowledgeability of the laws of war within national armies is not as common as it should be, and adds:

> 'par conséquent, il peut se faire dans beaucoup des cas, que, de très bonne foi, les subalternes aient cru qu'ils n'avaient qu'à obéir et qu'ils agissaient correctement en le faisant'.[150]

This, then, is Renault's first real contribution to the fabric woven by Oppenheim: he asserts that the doctrine of *respondeat superior* is based not only on the demands of military discipline but also on the element of *bona fide* mistake of law on the part of the recipient of the order.[151]

No one can contest the fact that the laws of war are not engraved upon the memory of every soldier. But, as indicated above,[152] the question whether the plea of *ignorantia juris* could and should serve as a basis for a defence against criminal prosecution under international law is not easy to answer. Anyway, even on the assumption that mistake of law ought to bring about discharge from responsibility under international law, Renault's argument fails to steer the doctrine of *respondeat superior* safely into harbour. To understand the reason for that, it is perhaps advisable to compare Renault's statement with that of another partisan of the same doctrine, namely, Eagleton:

> 'it is repugnant to the average person to think of punishing a soldier who, in the first place, would be ignorant of the legality or illegality of his act'.[153]

Eagleton apparently holds the view that in each and every case of obedience to orders the subordinate is afflicted with ignorance of the law. Such a view is undoubtedly erroneous. We have already pointed out that there is no inherent link between obedience to orders and

149. As for the argument that authorizing the soldier to judge the legality of superior orders is tantamount to undermining military discipline, see Boissier, *op. cit.*, pp. 45–46, 61–62; Knieriem, *op. cit.*, p. 244. Cf. Donnedieu de Vabres, 'La Théorie des Délits de Droit des Gens en Droit Pénal Interétatique', *I.L.R.*, vol. 28 (1950), pp. 159–172 at p. 160.
150. Renault, *op. cit.*, (*Clunet*), p. 341. Cf. Mérignhac, 'Sanction', p. 50.
151. This is also the way Daniel interprets Renault's statement (see Daniel, *op. cit.*, p. 166 n. 336).
152. See *supra*, p. 33.
153. Eagleton, 'Punishment of War Criminals by the United Nations', *op. cit.*, p. 497.

ignorance of the law: on the one hand, a soldier acting pursuant to an order may know right well that it is illegal; on the other, a soldier acting on his own may be ignorant of the law.[154] Unlike Eagleton, Renault perceives the possibility of a subordinate being aware of the illegality of the order carried out by him, and he realizes that in such case acquittal of the soldier on the basis of *ignorantia juris* is out of the question. Yet the doctrine of *respondeat superior* establishes automatic relief from responsibility in every instance of an offence being committed in compliance with orders. If the doctrine is founded on the basis of mistake of law, the question ought to be put why a soldier, obeying an illegal order with full knowledge of the law, is also entitled to be exculpated.

Here Renault submits that the second principal factor comes into operation. To quote the original:

> 'Puis, il y a autre chose: quand même, le cas échéant, les subalternes seraient convaincus de l'illégalité de l'ordre qui leur est donné, cela suffirait-il pour les rendre punissables? Il faut tenir compte de ce que le subalterne n'a pas la faculté d'obéir ou de ne pas obéir, il agit sous une contrainte immédiate; il sera souvent exécuté sur le champ s'il n'obéit pas, ou, dans tous les cas, il sera exposé à une peine grave. Il peut alors invoquer le fait de la *contrainte*'.[155]

This is the cardinal consideration of the compulsion element, which constitutes the focal point in Renault's theory. Indeed, many other writers follow him in this respect, and regard the concept of compulsion as the genesis of the doctrine of *respondeat superior*.[156] The protagonists of this school contend that it is 'practically impossible' for a soldier to refuse to obey an order.[157] Military discipline is very strict, and it threatens insubordination with inexorable sanctions, so that the soldier has practically no alternative (especially, though not necessarily, in times of war) but to obey the order *nolens volens*.[158] After all, as Maugham argues:

154. See *supra*, pp. 34ff.
155. Renault, *op. cit.*, (*Clunet*), pp. 341–342. Cf. Mérignhac, 'Sanction', p. 50; Poljokan, *op. cit.*, p. 154. Cf. also Garner, 'Articles', p. 138; Garner, *International Law*, vol. 2, p. 484; Garner, 'Punishment', p. 84.
156. See Belgion, *op. cit.*, p. 143; Birkenhead, *op. cit.*, p. 302; Dumas, *op. cit.*, p. 30; Eagleton, 'Punishment of War Criminals by the United Nations', *op. cit.*, p. 497; Rivière, *op. cit.*, p. 491; H. Smith, 'Nuremberg', p. 204. See also Boissier, *op. cit.*, pp. 59–60; Poljokan, *op. cit.*, pp. 156–158. Cf. Daniel, *op. cit.*, p. 167; Franklin, *op. cit.*, p. 161; Garçon, *op. cit.*, p. 478; Glaser, *Introduction*, p. 115; Glaser, 'L'Ordre', p. 306; Greenspan, *op. cit.*, p. 495; Levontin, *The Myth of International Security* (1957), p. 260; Maunoir, *op. cit.*, pp. 277, 302.
157. Both Belgion and H. Smith use these words (see Belgion, *op. cit.*, p. 143; H. Smith, 'Nuremberg', p. 204).
158. See Boissier, *op. cit.*, pp. 59–60; Borchard, *op. cit.*, p. 107 n. 1; Schick, 'Nuremberg', p. 198.

'A man ought not to be required to behave as a hero in order to escape death or imprisonment at the hands of an enemy tribunal'.[159]

Sometimes it is even alleged that the soldier carrying out orders acts not only out of external compulsion, that is, out of fear of the sanctions to which he is liable in case of disobedience, but also out of an internal compulsion which permeates him to the very marrow of his bones. Carlyle expresses this conception by saying:

'If a man becomes a soldier, his soul and his body thereby become the property of his commanding officer'.[160]

According to this approach, the training of the soldier and his mentality, the habit of obedience which military discipline infuses into his blood after recurrent drilling and which in time becomes second nature,[161] paralyze all his independent will-power and thinking capacity, and convert him into a sort of a puppet reacting automatically to any whim of its master who is pulling the strings. When the soldier is confronted with a superior order, he is driven or, from this point of view, virtually forced to obey, just as the robot is mechanically forced to obey the instructions of its master. The soldier, so runs the argument, is nothing but a tool or an instrument in the hands of a superpower. Daniel gives voice to this line of thought in the following way:

'Certains auteurs ne voient dans les soldats que des instruments matériels toujours dociles au commandement, abdiquant leur caractère et leur intelligence'.[162]

There is, perhaps, no need to elaborate upon the fallacy of the conception according to which every soldier is a sort of tame, subhuman creature or mechanical contraption without self-control. Individual soldiers of that kind do exist, of course, and in certain armies possibly more than in others,[163] but there is no ground for

159. Maugham, *op. cit.*, p. 45. Cf. Boissier, *op. cit.*, p. 46; Winfield – Lawrence, *International Law*, p. 547.
160. Carlyle quoted in the Nuremberg trial, Final Plea for the High Command (by Laternser), *I.M.T.*, vol. 22, p. 45.
161. F. Pollock speaks about the 'habit of obedience and disposition to obey which are the result of discipline', although he himself does not regard this element as one justifying manifestly criminal acts (F. Pollock, *op. cit.*, p. 198). It is interesting to note that in the Llandovery Castle case the Leipzig Court proclaimed that the accused 'had acquired the habit of obedience to military authority and could not rid themselves of it', and mitigated their punishment for that reason (Llandovery Castle case, *A.J.I.L.*, vol. 16 (1922), p. 723). In this regard, see also Glueck, *War Criminals*, p. 142.
162. Daniel, *op. cit.*, p. 155. Cf. also Maunoir, *op. cit.*, pp. 273, 302.
163. The term 'Prussian' has become notorious as designating a war machine without human checks. In the course of his testimony in the Eichmann trial, the priest Grueber described the German mercenary in the following way: 'A German *Landsknecht*, the minute he dons his uniform, puts his mind and conscience aside; it is said that he deposits them in the cloakroom' (Eichmann trial (first instance) (Criminal Case 40/

the contention that whoever doffs his civilian clothes and dresses in military uniform undergoes a phase of metamorphosis and, either immediately or after a process of 'brain-washing', loses his human image. What is important to emphasize, however, is that even the interests of military discipline itself require that the soldier will not act, and will not be trained to act, as a machine, but, conversely, will use the glimmerings of understanding, intelligence, reason and will-power that were bestowed upon him. Blind obedience, without any qualification or reservation, undermines the efficiency of the army first of all, and consequently defeats its own purposes. The following statement by Stephen is well known:

> 'The doctrine that a soldier is bound under all circumstances whatever to obey his superior officer would be fatal to military discipline itself, for it would justify the private in shooting the colonel by the orders of the captain, or in deserting to the enemy on the field of battle on the order of his immediate superior'.[164]

Yet, once it is conceded that a soldier is not, and is not supposed to be, a robot, but a percipient, conscious and will-powered living being, we must follow this train of thought to its limit.

Undoubtedly, the combination of obedience to superior orders and the element of compulsion is based on solid foundations in the realm of reality. At times, especially in times of war, orders are issued at the point of the sword or the muzzle of the gun; and, even more frequently, orders are accompanied—again, particularly in war time—by the threat, express or implicit, that disobedience will entail capital punishment. But it is important to keep in mind that the followers of the doctrine of *respondeat superior* wish to exonerate the recipient of the illegal order in every case and *a priori*. If, then, the doctrine is based on the reason of compulsion, we must point out at once that this plea, just like the plea of mistake of law, does not necessarily have to be voiced by a soldier who has complied with orders. The fact that orders are sometimes attended with compulsion does not signify that every obedience to orders is invariably accompanied by compulsion, or that compulsion may not take place unless it is a concomitant of obedience to orders. Obedience to orders is possible without compulsion, and compulsion is feasible without obedience to orders. Compulsion may occur without any distinction of rank

61, Attorney General v. Eichmann), Minutes (mimeographed, English), Session No. 41, p. Bbi. The present translation is taken from the Eichmann trial (first instance), Judgment, *op. cit.*, s. 225.

164. Stephen, *A History of the Criminal Law of England* (1883), vol. 1, p. 205. Cf. Daniel, *op. cit.*, p. 155; Dunbar, *op. cit.*, p. 260; Finch, 'Superior Orders', p. 443; Glaser, 'L'Ordre', p. 295; Janeczek, *op. cit.*, p. 76; Myerson, *op. cit.*, pp. 155–156; Eichmann trial (first instance), Minutes, *op. cit.*, Session No. 112, p. Z1; Kafr Kassem case (first instance), *op. cit.*, p. 410.

between the compeller and the one compelled; compulsion may even happen when the compeller is a private armed with a deadly weapon and the victim an unarmed senior officer. And a soldier may obey the orders of his commanders, not willy-nilly, but gladly and of his own volition. This last point is of great importance, and it therefore merits particular attention.

Garner has already noted that it is not easy to detect the motives which really induce the soldier to act when he is confronted with a superior order.[165] Mérignhac expresses the opinion that, in most cases when subordinates commit war crimes in pursuance of an order and the commander who issued the order does not personally supervise the performance of the actions ordered, the subordinates actually act of their own free will, and it is impossible to talk about compulsion.[166] In fact, the possibilities of committing a war crime pursuant to superior orders, while the perpetrator is happy to carry out the orders to the letter and even enjoys reaping the fruits of his action, are numerous and diverse, and it is difficult to classify them within definite categories.

Let us suppose several hypothetical instances of obedience to orders in different echelons and different circumstances so as to demonstrate the unreality of the sweeping generalization that every obedience to superior orders is involved with compulsion:

(a) Suppose that soldier A., who is stationed in an occupied area, mortally hates B., who is one of the local inhabitants. A. makes up his mind to lie in wait for B. and murder him. A. meticulously prepares the place and time of the ambush, takes his gun and is on his way to carry out his plot, when his commander, C., approaches and orders him to arrest B. on suspicion of having joined a resistance movement against the occupying authorities and to shoot him without ceremony. A. relinquishes his previous scheme of action, and kills B. in conformity with the minute instructions of C. When charges are preferred against A. on this account after the war, he claims in defence that he acted in compliance with the order of C.

(b) Suppose that a platoon of soldiers is accompanying a group of enemy prisoners-of-war on their way from the front-line to a prison camp located in the rear. The commander of one of the squads on guard, John Black, who is disgusted with the job, turns to his superior officer, Henry White, and proposes that all prisoners be shot there and then without more ado. Henry White vacillates, but

165. Garner, *International Law*, vol. 2, pp. 484–485; Garner, 'Punishment', pp. 84–85. Garner, however, is interested in this question from the outlook of the law of evidence.
166. Mérignhac, 'Sanction', p. 51; Mérignhac and Lémonon, *op. cit.*, vol. 2, p. 568.

finally makes up his mind in favour of the idea, and instructs John Black accordingly. John Black carries out the order. When he is caught, and arraigned as a war criminal, he claims that he obeyed a superior order, explaining that had he not received the order to shoot the prisoners he would not have committed the act, and this is the distinction between this case and the previous one. The fact that the whole idea originated with him is to John Black's mind irrelevant: an order was issued to him, and he complied with it.

(c) Suppose that a conference of the general staff of the army of Arcadia takes place. The commander-in-chief of the armed forces places on the agenda the subject of starting an aggressive war against Utopia. The participants in the conference, each in his own special field, survey the potentialities with a view to a quick subjugation of Utopia, and declare themselves in favour of war. The commander-in-chief, having listened to the proceedings, decides that war should be waged, and issues an order to that effect. At the end of the war, one of the corps commanders, who took part in the conference, is indicted for a crime against peace. He explains that he went to war only pursuant to, and because of, the order that he had received; that he did not conceive the idea of starting the war (and this is the line of distinction between this case and the foregoing one); and that the fact that he may have contributed to the decision taken by the commander-in-chief is immaterial. He only obeyed an order.

(d) Suppose that the officer X., whose post is with an army of occupation, receives an order from the military governor, Y., to destroy a public place of worship of people belonging to a certain religion. X. took no part in the decision-making process, but, owing to religious fanaticism or racial hatred, he carries out the order with ardour and zeal. When criminal proceedings are instigated against him at the end of the war, X. points out that he only acted the way he did because he had received an order from Y.; he explains that he did not conceive the idea or contribute at any stage to its crystallization, and in this regard this case is distinguished from the preceding one. The fact that he gladly acquiesced in the order does not, in X.'s opinion, bear upon the issue: all he did was to act pursuant to an order.

These are isolated instances taken at random from the infinite gamut of human experience; the common denominator of them all is that they deal with soldiers acting in obedience to superior orders, but the distinctive mark of our specific defendants is that, like Guildenstern and Rosencrantz, it may be said about them that

> 'they did make love to this employment'.[167]

167. Shakespeare, *Hamlet*, Act V, Scene 2. Cf. also Daube, *op. cit.*, p. 503.

If the doctrine of *respondeat superior* regards the soldier acting in submission to superior orders as a tool or an instrument, these are 'willing instruments',[168] and, assuming that they did not act in mistake of law, the doctrine does not offer any good reason for their discharge from responsibility.[169] It is certainly not reasonably possible in these cases to regard obedience to orders as derivative from compulsion. And when the engine of compulsion is shut off, the craft of the doctrine of *respondeat superior* runs aground. After all, once it is possible to indicate a list of cases in which soldiers obeying orders are not subject to compulsion, and no recourse to mistake of law is feasible, the doctrine stands in a *cul-de-sac*. It cannot reconcile the rigidly sweeping proposition that every obedience to superior orders automatically creates a full defence from criminal prosecution with the rationalization of that proposition.

It is possible, perhaps, graphically to describe the difficulties with which the doctrine of *respondeat superior* is faced as follows:

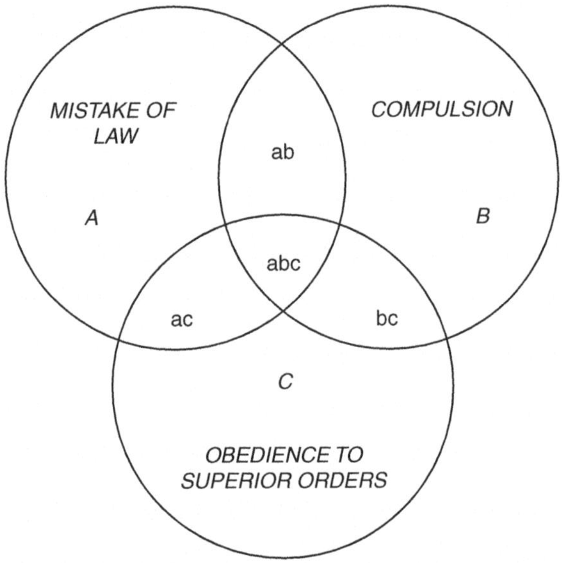

Circle *A* signifies the group of cases in which an international offender acts under mistake of law; circle *B* the line of cases in which such an offender acts under compulsion; and circle *C* all those cases in which he acts in obedience to superior orders. The two-fold premise on which the doctrine of *respondeat superior* is actually based is that mistake of law and compulsion constitute a rampart against criminal

168. To use Greenspan's words (see Greenspan, *op. cit.*, p. 494).
169. Cf. Glueck, *War Criminals*, p. 144; Greenspan, *op. cit.*, p. 494.

prosecution under international law. Let us assume that this basic premise is correct. In that case, all those whose acts fall within the circumferences of circles *A* and *B* ought to be relieved of responsibility. There are many instances in which these circles overlap circle *C*: an offender may act as a result of a combination of obedience to superior orders and mistake of law (though not under compulsion), and that is the case graphically expressed by enclosure 'ac'; likewise, an offender may act in consequence of a mixture of obedience to superior orders and compulsion (though not under mistake of law), and that is the case delineated by enclosure 'bc'; finally, the offender may act in such circumstances that all three elements—obedience to orders, compulsion and mistake of law—exist side by side, and that is the case indicated by enclosure 'abc'. As long as the doctrine of *respondeat superior* relates to a situation in which the component of obedience to orders coexists with at least one of the two other factors, of mistake of law and compulsion, it ought to be admitted, on the basis of the presupposition instanced, that the offender is indeed entitled to be clothed in immunity. But we ought always to recall that the two decisive elements in respect of discharge from responsibility are mistake of law and compulsion. Hence, even when the delinquent acts only under mistake of law (case *A*), or only under compulsion (case *B*), or under a combination of these two components (case 'ab'), without any obedience to superior orders, he should not be held responsible. On the other hand, and this is the main point, it does not follow that impunity is granted also to the offender whose case falls within the circumference of circle *C*, namely, an offender acting in obedience to orders, but outside the ambit of circles *A* and *B*, that is to say, one acting neither under mistake of law nor under compulsion. Here the doctrine of *respondeat superior* reaches the logical impasse of *non sequitur*. It is unable to answer the question why the defence that it purports to bestow upon offenders acting pursuant to orders is automatic and all-embracing, why impunity is applicable when mistake of law and compulsion are unavailing.

3. THE DISTINCTION BETWEEN THE DOCTRINE OF *RESPONDEAT SUPERIOR* AND THE ACTS OF STATE DOCTRINE

The doctrine of *respondeat superior* has a certain external resemblance to another theory, namely, the acts of State doctrine. What is the meaning of the latter doctrine? For an answer to the question, we must turn to the writings of Kelsen, who is the most important scholar actively pursuing this doctrine, examining its grounds and implications, and advocating its general recognition within the compass of international law.

According to Kelsen, the general principle obtaining in international law, subject to certain exceptions, is that no State has jurisdiction over the acts of another State, and consequently, when an individual violates the provisions of international law in his capacity as an organ of a certain State, the delict ought to be imputed to that State; the individual must not be brought to trial for the act, which is an 'act of State', before a court of a foreign State or a tribunal common to several foreign States, and must not be held personally responsible for it, save with the consent of the State on behalf of which he acted.[170] When can it be said than an individual acts in his capacity as an organ of the State and performs acts of State? Kelsen answers that as follows:

> 'Acts of State are acts of individuals performed by them in their capacity as organs of State, especially by that organ which is called the Government of the State. These acts are performed by individuals who belong to the Government as the head of State, or members of the cabinet, or are *acts performed at the command or with the authorization of the Government*'.[171]

The question whether the acts of State doctrine is really valid within positive international law, with or without qualifications, is of no concern to us in the purview of this study. What does concern us is that the doctrine has some pertinence to the subject of obedience to superior orders, as the italicized words in the passage quoted clearly indicate. Plainly, when an individual commits an offence by order of his Government, his act is regarded by Kelsen as an act of State, and the conclusion to be drawn, in accordance with Kelsen's theory, is that he should not incur responsibility for the act. At this point the acts of State doctrine is tangential to the doctrine of *respondeat superior*, as the latter also prescribes that this individual ought to be relieved of responsibility for the act, though not from the act of State angle, but on account of the element of obedience to an order.

Kelsen himself contends that there is no actual point of contact between the two doctrines, for to his mind

> 'The fact that an act is an act of State constitutes, in the first place, a problem of general international law which, as a rule, excludes individual responsibility for an act of State. The fact that an act is performed at a superior command constitutes a problem of national criminal law'.[172]

170. See Kelsen, 'Acts of State', pp. 230–231; Kelsen, *Peace*, pp. 81–84; Kelsen, *Principles*, pp. 235–238; Kelsen, 'Responsibility', pp. 539–541; Kelsen, *Theory*, p. 355.
171. Kelsen, 'Acts of State', p. 228. Italics supplied.
172. Kelsen, *Peace*, p. 104. Cf. Kelsen, 'Responsibility', p. 556.

In other words, Kelsen maintains that national law alone is involved with the problem arising from obedience to superior orders, whereas the sole interest of international law is the distinction between acts of State and ordinary acts.[173] As a consequence, Kelsen reaches the following conclusion:

> 'From the point of view of general international law, the difference between an act performed at superior command and an act performed on the own initiative of the acting individual is irrelevant. Only the question whether the act is or is not an act of state is decisive'.[174]

In my opinion this conclusion is mistaken. Both the theory and the practice of international law clearly demonstrate that this law is concerned with, and even vexed by, the problem of obedience to superior orders; and I think that almost every page in this study bears testimony to the fact. The discussion relating to the subjects of acts of State and obedience to superior orders should, therefore, and can, take place not on two separate planes—of different legal systems—but on the same level.

But the mere fact that both subjects are of interest to international law does not denote that the doctrine of *respondeat superior* and the acts of State doctrine are identical or even essentially similar. On the contrary, the two are different in their starting-points, different in their conclusions and different in their applicability.

The starting-points are plainly remote from each other. While the doctrine of *respondeat superior* is based, as we noticed in the last two sections, on the demands of military discipline, on the one hand, and on the elements of mistake of law and compulsion, on the other, the acts of State doctrine is founded on the general principle that no State has jurisdiction over another State: *par in parem non habet imperium.*[175]

As for the conclusions drawn from the two doctrines, it is true that both of them lend international offenders a mantle of immunity from responsibility; each, however, guides the missile of responsibility towards another target. The acts of State doctrine imputes the international delict, performed by the individual in his capacity as an organ of the State, to the State itself, and declares that the only applicable sanctions are those directed against the State—according to Kelsen: reprisals and war.[176] Conversely, the doctrine of *respondeat*

173. Apparently Levontin tends to agree with this conclusion. See Levontin, *op. cit.*, p. 254.
174. Kelsen, *Principles*, p. 136. Cf. Lauterpacht, 'Book Review (on Kelsen, *Principles*)', *B.Y.B.I.L.*, vol. 29 (1952), pp. 509–513 at p. 511.
175. See Kelsen, 'Acts of State', p. 230.
176. See Kelsen, *Peace*, pp. 81–82; Kelsen, *Principles*, pp. 235–236; Kelsen, 'Responsibility', pp. 539–540; Kelsen, *Theory*, p. 355.

superior removes the responsibility from the shoulders of one person, the recipient of the order, and places it on the shoulders of another, the superior who issued the order; and this transfer is vividly brought out by the actual meaning of the words '*respondeat superior*'. Svarlien expresses this idea as follows:

> 'it is well to remember that the maxim *respondeat superior* is a twin-edged blade which cuts in both directions. Whenever it is successfully invoked by a subordinate, the liability for the commission of the crime is not extinguished but is transferred to the superior who issued the order'.[177]

Finally, the main distinction between the two doctrines comes to light in the area of their actual application. Kelsen states:

> 'An act performed at superior command may or may not be an act of state. It is not an act of state if the command is not an act of state'.[178]

And he adds in another place:

> 'It is an act of State only if the command itself is an act of State, and that is the case only if the command was issued by the government (Head of State, cabinet, member of cabinet, parliament), or issued at the command or with the authorization of the government'.[179]

The distinction drawn here consequently hinges on the difference between general superior orders and specific superior orders, namely, orders of the Government.

This last distinction suggests that Oppenheim, in the above-cited passage from his treatise,[180] besides advocating the doctrine of *respondeat superior* (as is clearly indicated by his observation that, when the laws of war are violated in obedience to ordinary orders, the commanders issuing the orders are alone responsible as war criminals), also voiced and supported the acts of State doctrine (as may be inferred from his statement that, when the laws of war are violated in obedience to orders of the Government, it is impossible to talk about the commission of war crimes and the only available sanction is reprisals against the enemy).[181] Indeed, Kelsen regards the latter

177. Svarlien, *op. cit.*, p. 409. In respect of the responsibility of the superior see, e.g., Oppenheim's statement above (p. 38)—in the second half of the passage quoted. See also particularly Garner, *International Law*, vol. 2, p. 488; Garner, 'Punishment', pp. 87–88. Kelsen poses the question relating to the commission of an offence in obedience to superior orders in the following way: 'whether the perpetrator who executed the command, or only the individual who issued the command, can be made responsible and be punished for the act' (Kelsen, *Peace*, p. 104; Kelsen, 'Responsibility', p. 556).

178. Kelsen, *Principles*, p. 136. Cf. Lauterpacht, 'Book Review', *op. cit.*, p. 511.

179. Kelsen, *Peace*, p. 104; Kelsen, 'Responsibility', p. 556.

180. See *supra*, p. 38.

181. It is sometimes contended that Oppenheim did not distinguish between the doctrine of *respondeat superior* and the acts of State doctrine (see Glueck, *War Criminals*, pp. 229 n. 1, 233–234 n. 1; Hostage case, Opening Statement for Defendant

statement as reflective of the acts of State doctrine.[182]

A good example of the distinction that ought to be made in practice between the doctrine of *respondeat superior* and the acts of State doctrine may be found in the facts that were unravelled in the Dover Castle and Llandovery Castle cases, discussed above in the context of the Leipzig trials.[183] In the Dover Castle case, it will be recalled, a German submarine commander named Neumann was brought to trial for having torpedoed a British hospital-ship under the instructions of the German Admiralty; in the Llandovery Castle case, two German officers, Dithmar and Boldt, were arraigned for having taken part in the killing of survivors from another British hospital-ship, by order of their submarine commander, Patzig, who, on his part, had not been authorized by his superiors to commit the act. The Leipzig Court did not, in these cases, apply either the acts of State doctrine[184] or the doctrine of *respondeat superior*. Furthermore, it was a national court, applying national law to the defendants.[185] But suppose that the same facts were brought to light before a court of a foreign State, applying international law. In such a case,

(a) had the court subscribed to the doctrine of *respondeat superior*, all three defendants—Neumann, Dithmar and Boldt—would have had to be acquitted, because they all obeyed superior orders. The only one, under this doctrine, who should have incurred criminal responsibility for his acts, is Patzig, who acted on his own initiative but was not prosecuted;

(b) had the court admitted the validity and applicability of the acts of State doctrine, Neumann would have been entitled to immunity from the court's jurisdiction, because he complied with the instructions of the German Admiralty and Government (and this is supposedly a court of a foreign State). On the other hand, Dithmar and Boldt would not have been able to avail themselves of that doctrine, as their act was not an act of State; it was not vested with a character of one because the order that they received from Patzig was not an act of State.

List (by Laternser), *N.M.T.*, vol. 11, p. 857). This contention may, perhaps, have some formal validity in the sense that Oppenheim did not expressly state that he had in mind two distinct doctrines. Intrinsically, however, it is evident that Oppenheim drew a most definite distinction between obedience to orders of the Government and obedience to ordinary orders. When Glueck says that Oppenheim did not make a 'distinction between the government and a military superior as the source of the order' (Glueck, *War Criminals*, pp. 233–234 n. 1), he is misconstruing Oppenheim's proposition completely.

182. Kelsen, *Peace*, pp. 96–97; Kelsen, 'Responsibility', p. 550.
183. See *supra*, Part I, Chapter 2.
184. This was stressed by Glueck (*War Criminals*, p. 233 n. 15).
185. See *supra*, p. 19.

It should be noted that the acts of State doctrine is not confined to orders of a certain category, to wit, orders of the Government, and cannot be regarded as merely one facet of the aggregation of problems relating to obedience to superior orders. The doctrine of *respondeat superior* is, indeed, broader in scope, in the sense that it establishes that whoever obeys superior orders, no matter what their source is—inside or outside the Government—is relieved of responsibility. But the acts of State doctrine is broader in scope in another sense, namely, that it establishes that whoever acts on behalf of the Government—whether the act is performed in obedience to the Government's order or is committed subsequent or prior to mere authorization by the Government,[186] or even if the perpetrator acts on his own, being a member of the Government in the comprehensive meaning of the term—is not to bear responsibility.

For the purpose of further elucidation, let us suppose a case in which General A., a senior commander in the army of Arcadia, orders his troops, with the authorization of B., the Minister of Defence of Arcadia, to execute prisoners-of-war from Utopia, and officer C. carries out this order. When the war comes to an end, criminal proceedings are instigated against all three before a Utopian military tribunal. From the standpoint of the doctrine of *respondeat superior*, officer C. ought to be discharged from responsibility, because he obeyed orders, but not so General A., who issued the order, or Minister B., who authorized it. Contrariwise, from the point of view of the acts of State doctrine, all three ought to enjoy immunity from responsibility, for they all acted in their capacity as organs of the State.

It can be deduced from the foregoing that the distinction between the doctrine of *respondeat superior* and the acts of State doctrine stretches along an extended arc and is outlined in sharp contours.[187]

186. In the Eichmann trial, the Supreme Court emphasized particularly the dividing line between issuance of orders and authorization as the distinguishing factor between the doctrine of *respondeat superior* and the acts of State doctrine. Thus it pronounced: '"Act of State" does not necessarily mean that the person who performed the mission acted under a ministerial direction, which left him no margin of discretion, but it is rather the fact that the act performed was within the scope of the authority given which suffices to vest it with that character. On the other hand, the defence that the act was done in obedience to superior orders means—*ex hypothesi*—that the person who performed it had no alternative . . . but to carry out the order he received from his superior' (Eichmann trial (second instance), Judgment, *op. cit.*, p. 131).

187. The various aspects of the distinction are discussed by the following writers besides Kelsen: Glueck, *War Criminals*, p. 133; Graven, 'Crimes', p. 575; Keenan and Brown, *op. cit.*, p. 132; Levontin, *op. cit.*, p. 254; Sack, 'War Criminals and the Defense of Act of State in International Law', *L.G.R.*, vol. 5 (1945), pp. 288–300 at p. 288; Schafer, *op. cit.*, p. 139; Schick, 'War Criminals', p. 51; Woetzel, *op. cit.*, p. 68 n. 31. See also Eichmann trial (second instance), Judgment, *op. cit.*,

Nevertheless, writers who entirely reject the two doctrines jointly and severally again and again ignore this distinction and confuse the issues. At times the confusion is self-evident: thus one may find the following statement regarding the defences based on the two doctrines in Appleman's book:

> 'These defenses are allied, if not identical, in the eyes of the law'.[188]

At other times, only scrupulous scrutiny of the material reveals the confusion.[189]

Lack of clear distinction between the two doctrines is frequent when writers discuss the conclusions implied from the concept of *respondeat superior* with regard to possible upward shifting of responsibility in the hierarchy of command. As we shall see below, many jurists point out that the doctrine of *respondeat superior* may be invoked not only by the person who commits an offence in obedience to the order of his commander but also by the commander himself, inasmuch as the latter, on his part, complied with instructions from his own superiors, and thus the responsibility is passed from one echelon of command to another while everyone hides behind the back of his superior and enjoys impunity.[190] It may be argued that this movement up the hierarchical ladder must stop at one rung or another, and that, as soon as the origin of the prime order is traced, the focus of responsibility will be located. At this point, however, quite a few writers intervene, asserting that such is not necessarily the case. They contend that the origin of the order may be the Head of State himself, who, according to a certain doctrine in international law, is entitled to personal immunity; as a consequence, everyone is relieved of responsibility: the Head of State on account of the doctrine regarding his personal immunity, and all those subject to his authority—owing to the doctrine of *respondeat superior.*[191]

pp. 130–131; Hostage case, Opening Statement for Defendant List (by Laternser), *N.M.T.*, vol. 11, p. 857.

188. Appleman, *op. cit.*, p. 54. Characteristically, in the index of this book, under the item: 'Act of State, As Defense', it is simply stated: 'See *Respondeat Superior*' (*ibid.*, p. 385).
189. See e.g. Maynard, 'Crimes et Criminels de Guerre, Problème Etudié par un Groupe de Juristes aux Etats-Unis', *R.I.D.P.*, vol. 17 (1946), pp. 333–342 at p. 340; Q. Wright, 'War Criminals', *op. cit*, pp. 272, 278, 282. Cf. Q. Wright, 'Book Review (on *L.R.U.N.W.C.C.*, vol. 1)', *J.C.L.C.*, vol. 38 (1947–1948), pp. 400–401 at p. 401; Q. Wright, 'The Nuernberg Trial', *J.C.L.C.*, vol. 37 (1946–1947), pp. 477–478 at p. 477; Q. Wright, 'The Outlawry of War', *op. cit.*, p. 79; Q. Wright, 'The Outlawry of War and the Law of War', *A.J.I.L.*, vol. 47 (1953), pp. 365–376 at p. 373.
190. See below, Chapter 3.
191. See Bauer quoted by Glaser, 'L'Ordre', p. 310; Coste-Floret, *op. cit.*, p. 21; Daniel, *op. cit.*, p. 152; Eustathiades, 'Ordres', p. 397; Glaser, 'L'Ordre', pp. 306 n. 54, 322; Glueck, 'By What Tribunal Shall War Offenders be Tried?', *op. cit*,

Lauterpacht sums it up in the following words:

> 'To limit liability to the person responsible for the order may frequently amount, in practice, to concentrating responsibility on the head of the State whose accountability... is controversial'.[192]

The emphasis is laid here on the far-fetched conclusion of total dissolution of responsibility, what Glueck calls 'the Alice-in-Wonderland consequence',[193] produced by the combination of the doctrine of *respondeat superior* and that of the personal immunity of the Head of State. Several scholars, however, claim that similar results are derived from a combination of the former doctrine with the acts of State doctrine. The first step in this direction was made by Mérignhac, in 1917, when he stated, while repudiating the doctrine of *respondeat superior*:

> 'Enfin, si l'on pousse les choses à l'extrême, en remontant de grade en grade, on ne trouvera guère plus que le Kaiser comme responsable... Mais il... n'accomplit pas un acte personnel mais un acte *collectif*, un *acte de gouvernement*...
>
> 'Au fond des choses, c'est donc la nation entière qui est coupable'.[194]

In a book which he published subsequently (in 1921), in conjunction with Lémonon, Mérignhac spoke in this context not only about the German Kaiser but also of his staff officers.[195] A quarter of a century later, Jackson, in his opening speech for the prosecution in the Nuremberg trial, referring directly and simultaneously to the

p. 1088; Glueck, *War Criminals*, p. 141; Herzog, *op. cit.*, p. 287; R. Jackson, 'Report to the President (1945)', *International Conference*, pp. 42–54 at p. 47; Lauterpacht, 'War Crimes', p. 70; Lauterpacht – Oppenheim, *International Law*, vol. 2 (7th ed., 1952), p. 569; Maxwell-Fyfe, 'Foreword' to *W.C.T.S.*, *op. cit.*, p. xxi; Sack, 'Punishment', p. 63; Sack, 'Superior Order', p. 11; Sack, 'War Criminals and the Defense of Act of State in International Law', *op. cit.*, p. 288; Stevens, 'Introduction' to *W.C.T.S.*, vol. 6 (Falkenhorst trial), p. xxxvii; Lord Wright, 'War Crime under International Law', *History of U.N.W.C.C.*, Appendix VI, pp. 547–556 at p. 550; Q. Wright, 'War Criminals', *op. cit.*, p. 278; Hadamar trial, Opening Argument for the Prosecution, *W.C.T.S.*, vol. 4, p. 209; Hadamar trial, Closing Argument for the Prosecution, *W.C.T.S.*, vol. 4, p. 244. Cf. Harris, *op. cit.*, p. 13; *History of U.N.W.C.C.*, pp. 274, 276; Peleus trial, Address to the Court by Wegner, *W.C.T.S.*, vol. 1, p. 100.

192. Lauterpacht – Oppenheim, *International Law*, vol. 2 (7th ed., 1952), p. 569. Cf. Belsen trial, Summing-Up by the Judge Advocate, *L.R.U.N.W.C.C.*, vol. 2, p. 118; *W.C.T.S.*, vol. 2, p. 632.
193. Glueck, *War Criminals*, p. 141.
194. Mérignhac, 'Sanction', pp. 51–52. Schafer stated to the same effect: 'The defense of superior orders... illustrates the absurdity of the doctrine according to which the head of a State can never be held personally responsible for his acts because he is carrying out acts of State. When called to account, all the members of the State throw the responsibility on him. Yet he is immune. Who is responsible? No one' (Schafer, *op. cit.*, p. 142).
195. Mérignhac and Lémonon, *op. cit.*, vol. 2, p. 568.

doctrine of *respondeat superior* and the acts of State doctrine, stated:

> 'These twin principles working together have heretofore resulted in immunity for practically everyone concerned in the really great crimes against peace and mankind. Those in lower ranks were protected against liability by the orders of their superiors. The superiors were protected because their orders were called acts of state'.[196]

Here the immunity, personal or otherwise, of the Head of State was not mentioned, and Jackson explicitly underlined the perils lying in wait for international criminal law should the validity of the doctrine of *respondeat superior* and the acts of State doctrine not be contested.[197] Jackson's conclusion was that

> 'Modern civilization... cannot tolerate so vast an area of legal irresponsibility'.[198]

This argumentation, designed to gather the two doctrines in its net and discard them both, has found favour in the eyes of several writers, who have adopted it in its original form or with some slight modifications.[199] The trouble is that it is entirely faulty from a conceptual point of view. Whoever wishes to attack the doctrines and show that their combination brings about incongruous results must first of all take into consideration the major premises of each one of them and make sure that his criticism is directed at the doctrines as they are, and not as he might have liked them to be.

From the standpoint of the doctrine of *respondeat superior*, Jackson was apparently led astray, because it seems from his statement that the applicability of the doctrine is confined to persons in lower ranks only. In effect, the decisive factor is not the respective rank, lower or higher, of the one issuing the order and the one receiving it, but the very obedience to the order. Under this doctrine, every obedience to orders entails discharge from responsibility, be the rank whatever it may. Only one rank is actually excluded *a priori* from applicability of the doctrine, and that is the apex of the hierarchical pyramid, the rank of the one who serves no master, namely, the Head of State.

196. Nuremberg trial, Opening Speech for the Prosecution (by Jackson), *I.M.T.*, vol. 2, p. 150.

197. It is to be noted that, in a report which he prepared in 1945, prior to the beginning of the Nuremberg trial, Jackson emphasized the potential danger that may result from combining the doctrines of *respondeat superior* and the personal immunity of the Head of State, whereas he did not refer at all to the acts of State doctrine (R. Jackson, 'Report to the President (1945)', *op. cit.*, p. 47).

198. Nuremberg trial, Opening Speech for the Prosecution (by Jackson), *I.M.T.*, vol. 2, p. 150.

199. See Appleman, *op. cit.*, p. 54; Descheemaeker, *op. cit.*, p. 235; Eustathiades, 'Ordres', p. 397; Merle, *op. cit.*, p. 99.

From the outlook of the acts of State doctrine, again there is no foundation for the presupposition, inferable from Jackson's statement, that the applicability of the doctrine is restricted, as it were, to persons of higher ranks only. As a matter of fact, the decisive factor is not the rank, higher or lower, of the person committing the act but the possibility of imputing the act to the State. If the act was not performed by any individual in his capacity as an organ of the State, and consequently does not constitute an act of State, the doctrine is not applicable, and there is no reason for exemption from responsibility. On the other hand, if we really have before us an act of State, the doctrine creates a shelter from individual responsibility, and in such case it desires to gather under its wings all those connected with the act. That is to say: if the Government, in the broad sense of the term, including the Head of State, issues an order to violate the laws of war, and this order is relayed down the channels of command and is carried out by certain soldiers, the delict should be imputed to the State, and no individual is liable to be brought to trial for it before a foreign court—neither the soldiers who executed the order nor the various officers who transferred the order downwards from echelon to echelon, nor, for that matter, the members of the Government, such as the Head of State. Hence, the acts of State doctrine does not need any aid from the doctrine of *respondeat superior* to cancel the individual responsibility of persons of both lower and higher ranks for a violation of international law. It is perfectly able to achieve that end by itself and of itself. Actually, the acts of State doctrine alone, in case of an offence committed pursuant to orders which originate in the Head of State acting in his capacity as an organ of the State, produces the same result as would have been the composite effect of the doctrine of *respondeat superior* and that of the personal immunity of the Head of State operating in conjunction with each other,[200] even though the theoretical basis was completely different in each case.

We shall close the discussion on this subject by pointing out that deep confusion between the doctrine of *respondeat superior* and the acts of State doctrine is discernible in the oral pleadings of the Attorney General in the Eichmann trial (in the first instance). Addressing the Court, he referred to Kelsen's theory regarding acts of State, and said:

> 'It is clear that there is artificiality here, in this defence, because, had this defence been accepted, in dictatorial conditions like those prevailing in Germany there could have been only one defendant, namely Hitler; and when this person is no more, all the other persons accused of having com-

200. This is also pointed out by Sack ('War Criminals and the Defense of Act of State in International Law', *op. cit.*, p. 288).

mitted war crimes could say: our hands did not shed this blood, and our eyes did not see, for he was the only person authorized to issue orders, and we are all his soldiers, obliged to comply, to obey'.[201]

When this passage is read out of context, it looks as if it clearly referred to the doctrine of *respondeat superior*, but in fact the defence that the Attorney General had in mind was that of acts of State. Since, in accordance with the acts of State doctrine, responsibility is transferred from the individual to the State, and not to the Head of State, it is no wonder that at this point Judge Halevi interjected:

'He could also be immune as head of the Government'.[202]

But, strangely enough, the Attorney General replied as follows:

'He could have been immune by virtue of "Act of Sovereign". I do not wish to dwell upon the question as to what extent a Head of State is immune . . . If we accept the theory of "Act of State" as a defence, whoever executed Hitler's orders would have had a justification for the most atrocious crimes'.[203]

Unquestionably, according to the acts of State doctrine, the Head of State, not less than any other organ of the State, is immune from prosecution before a foreign court for acts committed by him in that capacity.[204] The Attorney General's restriction of his statement to persons executing the orders of the Head of State, in contradistinction to the Head of State himself, constitutes the betraying 'shibboleth': the words with which he chose to challenge the acts of State doctrine are derived from the vocabulary of the doctrine of *respondeat superior*. And it is needless to say, perhaps, that an attempt to fight one of these two doctrines with weapons designed against the other misses the mark.

201. Eichmann trial (first instance), Minutes, *op. cit.*, Session No. 5, p. C1 (Attorney General). As the English version of the transcript is most inexact here, I have inserted several corrections in the translation in line with the original Hebrew text (p. 7 of the Hebrew minutes of the session)
202. *Ibid.* (Judge Halevi) (translation corrected).
203. *Ibid.* (Attorney General) (translation corrected).
204. See Kelsen, 'Acts of State', p. 231; Kelsen, *Peace*, pp. 84–85; Kelsen, 'Responsibility', pp. 541–542.

CHAPTER 3

THE DOCTRINE OF ABSOLUTE LIABILITY

A great number of scholars tend to the view that the doctrine of absolute liability, according to which the fact of obedience to superior orders may not play any role for purposes of defence from criminal prosecution, correctly reflects positive international law.[205] The meaning of this doctrine, in its purity, is that the fact of obedience to orders does not create a defence *per se*, nor can it be taken into account within the compass of any other defence. This is the antithesis, the direct opposite, of the doctrine of *respondeat superior*.

The doctrine of absolute liability is sometimes explained along

205. See Anonymous ('Correspondent'), *op. cit.*, p. 154; April, 'An Inquiry into the Juridical Basis for the Nuernberg War Crimes Trial', *Minn.L.R.*, vol. 30 (1946), pp. 313–331 at p. 325; Bartlett, 'Liability for Official War Crimes', *L.Q.R.*, vol. 35 (1919), pp. 177–192 at pp. 189, 191; Bellot, 'A Permanent International Criminal Court', *op. cit.*, pp. 73, 78; Bellot, 'Punishment', pp. 45–47; Brand, 'The War Crimes Trials and the Laws of War', *B.Y.B.I.L.*, vol. 26 (1949), pp. 414–427 at p. 416; Coste-Floret, *op. cit.*, pp. 21–22; Goodhart, 'Questions and Answers concerning the Nuremberg Trials', *I.L.Q.*, vol. 1 (1947), pp. 525–531 at p. 527; Janeczek, *op. cit.*, pp. 76–77; Malézieux, 'Le Statut International des Criminels de Guerre', *R.G.D.I.P.*, vol. 49 (1941–1945), t. II, pp. 167–180 at pp. 172–173; Merle, *op. cit.*, pp. 96–99; Morgan, *Assize*, pp. 3, 11–15; Morgan, 'Nuremberg', pp. 320, 328–332; Pella, 'Le Code des Crimes contre la Paix et la Sécurité de l'Humanité (Observations et Réflexions)', *I.L.R.*, vols. 30 (1952), pp. 337–354; 31 (1953), pp. 125–150, 257–271, 353–362; 32 (1954), pp. 3–11, 111–118, 231–240, 351–360; 33 (1955), pp. 13–25, 243–252, 329–339; 34 (1956), pp. 33–47, 161–172, 372–385, in vol. 32, p. 240; Phillipson, *op. cit.*, pp. 260–261; Phillipson – Wheaton, *International Law*, pp. 478–479; Schneeberger, 'The Responsibility of the Individual under International Law', *G.L.J.*, vol. 35 (1946–1947), pp. 481–489 at p. 488; Schwarzenberger, *A Manual of International Law* (2nd ed., 1950), p. 90, (4th ed., 1960), vol. 1, p. 199; Schwarzenberger, 'Inductive Approach', p. 546; Schwarzenberger, *International Law*, vol. 1 (2nd ed., 1949), p. 323; Schwarzenberger, 'The Judgment of Nuremberg', *T.L.R.*, vol. 21 (1947), pp. 329–361 at pp. 354–355; Schwarzenberger, 'The Judgment of Nuremberg', *Y.B.W.A.*, 1948, pp. 94–124 at pp. 117–118; Sibert, *op. cit.*, vols. 1 (p. 97), 2 (p. 592); Spaight, *op. cit.*, (1st ed., 1924), p. 47; Stevens, *op. cit.*, p. xxxvii; Stowell, *International Law* (1931), p. 500; Weinstein, 'Book Review (on *W.C.T.S.*, vol. 8)', *I.L.Q.*, vol. 4 (1951), pp. 528–530 at p. 530; Woetzel, *op. cit.*, pp. 118–119, 188; Lord Wright, *op. cit.*, p. 551; Q. Wright, 'War Criminals', *op. cit.*, p. 282 (re: offences against the law of peace). Cf. Parker, 'The International Trial at Nuremberg: Giving Vitality to International Law', *A.B.A.J.*, vol. 37 (1951), pp. 493–496, 549–555 at p. 551; Spaight, *op. cit.*, (3rd ed., 1947), pp. 56–57; Lord Wright, 'Introductory Chapter' to *History of U.N.W.C.C.*, p. 11.

the line that the duty of the soldier to obey superior orders exists only when lawful orders are involved;[206] and only such orders, therefore, relieve the person who obeys them of criminal responsibility.[207] As for the first part of this explanation, it is poles apart from the concept subscribed to by Oppenheim and put forward by him—as we have noticed and expounded above[208]—as the reasoning underlying the doctrine of *respondeat superior*, namely, that international law imposes upon a soldier the duty to obey any order whatever, no matter what its content is. But just as we have objected to Oppenheim's proposition, we must also object to this manner of explanation by the advocates of the doctrine of absolute liability.[209] We have to distinguish carefully here between two unrelated questions: (a) When does the duty of obedience to superior orders exist *ab origine*? (b) When, if at all, is it possible to predicate a defence against criminal prosecution on the fact of actual obedience to orders? We are concerned not with question (a) but with question (b); and these are two independent questions, which necessitate disparate answers. One should not think that an answer given to question (a) must needs determine the tenor of the answer to question (b). Even if it be argued, in reply to question (a), that the soldier is in duty bound to obey only lawful orders, it is not logically inconceivable that actual obedience to an unlawful order which the soldier was not originally obliged to obey will relieve him of responsibility. Thus, for instance, a person is not bound to act out of insanity, but if he actually did so act the fact may prevent his conviction.

With regard to the second half of the foregoing explanation, it should be pointed out that a declaration to the effect that obedience to superior orders frees from responsibility only the executor of a lawful order makes a mockery of the dilemma confronting the recipient of an illegal order. When does a person need to make a plea for his defence? Obviously only when he is called to account for an illegal act, an offence, which he committed. When a person obeys a lawful order, *ex hypothesi* he does not perform any illegal act, and hence does not have to seek high and low for any defence, be it the defence of obedience to superior orders or another defence.[210] To

206. See Bartlett, *op. cit.*, p. 189.
207. See *ibid.*; Janeczek, *op. cit.*, pp. 76–77; Merle, *op. cit.*, p. 98.
208. See *supra*, p. 41.
209. One should not equate the conception expressed above (p. 21), that international law refrains from imposing an obligation of obedience to superior orders within the national army, to the notion that international law does impose such an obligation but only in case lawful orders are concerned.
210. See Appleman, *op. cit.*, p. 312; Eustathiades, 'Ordres', p. 407; *L.R.U.N.W.C.C.*, vol. 15 (Digest), pp. 157–158. See also Knieriem, *op. cit.*, p. 242.

quote the editors of the Law Reports of the United Nations War Crimes Commission:

> 'if the order is legal under international law, it is difficult to show how an act committed in obedience to it could be illegal under that system. If the act were thus legal in itself, there would be no need for an accused to have recourse to the defence of superior orders'.[211]

The question whether obedience to superior orders relieves the obeyer of responsibility or not consequently arises only in respect of a person who commits an offence pursuant to an illegal order.[212] He is the one whose protection from criminal prosecution is desired by the doctrine of *respondeat superior*, and the one whom the doctrine of absolute liability wishes to expose to such prosecution.

To hold the offender who obeyed (illegal) orders responsible for his acts, the doctrine of absolute liability has to proceed from the starting-point of the preservation of the interests of the supremacy of the law. That is, in fact, the starting-point of every objection to the doctrine of *respondeat superior*, though not necessarily within the ambit of the doctrine of absolute liability.[213] The law—that is, international criminal law generally, and the laws of war in particular—requires a certain conduct by way of commission or omission. The supremacy of the law requires the imposition of sanctions in case of a violation of its provisions. Not sanctions on paper; not theoretical sanctions; but real, down-to-earth sanctions. And in the opinion of the opponents of the doctrine of *respondeat superior*, the protagonists of the doctrine of absolute liability included, if an offender is not accountable for his act in any case of obedience to superior orders the supremacy of the law is frustrated. These scholars dwell markedly upon the potentially perilous consequences produced by an escalating shift of responsibility in the hierarchy of command:[214] they sound the alarm regarding the possibility of 'passing the buck'[215]

211. *L.R.U.N.W.C.C.*, vol. 15 (Digest), pp. 157–158.
212. See Appleman, *op. cit.*, p. 312; Eustathiades, 'Ordres' p. 407.
213. As we shall presently see, many writers adopt the course of emphasizing the necessity to preserve the interests of the supremacy of the law, in order to repudiate the validity of the doctrine of *respondeat superior*, even though at a later stage in the progress of the legal analysis they abandon the line of thought of absolute liability. At that stage they shift ground to another way of rejecting the doctrine of *respondeat superior* (such as the personal knowledge principle), out of consideration for various factors (such as ignorance of the law) which in their opinion turn the scale. But, as there is full consensus in the initial stage between them and the adherents of the doctrine of absolute liability, we shall have to take into account—during our discussion of the subject of the supremacy of the law—views expressed by all the opponents of the doctrine of *respondeat superior* without distinction between them.
214. See *supra*, p. 63.
215. To reiterate the expression very aptly used here by Appleman (*op. cit.*, p. 54).

and the swinging of responsibility from one echelon of command to another with everyone relying on the instructions of his superior and hiding behind him, of which the result is all but total immunity or '*reductio ad absurdum*'[216] of the subjection to the supremacy of the law.[217] Appleman describes this state of things in the following way:

> 'The soldier says, "I shoot this man upon the sergeant's orders." The sergeant says, "Captain Hirsch issued a general order covering this situation." Captain Hirsch refers to Major Blank, Major Blank to Colonel Jacobs, Colonel Jacobs to Lieutenant General Abrams, and Abrams refers to a directive of Goering. Goering says, "Ah yes, but the Führer ordered it"'.[218]

It is no wonder that Phillipson reaches a resounding conclusion:

> 'The safety and stability of a . . . family of nations are incompatible with such an exaggerated and preposterous notion of vicarious liability'.[219]

This argument regarding the upward transfer of responsibility and the creation of global immunity is interrelated with another argument to the effect that the doctrine of *respondeat superior* might enable an unconscientious and insidious Government to contrive and carry out a systematic transgression of the whole international legal system, while rendering the executive arms, the soldiers and civilians obeying its orders, immune from responsibility for their crimes by virtue of this obedience.[220] The inference is that the doctrine of *respondeat superior* incites 'international lawlessness'[221] on a large scale.

216. This fitting Latin term is popular with writers in this context. See Dickinson, *op. cit.*, p. 49; Finch, 'The Nuremberg Trial and International Law', *op. cit.*, p. 21; Finch, 'Three Problems of International Law', *op. cit.*, p. 13; Lachs, *op. cit.*, p. 84.
217. See Bauer quoted by Glaser, 'L'Ordre', p. 310; Bellot, 'Punishment', pp. 46, 49; Berger, *op. cit.*, p. 1203; Coste-Floret, *op. cit.*, p. 21; Daniel, *op. cit.*, p. 152; Dickinson, *op. cit.*, p. 49; Eustathiades, 'Ordres', pp. 396–398; Glaser, 'Nuremberg', p. 31; Lauterpacht, 'War Crimes', p. 70; Maxwell-Fyfe, 'Foreword' to *W.C.T.S.*, *op. cit.*, p. xxi; Phillipson, *op. cit.*, pp. 260–261; Phillipson – Wheaton, *International Law*, pp. 478–479; Sack, 'Punishment', p. 63; Sack, 'Superior Order', p. 11; Spaight, *op. cit.*, (3rd ed., 1947), p. 56; Lord Wright, 'War Crime under International Law', *op. cit.*, pp. 550–551; *L.R.U.N.W.C.C.*, Notes, Stalag Luft III case, vol. 11, p. 47. See also Finch, 'The Nuremberg Trial and International Law', *op. cit.*, p. 21; Finch, 'Three Problems of International Law', *op. cit.*, pp. 13–14; Merle, *op. cit.*, p. 99. Cf. Bellot, 'War Criminals', vol. 36, p. 765; Finch, 'Superior Orders', p. 442; Garner, *International Law*, vol. 2, p. 486; Garner, 'Punishment', p. 86; Glaser, *Introduction*, p. 116; Glaser, 'L'Ordre', pp. 305–306 n. 54, 308; *History of U.N.W.C.C.*, pp. 275–276; Janeczek, *op. cit.*, p. 77; Hadamar trial, Closing Argument for the Prosecution, *W.C.T.S.*, vol. 4, p. 244.
218. Appleman, *op. cit.*, p. 56.
219. Phillipson, *op. cit.*, p. 261. Cf. Finch, 'Superior Orders', p. 442.
220. See Malézieux, *op. cit.*, p. 173; Sack, 'Punishment', p. 68; Sack, 'Superior Order', p. 15; Schafer, *op. cit.*, pp. 141, 144. See also Berger, *op. cit.*, p. 1207. Cf. Winfield – Lawrence, *International Law*, pp. 546–547.
221. See R. Jackson, 'Nuremberg in Retrospect: Legal Answer to International Lawlessness', *A.B.A.J.*, vol. 35 (1949), pp. 813–816, 881–887 at p. 813.

For all these reasons, many writers are of opinion that recognition of obedience to superior orders as an automatic armour from responsibility is liable to incapacitate any possible criminal policy in international law, particularly in the sphere of the laws of war.[222] Eustathiades states it very simply, saying that the very same reason underlying the principle of the criminal responsibility of the individual on the international plane, that is, the need to impose efficacious sanctions on the actual offender, requires the repudiation of the doctrine of *respondeat superior*.[223] In other words, that doctrine prevents the application of real sanctions against the actual offender and undermines the foundations of the principle of the international responsibility of the individual, and must consequently be rejected.[224] There are those who take a further step and assert that eventually the doctrine of *respondeat superior* brings about the 'negation' of the whole international legal system.[225] Glaser phrases this idea as follows:

> 'il est certain que la doctrine attribuant à l'ordre hiérarchique une force justificative, n'est pas compatible avec la nature même du droit et avec son but essentiel'.[226]

All this argumentation has much merit. Ultimately, it exposes and emphasizes what Oppenheim sought to disguise when he propounded the doctrine of *respondeat superior*:[227] the essential need to ensure the supremacy of the law in the international realm generally and in the province of the laws of war in particular. The preceding considerations manifestly prove that not only disregard of military discipline is apt to produce dire consequences, to wit, anarchy in the military order; disregard of the supremacy of the law is also liable to bring about a calamitous aftermath, for it entails chaos and anarchy in the legal order. When the interest of preventing crimes collides with the interest of maintaining military discipline, they balance each other and create the dilemma dwelt upon above.[228] Within the international legal system, where it may be said that the interest of maintaining discipline in national armies has no legitimate status,[229] it even stands to reason that the demands of the supremacy

222. See Stevens, *op. cit.*, p. xxxvii. See also Finch, 'Superior Orders', p. 445; Glaser, *Introduction*, p. 116; Glaser, 'L'Ordre', p. 322; Harris, *op. cit.*, p. 557. Cf. Boissier, *op. cit.*, p. 39.
223. Eustathiades, 'Ordres', p. 396.
224. *Ibid.*, p. 397.
225. See Bellot, 'A Permanent International Criminal Court', *op. cit.*, p. 78. Cf. Weber quoted by Maunoir, *op. cit.*, p. 218.
226. Glaser, *Introduction*, p. 118. Cf. Glaser, 'L'Ordre', p. 312.
227. See *supra*, p. 42.
228. See *supra*, pp. 6–7.
229. See *supra*, pp. 21, 41.

of the law must prevail. But anyhow it must be concluded that the doctrine of *respondeat superior*, as put forward by Oppenheim, is inept, for it bows down before the Moloch of military discipline and, arbitrarily, pays no heed to the interest—which is not less, and perhaps even more, important—of preventing crimes.

Still, rejection of the doctrine of *respondeat superior* does not necessarily mean affirmation of the doctrine of absolute liability. After all, the soldier receiving an order to commit an act constituting an offence is caught between two fires and risks his life whether he obeys the order or acts counter to it. The principle of the supremacy of the law does not, in itself, answer his plaint, and it is unable to prevent his being ground between the upper and the nether millstone. We cannot, therefore, regard the principle of the supremacy of the law as the panacea in the realm of obedience to superior orders. As observed above,[230] even if international law is not confronted with a theoretical dilemma, the soldier is unquestionably driven on to the horns of a very acute practical one. And we must be wary of the state of things expressed by *summum jus summa injuria:* laws of war which the combatants are unable to live with and withstand are doomed to be nullified.

We have already seen how Renault and those following his lead transferred the emphasis in the doctrine of *respondeat superior* from the demands of military discipline to the hardships of the soldier, and sought to avail themselves of the considerations of mistake of law and compulsion.[231] We have pointed out that their theory is defective inasmuch as it starts from the presupposition that in every case of obedience to superior orders one or other of these two considerations must inevitably produce the discharge of the offender from responsibility. Well, the doctrine of absolute liability is also defective, though in a converse way, for it starts from the presupposition that in no case may obedience to orders contribute to relieving the offender of responsibility. This defect is conspicuous, and many scholars take note of it. We have seen how some of them, impelled by the wish to establish the factor of mistake of law in its proper place (from their viewpoint) in the sphere of obedience to orders, end by supporting either the manifest illegality principle or the personal knowledge principle.[232] We shall see below how others attempt to find a remedy for the problems that stem from the combination of obedience to orders and the element of compulsion.[233]

230. See *supra*, p. 22.
231. See *supra*, Chapter 2, Section 2.
232. See *supra*, notes 59 and 70.
233. See below, Chapter 4, Section 1.

The common cause of all these is that they rally round the flag of the interest of the supremacy of the law and challenge the doctrine of *respondeat superior*, but nonetheless they do not subscribe to the doctrine of absolute liability, striving instead to find a *via media* between the two extreme theories.

Should it be concluded that the doctrine of absolute liability totally denies the factors of mistake of law and compulsion any substance? By no means. At this point we ought, first, to bear in mind the explicit argument of the adherents of the doctrine, and, secondly, to consider what may be inferred by implication from their theory even though it is not expressly voiced.

The explicit argument of the proponents of the doctrine of absolute liability is that the fact of obedience to orders under mistake of law or compulsion, although not sufficient to justify the acquittal of an offender, should be taken into account among other extenuating circumstances when sentence is passed.[234] This argument constitutes a part of the general proposition, under the doctrine of absolute liability, that the fact of obedience to orders may play a part in mitigation of punishment, even though it cannot prevent criminal conviction as such.[235] Indeed, many writers who do not endorse the doctrine of absolute liability but, on the other hand, do not adopt the doctrine of *respondeat superior* either, concur with the protagonists of the former doctrine that alleviation of punishment is possible as a consequence of obedience to orders especially when the ingredients of mistake of law and compulsion are present.[236] Thus states F. Pollock:

> 'It remains to add that ... facts alleged in defence but not sufficient for justification or excuse are not to be wholly disregarded. They may still have their effect in mitigating the sentence. The propriety and the measure of such

234. See Brand, *op. cit.*, p. 416; Janeczek, *op. cit.*, pp. 76–77; Sibert, *op. cit.*, vol. 2, pp. 592–593; Woetzel, *op. cit.*, pp. 118–119, 188; Lord Wright, 'War Crime under International Law', *op. cit.*, p. 551. Cf. Goodhart, *op. cit.*, pp. 527–528.

235. See Merle, *op. cit.*, p. 99; Schneeberger, *op. cit.*, p. 488; Schwarzenberger, *A Manual of International Law* (2nd ed., 1950), p. 90; Lord Wright, 'Introductory Chapter' to *History of U.N.W.C.C.*, p. 11. Cf. Parker, *op. cit.*, p. 551; Schwarzenberger, *A Manual of International Law* (4th ed., 1960), vol. 1, p. 199; Schwarzenberger, *International Law*, vol. 1 (2nd ed., 1949), p. 323; Schwarzenberger, 'The Judgment of Nuremberg' (*T.L.R.*), *op. cit.*, pp. 354–355; Schwarzenberger, 'The Judgment of Nuremberg' (*Y.B.W.A.*), *op. cit.*, pp. 117–118.

236. See Berger, *op. cit.*, p. 1208; Castrén, *op. cit.*, p. 88; Daniel, *op. cit.*, p. 172; Dunbar, *op. cit.*, p. 257; Eustathiades, 'Ordres', p. 419; Glaser, *Introduction*, pp. 119, 121, 124–125, 131; Glaser, 'L'Ordre', pp. 313, 316, 321–322, 329–330; Glueck, *War Criminals*, pp. 156–157, 183; Greenspan, *op. cit.*, p. 495; Higgins, *op. cit.*, p. 105; Lauterpacht – Oppenheim, *International Law*, vol. 2 (7th ed., 1952), p. 571; Maunoir, *op. cit.*, pp. 204, 256; Paston, *op. cit.*, p. 4; F. Pollock, *op. cit.*, p. 198; Sack, 'Punishment', p. 68; Sack, 'Superior Order', p. 15; Q. Wright, 'Book Review', *op. cit.*, p. 401. Cf. Lawrence, *op. cit.*, p. 156; Stone, *op. cit.*, p. 363.

> mitigation—extending, it may be, to the imposition of a merely nominal penalty—are in the judicial discretion of the Court and not definable by rule'.[237]

It should, however, be recalled that, whereas the proponents of the doctrine of absolute liability regard the fact of obedience to orders only as a reason for mitigating the punishment in certain cases, and no more, the other writers regard this fact both as an extenuating reason in certain cases, and as a factor which may bring about total exculpation in other cases.

The strictly and stubbornly negativistic approach of the doctrine of absolute liability towards the idea of obedience to orders as a defence should not prompt us to think that in no case may the defendant who obeyed orders be acquitted. All that the doctrine establishes is that the fact of obedience may never be used for defence purposes. That is to say, whatever the defence of the offender may be, it will fail if it rests on the foundation of obedience to orders. But if the defendant who obeyed orders may build the structure of his defence in such a way that the fact of obedience to orders will not be a part of it, it is obvious that the doctrine does not, and cannot, intend to stand in his way. In other words: suppose that international law recognizes the validity of the defence of mistake of law. Suppose further that John Doe is brought to trial for having committed a certain act pursuant to an order issued by Richard Roe, and John Doe proves that he did not know that this act constitutes a war crime. In accordance with the doctrine of absolute liability, the fact of obedience to orders cannot bring about the acquittal of John Doe, either as an independent defence or as a part of the defence of mistake of law. But, if John Doe can manage to devise the defence of mistake of law without any relation to the fact of obedience to orders, I do not see how it may be contended that the doctrine of absolute liability will obstruct the success of that defence. The doctrine of absolute liability is powerful enough to exclude the fact of obedience to orders from the armoury of the defence. But if, despite that, the defendant is credited with an admissible defence, the doctrine may not form a stumbling-block in his way.

Yet the question may well be asked whether even this conclusion is reasonable; whether it is sensible or desirable that a certain item of the factual complex, to wit, the fact of obedience to superior orders, shall not be taken into account by the court, even within the framework of another defence. But as to that, we shall speak in the next chapter.

237. F. Pollock, *op. cit.*, p. 198.

CHAPTER 4

THE *MENS REA* PRINCIPLE

1. MISTAKE OF LAW AND COMPULSION

If we take a brief look backward at this point and survey the ground covered so far, our attention is at once attracted by two elements, namely, mistake of law and compulsion, which are sometimes concealed below the surface and at other times distinctly exposed to view, but again and again they magnetize the course of the discussion. The question is whether those two elements may not perchance extricate us from the quagmire of the problems pertaining to the subject of obedience to superior orders and serve as a guidepost for our thoughts.

As for mistake of law, we have already observed that it is not necessary, within the scope of this study, to determine whether positive international law recognizes or repudiates the well-known maxim *ignorantia juris non excusat.*[238] If international law does acknowledge the validity of this maxim, every offender acting under mistake of law ought to be criminally convicted, whether he obeyed superior orders or not. On the other hand, if international law disavows this maxim, particularly in the field of the laws of war—that is, if mistake of law constitutes a valid defence under international law—I think that in appropriate cases the fact of obedience to orders may figure, in conjunction with the other circumstances of the given case, in the scope of that defence. I see no reason for the contention that the fact of obedience to orders must never be taken into account as a component in the formation of the defence of mistake of law. Just as the court is entitled to take other facts into consideration, it must also be empowered to pay heed to the fact of obedience to orders when it is weighing the circumstances of the case in the light of the defence of mistake of law. There is no reason why the fact of obedience to orders should occupy a specially inferior position, and there is no cause for the court to disregard it. To that extent the fact of obedience to orders may, and should, contribute to the exemption of the defendant from responsibility, and not only to the reduction of his sentence. But there is no reason, either, for attributing to the fact

238. See *supra*, p. 33.

of obedience to orders a specially superior position,[239] and it should not be regarded as more than a factual aspect of another defence, to wit, that of mistake of law. Now and then, the fact of obedience to orders, in conjunction with other facts, may bring about the acquittal of a defendant owing to mistake of law, but at other times it may fail to accomplish that. Of itself, the fact of obedience to orders is not sufficient to relieve the accused automatically of responsibility on account of mistake of law.

The factor of compulsion plays a similar role *vis-à-vis* obedience to orders. We have already dwelt at some length upon the fallacy in the contention that, in every case of obedience to orders, the offender is entitled to exculpation for reasons of compulsion.[240] But inasmuch as a defence based on compulsion is admissible under positive international law, it seems to me that the fact of obedience to orders may be taken into consideration in appropriate cases side by side with other facts within such a defence. Actually, to draw an analogy from national law, it is, perhaps, possible to speak about obedience to orders in the context of two different defences derived from the factor of compulsion, namely, duress (or constraint or coercion)[241] and necessity.[242] Indeed, many writers hold the view that in appropriate cases, especially in time of war, international law grants discharge from responsibility to a soldier who obeyed illegal orders under necessity[243] or duress.[244]

239. As regards the assertion that mistake of law in case of obedience to orders is unlike ordinary mistake of law, see *supra*, pp. 34ff.
240. See *supra*, pp. 53–56.
241. This defence is prescribed in Section 17 of the Israel Criminal Code Ordinance, 1936, as follows: '*Constraint.* Except murder and offences against the state punishable with death, no act is an offence which is done by a person who is compelled to do it by threats which at the time of doing it reasonably cause the apprehension that instant death or grievous harm to that person will otherwise be the consequence; Provided that the person doing the act did not, of his own accord, place himself in the situation by which he became subject to such constraint'.
242. This defence is laid down in Section 18 of the Israel Criminal Code Ordinance, 1936, as follows: '*Necessity.* An act or omission which would otherwise be an offence may be excused if the person accused can show that it was done or omitted to be done only in order to avoid consequences which could not otherwise be avoided, and which if they had followed would have inflicted grievous harm or injury to his person or to his honour or his property or to the person or honour of others whom he was bound to protect or to property placed in his charge; Provided that in so acting he did no more than was reasonably necessary for that purpose, and that the harm inflicted by the act or omission was not disproportionate to the harm avoided'.
243. See Eustathiades, 'Ordres', pp. 415–417, 419, 421; Glaser, *Introduction*, pp. 124–125; Glaser, 'L'Ordre', pp. 286, 321; Glaser, 'Nuremberg', p. 30; Graven, 'Code', p. 375; Graven, 'Crimes', p. 582. Cf. Levontin, *op. cit.*, pp. 259–260.
244. See Cave, *op. cit.*, p. xxiii; Daniel, *op. cit.*, pp. 167, 172; Donnedieu de Vabres,

It should be noted, however, that some jurists are of opinion that the factor of compulsion is never, and hence not even in the specific case of obedience to orders, a reason for the acquittal of an offender, as distinct from mitigation of punishment.[245] Glueck supports the latter view when the military are concerned, adducing the following argument:

> 'It is clear that if and when coercion is a justification the reason lies in the recognition of the strength of the instinct of self-preservation, *i.e.*, a recognition of human frailty; but a soldier's entire work involves the suppression of the instinct of self-preservation'.[246]

By the same token, April maintains that

> 'It may be conceded that if he had refused to obey he might have been shot for insubordination; but it has always been known that the military profession was an extrahazardous occupation'.[247]

As regards the conception espoused by Glueck and April, there seems to be an over-simplification. First of all, there is a latent preconception in their way of thinking, which is apparently identical with the unwarranted assumption that underlies the diametrically opposed line of thought of some of the adherents of the doctrine of *respondeat superior*, namely, that, as soon as a person chooses to be a soldier and is dressed in a uniform, he stops being an ordinary human being and is possessed of sub-human instincts.[248] Secondly, in modern conditions of total war with the whole nation up in arms, it is impossible to regard soldiers as belonging to a unique profession or class and demand of them submission to certain *risques du métier.*

In respect of the more general approach of denying to one and all the validity of the compulsion factor as a reason for exemption from responsibility, it is interesting to follow the vacillations of one important jurist, Lauterpacht, in this matter. In an article published in 1944,[249] he wrote:

'Nuremberg', pp. 569–571; Dunbar, *op. cit.*, p. 255; Eustathiades, 'Ordres', pp. 415–417, 419, 421; Glaser, *Introduction*, pp. 124–125; Glaser, 'L'Ordre', pp. 285–286, 321; Graven, 'Code', p. 375; Graven, 'Crimes', p. 582; Maunoir, *op. cit.*, pp. 256, 277, 288, 297, 302, 311; Paston, *op. cit.*, p. 6. Cf. Berger, *op. cit.*, p. 1208; Calvocoressi, *op. cit.*, p. 73; Coste-Floret, *op. cit.*, p. 21; Harris, *op. cit.*, p. 557; Mérignhac, 'Sanction', p. 51; Mérignhac and Lémonon, *op. cit.*, vol. 2, p. 568; Normand, Speech, *R.P.D.P.*, vol. 39 (1915), p. 470; Rochette, *op. cit.*, p. 135; Scelle, *op. cit.*, pp. 985–986; Schafer, *op. cit.*, p. 144; *S.G. Memorandum*, p. 42; Q. Wright, 'The Outlawry of War and the Law of War', *op. cit.*, p. 373.

245. See Greenspan, *op. cit.*, pp. 494, 501; Sack, 'Punishment', p. 64; Sack, 'Superior Order', p. 12.
246. Glueck, *War Criminals*, p. 242 n. 45.
247. April, *op. cit.*, p. 325.
248. See *supra*, p. 52.
249. In regard to this article, see below, note 336.

'such a degree of compulsion as must be deemed to exist in the case of a soldier or officer exposing himself to immediate danger of death as the result of a refusal to obey an order excludes *pro tanto* the accountability of the accused'.[250]

He did, in fact, add the following qualification:

'unless, indeed, we adopt the view, which cannot lightly be dismissed, that the person threatened with such summary punishment is not entitled to save his own life at the expense of the victim or, in particular, of many victims'.[251]

In the sequel, however, Lauterpacht made it abundantly clear that, despite this qualification, he was firmly entrenched in his position regarding the element of compulsion as a reason for relieving an offender who complied with superior orders of responsibility in appropriate cases.[252] That was his opinion during the Second World War; but after the Allied victory—after the Nazi atrocities had been fully disclosed and the major war criminals, having been brought to trial, had voiced their pleas in defence—he changed his mind. When, in 1952, he published the seventh edition of the second volume of Oppenheim's treatise, he made the following unequivocal statement:

'No principle of justice and, in most civilized communities, no principle of law permits the individual person to avoid suffering or even to save his life at the expense of the life—or, as revealed in many war crimes trials, of a vast multitude of lives—or of sufferings, on a vast scale, of others'.[253]

At this stage, he was ready to take the element of compulsion into consideration in appropriate cases with a view only to mitigating punishment.[254]

In my opinion, Lauterpacht's later view suffers from overstringency. Apparently, he was led to this extreme position on a rebound from the impact of a vexatious *dictum* in the judgment rendered by an American Military Tribunal at Nuremberg in the Einsatzgruppen case:

'there is no law which requires that an innocent man must forfeit his life or suffer serious harm in order to avoid committing a crime which he condemns'.[255]

250. Lauterpacht, 'War Crimes', p. 73. Cf. *History of U.N.W.C.C.*, p. 277; J. Robinson, 'Lauterpacht's Contribution to the Development of International Criminal Law' (Hebrew), *Studies in Public International Law in Memory of Lauterpacht* (ed. by Feinberg, 1961), pp. 84–91 at p. 88.
251. Lauterpacht, 'War Crimes', p. 73. Cf. J. Robinson, *op. cit.*, p. 88.
252. Lauterpacht, 'War Crimes', p. 73.
253. Lauterpacht – Oppenheim, *International Law*, vol. 2 (7th ed., 1952), pp. 571–572.
254. *Ibid.*, pp. 570–571.
255. Einsatzgruppen case, Judgment, *N.M.T.*, vol. 4, p. 480. This passage was quoted by Lauterpacht (Lauterpacht – Oppenheim, *International Law*, vol. 2 (7th ed., 1952), pp. 571–572 n. 2).

In this case, criminal proceedings were instituted against the principal commanders of the extermination gangs that had cut a swathe of death across the territories occupied by the Nazis. The Tribunal actually rejected the plea of the defence which had been based on a combination of obedience to superior orders and compulsion, as it found that the accused had committed their monstrous crimes willingly and zealously.[256] All of them, without exception, were found guilty.[257] Yet, for one reason or another, the Tribunal saw fit to remark, for the benefit of the historical record, that it would have acquitted the defendants had they acted under a threat that was 'imminent, real and inevitable'.[258] Admittedly, in the context of the Einsatzgruppen case, these *dicta* were most unfortunate, and Lauterpacht was entirely justified when he wrote that

> 'There is . . . serious objection to this reasoning of the Tribunal'.[259]

It is in the nature of things that the defence based on compulsion, whether duress or necessity, must have limitations, and even very serious ones.[260] No amount of compulsion, be it as imminent, real and inevitable as events may prove it to be, can relieve the perpetrators of heinous and diabolical crimes of responsibility; hence the commanders of the extermination squads could not enjoy this defence in any way, shape or form. But it appears that Lauterpacht completely overlooked the fact that the crimes of these defendants fell into a very particular category, and that not all violations of the laws of war consist of wholesale, or even solitary, murder. A war criminal may also, for instance, be a soldier who plunders private or public property, without any harm or danger to human life. If such a delinquent acts in obedience to superior orders and under compulsion, there is no persuasive explanation in Lauterpacht's statement why this fact will not be taken into account for the purposes of the defence but only for alleviation of sentence.

There is really no need, within the purview of this study, to resolve the question whether international law recognizes the validity of any defence based on compulsion, and, if so, what are its limitations. Suffice it to establish that, if such a defence does not obtain in international law, the offender who obeyed a superior order under compulsion must also incur responsibility for his act. On the other hand,

256. Einsatzgruppen case, Judgment, *N.M.T.*, vol. 4, p. 480.
257. *Ibid.*, pp. 587–589.
258. *Ibid.*, p. 480. Lauterpacht quoted these words also (Lauterpacht – Oppenheim, *International Law*, vol. 2 (7th ed., 1952), p. 571 n. 2).
259. Lauterpacht – Oppenheim, *International Law*, vol. 2 (7th ed., 1952), p. 572 n. 2.
260. Such limitations are conspicuous, for instance, in the formulation of Sections 17 and 18 of the Israel Criminal Code Ordinance, 1936, cited *supra*, notes 241–242.

if such a defence is applicable under international law, there must be the possibility to take into account, within its compass, all relevant facts, including the fact of obedience to orders. To my mind, the proposition flowing from the doctrine of absolute liability—according to which, even if the legitimacy of a defence based on compulsion is conceded, the fact of obedience to orders may still not be considered for the purposes of such a defence—is unacceptable. To reiterate what we have said with regard to the subject of mistake of law: the fact of obedience to orders does not occupy a specially inferior position in relation to other pertinent facts, just as it is not vested with a specially superior position either.

To sum up now, on a tentative basis, our findings up to this point, it seems that we may conclude that the fact of obedience to superior orders may be taken into account in appropriate cases for the purposes of defence, but only within the scope of other defences, namely, those of mistake of law and compulsion, insofar as the latter really constitute valid defences under international law. The fact of obedience to orders does not constitute a condition precedent to the applicability of these defences, and it certainly does not form a separate defence of obedience to orders *per se*. In itself and of itself it does not protect offenders from the arm of the law, but it may contribute, in conjunction with other facts, to the substantiation of a defence recognized in the international sphere.

As this tentative conclusion will guide our path in the ensuing examination of the problem of obedience to orders, we should refrain from any equivocation. In my opinion, both the doctrine of *respondeat superior* and the doctrine of absolute liability ought to be rejected. By the same token, we should reject intermediate solutions which deny to the fact of obedience to orders the status of an automatic, *a priori* defence, but nevertheless recognize it as a defence *per se* under appropriate circumstances. Such intermediate solutions are endorsed by many writers, who contend, expressly or by implication,[261] that obedience to superior orders should be accepted as a defence, though only when the orders involved are not manifestly illegal, or when the offender complying with the orders acts without being aware of the fact that he was ordered to perform an illegal act or when the offender acts under compulsion.[262] An illustration of

261. This is done by implication when writers maintain—for example—that obedience to superior orders does not constitute a defence if the orders involved are manifestly illegal (see e.g. Maugham's definition quoted *supra*, p. 26). The implication is that, when the orders are not manifestly illegal, obedience thereto does constitute a defence.
262. The contention is expressly made by Berger, *op. cit.*, pp. 1207–1208; Daniel, *op. cit.*, pp. 152, 164–167, 172; Dunbar, *op. cit.*, pp. 250–255, 259, 261; Higgins, *op. cit.*, pp. 104–105; Knieriem, *op. cit.*, p. 244; Lachs, *op. cit.*, p. 84; Lauterpacht,

such an approach may be found in the following extract from Daniel's book:

> 'celui qui commet volontairement un crime de guerre en est responsable, même s'il a reçu des ordres de ses supérieurs de le faire; aucune irresponsabilité "a priori" ne peut être admise de ce chef.
>
> '...l'ordre d'un supérieur ne saurait être constitutif d'excuse ou servir de base à l'admission des circonstances atténuantes (suivant les cas) que lorsqu'il entraîne pour l'inculpé une erreur de bonne foi ou une contrainte irrésistible'.[263]

It is wrong, however, to regard obedience to orders as a defence *per se*—even when the defence referred to is not one that is automatically valid *a priori* but one applicable *a posteriori* under appropriate circumstances. After all, if the plea of obedience to orders may only be taken into account for defence purposes in appropriate cases of mistake of law and compulsion—and this is ultimately conceded by Daniel and those who are in accord with him—and if the defences of compulsion and mistake of law may be available not merely in cases of obedience to orders, it stands to reason that the actual defence is that of mistake of law or compulsion, and not that of obedience to orders. A reference to the fact of obedience to orders as a defence simply confuses the real issue. A subordinate who commits an offence pursuant to orders cannot count on the fact of obedience to them of itself to confer impunity upon him. He can only rely on the defence of compulsion or mistake of law, in the context of which he may, if the circumstances of the case warrant it, interpose the plea of having acted in compliance with orders.

Indeed, many jurists note that obedience to superior orders does not constitute a defence, but only a factual element that may be weighed, in conjunction with the other circumstances of the concrete case, when the offender acts under mistake of law or compulsion.[264]

'War Crimes', pp. 73–74; Sack, 'Punishment', pp. 64, 68; Sack, 'Superior Order', pp. 12, 15. By implication the contention is made by Appleman, *op. cit.*, pp. 54–56, 312; Calvocoressi, *op. cit.*, p. 73; Glueck, *War Criminals*, p. 183; Greenspan, *op. cit.*, p. 495; Keenan and Brown, *op. cit.*, pp. 132–133; Lande, *op. cit.*, p. XI; Levontin, *op. cit.*, pp. 259–260; Maugham, *op. cit.*, p. 48; Maxwell-Fyfe, 'Foreword' to *W.C.T.S.*, *op. cit.*, p. xx; *N.L.G. Report*, p. 21; Q. Wright, 'War Criminals', *op. cit.*, p. 278 (re: offences against the law of war).

263. Daniel, *op. cit.*, p. 172.
264. See and cf. Donnedieu de Vabres, 'Nuremberg', pp. 569–572; Eustathiades, 'Ordres', pp. 395, 397–398, 400, 404–405, 407, 411–413, 415–417, 419, 421; Glaser, *Introduction*, pp. 113–115, 118–119, 121, 124–125, 131; Glaser, 'L'Ordre', pp. 285–286, 302, 305–306, 310, 312–313, 316, 319–322, 325, 329–330; Glaser, 'Nuremberg', pp. 29–30; Graven, 'Code', pp. 374–375; Graven, 'Crimes', pp. 580–582; Maunoir, *op. cit.*, pp. 239, 256, 274–275, 277, 311; Paston, *op. cit.*, pp. 4–6; Scelle, *op. cit.*, pp. 984–985.

Glaser reflects this conception when he emphasizes that

> 'l'ordre reçu ne constitue pas, en soi-même, une cause justificative'.[265]

And he elaborates this idea as follows:

> 'il est certain qu'une règle consacrant l'ordre reçu comme une cause de justification, serait incompatible avec les principes modernes de la responsabilité pénale. Pourtant, il n'en résulte pas qu'une telle situation, l'infraction commise par ordre, ne pourrait ou ne devrait jamais justifier son auteur, c'est-à-dire le dispenser de la responsabilité. Mais ce que nous prétendons, c'est que la responsabilité de l'auteur d'un crime commis par ordre devrait être examinée dans chaque cas particulier, d'après les règles générales concernant la responsabilité. Il peut, en effet, se produire que l'auteur d'un crime de guerre agisse sans culpabilité, étant dans l'ignorance de l'illégalité de son acte, ou bien qu'il agisse dans une situation qu'on désigne comme l'état de nécessité'.[266]

The real defence in such a case is the defence of mistake of law or compulsion.

2. MISTAKE OF FACT VS. MISTAKE OF LAW

We ought to inquire now whether the two defences of mistake of law and compulsion, both controversial themselves, are the only defences in whose substantiation the fact of obedience to superior orders may play its part. I think that the answer to this question is in the negative, that there is another defence within the scope of which the fact of obedience to orders may well operate, and that this one is not controversial at all. This is the defence of mistake of fact, based on the generally accepted maxim *ignorantia facti excusat.*[267] Glueck has already noted, and rightly so, that

> 'the defense of "ignorance or mistake of fact" ... is of course ... available to soldiers',[268]

and he has correctly indicated the possibility of

> 'using the fact of obedience to orders as a stepping-stone to proof of ignorance or mistake of fact'.[269]

265. Glaser, *Introduction*, p. 131; Glaser, 'L'Ordre', p. 329.
266. Glaser, 'Nuremberg', p. 30.
267. To draw an analogy from national law, it may be mentioned here that this defence is prescribed in Section 12 of the Israel Criminal Code Ordinance, 1936, as follows: '*Mistake of Fact.* (1) A person who does or omits to do an act under an honest and reasonable, but mistaken, belief in the existence of any state of things is not criminally responsible for the act or omission to any greater extent than if the real state of things had been such as he believed to exist.' See also Kafr Kassem case (second instance), *op. cit.*, p. 413.
268. Glueck, *War Criminals*, p. 244 n. 49.
269. *Ibid.*

Admittedly, writers in general refrain, for one reason or another, from examining the question of obedience to superior orders in the context of mistake of fact; but if the fact of obedience to orders may be taken into account within the purview of the dubious defence of mistake of law, surely it may just as well contribute, together with the other circumstances of the case, to the formation of the undisputed defence of mistake of fact.[270]

When the relative position of the fact of obedience to orders within the confines of mistake of law or fact is established, the way is paved to come to grips with the problem which has vexed many a scholar, namely, how to handle an offender who violated the laws of war pursuant to orders that had purported, without ground, to justify the offence under the pretext of its constituting a reprisal for the enemy's crimes. The problem is defined by Lauterpacht as follows:

> 'The element of reprisals may have a significant and perplexing bearing upon the plea of superior orders... The subordinate may be expected, when confronted with an order utterly and palpably contemptuous of law and humanity alike, to assert, at the risk of his own life, his own standard of law and morality. This is an exacting though unavoidable test. But no such independence of conviction and action may invariably be expected in cases where the soldier or officer is confronted with a command ordering an act admittedly illegal and cruel but issued as a reprisal against the similarly reprehensible conduct of the adversary. We may attribute to the accused a rudimentary knowledge of the law and an elementary standard of morality, but it may be more difficult to expect him to be in possession of the necessary information to enable him to judge the lawfulness of the retaliatory measures in question in relation to the circumstances alleged to have given rise to them'.[271]

Lauterpacht refers somewhere else to the case of a violation of the laws of war, perpetrated 'in obedience to orders conceived as a measure of reprisals', and concludes:

> 'Such circumstances are probably in themselves sufficient to divest the act of the stigma of a war crime'.[272]

Dunbar is also of opinion that an offender who acted in compliance with superior orders representing the offence as an act of reprisal ought to be freed from responsibility.[273]

It is not entirely clear when precisely, according to Lauterpacht

270. Illustrations from war crimes trials of the application of the defence of mistake of fact in case of obedience to orders will be given below, Part IV, Chapter 2.
271. Lauterpacht, 'War Crimes', p. 76. Cf. Dunbar, *op. cit.*, pp. 256–257; Maunoir, *op. cit.*, p. 269; *L.R.U.N.W.C.C.*, Notes, Mackenzen and Maelzer trial, vol. 8, p. 7.
272. Lauterpacht – Oppenheim, *International Law*, vol. 2 (7th ed., 1952), p. 569. Cf. Maunoir, *op. cit.*, pp. 247, 275.
273. Dunbar, *op. cit.*, p. 256.

and Dunbar, the offender who obeyed an order falsely pretending to be a measure of reprisal is entitled to discharge from responsibility. But, inasmuch as it is implied in their statements that automatic discharge from responsibility must follow whenever the superior bothers to fasten a label of reprisal to his order, this proposition must be rejected. Lauterpacht and Dunbar themselves rely on the judgment delivered at Leipzig in the Dover Castle case[274] to illustrate the need to acquit an offender obeying orders in such circumstances.[275] But this case provides a good example for the non-acceptance of that proposition. Here, it will be recalled, the commander of a German submarine, who had torpedoed a British hospital-ship upon the instructions of the German Admiralty, was found not guilty. The German Court did not acquit the accused merely because these instructions had represented a violation of the laws of war (by sinking a hospital-ship) as an act of reprisal, but because the defendant himself had actually believed that he was indeed carrying out legitimate reprisals.[276] The fact that a superior commands a subordinate to contravene the laws of war, and, in phrasing the order, classifies this contravention as a reprisal, cannot of itself immunize the subordinate against responsibility. The decisive question is whether the subordinate really believes *bona fide*, in the light of the explanations of the superior and the other circumstances of the case, that he is performing a legitimate act of reprisal.[277] As formulated by Guggenheim,

> 'Il faut . . . examiner si le subordonné pouvait croire en toute bonne foi que l'acte illicite commis par lui avait le caractère de représaille'.[278]

One may share Lauterpacht's view that, ordinarily, it is not easy for the subordinate to pass judgment whether and when an act is legitimately vested with retaliatory character. But one cannot pronounce conclusively that the subordinate is never able to determine the nature of his act in this regard. The question posed by Kelsen and others

> 'How can a soldier know that a command that violates the rules of warfare is not a reprisal and therefore permitted?',[279]

274. See *supra*, p. 12.
275. Dunbar, *op. cit.*, p. 256; Lauterpacht, 'War Crimes', p. 77; Lauterpacht – Oppenheim, *International Law*, vol. 2 (7th ed., 1952), p. 569 n. 1.
276. See *supra*, p. 13. Cf. Glaser, *Introduction*, p. 115; Glaser, 'L'Ordre', p. 305; *History of U.N.W.C.C.*, p. 287.
277. See Guggenheim, *op. cit.*, vol. 2, p. 48 n. 1; *L.R.U.N.W.C.C.*, Notes, Falkenhorst trial, vol. 11, p. 26.
278. Guggenheim, *op. cit.*, vol. 2, p. 48 n. 1.
279. Kelsen, *Peace*, p. 107. Cf. Kelsen, 'Responsibility', p. 558; Schick, 'War Criminals', p. 47.

ought to be answered by saying that in quite a number of cases the subordinates may know that the professed excuse of reprisals is a vain pretext, either unsubstantiated by facts or lacking legal foundation. Every case should be determined according to its own merits and, if the subordinate believed *bona fide* that he was really carrying out a legitimate reprisal, he may base his defence on the mistake factor: mistake of law,[280] or mistake of fact, or even both.

To render this general thesis readily perceptible, let us exemplify the case of the soldier executing prisoners-of-war in pursuance of an order that depicted the act as a reprisal for similar misconduct of the enemy. Lauterpacht himself is troubled by this very case, saying:

> 'An example will illustrate the position: No person can be allowed to plead that he was unaware of the prohibition of killing prisoners of war... But the situation is more complicated when the accused pleads not only an order, but the fact that the order was represented as a reprisal'.[281]

As for myself, I feel constrained to say that I fail to comprehend in what way the representation of the act as a reprisal complicates the situation. If a defendant who obeyed an order to execute prisoners-of-war owing to an erroneous belief that he was carrying out an act of reprisal is acquitted—and the supposition is highly questionable[282]—this will be a classical case in point for the application of the defence of mistake of law, as international law expressly proscribes the use of reprisals against prisoners-of-war. Article 13 of the Geneva Convention relative to the Treatment of Prisoners of War, signed on 12 August 1949, provides very clearly that

> 'Measures of reprisal against prisoners of war are prohibited'.[283]

And a similar injunction appeared in Article 2 of the corresponding Geneva Convention concerning the Treatment of Prisoners of War signed in 1929.[284] In contradistinction, however, to the case of prisoners-of-war, there are other cases in which international law permits in principle recourse to reprisals if and when certain

280. See and cf. Daniel, *op. cit.*, p. 166; Glaser, *Introduction*, p. 124; Glaser, 'L'Ordre', p. 319; Maunoir, *op. cit.*, pp. 268–270, 273.
281. Lauterpacht, 'War Crimes', pp. 76–77. Cf. Maunoir, *op. cit.*, p. 269; *L.R.U.N.W.C.C.*, Notes, Dostler trial, vol. 1, p. 31; *L.R.U.N.W.C.C.*, Notes, Mackenzen and Maelzer trial, vol. 8, p. 7.
282. The editors of the Law Reports of the United Nations War Crimes Commission state categorically (and with good reason): 'No soldier... can be heard to say that he considered the summary shooting of prisoners of war legitimate as a reprisal' (*L.R.U.N.W.C.C.*, Notes, Dostler trial, vol. 1, p. 31).
283. *Kitvei Amana* (Israel Treaty Series), vol. 1, No. 30, p. 453 at p. 461.
284. Hudson, *International Legislation* (1936), vol. 5, p. 20 at p. 26. See also Maunoir, *op. cit.*, p. 270; *L.R.U.N.W.C.C.*, Notes, Dostler trial, vol. 1, p. 31.

conditions are fulfilled. In these latter cases, when an order to commit an offence is issued under the groundless pretext that the act is permitted as a measure of reprisal, and when the offender complying with the order erroneously believes that the conditions precedent required by law for recourse to reprisals have been met, he may found his defence either on mistake of fact or on a combined mistake of both fact and law.

Indeed, once the question of obedience to superior orders and reprisals is regarded from the angle of the defence of mistake of law or fact, it becomes quite obvious that there is no basis for the following despondent declaration by the editors of the Law Reports of the United Nations War Crimes Commission:

> 'Possibly there is no more difficult subject in the ambit of the law relating to war crimes than a correct application of the principles in a case where reprisal and superior orders are raised by the defence in respect of one and the same order which the defendant is alleged to have carried out'.[285]

3. A PROPOSED SOLUTION OF THE PROBLEM OF OBEDIENCE TO SUPERIOR ORDERS

Now that we have discerned the possibility of taking the fact of obedience to superior orders into account within the scope of the defences of mistake—of law and fact—and of compulsion, insofar as these defences are valid under international law, it is befitting that we search out their common denominator and thereby the bounds of the admissibility of the fact of obedience to orders for defence purposes. And what is the common denominator of mistake and compulsion if not lack of *mens rea*?

Not a few scholars have pointed out that the solution of the question of obedience to orders in international law ought to be sought, in accordance with the basic tenets of criminal law, by way of exploring the *mens rea* of the individual defendant in the concrete case. First to embark upon this promising route was apparently Lauterpacht, who in 1942[286] made the following significant and striking statement:

> 'it is necessary to approach the subject of superior orders on the basis of general principles of criminal law, namely, as an element in ascertaining the existence of *mens rea* as a condition of accountability'.[287]

285. *L.R.U.N.W.C.C.*, Notes, Falkenhorst trial, vol. 11, p. 27.
286. This statement was published as a part of an article in 1944. See below, note 336.
287. Lauterpacht, 'War Crimes', p. 73. Cf. *History of U.N.W.C.C.*, p. 277; J. Robinson, *op. cit.*, p. 88.

One year later, Dickinson referred to the problem of obedience to orders and said:

> 'It may be suggested . . . that the problem is chiefly one concerning the *mens rea*'.[288]

And other writers followed suit.[289] The trouble is that none of these jurists have drawn the full consequences that to my mind are inferable from examination of the question of obedience to superior orders through the lens of *mens rea*. If the existence of *mens rea* is the signpost that ought to direct our thoughts and guide us in the attempt to solve the problem of obedience to superior orders, it is clear that the mere fact of obedience is of secondary importance only. The rule that ought to be deduced is, in my opinion, as follows: the fact of obedience to orders constitutes not a defence *per se* but only a factual element that may be taken into account in conjunction with the other circumstances of the given case within the compass of a defence based on lack of *mens rea*, that is, mistake of law or fact or compulsion. Only lack of *mens rea*, of which obedience to orders constitutes circumstantial evidence, serves to protect from criminal responsibility in this case.

This, I think, is the proper, logical and effective solution of the question of obedience to superior orders in international law, and it may be termed 'the *mens rea* principle'. According to this principle, obedience to orders should be regarded as a factual detail germane to the offence, just like the time when, and the place where, the offence was committed; just like the weapon by which it was carried out; and just like myriads of other circumstantial minutiae. None of these factual details standing alone and out of context is endowed with special traits which radiate special legal significance. When the only thing that we know about a particular offence is that it was performed pursuant to orders, the knowledge does not get us, legally speaking, any farther than if the only thing that we knew were that the offence was committed, for instance, at 6 o'clock p.m. It would have been rash and impetuous on our part, if, on the basis of this knowledge alone, we had jumped to the conclusion that when the offender is brought to trial he must needs be relieved of responsibility. No particularly immunizing ingredient is inherent in the mere fact that the offender obeyed an order, just as no specially exculpating component is inherent in the fact that the offence was committed at 6 o'clock p.m. Of course, when the scope of our knowledge in respect of the circumstances of the case

288. Dickinson, *op. cit.*, p. 49.
289. See Dunbar, *op. cit.*, p. 234; Janeczek, *op. cit.*, p. 76; Levontin, *op. cit.*, p. 260; Starke, *op. cit.*, p. 370. Cf. Sack, 'Punishment', p. 64; Sack, 'Superior Order', p. 12.

broadens and all the facts are assembled and evaluated, the fact that the offence was carried out in submission to orders may contribute to the discharge of the defendant from responsibility, just as the fact that the offence was committed at 6 o'clock p.m. may be material in the achievement of the same result. In the latter case, evidence to the effect that the offence was committed at 6 o'clock p.m., and not at 7 o'clock p.m. or 6 o'clock a.m., may contribute to the acquittal of the defendant when it combines with the other findings of the court, according to which, for example, the defendant at that definite time, on that specific day, was in a certain place far away from the spot where the offence was committed, so that he was unable to commit it and may avail himself of the plea of alibi. In the former case, the fact that the offence was committed in pursuance of superior orders may contribute to the acquittal of the defendant when it combines with the other findings of the court, in accordance with which, for example, the defendant had been forewarned that unless he complied with the orders he would be shot there and then.

All that is the factual background to the acquittal of the accused. When we try to rationalize the two different cases that culminated in acquittal and draw the necessary legal conclusions from them, we cannot possibly claim that the court laid down the rule that offences committed at 6 o'clock p.m., or in obedience to orders, are not punishable. The *ratio decidendi* in the one case is that the prosecution cannot successfully bear the *onus probandi* unless it proves that the person in the dock was factually able to commit the offence with which he is charged. The *ratio decidendi* in the other case is that the defendant ought to be relieved of responsibility in certain circumstances if he acts under compulsion: lack of *mens rea*, and not obedience to orders, is the real reason for acquittal in this instance.

To conclude, the mere fact that a defendant obeyed orders does not render him immune from criminal prosecution under international law. Superior orders are not a magical talisman which wards off the spirit of justice. They do not serve as a 'Close-sesame' password to an enchanted mountain to hide the robbers of the Arabian Nights from the arm of the law. If they ever did, it is high time to realize that the Thousand and One Nights have come to an end, and that talismans and other charms are behind the times. From the viewpoint of international legal theory, obedience to orders ought not to create any defence *per se*. If a subordinate commits an offence against international law in compliance with orders, he may be convicted just as he may be acquitted. The choice between conviction and acquittal is dependent upon the circumstances of the case and is derived from them. The fact of obedience to orders constitutes only one of these circumstances, and it is interwoven with the others. Standing alone, the fact of obedience to orders should not have any special significance in international law. In conjunction with the other circumstances of the case, it may contribute to the proof of lack of *mens rea* and consequently bring about the acquittal of the accused.

The foregoing conclusion relates to the theory of international law. Evidently, however, the Contracting Parties to an international treaty, and courts entrusted with international legal proceedings, may elect to breathe life into the fossil of obedience to orders and then place this factual element on the pedestal of a legitimate defence *per se*. Such a result, to my mind, would shackle logic and law to a Procrustean bed, by arbitrarily stretching obedience to orders beyond its natural, factual dimensions. Nevertheless, if this is the general tenor of international practice, we have no option but to submit to it as reflective of positive international law. The *mens rea* principle, as proposed here, like all other competing doctrines and principles pertaining to the subject of obedience to orders, must stand or fall in the light of its own and of their applicability in practice. Shrewd distinctions and methodological deductions may help us in understanding the *lex lata* and certainly in consolidating the *lex ferenda*, but in the final analysis we must consider the law as it is, and not, or not only, as it should be. Bearing this in mind, let us proceed now to examine international practice and see the extent to which it confirms the validity of the *mens rea* principle and other principles discussed heretofore.

PART III: INTERNATIONAL LEGISLATION, 1919–1945

THIS part of the study is dedicated to an analysis of international instruments, drafted in the period from 1919 to 1945 and containing provisions relative to the subject of obedience to superior orders. In the first chapter, we shall consider the instruments drafted between the two World Wars; and let it be immediately stated that the common ground of them all is that they can be interpreted in diverse ways, mutually contradictory, and cannot settle the waverers or guide the perplexed. In the second chapter, we shall trace the numerous proposals crystallized during the Second World War and immediately thereafter, with a view to formulating a valid international instrument repudiating the plea of obedience to orders. Taking note of the various modifications undergone by these proposals, we shall be able to examine the Charter of the International Military Tribunal, which served as the basis of the trial of the major war criminals in Europe, and which has a significance over and above the scope of its direct factual application.

CHAPTER I

INITIAL IRRESOLUTION

I. THE PEACE CONFERENCE, 1919

A. *The Birkenhead Committee*

In 1918, the British Government appointed a Committee of Enquiry into War Crimes, headed by Lord Birkenhead and including such members as Lord Caldecote, Lord Hanworth, Russell, F. Pollock, Macdonnell and Higgins.[290] The Committee dealt, *inter alia*, with the question of obedience to orders and ultimately

> 'unanimously recommended that no plea of superior orders should be accepted in the trial of German war criminals if it could be proved that "the act charged was flagrantly and obviously contrary to the laws and customs of war"'.[291]

This recommendation clearly endorsed the manifest illegality principle as the one obtaining in the area of obedience to orders of war criminals.[292] But the Birkenhead Committee was merely an internal-British organ, and when the Allied Powers faced the need to outline their policy in regard to vanquished Germany they did not content themselves with the findings of that Committee.

B. *The Commission on the Responsibilities of the Authors of the War and on Enforcement of Penalties*

The Preliminary Peace Conference in Paris decided to inquire into the question of the responsibility relating to the First World War and to explore the possibilities of punishing war criminals, and

290. See Morgan, *Assize*, pp. 12–13; Morgan, 'Nuremberg', pp. 329–330. Cf. Dunbar, *op. cit.*, p. 243.
291. Morgan, *Assize*, p. 13; Morgan, 'Nuremberg', p. 330. Cf. Dunbar, *op. cit.*, p. 243.
292. It is of interest that Bellot—one of the most outspoken opponents of the doctrine of *respondeat superior* (see *supra*, p. 40)—maintains that during the First World War the British Government held the view that it was not permissible to bring to trial German war criminals who had acted in obedience to superior orders (see Bellot, 'Punishment', p. 45; Bellot, 'War Criminals', vol. 36, p. 763. Cf. Hostage case, Opening Statement for Defendant List (by Laternser), *N.M.T.*, vol. 11, p. 860). If that was so, the findings of the Birkenhead Committee ought to be regarded as an important turnabout in the official British approach to the subject.

for that dual purpose it set up, on 25 January 1919, a Commission on the Responsibilities of the Authors of the War and on Enforcement of Penalties.[293] The Commission was composed of fifteen members: two from each of the five Great Powers—the United States, Britain, France, Italy and Japan—and the others from Belgium, Greece, Poland, Rumania and Serbia.[294] The American Secretary of State, Lansing, was elected as chairman of the Commission, and among its other members we should particularly mention Scott (from the United States), Hewart (from Britain), Larnaude (from France) and Politis (from Greece).[295]

Like the Birkenhead Committee, the Commission of fifteen attended to the problem of obedience to orders, but, unlike its predecessor, it stated the following in its Report submitted on 29 March 1919:

> 'It will be for the court to decide whether a plea of superior orders is sufficient to acquit the person charged from responsibility'.[296]

This statement is susceptible of interpretation in any one of the following ways:

(1) It may be asserted that the Commission accepted in principle, as a matter of law, the defence of obedience to orders, and only indicated that the competent court would determine, as a matter of fact, whether there was room for the application of that defence in the concrete case in adjudication.[297] This line of thought may be pursued from a strictly logical standpoint, but actually it is difficult to suppose that it correctly reflects the Commission's view on the subject. It goes without saying that, even if the defence of obedience to orders were legally valid, the mere claim by the defendant that he is entitled to the benefit of it is not conclusive of the criminal proceedings and the court is bound further to examine whether the evidence confirms that the defendant indeed obeyed superior orders. It is, therefore, difficult to comprehend why the Commission bothered to emphasize this self-evident rule.

(2) It may be contended that the Commission evaded the issue and simply left it to the court to decide in principle, as a matter of law, whether obedience to orders may or may not shield offenders from punishment.[298]

293. *C.R. Report*, p. 95. Cf. *History of U.N.W.C.C.*, p. 32; Lansing, 'Some Legal Questions of the Peace Conference', *A.J.I.L.*, vol. 13 (1919), pp. 631–650 at p. 642; Levy, *op. cit.*, pp. 1056–1057.

294. *C.R. Report*, pp. 95–96. Cf. Lansing, *op. cit.*, p. 642.

295. *C.R. Report*, pp. 96–97. Cf. Lansing, *op. cit.*, p. 642.

296. *C.R. Report*, p. 117.

297. See Manner, *op. cit.*, p. 417.

298. See Einsatzgruppen case, Closing Statement for Defendant Naumann (by

(3) It may be argued that the Commission rejected in principle the plea of obedience to orders as an *a priori* reason for automatic acquittal of defendants and that it wished the court to determine, in each and every case on its own merits, whether the particular defendant who acted pursuant to orders ought to be convicted or exculpated.[299]

Interpretation of the Commission's statement is not made any easier when the following sentence, appearing in its Report immediately prior to the above citation, is taken into account:

> 'We desire to say that civil and military authorities cannot be relieved from responsibility by the mere fact that a higher authority might have been convicted of the same offence'.[300]

This sentence may be construed, standing by itself, as simply repetitive of the well-known principle that a defendant is not to be absolved of guilt just because another person could have also been accused of the self-same offence.[301] On the other hand, it is possible to read the sentence together with the immediately ensuing statement relative to the subject of obedience to orders and regard both parts as making up a composite whole. If the latter course is taken, greater force is given to the argument that the Commission's recommendation should be regarded as excluding in principle the plea of obedience to orders as an *a priori* defence, in the light of the last of the three foregoing interpretations.[302]

C. *The Peace Treaty of Versailles, 1919*

The Peace Treaty of Versailles, as adopted by the Peace Conference of Paris and signed on 28 June 1919, laid down in Article 228 that

> 'The German Government recognizes the right of the Allied and Associated Powers to bring before military tribunals persons accused of having committed acts in violation of the laws and customs of war'.[303]

Gawlik), *N.M.T.*, vol. 4, pp. 331–332. Cf. Hostage case, Closing Statement for Defendant List (by Laternser), *N.M.T.*, vol. 11, p. 1225.

299. See Daniel, *op. cit.*, p. 165; Dunbar, *op. cit.*, pp. 243, 246; Glaser, *Introduction*, pp. 114, 128; Glaser, 'L'Ordre', pp. 303, 322–323; Glaser, 'Nuremberg', p. 29; Lauterpacht, 'War Crimes', p. 69; Maunoir, *op. cit.*, pp. 216, 229; Schwarzenberger, *Lawlessness*, pp. 69–70, 73; Schwarzenberger, 'War Crimes', pp. 77–78, 81. Cf. Levy, *op. cit.*, pp. 1079–1080; J. Robinson, *op. cit.*, pp. 87–88.
300. *C.R. Report*, p. 117.
301. This is apparently the way Manner reads the sentence under discussion (Manner, *op. cit.*, p. 417). The difficulty intrinsic in the interpretation of this sentence is particularly noticed by Glaser (*Introduction*, p. 114 n. 1; 'L'Ordre', p. 303).
302. Those subscribing to this last interpretation (see note 299) do, in fact, read the two sentences conjunctively.
303. *A.J.I.L.*, vol. 13 (1919), Supp., p. 151 at pp. 250–251 (see *supra*, pp. 10–11). Parallel provisions also appeared in the other Peace Treaties of Paris: Article 173

No express provision in the Treaty of Versailles in general or in Article 228 in particular dealt with the question of obedience to orders. Glaser holds that what was not explicitly stated is nevertheless implicitly meant, and he reaches the following conclusion:

> 'Il était certainement dans l'intention des auteurs de cette clause de rendre responsables les coupables de ces violations sans égard au fait qu'ils avaient agi ou non sur l'ordre d'un supérieur hiérarchique'.[304]

It may be assumed that the Peace Conference primarily wished to follow the recommendation of the Commission of fifteen with regard to obedience to orders. The trouble is that this recommendation, as we have just seen, may be interpreted in various ways, so that the silence of the Treaty of Versailles may also be given more than one explanation. Manner, who maintains that the Commission admitted, in principle, the validity of the defence of obedience to orders, propounds, for instance, as follows:

> 'It seems that in the light of this recommendation, and in the absence of express provisions showing a contrary intent, the penal clauses of the treaties of peace of 1919–1920 . . . should not be construed as invalidating this defense although they are silent on this point'.[305]

Conversely, Daniel—who is of opinion that the sense of the recommendation of the Commission of fifteen was a rejection, in principle, of the plea of obedience to orders as an automatic defence and an authorization of the court to adjudicate each case according to its merits—submits that the Peace Conference intended to take the same path.[306] Finally, if the recommendation is interpreted as meaning that the Commission simply preferred to follow the line of least resistance and leave it to the competent court to decide in respect of the validity of the defence of obedience to orders, one may regard the formulation of Article 228 of the Treaty of Versailles as corroborating this view as well.[307]

of the Treaty of Saint Germain, signed with Austria on 10 September 1919 (*A.J.I.L.*, vol. 14 (1920), Supp., p. 1 at p. 55); Article 118 of the Treaty of Neuilly, signed with Bulgaria on 27 November 1919 (*A.J.I.L.*, vol. 14 (1920), Supp., p. 185 at p. 221); Article 157 of the Treaty of Trianon, signed with Hungary on 4 June 1920 (*A.J.I.L.*, vol. 15 (1921), Supp., p. 1 at p. 48); and Article 226 of the Treaty of Sèvres, signed with Turkey on 10 August 1920 (*A.J.I.L.*, vol. 15 (1921), Supp., p. 179 at p. 234). It should be noted, though, that the Treaty of Sèvres did not come into force, but was superseded by the Treaty of Lausanne, which did not include a corresponding provision. See Schwelb, 'Crimes against Humanity', *B.Y.B.I.L.*, vol. 23 (1946), pp. 178–226 at p. 182.

304. Glaser, *Introduction*, p. 114. See also Glaser, 'L'Ordre', p. 303. Cf. Maunoir, *op. cit.*, pp. 216–217.
305. Manner, *op. cit.*, p. 417. Cf. Daniel, *op. cit.*, p. 165.
306. Daniel, *op. cit.*, p. 165.
307. Cf. Scott, *op. cit.*, pp. 247–248.

Actually, as we have seen,[308] the German war criminals were not surrendered to the Allied Powers, and accordingly the problem of the interpretation of Article 228 in the light of the issue of obedience to orders did not in fact arise.

2. THE WASHINGTON CONFERENCE, 1922

A. *The Treaty in relation to the Use of Submarines and Noxious Gases in Warfare*

On 6 February 1922, the United States, Britain, France, Italy and Japan signed at Washington the Treaty in relation to the Use of Submarines and Noxious Gases in Warfare.[309] The Treaty was formulated in the Conference on the Limitation of Armament, and in accordance with a proposal submitted by the American representative, Root,[310] the following provision was inserted in it as Article III:

> 'The Signatory Powers, desiring to insure the enforcement of the humane rules of existing law declared by them with respect to attacks upon and the seizure and destruction of merchant ships, further declare that any person in the service of any Power who shall violate any of those rules, *whether or not such person is under orders of a governmental superior*, shall be deemed to have violated the laws of war and shall be liable to trial and punishment as if for an act of piracy and may be brought to trial before the civil or military authorities of any Power within the jurisdiction of which he may be found'.[311]

It is manifest that this Article repudiates the doctrine of *respondeat superior.*[312]

308. See *supra*, p. 11.
309. *A.J.I.L.*, vol. 16 (1922), Supp., p. 57.
310. See Buell, *The Washington Conference* (1922), pp. 219ff.
311. *A.J.I.L.*, vol. 16 (1922), Supp., pp. 58–59. Italics supplied.
312. See Birkenhead, *op. cit.*, p. 302; Cave, *op. cit.*, pp. xxix–xxx; Daniel, *op. cit.*, pp. 164–165; Dunbar, *op. cit.*, pp. 246–247; Eustathiades, 'Ordres', pp. 402–403; Fenwick, *op. cit.*, p. 669; Glaser, *Introduction*, pp. 114–115; Glaser, 'L'Ordre', p. 304; Glaser, 'Nuremberg', pp. 29–30; Glueck, *War Criminals*, pp. 154–155; Higgins – Hall, *International Law*, pp. 499, 627–628; Keenan and Brown, *op. cit.*, p. 134; Maunoir, *op. cit.*, p. 217; Pella, 'Le Code des Crimes contre la Paix et la Sécurité de l'Humanité', *op. cit.*, p. 355; Roxburgh, *op. cit.*, pp. 150–151, 154; Schwarzenberger, *Lawlessness*, pp. 63, 72–73; Schwarzenberger, 'War Crimes', pp. 72, 80–81; Spaight, *op. cit.*, (3rd ed., 1947), p. 57; Kharkov trial, Prosecution, *People's Verdict*, p. 114. Cf. Colby, 'War Crimes', p. 607 n. 133; Genet, *op. cit.*, pp. 255–256; Guggenheim, *op. cit.*, vol. 2, p. 47 n. 3; Janeczek, *op. cit.*, p. 77 n. 3; Lauterpacht – Oppenheim, *International Law*, vol. 2 (7th ed., 1952), p. 569 n. 2; Levy, *op. cit.*, pp. 1079–1080; Manner, *op. cit.*, p. 417; Morgan, *Assize*, p. 15, note; Morgan, 'Nuremberg', p. 332, note; Sack, 'Punishment', p. 67; Sack, 'Superior Order', p. 15; Schick, 'War Criminals', p. 50; Winfield – Lawrence, *International Law*, p. 547; Q. Wright, 'The Outlawry of War', *op. cit.*, p. 79 n. 15; Einsatz-

To come into force, the Treaty of Washington required ratification by all its five Contracting Parties, and, as one of the five—France—refused to ratify, it failed to mature and remained abortive.[313] After renewed negotiations, the five Powers, on 22 April 1930, signed the Treaty of London for the Limitation and Reduction of Naval Armament.[314] Part IV of the Treaty of London parallels, in its stipulations, the inoperative Treaty of Washington, but the main link is missing from the chain: no clause corresponding to Article III of the Treaty of Washington appears in the new instrument.

The question presents itself why France abstained from ratifying the Treaty of Washington and thus putting life into it. Gawlik, defence counsel for the accused Naumann in the Einsatzgruppen case, asserted that

> 'France especially declined to ratify this Agreement just because of the provision in it that the plea of superior orders should not be admissible'.[315]

But he based this statement of his on the following quotation from an article written by Genet:

> 'During the negotiation of the treaty signed at Washington, France (which, however, did not ratify) had contended that the commanders of submarines could not be held personally responsible for orders which they had received from their hierarchic superiors'.[316]

And in this passage, even though Genet refers to the initial objection raised by France with regard to the inclusion of the provision

gruppen case, Closing Statement for Defendant Naumann (by Gawlik), *N.M.T.*, vol. 4, p. 330; Hostage case, Opening Statement for Defendant List (by Laternser), *N.M.T.*, vol. 11, p. 860; Nuremberg trial, Opening Speech for the Prosecution (by Rudenko), *I.M.T.*, vol. 7, p. 150. It should be noted that several jurists hold the view that Article III pertains to the acts of State doctrine (discussed *supra*, pp. 57ff). See e.g. Kelsen, 'Acts of State', pp. 232–233; Kelsen, *Peace*, pp. 78–79; Kelsen, 'Responsibility', p. 537; Svarlien, *op. cit.*, pp. 397–398. And cf. Glaser, *Introduction*, p. 75; Glaser, '"L'Acte d'Etat" et le Problème de la Responsabilité Individuelle', *R.D.P.C.*, vol. 31 (1950–1951), pp. 1–17 at p. 15; Glaser 'Nuremberg', p. 20; Glueck, *The Nuremberg Trial and Aggressive War* (1946), p. 58 n. 20.

313. In Britain, the Treaties of Washington Act, 1922 (12 & 13 Geo. 5 c. 21), was enacted, and Section 4 thereof made Article III of the Treaty of Washington operative on a national level. Subsequent to the signature of the Treaty of London, 1930, the British Parliament passed the London Naval Treaty Act, 1930 (20 & 21 Geo. 5 c. 48), of which Section 2 repealed Section 4 of the 1922 Act. As to the effect of Section 4 in the interval between 1922 and 1930, see McNair, 'When Do British Treaties Involve Legislation?', *B.Y.B.I.L.*, vol. 9 (1928), pp. 59–68 at pp. 65–66.
314. *A.J.I.L.*, vol. 25 (1931), Supp., p. 63.
315. Einsatzgruppen case, Closing Statement for Defendant Naumann (by Gawlik), *N.M.T.*, vol. 4, p. 330.
316. Genet, *op. cit.*, p. 256.

rejecting the plea of obedience to orders in the Treaty of Washington, there is no allusion to the alleged fact that France ultimately withheld its ratification on account of its objection to that provision in particular. Moreover, Glueck categorically declares that France declined to ratify

> 'for a reason other than elimination of the defense of superior orders'.[317]

And he is not the only one who maintains that.[318]

Although Article III of the Treaty of Washington remained a dead letter, we must not underestimate the fact that five major Powers at least signed the instrument containing it and four of them ratified the Treaty as it was. One may, therefore, ask whether the repudiation of the doctrine of *respondeat superior* in Article III proves anything with respect to the legal force of this doctrine under international law. In posing this question we do not wish, of course, to detract from the significance of the fact that the Treaty of Washington applied to certain offences only and that at any rate it was signed by five Powers alone, no matter how important they were, so that, even had they all ratified the Treaty, it would not have been universally valid.[319] All that we want to enquire is whether those five Powers originally wished merely to crystallize, in an agreement between them, a legal principle which anyhow obtains in general international law, or, alternatively, whether they wanted to adopt for themselves a special provision which is an exception to the rules accepted on the international plane.

The latter alternative is endorsed by Manner, who contends that

> 'the attempt made in Article 3 of the Washington Treaty of February 6, 1922, to set aside expressly this defense in so far as applicable to acts connected with unrestricted submarine warfare furnishes evidence of its validity after the last war'.[320]

Daniel, on the other hand, espouses the converse proposition,[321] relying on Article I of the Treaty of Washington, which provides:

> 'The Signatory Powers declare that . . . the following are to be deemed an established part of international law:
> ' . . . '.[322]

317. Glueck, *War Criminals*, p. 155.
318. See Sack, 'Punishment', p. 67; Sack, 'Superior Order', p. 15.
319. This point is particularly emphasized by Schick ('War Criminals', p. 50). See also Padelford, 'Foreign Shipping during the Spanish Civil War', *A.J.I.L.*, vol. 32 (1938), pp. 264–279 at p. 274.
320. Manner, *op. cit.*, p. 417. Cf. Dunbar, *op. cit.*, p. 246 n. 34; Fenwick, *op. cit.*, (2nd ed., rev. enl., 1934), pp. 583–584; Hostage case, Opening Statement for Defendant List (by Laternser), *N.M.T.*, vol. 11, p. 860.
321. Daniel, *op. cit.*, pp. 164–165.
322. *A.J.I.L.*, vol. 16 (1922), Supp., p. 58.

As the Treaty itself refers here to rules regarded by the Contracting Parties as 'an established part of international law', Daniel asserts that

> 'L'intention n'était donc pas d'innover en adoptant une règle différente du droit commun, mais au contraire de préciser un point de droit international sur lequel des doutes avaient pu naître'.[323]

Article I itself, however, enumerates the rules which, in the opinion of the Signatory Powers, ought to be considered as 'an established part of international law'; and nowhere does the Treaty state that Article III, which was designed to ensure the enforcement of those rules, is also indicative of legal tenets that are part of pre-existing law. The innate character of the rules specified in Article I does not necessarily bear upon the legal nature of the measures mentioned in Article III, which were contemplated with a view to enforcing submission to those rules. Relying on Article I consequently means leaning on a broken reed. On the other hand, it should be noted that the Treaty of Washington in no way alludes to the exclusion of the plea of obedience to orders in Article III as a departure from the rules of positive international law. Hence, even without resort to Article I for support, the view is not untenable that the express denial of that plea is, in the opinion of the Contracting Parties, in line with the accepted principles of general international law.[324]

Finally, we ought here to raise the question whether one may draw any conclusion relative to the validity of the doctrine of *respondeat superior* under international law from the fact that the Treaty of London lacks any clause corresponding to that of Article III of the Treaty of Washington rejecting the excuse of obedience to orders. Indeed, it is argued on the basis of this fact that at London the five Powers, as it were, recognized that a mistake had been made at Washington and therefore deleted the stipulation conflicting with the doctrine of *respondeat superior.*[325] But this argument will not hold water. At London, the whole subject of punishment of offenders was excised from the Treaty and naturally the passage dealing with obedience to orders was done away with, together with the other portions of the provision contained in Article III. There is no reason to regard this particular passage as refuted; it is self-evident that, with the disappearance of the whole penal complex from the Treaty, no room was left for the component of obedience to orders.

323. Daniel, *op. cit.*, p. 165.
324. See Maunoir, *op. cit.*, pp. 217–218.
325. See Hostage case, Opening Statement for Defendant List (by Laternser), *N.M.T.*, vol. 11, pp. 860–861. Cf. Dunbar, *op. cit.*, p. 247; Spaight, *op. cit.*, (3rd ed., 1947), p. 57.

B. *The Rules for the Control of Radio in Time of War*

On 4 February 1922, the Washington Conference on the Limitation of Armament decided to set up a Commission of Jurists to consider the Revision of the Rules of Warfare.[326] At a later stage, the scope of the task assigned to the Commission was confined to the formulation of rules relating to aerial warfare and the use of radio in time of war.[327] The Commission comprised representatives of the five Powers taking part in the Washington Conference, with the addition of the Netherlands; it was under the chairmanship of Moore from the United States, and included such prominent members as Hurst, Lapradelle and Basdevant.[328] The Report of the Commission containing the rules which it had been asked to prepare was submitted on 19 February 1923,[329] but the rules never came into force.[330]

In the set of Rules for the Control of Radio in Time of War, the Commission included in Article 10 a prohibition of the abuse of distress signals as a *ruse de guerre* and laid down that offenders would be held personally responsible under international law.[331] Nevertheless, Article 12 of the Rules prescribes:

> 'Radio operators incur no personal responsibility from the mere fact of carrying out the orders which they receive in the performance of their duties as operators'.[332]

In an explanatory note, the Report expounded as follows the decision to embrace the provision of Article 12 as part of the set of Rules:

> 'The operator works in his cabin where he executes the orders of those above him. Consequently it is right that he should incur no personal responsibility merely because he has executed orders which he has received in the discharge of his duties as radio operator'.[333]

This explanation is most perplexing. Had the Commission established the rule that in every case of obedience to orders the offender is automatically relieved of responsibility, it would have been comprehensible that its members upheld the doctrine of *respondeat superior*. But the note pertains to the radio operator exclusively, so as to create the impression that his position is not akin to that of an

326. General Report of Commission of Jurists to Consider and Report upon the Revision of the Rules of Warfare, *A.J.I.L.*, vol. 32 (1938), Supp., pp. 1–56 at p. 1.
327. *Ibid.*
328. *Ibid.*, pp. 1, 56.
329. *Ibid.*, p. 1.
330. See Hackworth, *op. cit.*, vol. 4, p. 315.
331. General Report of Commission of Jurists, *op. cit.*, p. 10.
332. *Ibid.*, p. 11.
333. *Ibid.*

ordinary offender. It is difficult to perceive the basis for this peculiar conception of the Commission. Does the fact that the radio operator is secluded in the communications cabin instil a special fear in him, so that he feels himself compelled to submit to any outrageous demand of his superior? The cabin in which the operator works is not a Gestapo cellar and the radio transmitter is not the torture rack of the Inquisition. If the operator commits an offence inside his cabin pursuant to the orders of his superiors, the fact that he performs the act when withdrawn in an isolated cabin, and not, for instance, while under fire on the control bridge, may increase instead of diminishing its gravity. Can it be argued, though, that his seclusion in the communications cabin prevents him from being able to discern what is happening in the outside world? The best answer to this question is given by one of the professed protagonists of the doctrine of *respondeat superior*:

> 'Obviously, a radio operator when sending radio distress signals will, in nearly all cases, know whether or not the ship is in distress. Yet, even if he is aware that his act constitutes a "ruse of war", declared a violation of international law by the . . . draft convention, he cannot be held responsible for carrying out such a superior order'.[334]

Whatever be the explanation of the principle which the Commission of Jurists gave vent to, we ought to query what bearing the principle has upon general international law. There are those who contend, in reply, that Article 12 reaffirms a pre-existent rule in international law, under which obedience to orders constitutes a legitimate defence for international offenders.[335] The assertion is, however, vulnerable in view of the fact that the Commission treated the radio operator as if he were *sui generis*. With this in mind, it stands more to reason that the Commission desired to create an exception to the rule, apparently regarded by it as generally accepted under international law, according to which obedience to orders does not constitute an automatic defence. But we should not attempt to determine the question conclusively, for we have only the Report of the Commission to rely upon and that is too obscure to allow certitude in this regard.

To summarize the instruments from the period between the two World Wars, dealt with in this chapter, we are bound to state that

334. Schick, 'War Criminals', pp. 48–49.
335. This contention is set forth by Manner and Schick (Manner, *op. cit.*, p. 417; Schick, 'War Criminals', p. 48). See also Colby, 'War Crimes', p. 607; Hostage case, Opening Statement for Defendant List (by Laternser), *N.M.T.*, vol. 11, p. 861. Cf. Daniel, *op. cit.*, p. 164; Dunbar, *op. cit.*, p. 247. Cf. also Greenspan, *op. cit.*, p. 495 n. 351.

they do not carry the discussion of the subject of obedience to orders much further forward. Here and there it is, admittedly, possible to find in them traces of a trend to exclude the doctrine of *respondeat superior*, but these traces are somewhat blurred and indistinct, and the trend is too uncertain to serve as a beacon in this issue. Only when the holocaust of the Second World War befell the world and shook the foundations of international law did the problem of obedience to orders approach its solution in international legislation.

CHAPTER 2

THE NEGATION OF THE PLEA OF OBEDIENCE TO SUPERIOR ORDERS

1. THE DELIBERATIONS OF THE COMMISSIONS OF THE UNITED NATIONS, 1942–1945

In all the deliberations which took place during the Second World War with respect to the question of the punishment to be meted out to the Nazi war criminals, the subject of obedience to superior orders played a central role. An important contribution to these discussions was made by Lauterpacht, who in 1942 submitted a memorandum to a Committee established by the International Commission for Penal Reconstruction and Development.[336] Lauterpacht's findings won 'general approval' from the Commission, as well as from various Governments of the United Nations, to which the Commission reported them.[337] Lauterpacht entirely rejected both extreme doctrines of *respondeat superior* and absolute liability, for the following reasons:[338]

> 'There ought to be no doubt that should courts entrusted with the trial of war crimes disregard altogether the plea of superior orders, they would be adopting a course which could not be regarded as defensible. On the other hand, . . . the fact of superior orders . . . need not warp the effectiveness of the law in a manner which may rightly be regarded as a perversion of justice'.[339]

The solution put forward by him was that the defence of obedience to orders would be available to the offender only if he acted under compulsion or a legitimate mistake of law; and he emphatically

336. This international Commission was a semi-official body set up in Cambridge, in 1941, by several of the United Nations (*History of U.N.W.C.C.*, p. 266). Lauterpacht's memorandum (Lauterpacht, 'Punishment of War Crimes', Memorandum submitted to the Committee on Crimes against International Public Order (1942) (mimeographed)) grew into the article: 'The Law of Nations and the Punishment of War Crimes', published by the author in 1944 in *B.Y.B.I.L.* (that is the article referred to—throughout this study—by the abbreviation: Lauterpacht, 'War Crimes'). See *History of U.N.W.C.C.*, p. 275 n. 1; Lauterpacht, 'War Crimes', p. 58 n. 1.

337. See *History of U.N.W.C.C.*, pp. 275, 277. Cf. Glaser, 'L'Ordre', p. 323 n. 113.

338. Citations and references will be from and to the article: Lauterpacht, 'War Crimes'.

339. Lauterpacht, 'War Crimes', p. 73. Cf. J. Robinson, *op. cit.*, p. 88.

pointed out that, when orders are manifestly illegal, there is no room for mistake of law and the plea of compulsion cannot be always at the disposal of the defendant in this case either.[340]

Lauterpacht's analysis has, to my mind, this defect: that it ascribes to obedience to orders the status of a defence under appropriate circumstances—although not an automatic defence—instead of considering it as a factual aspect of another defence. Nevertheless we must keep in mind that Lauterpacht took note in his memorandum of the need to examine the question of obedience to orders from the outlook of *mens rea*,[341] and thus he piloted the discussion of this subject in the right channel. We may consequently say that Lauterpacht touched upon the correct solution of the problem, that is, taking the fact of obedience to orders into account among the other circumstances of the case within the compass of a defence based on lack of *mens rea*, but failed to grasp it entirely.

It is interesting to compare Lauterpacht's line of thought with the text of the following Resolution, adopted in 1943 by another international body, the London International Assembly:[342]

> '(a) That an order issued by a superior to a subordinate to commit an act violating international law was not in itself a defence, but that the courts were entitled to consider whether the accused was placed in a "state of compulsion" to act as ordered, and acquit him or mitigate the punishment accordingly.
>
> '(b) That such exculpating or extenuating circumstances should in all cases be disregarded... when the act was so obviously heinous that it could not be committed without revolting the conscience of an average human being'.[343]

Here it is rendered transparently clear that the fact of obedience to orders does not 'in itself' constitute a defence, but that the competent court is empowered to take it into account within the scope of another defence, namely, that of compulsion. The trouble is that the Resolution overlooks the availability of the defence of mistake of law or fact, and even the reference to manifestly illegal orders in sub-section (b) is made so as to set limits to the use of the fact of obedience to orders within the orbit of the defence of compulsion. Admittedly, Lauterpacht, as just mentioned, qualified in a similar way the efficacy of the plea of compulsion, but he also, and mainly, tackled the question of the manifest illegality of orders

340. Lauterpacht, 'War Crimes', pp. 73–74. Cf. Glaser, 'L'Ordre', p. 325 n. 118; *History of U.N.W.C.C.*, p. 277; J. Robinson, *op. cit.*, p. 88.
341. See *supra*, p. 87.
342. The Assembly was formed in 1941 under the auspices of the League of Nations Union, but most of its members were appointed by the Governments of the United Nations (*History of U.N.W.C.C.*, p. 266).
343. *History of U.N.W.C.C.*, p. 275. Cf. Eustathiades, 'Ordres', p. 402 n. 23; Glaser, 'L'Ordre', p. 323 n. 112; Maunoir, *op. cit.*, p. 229.

in the context of mistake of law.[344] One may, therefore, say that the Resolution of the London International Assembly brings the real issue into focus by denying the status of a defence *per se* to the fact of obedience to orders, but that its range of vision is somewhat restricted in that it disregards the subject of mistake.

In the United Nations War Crimes Commission established on 20 October 1943 by seventeen States,[345] the question of obedience to orders was simultaneously explored by two different Committees. One of them, the Legal Committee, dealt with the subject with a view to attaining an approximation of the relevant national laws of the United Nations, so that the national courts charged with the trial of war criminals would apply one legal principle in this regard.[346] The other, the Committee on Enforcement, considered the problem with a view to including a provision about it in a Draft Convention on the Trial and Punishment of War Criminals, which was supposed to create an international Court of the United Nations for the punishment of war criminals.[347]

To the Committee on Enforcement the American delegate submitted the following draft provision, proposing that it be inserted in the contemplated Convention (Article 30):

> '(1) The plea of superior orders shall not constitute a defence . . . if the order was so manifestly contrary to the laws of war that a person of ordinary sense and understanding would know or should know, given his rank or position and the circumstances of the case, that such an order was illegal.
>
> '(2) It shall be for the Tribunal . . . to consider to what extent irresistible compulsion shall be a ground for mitigation of the penalty or for acquittal'.[348]

The text of the American proposal departs from the proposition endorsed by the London International Assembly that obedience to orders is not a defence *per se* but a factual element that may be taken into account within the compass of another defence. The first paragraph of the American proposal implies that obedience to

344. See Lauterpacht, 'War Crimes', p. 73.
345. *History of U.N.W.C.C.*, pp. 112–113. Regarding the Commission in general, see *History of U.N.W.C.C.*, *passim*, and also Bathurst, 'The United Nations War Crimes Commission', *A.J.I.L.*, vol. 39 (1945), pp. 565–570, *passim*; Schwelb, 'The United Nations War Crimes Commission', *op. cit.*, *passim*. The Commission was headed initially by Hurst, and at a later stage by Lord Wright. Of the principal Allied Powers, the Soviet Union alone declined to participate in the work of the Commission, because its demand that each of the Soviet Republics be independently represented in the membership had been rejected (see Taylor, 'Nuremberg Trials, War Crimes and International Law', *Int. Con.*, No. 450 (1949), pp. 121–346 (reprint) at p. 128).
346. *History of U.N.W.C.C.*, p. 278.
347. *Ibid.*
348. *Ibid.*

orders may constitute a defence under certain conditions, to wit, when the orders in question are not manifestly illegal, and we revert here, in point of fact, to the conception underlying Lauterpacht's memorandum. As for the second paragraph, we ought to note that, as a reference was properly made here directly to the defence of compulsion, without any particular allusion to the phenomenon of obedience to orders, while in the preceding paragraph a reference was improperly made to a seemingly independent defence of obedience to orders, the two paragraphs do not appear to be intrinsically linked to each other. Ostensibly, the plea of obedience to orders seems to fall only within the ambit of the first paragraph, whereas the second paragraph looks as if it dealt with an entirely different subject. Yet there is every indication that this is a result of a mere optical illusion due to imperfect drafting and that the two paragraphs really concern themselves with two different aspects of the same subject-matter, namely, obedience to orders, and that is why they were attached to one another. A further remark which is called for in regard to the second paragraph is that, like the text of the recommendation of the Commission of fifteen on the Responsibilities of the Authors of the First World War,[349] it does not clarify whether the Tribunal mentioned therein is authorized to determine in principle as a matter of law the question of the validity of the defence under discussion, or, alternatively, whether it is only authorized to decide as a matter of fact when to apply a defence whose legal validity is not subject to doubt.

The American draft submitted to the Committee on Enforcement served as a basis for a report sent in to the Commission by the majority of the Legal Committee. But, perhaps as a result of the distinction in the American proposal between two seemingly independent defences of obedience to orders and compulsion, the question of compulsion was left out of the orbit of obedience to orders in the report. Here the majority of the Legal Committee recommended to the Commission that it adopt a formulation similar to that of the first paragraph of the American proposal as the principle applicable under international law to the subject of obedience to orders. The recommendation read:

> 'The Commission is satisfied that the following rule is in accordance with general international practice and is consistent with international law:
>
> 'The defence of obedience to superior orders shall not constitute a justification for the commission of an offence against the laws and customs of war, if the order was so manifestly contrary to those laws and customs that, taking into account his rank or position and the circumstances surrounding the

349. See *supra*, p. 94.

commission of the offence, an individual of ordinary understanding should have known that such an order was illegal'.[350]

This recommendation was contested by the Czech representative, who still clung to the conception of the London International Assembly and consequently held the opinion that the Commission ought to adopt the following rules:

> '1. An order given by a superior to an inferior to commit a crime is not in itself a defence.
>
> '2. The court may consider in individual cases whether the accused was placed in a state of irresistible compulsion and acquit him or mitigate the punishment accordingly.
>
> '3. The defence that the accused was placed in a state of compulsion is excluded... [i]f the crime was of a revolting nature'.[351]

Before the Commission settled its position with regard to these recommendations of the majority and the minority in the Legal Committee, the Committee on Enforcement put forward the proposal, accepted by the Commission, that, instead of including a provision on obedience to orders in the planned Convention concerning the international Court vested with the power to try war criminals, the following statement should be transmitted to the Governments of the United Nations:

> 'The Commission has considered the question of "superior orders". It finally decided to leave out any provision on the subject... The Commission considers that it is better to leave it to the court itself in each case to decide what weight should be attached to a plea of superior orders. But the Commission wants to make it clear that its members unanimously agree that in principle this plea does not of itself exonerate the offenders'.[352]

At first glance, there appears to be an outward resemblance between this statement and the recommendation of the Commission of fifteen on the Responsibilities of the Authors of the First World War, for in both cases the question of obedience to orders is referred to the competent court. But, unlike the recommendation of the Commission of fifteen, the statement of the United Nations War Crimes Commission is susceptible of one, and only one, interpretation, namely, that the Commission did not regard obedience to orders as a defence *per se*, but only as a fact to be weighed by the court in conjunction with the rest of the evidence in the concrete case. In this decisive respect the United Nations War Crimes Commission took the trodden path of the London International Assembly and the minority in the Legal Committee.

350. *History of U.N.W.C.C.*, p. 279.
351. *Ibid.*
352. *Ibid.*, pp. 279–280, 449. Cf. Eustathiades, 'Ordres', p. 399.

This view of the Commission was reaffirmed by it anew, and finally, in March 1945, when it deliberated the recommendations of the Legal Committee. On that occasion the Commission pronounced:

> 'Having regard to the ... consideration that the question how far obedience to the orders of a superior exonerates an offender or mitigates the punishment must depend on the circumstances of the particular case, the Commission does not consider that it can usefully propound any principle or rule.
>
> 'The Commission unanimously maintains the view which it expressed in connection with the United Nations War Crimes Court that the mere fact of having acted in obedience to the orders of a superior does not of itself relieve a person who has committed a war crime from responsibility'.[353]

Notwithstanding the Commission's very modest pretension that it did not lay down any rule in this matter, in effect it established most conclusively the basic tenet that the fact of obedience to orders does not 'of itself' justify acquittal of an offender, so that it does not constitute a defence *per se* but may be taken into account among the other circumstances of the case for the purposes of either discharge from responsibility or mitigation of punishment.[354]

2. THE CHARTER OF THE INTERNATIONAL MILITARY TRIBUNAL, 1945

A. *The United States Proposal*

The attitude of the United Nations War Crimes Commission towards the subject of obedience to orders seems to have influenced the proposal presented by the United States, during the San Francisco Conference in April 1945, to the Foreign Ministers of the United Kingdom, the Soviet Union and France. This proposal, relative to the question of the trial of the major war criminals in Europe, provided as follows (Article 11):

> 'The fact that a defendant acted pursuant to order of a superior or government sanction shall not constitute an absolute defense but may be considered either in defense or in mitigation of punishment if the tribunal before which the charges are being tried determines that justice so requires'.[355]

This stipulation was in substance incorporated in a subsequent American draft of 14 June 1945, transmitted to the Embassies of those three Powers in Washington to form a basis for discussion in

353. *History of U.N.W.C.C.*, p. 280. Cf. Dunbar, *op. cit.*, p. 248; Glaser, *Introduction*, p. 128 n. 3; Glaser, 'L'Ordre', p. 323 n. 114.
354. See Glaser, *Introduction*, p. 128; Glaser, 'L'Ordre', p. 323.
355. American Draft of Definitive Proposal, *International Conference*, p. 22 at p. 24.

a special conference to be convened with a view to resolving the problem of bringing the major war criminals to trial. The new, revised proposal prescribed as follows (Article 15):

> 'In any trial before an International Military Tribunal the fact that a defendant acted pursuant to order of a superior or government sanction shall not constitute a defense *per se*, but may be considered either in defense or in mitigation of punishment if the Tribunal determines that justice so requires'.[356]

The most important modification here is reflected in the replacement of the words 'an absolute defense' which appeared in the original text by the words 'a defense *per se*'. The new version is stylistically superior to the initial one, for the amendment renders the meaning of the Article clearer: the fact of obedience to orders constitutes a factor which may be considered 'in defense', but it does not form a defence *per se*.

The distinction between these American proposals and the draft submitted by the United States delegate to the Committee on Enforcement of the United Nations War Crimes Commission speaks for itself. Evidently, under the formulation of April – June 1945, it is not sufficient for an accused to prove to the tribunal that he obeyed superior orders, for such obedience does not constitute a defence *per se*. The defendant must convince the tribunal of the existence of other circumstances, which will enable the judges to determine in the light of all the evidence that he ought to be acquitted, as 'justice so requires'. And what circumstances can be envisaged in this regard but those substantiating, one way or another, the fact that the defendant acted without *mens rea*?

B. *The Jackson Report*

To shed light on the American state of mind at the time of the drafting of the two proposals of April – June 1945, one may perhaps turn to a Report transmitted to the President of the United States on 6 June of that year by Jackson, American chief of counsel in the prosecution of the principal Axis war criminals.[357] The Report had this remark to make in respect of obedience to orders:

> 'There is doubtless a sphere in which the defense of obedience to superior orders should prevail. If a conscripted or enlisted soldier is put on a firing squad, he should not be held responsible for the validity of the sentence he carries out. But the case may be greatly altered where one has discretion

356. Revision of American Draft of Proposed Agreement, *International Conference*, p. 55 at p. 58. Cf. Spiropoulos, 'Code (1st Report)', p. 271; Spiropoulos, 'Principles', p. 182.
357. R. Jackson, 'Report to the President (1945)', *International Conference*, pp. 42–54.

because of rank or the latitude of his orders... An accused should be allowed to show the facts about superior orders. The Tribunal can then determine whether they constitute a defense or merely extenuating circumstances, or perhaps carry no weight at all'.[358]

Unfortunately, this passage is far from being Jackson's consummate piece of writing. The pivotal part here is embodied in the example of the soldier assigned to a firing-squad, and presumably this example was put forward as an index of a generally applicable rule. Instead of elucidating matters, however, it only tends further to cloud the issue. Jackson stated that the soldier could not incur responsibility for the validity of the sentence carried out by him. In fact, this statement misses its mark, as no attempt is made to hold the soldier accountable for the court's verdict. On the contrary, it is the soldier brought to trial for shooting a person to death who relies on the sentence of the court for his defence, and the only question that may be raised is whether the judicial decree can be of help to him. But even when Jackson's statement is regarded as relating to the latter question, as well as replying to it in the affirmative, its meaning is still obscure. Does the soldier plead mistake, of law or of fact? That is the opinion held by Maunoir, who interprets Jackson's statement in the following way:

'Si l'ordre d'exécution émanait d'un chef militaire compétent pour le donner, cette apparence de légalité devait suffire à le justifier'.[359]

And Donnedieu de Vabres also seems to maintain that the soldier in the firing-squad is not criminally responsible for the execution in which he participated, on account of the element of mistake of law.[360] Yet one execution is not necessarily similar to another, and not in every case can the soldier claim that he erred, thinking that he was acting pursuant to a lawful decree. As F. Pollock put it, a quarter of a century before the Jackson Report:

'Elementary examples: the men of a firing-party told off to shoot a deserter have not to satisfy themselves of the facts, or that the process of the court-martial was correct. But if the same men are ordered to shoot unarmed priests, women and children, they must know that this is not a usual act of war, and further questions then arise'.[361]

Did Jackson have in mind only one of Pollock's 'elementary examples' when he prepared his Report to the President? If he did, he

358. *Ibid.*, p. 47. Cf. Descheemaeker, *op. cit.*, p. 217; Guggenheim, *op. cit.*, vol. 2, p. 48 n. 1; Maunoir, *op. cit.*, p. 249; Nuremberg trial, Final Plea for the High Command (by Laternser), *I.M.T.*, vol. 22, p. 85.
359. Maunoir, *op. cit.*, p. 249. See also *ibid.*, p. 274.
360. Donnedieu de Vabres, 'Nuremberg', p. 571.
361. F. Pollock, *op. cit.*, p. 197.

did not say so. And if he thought that a soldier in a firing-squad should never bear responsibility for an execution, being divested of all discretion, we should inquire why discretion is perforce eliminated.

Jackson emphasized the rank of the soldier in the firing-squad, and Schick indeed asserts:

> 'It is only with regard to military personnel of inferior rank that Justice Jackson was willing to accept superior orders as a possible plea for defence'.[362]

Jackson's Report clearly suggests, however, that the rank of the soldier in the firing-squad constitutes merely one consideration out of the many leading to his exemption from responsibility. Furthermore, if every offender of low rank has to be absolved of guilt, why did Jackson qualify his statement, confining its applicability to the bounds of the firing-squad? What is the difference between a firing-squad and, say, a demolition-squad for that matter? Would it not have been better to declare simply and generally that the plea of obedience to orders is available to every private or non-commissioned officer wherever he is and whatever his particular assignment may be? There must be another factor, besides the rank of the soldier in the firing-squad, which, by rendering this particular soldier devoid of discretion, caused Jackson to say what he said. Is that factor derived from the circumstance that the soldier in the firing-squad is placed under constant threat that, should he refrain from squeezing the trigger of his rifle when ordered to open fire, he would himself be shot? Jackson did not say so;[363] but, assuming that his statement ought indeed to be construed in such a way that the threat constitutes the decisive consideration applying to the soldier in the firing-squad, the question arises whether the defence of this soldier stands, as a matter of law, on the footing of obedience to orders or of compulsion? And is the defence of compulsion allowed in the case of a person accused of causing death in general and mass-executions in particular? All these queries remain unanswered in Jackson's Report. All that we may say is that, for one reason or another, Jackson regarded the soldier in the firing-squad as entitled to an inherent right of impunity. And in view of the fact that the

362. Schick, 'War Criminals', p. 46 n. 67. That is also the way that Laternser interprets Jackson's statement (Nuremberg trial, Final Plea for the High Command (by Laternser), *I.M.T.*, vol. 22, p. 85).

363. Harris—one of Jackson's assistants in the Nuremberg trial—says: 'The soldier on the firing line cannot be held criminally responsible for carrying out an order to shoot a prisoner. He does not have a fair moral choice whether to comply with the order. But a person in high position in government may have the opportunity of resignation as an alternative to compliance with an order to commit a criminal act' (Harris, *op. cit.*, p. 557). As we shall see below, the term 'moral choice' relates mainly to the subject of compulsion.

sacrosanctity of the executioner is not as manifestly and obviously clear as Jackson apparently thought, his statement does not illuminate the subject of obedience to orders. Nor is it instructive in connection with the American proposals of April – June 1945, for they profess the principle, denied in the Jackson Report, that obedience to orders may never constitute a defence *per se.*

C. *The Soviet Union Proposal and the Compromise Formula*

The United States' attitude towards the question of obedience to orders by the Nazi war criminals was not acceptable to the Soviet Union. On 14 June 1945, the day when the Americans submitted their revised draft, the Russians proposed to replace the American formulation of April by the following provision (Article 7):

> 'The fact that the accused acted under orders of his superior or his government will not be considered as justifying the guilt circumstance'.[364]

This proposal is basically different from the American draft in that it

(a) does not deal at all with the problem of mitigation of punishment;

(b) rejects any possibility of regarding obedience to orders as a justification.

It should be noted here that it is a little curious that the Soviet proposal excludes compliance with orders as a justification of the 'guilt circumstance'. After all, it can hardly be contested that the fact of obedience to orders does not justify the crime itself, and the only question is whether it can justify the discharge of the criminal from responsibility. It may, however, be assumed that the intention was to reject the possibility of the tribunal taking the fact of obedience to orders into account so as to relieve the defendant of responsibility. That is to say, it is not enough that this fact does not create a defence *per se*; it cannot even free the accused from responsibility if adduced in another defence, that of compulsion, for instance. Thus the Soviet formulation gives faithful expression to the doctrine of absolute liability.

With regard to the second distinction between the Russian and American texts, we ought to remark that it may not be self-evident in all its sharpness when the Russian proposal is read independently. But a meticulous comparison of the two drafts indicates plainly what the Russians wished to attain by their counter-proposal.

On 26 June 1945, a Conference of the four Powers—the United

364. Aide-Mémoire from the Soviet Government, *International Conference*, p. 61 at p. 62. Cf. Spiropoulos, 'Code (1st Report)', p. 271.

States, the Soviet Union, the United Kingdom and France—was convened in London, to deliberate the subject of the trial of the major war criminals of the European Axis.[365] On 30 June, the American delegation to the Conference put forward a new formula relative to the question of obedience to orders (Article 17):

> 'The fact that a defendant acted pursuant to order of a superior or to government sanction shall not constitute a defense *per se*, but may be considered in mitigation of punishment if the Tribunal determines that justice so requires'.[366]

Thus the Americans left no doubt that they insisted on an explicit reference to the possibility of mitigating the punishment in the context of obedience to orders. In regard to superior orders as a cause for absolute discharge from responsibility, the Americans appear to have avoided the problem by way of obscure phrasing with an ambiguous meaning. On the one hand, the new draft no longer expressly prescribes, as the old proposals do, that the tribunal is authorized to consider the fact of obedience to orders 'in defense' when 'justice so requires'. On the other, the new formula continues explicitly to withhold from the fact of obedience to orders only the status of a defence *per se*, so that one may find in it an implicit authorization of the tribunal to take the fact of obedience to orders into account when other defences are contemplated.[367] According to this interpretation, the same result as is produced by the preceding American drafts is brought about by the newly revised one, even though it is not spelt out in so many words.

This solution did not satisfy the Soviet delegation. On 2 July, they presented to the London Conference a new proposal, which included the following stipulation (Article 29):

> 'The carrying out by the defendant of an order of his superior or government shall not be considered a reason excluding his responsibility for the crimes set out in Article... In certain cases, when the subordinate acted blindly in carrying out the orders of his superior, the Tribunal has a right to mitigate the punishment of the defendant'.[368]

Again, the Russians here demanded the adoption of the doctrine of absolute liability in all its extremeness, and the denial of any

365. On the Conference in general, see *International Conference, passim.*
366. Revised Draft of Agreement and Memorandum, Submitted by the American Delegation, *International Conference*, p. 119 at p. 124. Cf. Spiropoulos, 'Principles', p. 183.
367. In one of his reports to the International Law Commission, Spiropoulos made the following odd remark: 'The American drafts submitted to the London Conference of 1945... do not exclude the "superior orders" as a defence' (Spiropoulos, 'Principles', p. 193 n. 55). But the draft of 30 June expressly rejects obedience to orders as a defence *per se.*
368. Last Soviet Draft, *International Conference*, p. 165 at p. 181. Cf. Spiropoulos, 'Principles', p. 183.

significance to the fact of obedience to orders in the context of relieving the defendant of responsibility, no matter what his defence is, even if it be compulsion and such like. As for mitigation of punishment, the Russians would not accept the vague formula that the tribunal is empowered to pronounce a light sentence when 'justice so requires', and they preferred in its stead a wording clearly and emphatically denoting that only when the subordinate acts 'blindly' (that is, without *mens rea*) is there room for alleviation of punishment.

Eventually, a compromise was supposedly reached between the American and Russian positions, as the drafting sub-committee of the Conference formulated the following consolidated clause (Article 8) on 11 July:

> 'The fact that the defendant acted pursuant to order of a superior or to Government sanction shall not free him from responsibility but may be considered in mitigation of punishment if the Tribunal determines that justice so requires'.[369]

When this phrasing is set against the background of all the preceding drafts, one realizes that it follows the Soviet proposals insofar as discharge from responsibility, which is the heart of the problem, is concerned, for obedience to orders is now rejected not merely as a defence *per se* but as a reason for relieving the defendant of responsibility. The new provision follows the pattern of the American proposals only to the extent that mitigation of punishment, that is, a matter of secondary importance, is concerned.

On 23 July, the British suggested that the expression 'Government sanction'—appearing in all American proposals as well as in the formulation adopted by the drafting sub-committee—be substituted by the phrase 'order of his Government'.[370] The use of this version, in line with the Russian drafts, is more logical. The term 'Government sanction' is so broad that it encompasses *inter alia* the case of an offender who commits a war crime on his own, with the act subsequently enjoying retroactive sanction by his Government. This case is entirely beyond the scope of the subject of obedience to orders, although it does fall within the ambit of the acts of State problem.[371]

D. *Article 8 and its Meaning*

On 24 July 1945, the London Conference discussed the provision

369. Draft of Agreement and Charter, Reported by Drafting Subcommittee, *International Conference*, p. 194 at p. 197. Cf. Spiropoulos, 'Principles', p. 183.
370. Redraft of Charter, Submitted by British Delegation, *International Conference*, p. 348 at p. 352.
371. See *supra*, p. 62.

relating to obedience to orders in its ultimate form as Article 8.[372] On that occasion, the Russian representative, Nikitchenko, reiterated his delegation's negative attitude towards that section in the Article which dealt with mitigation of punishment, but he explained that the Soviet Union was not opposed, generally and in principle, to the consideration of obedience to orders as an extenuating circumstance; if it wished to delete that section from the Article, it was solely because the Agreement in question related to the *major* war criminals only, who were not entitled to benefit from this privilege.[373] At that late stage, Nikitchenko did not press further that the Soviet position in this regard be accepted, especially in view of the explanation given by the British representative, Maxwell-Fyfe, to the controversial passage:

> 'Suppose someone said he was threatened to be shot if he did not carry out Hitler's orders. If he wasn't too important, the Tribunal might let him off with his life. It seems to be a matter for the Tribunal'.[374]

This explanation is particularly noteworthy, for it places the whole Article in the correct light. If a defendant pleads that he acted pursuant to orders and that, had he not submitted to them, he would have been shot out of hand, the plea of obedience to orders, according to the Article drafted by the Conference, does not constitute a defence *per se* or play any part in the discharge of the defendant from responsibility in the context of another defence, namely, that of compulsion. This plea can be taken into account, even on the basis of compulsion, only within the bounds of mitigation of punishment; and it is within those bounds that Maxwell-Fyfe keeps it. We face the doctrine of absolute liability in all its purity.

Incidentally, we might observe that, in the course of the Conference's discussion on this subject, Jackson made the following statement:

> 'That is about what we proposed originally—not an absolute defense but a mitigation'.[375]

Here Jackson did not describe the legislative history of the Article accurately. The original American proposal submitted in April admittedly excluded obedience to orders as 'an absolute defense', but at the same time it expressly established that this fact 'may be

372. *International Conference*, pp. 367–368. Cf. Spiropoulos, 'Code (1st Report)', pp. 271–272.
373. *International Conference*, pp. 367–368. Cf. Spiropoulos, 'Code (1st Report)', p. 271.
374. *International Conference*, p. 368. Cf. Spiropoulos, 'Code (1st Report)', p. 271.
375. *International Conference*, p. 368. Cf. Spiropoulos, 'Code (1st Report)', p. 272.

considered... in defense' when justice so requires and does not merely constitute an extenuating circumstance. The revised draft of 14 June reproduced this rule in yet clearer terms, substituting for the words 'an absolute defense' the phrase 'a defense per se', and even the proposal of 30 June, as we have pointed out, may be interpreted in the same sense. Consequently, the Americans 'originally' regarded obedience to orders not as merely a reason for mitigation of punishment; and that is why their withdrawal under Soviet pressure is so remarkable.

The Article proposed by the drafting sub-committee was endorsed by the London Conference subject to the amendment put forward by the British, and was incorporated in the Charter of the International Military Tribunal annexed to the Agreement for the Prosecution and Punishment of the Major War Criminals of the European Axis.[376] The Agreement was signed by the four Powers at London on 8 August 1945, and was subsequently adhered to by nineteen other States.[377]

Article 8 of the Charter of the International Military Tribunal provides, in fine, as follows:

> 'The fact that the defendant acted pursuant to order of his Government or of a superior shall not free him from responsibility, but may be considered in mitigation of punishment if the Tribunal determines that justice so requires'.[378]

In view of the *travaux préparatoires* of this Article, I think that there is no escape from the conclusion that it precludes any possibility of taking the fact of obedience to orders into account for the purpose of relieving the defendant of responsibility in the context of any defence whatsoever, a defence based on lack of *mens rea* not excepted. The Soviet attitude towards exemption from responsibility—as distinct from the question of mitigation of punishment—is the one that prevailed in London, and, being adopted by the Conference, turned into *lex scripta*. Thus the doctrine of absolute liability was impressively confirmed, within the compass of the Charter, as the proper solution of the problem of obedience to orders. To my mind, this rigorous approach does not rest on solidly logical foundations; and the mere fact that the London Conference decided to draft Article 8 in a certain way cannot conclusively determine the issue of obedience to orders in general international law. From the standpoint of general international law, I think that there is more merit in the initial American proposals, which refuse the standing

376. *I.M.T.*, vol. 1, p. 9. Cf. *International Conference*, p. 420.
377. *I.M.T.*, vol. 1, p. 9, note.
378. *Ibid.*, p. 12. Cf. *International Conference*, p. 424.

of a defence *per se* to the fact of obedience to orders but confer upon the tribunal the right to take this fact into account among the other circumstances of the case within the purview of another defence. Of course, however, the fact that we are not satisfied with the strict and inelastic conception underlying Article 8 does not detract in any way from its legal validity in its sphere of application or warrant attempts to ascribe to it, unjustifiably, a more palatable meaning. Such an attempt is made, for instance, by Glaser, who maintains that under Article 8

> 'l'ordre hiérarchique ne constitue pas, en soi-même, c'est-à-dire de son propre chef, une cause justificative';

and adds, with increasing confidence and self-assurance, that according to this Article

> 'il semble d'être hors de doute qu'un tel ordre peut se traduire... dans l'irresponsabilité'.[379]

Glaser's statement correctly reflects, in my opinion, the rules of general international law, but not the special provision of Article 8 which disallows any consideration of the fact of obedience to orders for defence purposes. Glaser indeed is not the only one who endeavours to break down the confines of the Article,[380] and, as we shall see below, many efforts were made, in the course of the Nuremberg trial and afterwards, to evade its high-handed and sweeping provision by means of ingenious constructions, whose common denominator is that they are unfounded. But all such efforts are vain: Article 8 is moulded in a given and definite shape, and there is no sense in wishful-thinking interpretations.[381]

379. Glaser, 'L'Ordre', p. 325. Cf. *ibid.*, p. 330 n. 132; Glaser, *Introduction*, pp. 129, 131 n. 3.
380. In keeping with Glaser's interpretation see also Castrén, *op. cit.*, p. 88; Schick, 'Nuremberg', p. 197; Schick, 'War Criminals', p. 45; *L.R.U.N.W.C.C.*, Notes, Zuehlke trial, vol. 14, p. 151.
381. Usually writers dealing with the subject do not seek to scrutinize Article 8 carefully, and they content themselves with the remark that the Article rejects the fact of obedience to orders as a measure of defence, but permits taking it into account with a view to mitigation of punishment. See and cf. Bastid, *Cours de Droit International Public* (1956–1957), pp. 312–313; Belgion, *op. cit.*, p. 143; Calvocoressi, *op. cit.*, p. 73; Donnedieu de Vabres, 'La Théorie des Délits de Droit des Gens en Droit Pénal Interétatique', *op. cit.*, p. 160; W. E. Jackson, *op. cit.*, p. 558; Lauterpacht – Oppenheim, *International Law*, vol. 2 (7th ed., 1952), p. 570; Leventhal, Harris, Woolsey and Farr, 'The Nuernberg Verdict', *H.L.R.*, vol. 60 (1946–1947), pp. 857–907 at p. 870 n. 58; Maugham, *op. cit.*, p. 48; Merle, *op. cit.*, pp. 97–98; Morgan, *Assize*, p. 15; Morgan, 'Nuremberg', p. 332; Parker, *op. cit.*, p. 551; Reuter, 'Le Jugement du Tribunal Militaire International de Nuremberg', *Dalloz*, 1946, Chronique XX, pp. 77–80 at p. 79; Schafer, *op. cit.*, p. 141; Schwarzenberger, 'The Judgment of Nuremberg' (*T.L.R.*), *op. cit.*, p. 354; Schwarzenberger,

At all events, the negative aspects of the provision of Article 8 must not overshadow the fact that it nevertheless constitutes an important milestone in the development of international law in the sphere of obedience to orders. I feel that the authors of the Charter went astray by overshooting the mark and neglecting to set limits to criminal responsibility in this field. But let it be acknowledged, to their credit, that their line of thought was in the right direction of finding an outlet to demands based on the principle of the supremacy of the law, in repudiation of the doctrine of *respondeat superior.*

'The Judgment of Nuremberg' (*Y.B.W.A.*), *op. cit.*, p. 117; H. Smith, *The Law and Custom of the Sea* (3rd ed., 1959), p. 215; Spaight, *op. cit.*, (3rd ed., 1947), p. 57; Spiropoulos, 'Code (1st Report)', p. 272; Wechsler, 'The Issues of the Nuremberg Trial', *P.S.Q.*, vol. 62 (1947), pp. 11–26 at p. 13; Woetzel, *op. cit.*, p. 68 n. 31.

PART IV: THE CASES

AN analysis of the proceedings against war criminals which took place at the end of the Second World War demonstrates that

> 'The plea of superior orders has been raised by the Defence in war crime trials more frequently than any other'.[382]

In this part of the study we shall examine how this plea was treated by the tribunals that tried war criminals. We cannot trace the details of each of the vast number of cases in which the accused sought to find protection under the cloak of obedience to superior orders; but we shall attempt to arrive at the over-all upshot of the arguments of the defence, the rebuttal of the prosecution and the decisions of the courts. We shall distinguish, in the course of the discussion, between trials held before national courts and cases adjudicated by international tribunals. The latter include the first and foremost war crimes trial—that of the principal Nazi war criminals which was conducted under the London Agreement before an International Military Tribunal at Nuremberg. This landmark trial left its imprint on all which subsequently took place, and for that reason we shall single it out and pay particular heed to the rule laid down in it.

Although, as just mentioned, we shall mainly occupy ourselves in this part with trials held after the Second World War, we shall also consider a number of legal proceedings which occurred in the recent as well as distant past. These proceedings have this characteristic, that they do have a certain projection on the question of obedience to orders in international law, yet their contribution to its shaping is not of major significance. We shall, therefore, discuss them only for the sake of rounding off the picture and by way of an historical note.

382. *L.R.U.N.W.C.C.*, vol. 15 (Digest), p. 157; *L.R.U.N.W.C.C.*, Notes, Sawada trial, vol. 5, p. 13. Cf. Kelsen, *Principles*, p. 137 n. 27. Cf. also Eustathiades, 'Ordres', p. 404; Greenspan, *op. cit.*, p. 441; Levie, *op. cit.*, p. 463; Maunoir, *op. cit.*, p. 203; Stevens, *op. cit.*, p. xxxv; Weinstein, *op. cit.*, p. 530.

CHAPTER I

TRIALS BEFORE INTERNATIONAL TRIBUNALS

1. HISTORICAL NOTE

Before we dissect the two main trials that are to be the focus of our attention in this chapter, it may perhaps be worthwhile to linger upon two other trials, previous in time, that are connected to a certain extent with the subject of obedience to superior orders, so that our inquiry into the international judgments relating to this problem may be complete.

The first trial is that of Peter of Hagenbach, held in 1474 at Breisach on the Upper Rhine. For a long time this ancient trial had been consigned to oblivion, until Schwarzenberger came and directed the limelight onto it.[383] The facts of the Breisach case are as follows:[384] Peter of Hagenbach was the Governor (*Landvogt*) of the town of Breisach on behalf of the Duke of Burgundy, Charles *le Téméraire*. After an alliance of the Duke's enemies had taken the field, broken his power and vanquished Burgundy, Peter of Hagenbach was brought to trial before a tribunal of the victorious allies for having committed certain crimes. Schwarzenberger is of opinion that these 'would be called to-day crimes against humanity'.[385] Peter of Hagenbach's chief line of defence was that he had obeyed the orders of Duke Charles. His counsel put it in the following way:

383. Schwarzenberger first pointed out this trial in his article 'A Forerunner of Nuremberg—the Breisach War Crime Trial of 1474', *Manchester Guardian*, 28 September 1946, p. 4.
384. See Schwarzenberger, 'Inductive Approach', p. 548 n. 23; Schwarzenberger, *International Law*, vol. 1 (2nd ed., 1949), pp. 308–310. Cf. Birkett, *op. cit.*, p. 317; Gros, *Symposium*, p. 131; *History of U.N.W.C.C.*, p. 242 n. 1; Janeczek, *op. cit.*, p. 91; Muszkat, 'Problems of International Criminal Law', *op. cit.*, p. 336; Muszkat, *Theory and Realities in International Law* (1959) (Hebrew), vol. 1, p. 326; Scelle, *op. cit.*, p. 984 n. 2; Schwarzenberger, 'The Judgment of Nuremberg' (*T.L.R.*), *op. cit.*, p. 331; Schwarzenberger, 'The Judgment of Nuremberg' (*Y.B.W.A.*), *op. cit.*, p. 95; Weinstein, *op. cit.*, p. 530; Woetzel, *op. cit.*, pp. 19–20; Ministries case, Oral Argument of the Prosecution, *N.M.T.*, vol. 13, p. 97.
385. Schwarzenberger, *International Law*, vol. 1 (2nd ed., 1949), p. 309. Cf. Birkett, *op. cit.*, p. 317; Weinstein, *op. cit.*, p. 530; Ministries case, Oral Argument of the Prosecution, *N.M.T.*, vol. 13, p. 97.

'He had no right to question the orders which he was charged to carry out, and it was his duty to obey. Is it not known that soldiers owe absolute obedience to their superiors?'[386]

This defence was rejected by the tribunal: Peter of Hagenbach was convicted and sentenced to death.

Schwarzenberger maintains that the Breisach trial had an international character,[387] and he dwells upon this discovery of his with some relish. In his opinion, this is 'the first international trial for war crimes',[388] and it is 'a forerunner of the proceedings at Nuremberg'.[389] But other jurists contest the import of the Breisach trial as a precedent under international law: they contend that the tribunal sitting in judgment on Peter of Hagenbach cannot be regarded as an international tribunal and that the crimes with which he was charged cannot be considered as international crimes.[390]

I do not find it necessary to become involved in a barren controversy. After having sunk into the limbo of history and been completely lost sight of for half a millennium, the Breisach trial suddenly emerged from the depths of forgetfulness thanks to the research of an eminent scholar. Had the case come to light a few years earlier, it might (or might not) have been acknowledged as a precedent and have left its imprint upon international law. But it was discovered too late and did not contribute substantially to the pattern of the dispute that plagued the subject-matter of obedience to orders in international law. The wheels of international law did admittedly revolve in the general direction indicated at Breisach long before, but not by means or on account of the trial of Peter of Hagenbach. In these circumstances, there is little point in regarding the trial as more than an historical oddity.

The second case that ought perhaps to be mentioned here is that of the Casablanca Deserters: an arbitration between France

386. Schwarzenberger, *International Law*, vol. 1 (2nd ed., 1949), p. 309. Cf. Woetzel, *op. cit.*, p. 20.

387. Schwarzenberger, *International Law*, vol. 1 (2nd ed., 1949), p. 309. Cf. Gros, *Symposium*, p. 131; Muszkat, 'Problems of International Criminal Law', *op. cit.*, p. 336; Muszkat, *Theory and Realities in International Law* (1959) (Hebrew), vol. 1, p. 326; Ministries case, Oral Argument of the Prosecution, *N.M.T.*, vol. 13, p. 97.

388. Schwarzenberger, 'Inductive Approach', p. 548 n. 23. Cf. Gros, *Symposium*, p. 131; Schwarzenberger, *International Law*, vol. 1 (2nd ed., 1949), p. 308; Weinstein, *op. cit.*, p. 530.

389. Schwarzenberger, *International Law*, vol. 1 (2nd ed., 1949), p. 310; Schwarzenberger, 'The Judgment of Nuremberg' (*T.L.R.*), *op. cit.*, p. 331; Schwarzenberger, 'The Judgment of Nuremberg' (*Y.B.W.A.*), *op. cit.*, p. 95. Cf. *History of U.N.W.C.C.*, p. 242 n. 1.

390. Nussbaum, *A Concise History of the Law of Nations* (rev. ed., 1954), pp. 62, 320 n. 3; Woetzel, *op. cit.*, pp. 20–21.

and Germany that took place at the beginning of the present century before a panel of the Permanent Court of Arbitration.[391] In the Award, delivered in 1909, I have found the following *obiter dictum*:

> 'The Moroccan soldier at the Consulate, in aiding the deserters to embark, acted only in accordance with orders from his superiors and, by reason of his inferior position, could not have incurred any personal responsibility'.[392]

For all the laconic style, we have here a clear endorsement of the doctrine of *respondeat superior*, but, strange as it may seem, to the best of my knowledge none of the proponents of this doctrine and, for that matter, none of its opponents refers to this Award. As the *dictum* never formed part of the cycle of authorities used by the respective disputants in the field of obedience to orders in international law, I think that its significance is inconsiderable.[393]

2. THE NUREMBERG TRIAL

At Nuremberg more than a score of the leaders of the Third Reich and half a dozen Nazi organizations were criminally prosecuted by the four Allied Powers that had signed the London Agreement for the Prosecution and Punishment of the Major War Criminals of the European Axis. The trial started late in 1945, and the International Military Tribunal—composed of four judges and four alternates, one from each of the four Powers—rendered its judgment in the second half of 1946. During the long months of the trial, the prosecution and the defence crossed swords many times in the arena of obedience to orders, and the Tribunal seriously pondered the question. We shall examine in the first place what were the differing conceptions adopted by counsel for the prosecution and for the defence, and how far these conceptions were compatible with the provision of Article 8 of the Charter of the International Military Tribunal. Finally, we shall see what was the position taken by the Tribunal and what are the conclusions which arise from it.

A. *The Arguments of the Prosecution*

When the arguments of the prosecution in the Nuremberg trial are appraised, one must distinguish between the attitude of the American chief prosecutor, Jackson, towards the subject of obedi-

391. Casablanca Deserters case (France v. Germany), Scott, *The Hague Court Reports* (1916), p. 110.
392. *Ibid.*, p. 115.
393. It is to be observed that this *dictum* was pronounced after the first edition of Oppenheim's treatise had been published (in 1906).

ence to orders and the approach of his colleagues. In his opening speech, Jackson pointed out that under the Charter of the Tribunal no defence based on obedience to orders could be entertained, and then he added:

> 'Of course, we do not argue that the circumstances under which one commits an act should be disregarded in judging its legal effect. A conscripted private on a firing squad cannot expect to hold an inquest on the validity of the execution. The Charter implies common sense limits to liability just as it places common sense limits upon immunity'.[394]

This passage is very interesting and instructive. Ostensibly, Jackson reiterated here the view which he had expressed in his Report to the President of the United States[395] that a soldier in a firing-squad is entitled to impunity. Without repeating what I have already said on this proposition, I feel obliged to recall, and to stress, the fact that the Report to the President was submitted before the London Conference met and at a time when no one challenged the American proposal which authorized the competent tribunal to consider the fact of obedience to orders 'in defense'.[396] In the interval between that time and Jackson's opening speech at Nuremberg a new leaf was turned: the American proposal was superseded by another text, finally adopted in a binding international Agreement which generated the Nuremberg trial. That text, Article 8 of the Charter, as we have seen, does not allow the fact of obedience to orders to be taken into account in any manner for the purpose of relieving the defendant of responsibility. It can hardly be assumed that Jackson was willing or ready to make a blatant departure from the rule enunciated in an Article which he had helped to formulate. In his closing speech, for instance, he described the provision of Article 8 as one that 'corresponds with the justice and with the realities of the situation'.[397] One way or another, therefore, we must interpret Jackson's argument in the opening speech in conformity with the Charter's stipulation. The only way that I can see to do this would be to construe his argument in the sense that the defence of the soldier in the firing-squad is based not on the fact of obedience to orders but on the other circumstances of the case. In other words, Jackson did not attempt to contest the negation of the Tribunal's authority to take the fact of obedience to orders into account in the context of any defence whatever, but he did want to emphasize that

394. Nuremberg trial, Opening Speech for the Prosecution (by Jackson), *I.M.T.*, vol. 2, pp. 150–151.
395. See *supra*, pp. 110ff.
396. See *supra*, pp. 109–110.
397. Nuremberg trial, Closing Speech for the Prosecution (by Jackson), *I.M.T.*, vol. 19, p. 423.

the Tribunal must not overlook the other circumstances of the case. Hence, if the rule is that a war criminal who is forced to kill should be acquitted on account of compulsion,[398] the soldier in the firing-squad should also be acquitted if, for example, he shoots a person condemned to death because his superior holds a loaded pistol to his head and threatens him with instant death unless he squeezes the trigger of his rifle. The acquittal here is based only on the loaded gun, and it has no connection with the hierarchical relationship between the soldier and his superior. Had it not been the superior but someone else, of a rank equal or even inferior to that of the soldier in the firing-squad, standing behind him with the loaded gun, he should have been acquitted as well. This is in line with what was said above, when we discussed the doctrine of absolute liability: that doctrine cannot constitute an obstruction for an accused who acted pursuant to orders and yet does not rely on that fact when he is devising the pattern of his defence.[399] As the provision of Article 8 is reflective of the doctrine of absolute liability, one may make the very same remark about it; consequently, if this is the meaning of Jackson's argument, it cannot be looked upon as contradicting that provision.

The British chief prosecutor, Shawcross, in his closing speech, touched upon Article 8, stressing that it was merely declaratory of existing international law, and maintained:

> 'There is no rule of international law which provides immunity for those who obey orders which . . . are manifestly contrary to the very law of nature from which international law has grown'.[400]

The French chief prosecutor, Menthon, found support in the following statement, published in the Nazi Press by Goebbels himself, the Third Reich's Minister of Propaganda, at a time when he was attempting to justify, and even incite to, the lynching of those Allied pilots who happened to fall into the hands of the German population after having wrought havoc upon German cities by their devastating bombings:

> 'The pilots cannot validly claim that as soldiers they obeyed orders. No law of war provides that a soldier will remain unpunished for a hateful crime by

398. It is, however, difficult to accept the thesis that the defence of compulsion is available in the case where death is inflicted. We have already pointed out (*supra*, p. 80) that the defence based on compulsion must needs have serious limitations.
399. See *supra*, p. 75.
400. Nuremberg trial, Closing Speech for the Prosecution (by Shawcross), *I.M.T.*, vol. 19, pp. 465–466. A similar statement was made by Shawcross in his opening speech as well. See Nuremberg trial, Opening Speech for the Prosecution (by Shawcross), *I.M.T.*, vol. 3, p. 144. And cf. Harris, *op. cit.*, p. 176.

referring to the orders of his superiors, if their orders are in striking opposition to all human ethics, to all international customs in the conduct of war'.[401]

To that Menthon added a contribution of his own:

> 'Orders from a superior do not exonerate the agent of a manifest crime from responsibility'.[402]

The Soviet chief prosecutor, Rudenko, associated himself with his Western colleagues when he said, in his closing speech, that

> 'the authors of the Charter...made a special proviso to the effect that the execution of an obviously criminal order does not exonerate one from criminal responsibility'.[403]

This line of thought is a true reflection of the manifest illegality principle;[404] and, in the light of the London Charter, the argumentation based on that principle seems to be peculiarly out of place. The prosecution, admittedly, underscored only one aspect of the principle, namely, that a defendant should incur responsibility for his acts if he obeyed manifestly illegal orders; but there is also another side to the coin, for under the very same principle a defendant must be relieved of responsibility if he obeyed orders which are not manifestly illegal. We have already observed that the manifest illegality principle is logical only as far as it constitutes an auxiliary test designed to ascertain the personal knowledge of the accused regarding the illegality of the order,[405] and only if the fact

401. Nuremberg trial, Opening Speech for the Prosecution (by Menthon) *I.M.T.*, vol. 5, p. 418. Goebbels' harangue, published on 28 May 1944 in the official Nazi mouthpiece, *Völkischer Beobachter*—and also, in like language, in the *Deutsche Allgemeine Zeitung*—has often been quoted. See Appleman, *op. cit.*, p. 312; Coste-Floret, *op. cit.*, p. 22; Cowles, 'Trials of War Criminals (Non-Nuremberg)', *A.J.I.L.*, vol. 42 (1948), pp. 299–319 at p. 309; Dunbar, *op. cit.*, pp. 245–246; Eustathiades, 'Ordres', pp. 413–414 n. 56; Glaser, 'L'Ordre', p. 302 n. 45; Green, 'Book Review (on *L.R.U.N.W.C.C.*, vol. 1)', *op. cit.*, p. 106; Greenspan, *op. cit.*, p. 442; *History of U.N.W.C.C.*, p. 288; Kilmuir (Maxwell-Fyfe), *op. cit.*, p. 15; Maunoir, *op. cit.*, pp. 212–213; Stevens, *op. cit.*, pp. xxxix–xl; Almelo trial, Closing Address for the Prosecution, *L.R.U.N.W.C.C.*, vol. 1, p. 40; High Command case, Judgment, *N.M.T.*, vol. 11, p. 509.

402. Nuremberg trial, Opening Speech for the Prosecution (by Menthon), *I.M.T.*, vol. 5, p. 418.

403. Nuremberg trial, Closing Speech for the Prosecution (by Rudenko), *I.M.T.*, vol. 19, p. 577. Cf. *ibid.*, p. 592.

404. A similar line of thought in relation to Article 8 is pursued by Calvocoressi, *op. cit.*, p. 73; Graven, 'Code', p. 374.

405. It should be noted that one of the British prosecutors—Maxwell-Fyfe—gave direct expression to the personal knowledge principle when he argued, with respect to the German High Command, that 'They knew that they were doing what was wrong' (Nuremberg trial, Closing Speech for the Prosecution (by Maxwell-Fyfe), *I.M.T.*, vol. 22, p. 235). Taylor—from the American prosecution—

of obedience to orders is taken into account, among other facts, in the context of the defence of mistake of law.[406] But Article 8 expressly precludes the Tribunal from taking the fact of obedience to orders into account for the purpose of discharge from responsibility in the context of any defence whatever, including the defence of mistake of law. It can scarcely be supposed that the prosecution endeavoured to depart so pointedly from the provision of Article 8—especially in view of the fact that Shawcross, for instance, emphasized that the Article reflects existing law—and we must regard its proposition only as an historical explanation of Article 8. According to this interpretation, Article 8 was formulated in its present form because, in the opinion of the prosecution, it applies to certain acts enumerated in the Charter of the International Military Tribunal which the authors of the Charter regarded as manifestly illegal in the nature of things. That is to say, the prosecution's attitude ought to be comprehended as a general confirmation of the validity of the manifest illegality principle in the sphere of obedience to orders in international law. Article 8, in the view of the prosecution under this interpretation, reflects not the general rule but an exceptional case, for its application is restricted to acts which are *a priori* manifestly illegal. Shawcross, in his closing speech, explicitly pointed out that the orders under discussion in the Nuremberg trial were not ordinary orders:

> 'By every test of international law, of common conscience, of elementary humanity, these orders . . . were illegal'.[407]

Article 8 is consequently to be perceived as dealing with an extraordinary state of things, in which it is known in advance that the defendants cannot plead that they were unaware of the illegality of the acts which they performed pursuant to orders. One of the defence counsel in the Nuremberg trial—Kauffmann, representing the accused Kaltenbrunner—construed the prosecution's approach in the same way, saying:

> 'According to the Charter of this Tribunal one cannot plead higher orders for the purposes of avoiding punishment. The reasons given for this by the American chief prosecutor proceeded from the presumed knowledge of the crimes or their background in the minds of the higher leaders which, therefore, precluded them from pleading the existence of orders'.[408]

followed suit, contending that 'it is the duty of every soldier to refuse to obey orders which he knows to be criminal' (Nuremberg trial, Closing Speech for the Prosecution (by Taylor), *I.M.T.*, vol. 22, p. 291).

406. See *supra*, Part II, Chapter 1.

407. Nuremberg trial, Closing Speech for the Prosecution (by Shawcross), *I.M.T.*, vol. 19, p. 466.

408. Nuremberg trial, Final Plea for Defendant Kaltenbrunner (by Kauffmann), *I.M.T.*, vol. 18, p. 67.

Why this interpretation of Article 8 is attributed to the American chief prosecutor, of all others, is not clear to me; but this, to my mind, is the correct and precise interpretation of the argumentation put forward by the other prosecutors.

The statement that this is the correct interpretation of the prosecution's proposition is by no means meant to imply that the proposition itself is correct. On the contrary: whereas the attitude of the prosecution tallies with the letter of Article 8, I think that it conflicts with the spirit, for it has no factual basis in the legislative history of the Article, already discussed at great length. There is no least hint in the deliberations of the London Conference that the authors of the Charter regarded the manifest illegality principle as the one obtaining and binding under international law but resolved all the same, as it were, that the Charter dealt with manifestly illegal acts anyway and so they formulated Article 8 in a rigorous form. It is permissible to voice astonishment that the Nuremberg chief prosecutors themselves found it necessary to resort to an analysis of the Article which divests it of any significance as an authority in general international law. A suspicion hovers in the mind that they were not satisfied with the rigid wording of Article 8 as a general stipulation and accordingly interpolated an artificial rider which voids the Article of its content.

B. *The Arguments of the Defence*

In their attempt to absolve the accused of guilt and save them from the gallows, counsel for the defence made a far-reaching and variegated use of the plea of obedience to orders, namely, to Hitler's orders. As a first line of defence, they presented a uniform front, putting forward the contention that Article 8 of the Charter of the International Military Tribunal was entirely inapplicable to the *Führer*'s orders owing to the special circumstances prevalent in the Third Reich. Many of them, however, did not put their trust in this contention, being fully aware of its vulnerability to the prosecution's attacks. They sought, therefore, to create a second and third line of defence for the accused, and here all unison faded away and it was each man for himself: several counsel braced themselves and launched a frontal assault upon Article 8, leaving not an arrow in their quiver unsped. Others determined that at such a time it was a case of *sauve qui peut*, and therefore conceded that Article 8 had justification, or, at least, they admitted that it applied in principle to the defendants in the dock at Nuremberg but strove to clarify that their own clients, in contrast to their associates, were entitled to get off its hook. Finally, there were those who threw in their hand, submitting to the provision of the Article and contenting themselves with a plea for mitigation of punishment.

We shall classify below the different arguments of defence counsel, not according to the stratagem selected to ward off capital punishment, for that is of small import insofar as the present study is concerned, but in accordance with the doctrine embraced. At the outset, we shall discuss the arguments predicated on the manifest illegality principle and the personal knowledge principle; then we shall inquire into the assertions of the adherents of the doctrine of *respondeat superior*; finally, we shall examine the contention based on the special nature of the *Führer*'s orders.

(*1*) The Manifest Illegality Principle and the Personal Knowledge Principle

As we have just cited a passage from Kauffmann's pleading at the Nuremberg trial with regard to the interpretation of Article 8, we might as well start by presenting here his entire reasoning in this field. Kauffmann subscribed to the prosecution's analysis of the Article as a consequence of the supposition of the authors of the London Charter that the criminals brought to trial under it had been aware of the criminality of their acts, and hence were not entitled to benefit from the plea of obedience to orders for the purpose of discharge from responsibility.[409] Kauffmann took a further step and brought into the picture the element of compulsion ignored by the prosecution. There was no doubt, to his mind, that anyone refusing to comply with an order in the Third Reich, particularly during the last years of the war, had been in peril of his life, and therefore the plea of compulsion should have been available to the defendants.[410] Yet Kauffmann acknowledged the limitations inherent in such a plea, and he stated:

> 'there yet remains an absolute obligation to resist an order the purport of which, clearly recognizable to a subordinate, amounts to the materialization of evil... Even immediate danger to the life of the person receiving the order could not induce me to change my conviction'.[411]

His conclusion was that inasmuch as manifestly illegal orders were involved—and he agreed that such orders were in issue in the Nuremberg trial—the factor of compulsion could be taken into consideration only for the purpose of alleviation of punishment.[412] As a result, he confined his arguments in respect of obedience to

409. *Ibid.*
410. *Ibid.*, pp. 66–67.
411. *Ibid.*, p. 68.
412. *Ibid.*

orders by his client Kaltenbrunner to the question of the existence of extenuating circumstances.[413]

And Kauffmann was not the only defence counsel who trod the path of the manifest illegality principle. Sauter, counsel for the defendant Funk, followed suit, though with a completely different practical aim in mind. He analyzed Article 8 in the following way:

> 'if the official order obviously constitutes a breach of the law, it may in general be fully approved that the subordinate is not accorded the right to refer to his superior's official order as an excuse and to maintain that he was only carrying out that order. In that respect the stipulation of the Charter contains nothing essentially new'.[414]

But Sauter attempted to shield his client from the menacing thrust of the Article by claiming that he had obeyed not an ordinary order, to which the Article refers, but rather the law.[415] A somewhat similar approach was made by Nelte, counsel for the defendant Keitel, who admitted that his client had acted in pursuance of manifestly illegal orders, and agreed that a soldier is not obliged to obey such orders, but sought to escape the application of Article 8 by means of the plea based on the special nature of the *Führer*'s orders.[416]

All these counsel for the defence made common cause by endorsing the manifest illegality principle, without seeking to contest the strict provision of Article 8, maintaining, as did most of the prosecutors, that by its very nature the Article relates to orders that are manifestly illegal. They sought salvation either within the compass of Article 8, trying to put its proviso dealing with mitigation of punishment to good use, or without it, arguing that the Article was inapplicable to the case in issue as the offence had been committed in obedience to the law or to an order of a special character. It is interesting to compare this way of approach to that of Gawlik, counsel for the defence of the SD, as expressed in the following passage:

413. *Ibid.* The scope of the plea of obedience to orders was also limited to the field of mitigation of punishment by Servatius, counsel for the defendant Sauckel, who emphatically requested the Tribunal to apply to his client the provision of Article 8 of the London Charter (which includes a passage relating to leniency in punishment) and not another provision (Article 7, which does not contain such a passage) (Nuremberg trial, Final Plea for Defendant Sauckel (by Servatius), *I.M.T.*, vol. 18, p. 505).
414. Nuremberg trial, Final Plea for Defendant Funk (by Sauter), *I.M.T.*, vol. 18, p. 248.
415. *Ibid.*, p. 249.
416. Nuremberg trial, Final Plea for Defendant Keitel (by Nelte), *I.M.T.*, vol. 18, pp. 4–5. As regards the plea concerning the special nature of the *Führer*'s orders, see below, Sub-Section (3).

'The provision of Article 8 of the Charter merely eliminates superior orders as a general reason for exclusion from punishment; but it is possible for an order to exclude the cognizance of illegality in individual cases. He who has recognized the illegality of his action cannot, according to Article 8, justify himself by reference to an order. In a case, however, where a person considers his action right and legal by virtue of an order given him, he must be exonerated. The provisions of Article 8 of the Charter can only have this sense and this meaning'.[417]

Actually, Gawlik here presented the provision of Article 8 as a reflection of the personal knowledge principle. In his opinion, the Tribunal ought to inquire in each case whether the defendant knew that he was obeying an illegal order, and pass judgment accordingly. In view of the fact that the twin principles of personal knowledge and manifest illegality are, as noted above,[418] two different guises of what is essentially one and the same proposition, it looks, at first blush, as if Gawlik followed the footsteps of those preceding him. And indeed, in the sequel of his pleading, he adduced the passage quoted above from the argument of the French prosecutor Menthon[419] to promote his own interpretation of Article 8.[420] But, in point of fact, Gawlik devised a new construction of the Article, and the reliance on Menthon was inappropriate. Menthon and other members of the prosecution, as well as Kauffmann, wished to apply in effect, at Nuremberg, the uncompromising stipulation of Article 8, according to which the Tribunal may not consider the fact of obedience to orders save for the purpose of mitigation of punishment, without entering into the question whether this or that defendant had been aware of the criminality of his acts. In their view, the authors of the London Charter had already asked themselves that very question in regard to all the criminals and all the crimes dealt with by the Charter and had reached the global decision that the acts and orders involved were manifestly illegal. From the viewpoint of Menthon and his colleagues, therefore, no operative conclusion emerged from the espousal of the manifest illegality principle insofar as the Nuremberg defendants were concerned. Gawlik's attitude was entirely different. He wanted the Tribunal to apply to the Nuremberg defendants the personal knowledge principle in fact no less than in theory and to examine whether each defendant had really been aware of the illegality of his acts; to his mind, the London Charter had not precluded in advance the possibility of relieving the defendants of

417. Nuremberg trial, Final Plea for the S.D. (by Gawlik), *I.M.T.*, vol. 21, pp. 625–626.
418. See *supra*, Part II, Chapter 1.
419. See *supra*, p. 128.
420. Nuremberg trial, Final Plea for the S.D. (by Gawlik), *I.M.T.*, vol. 21, p. 626.

responsibility on account of mistake of law. Consequently, his interpretation of Article 8 does not fall into the category of a background explanation; it is a construction of operative significance that is liable utterly to transform the nature and the essence of the provision of the Article. I have already expressed my opinion that the conception of Menthon and his colleagues has no factual-historical foundation. Here I must add that Gawlik's contention does not even have a legal foundation. It is impossible to ignore the rigid wording of Article 8 completely, as if it had never existed.

Out of excessive loyalty to the personal knowledge principle, Gawlik tried in the course of his argument to condense the whole controversy that is raging in the international juristic literature on obedience to orders into the short and sharp question whether a subordinate, having complied with a superior order while being aware of its illegality, ought to bear responsibility for his act; as if there were universal agreement that obedience to an order without awareness of its illegality brings about exemption from responsibility.[421] Needless to say, this assertion, which ignores, *inter alia*, the doctrine of absolute liability in international legal theory, is entirely baseless. Yet the roots of the erroneous interpretation of Article 8, set out above, may be embedded in it.

There is more sense in another contention put forward by Gawlik in the continuation of his pleading:

> 'It could lead to an illogical result if one considered it inadmissible to cite an order as proof of the lack of illegality. He who carried out an act without an order would not be punished if he lacked the knowledge of its illegality. If, however, he commits the same deed on the strength of an order, he would have to be punished, unless one were to agree with my point of view'.[422]

The obvious presupposition underlying this passage is that lack of acquaintance with the law precludes criminal conviction; in other words, *ignorantia juris excusat.* Proceeding from this presupposition, Gawlik put the question how it was possible that an offender acting on his own instigation and out of mistake of law should be relieved of responsibility, whereas his colleague, also acting out of mistake of law but in pursuance of a superior order, should be convicted. This question may be answered, in line with Jackson's argument quoted above,[423] by saying that the doctrine of absolute liability, which is, in fact, challenged here by Gawlik, does not render conviction compulsory in case of obedience to orders and is not designed to bring to naught the defence of mistake of law or any other defence

421. *Ibid.*
422. *Ibid.*
423. See *supra*, p. 126.

available to the accused; the doctrine's only aim is to deny to the defendant the possibility of utilizing the fact of obedience to orders in the foundation of his defence. But this answer cannot completely solve the problem posed by Gawlik, for it does not reply convincingly to the question why the fact of obedience to orders is inadmissible in evidence in conjunction with the other circumstances of the case when the defence of mistake of law, or any other available defence, is raised. And indeed we have already seen that this is precisely the reason why the doctrine of absolute liability, and, equally, Article 8 of the London Charter, are inadequate.[424] Nevertheless, even if Gawlik's argument may impel us to the conclusion that Article 8 cannot be regarded as the *lex ferenda*, it is still incapable of explaining how the Nuremberg Tribunal could ignore the provision of the Article as the *lex lata*.

Being seized with the subject of mistake of law, it is fitting for us to mention the contention put forward by Kranzbühler, counsel for the defendant Doenitz, that his client had obeyed a certain order of Hitler, the notorious 'Commando Order', out of a belief that the act in question—merciless extermination of Commando prisoners-of-war—constituted, as the order had represented it to be, a measure of reprisal.[425] This plea might have had substance if it had been submitted within the limits of the defence of mistake of law or of fact.[426] But Kranzbühler cut the ground from under his own feet by stating as follows:

> 'Whether such reprisals were admissible at all according to the Geneva Convention, and to what extent, could not be judged by, nor did that come within the competence of, the recipient of the order. Every superior officer, at any rate, probably recognized that the order... was in itself an infringement of the rules of war. However, since the essence of any reprisal is to avenge a wrong on the part of the enemy with a wrong on one's own part, this does not prove anything concerning the legitimacy or illegitimacy of the reprisal order'.[427]

It seems that, when he expressed himself in this way, learned counsel forgot what was provided by the Geneva Convention of 1929 that he alluded to. Had the Convention merely pronounced that killing prisoners-of-war was prohibited, Doenitz might well have argued that while he had been aware, or ought to have been aware, of the illegality, in ordinary circumstances, of the acts

424. See *supra*, pp. 75–76, 117–118.
425. Nuremberg trial, Final Plea for Defendant Doenitz (by Kranzbühler), *I.M.T.*, vol. 18, p. 362.
426. See *supra*, pp. 84ff.
427. Nuremberg trial, Final Plea for Defendant Doenitz (by Kranzbühler), *I.M.T.*, vol. 18, p. 362.

enjoined by the 'Commando Order', nevertheless he had believed *bona fide* that, as reprisals, they were irreprehensible. But, as we have observed,[428] the Geneva Convention explicitly prohibited the use of measures of reprisals against prisoners-of-war. Hence, and in view of the fact that Kranzbühler openly conceded that his client, like every senior officer, had been aware of the laws of war on this subject, Doenitz could not argue that he had committed a mistake of law. And if no such mistake was committed by Doenitz, why does obedience to the 'Commando Order' differ from obedience to other illegal orders?

(2) The Doctrine of *Respondeat Superior*

Regardless of the interpretation of Article 8 of the Charter of the International Military Tribunal, it is undeniable that the Article looks upon the doctrine of *respondeat superior* as anathema. Yet this fact did not prevent several defence counsel at Nuremberg from putting their trust in the doctrine, as if it had been viable, recognized and accepted. These attorneys emphasized that a soldier is bound to obey orders without doubt or hesitation and that discipline is the backbone of the army; and, if that is the rule in general, then all the more so in time of war.[429] Insubordination on the part of a senior officer, so ran the argument, is a much graver phenomenon than disobedience on the part of an ordinary soldier (the soldier in the firing-squad, for instance, to use Jackson's illustration), for it is apt to shatter the whole structure of the army and the State.[430]

In respect of crimes against peace, several defence counsel contended that the power to determine the question of the legality of war is vested in the competent political authorities and is not the affair of the armed forces.[431] Siemers, counsel for the defendant Raeder, reached the conclusion that, as the decision between peace and war is beyond the scope of the armed forces,

> 'for an army the concept of war of aggression exists in the strategic sense only'.[432]

Exner, counsel for the defendant Jodl, set forth the argument that

428. See *supra*, p. 86.
429. See Nuremberg trial, Final Plea for the High Command (by Laternser), *I.M.T.*, vol. 22, pp. 45–46, 64–65, 83, 85–86. See also Nuremberg trial, Final Plea for Defendant Keitel (by Nelte), *I.M.T.*, vol. 18, p. 2.
430. See Nuremberg trial, Final Plea for the High Command (by Laternser), *I.M.T.*, vol. 22, p. 85.
431. See Nuremberg trial, Final Plea for Defendant Jodl (by Exner), *I.M.T.*, vol. 19, pp. 24–25; Final Plea for Defendant Raeder (by Siemers), *I.M.T.*, vol. 18, p. 426.
432. Nuremberg trial, Final Plea for Defendant Raeder (by Siemers), *I.M.T.*, vol. 18, p. 426.

no officer, not even the Chief of the General Staff in person, may refuse to comply with the resolve of the competent political leadership to wage war merely because in his opinion the war is in contravention of the rules of international law; otherwise, no war could be waged at all, and that includes not only aggressive war, but defensive war as well.[433] Furthermore, said Exner, suppose that the Security Council of the United Nations decides upon a punitive war—or, rather, a police action—in response to aggression, and the Commander-in-Chief of the United Nations forces refuses to implement the decision, alleging that to his mind no aggression justifying the countermeasure has taken place.[434] Exner then asked with specious self-righteousness:

> 'Would not the whole security apparatus in this case depend on the subjective opinion of a single nonpolitical person?'[435]

At first sight, the problem presented by Exner cannot be easily solved, for international law seems to be enmeshed in a choice between two evils: either to loosen its grip on the army and risk its participation in wars of aggression, or claim the legal pound of flesh from offenders and take the chance that defensive wars and collective police actions will fail owing to the hesitations of key officers. In both cases, the danger appears to loom that aggression will be crowned with success and as a result the whole modern international legal structure will disintegrate. But I think that these two cases do not form a parallelogram of forces, and the two horns of the dilemma are not made of the same stuff. Whereas the risk in the first case is most substantial, in the second there may be a blessing in disguise behind the risk. It is well known that, in reality, the distinction between aggressive and defensive wars is sometimes shrouded by the twilight of doubt, and there is a marked tendency of statesmen and States to cover malicious intents with a mask of innocence and conceal the serpent of aggression under the flower of purported defence. Precisely because it is essential to international

433. Nuremberg trial, Final Plea for Defendant Jodl (by Exner), *I.M.T.*, vol. 19, p. 21. Exner's argument particularly impressed Appleman, who posed the question whether a general—ordered by the President of his State to mass his troops along the border of a foreign State—is entitled to answer as follows: 'Now wait a minute... give me a complete history of all the incidents leading up to your order so that my attorney and I can judge whether to act or whether to refuse to obey your orders' (Appleman, *op. cit.*, p. 55). And see, in this context, also Grenfell's statement quoted in the High Command case, Closing Brief for Defendant Hollidt (by Fritsch), *N.M.T.*, vol. 11, p. 415.
434. Nuremberg trial, Final Plea for Defendant Jodl (by Exner), *I.M.T.*, vol. 19, p. 21.
435. *Ibid.*

law to war against wars of aggression and make sure that only defensive wars end with victory, international law must insist that soldiers called to the colours will not merely 'do and die' in submission to orders but start to 'reason why' war is being waged. We must bear in mind that in the illustrations drawn by Exner the generals disobey the political leadership which sends them, with their troops, into the line of fire, because they are apprehensive lest their service be abused. International law must encourage them in this attitude, and perhaps the rebelliousness of the generals will bring about the end of wars on earth. As for the example given by Exner in respect of a collective action of the Security Council, it seems that, in existing circumstances, even the label of police operation of the United Nations does not justify such an action, if attached to it improperly. It was demonstrated manifestly, during certain stages in the Congo crisis, that there is a possibility that forces—bearing aloft the flag of the United Nations—can be used for political purposes that are not to everyone's liking or above any least suspicion of being touched with a fleck of aggression. Consequently, refusal on the part of the commander of the United Nations forces to carry out such an action does not necessarily have to paralyze the international security apparatus. It is possible that in the future the international community will raise a real army of its own, in which event the legality of all its actions will perhaps be ensured in advance beyond reasonable doubt. If that happens, there may be room for the argument that officers serving in that army must unquestioningly carry out all their assignments. But an attempt to apply illustrations drawn from such a fictitious army to the army that Exner had in mind, namely, the *Wehrmacht*, verges on sacrilege.

Exner and his colleagues sought to support the argument based on the standpoint of military discipline and on the interests of the international legal system by relying on the factor of military ignorance of the law. In their view, it is impossible to impose upon an officer the obligation to probe into the legality of wars, for (a), as a matter of fact, only seldom will he be in a position to discern all relevant circumstances so as to determine in accordance therewith whether war is permissible; (b), as a matter of law, the definition of aggression is disputable even among scholars versed in international law, and who is the officer to determine such a subtle question?[436] The officer standing trial, they argued, is not a judge; he is not obliged, nor is he competent, to pronounce a verdict on

436. See *ibid.*, pp. 21–22. See also Nuremberg trial, Final Plea for Defendant Doenitz (by Kranzbühler), *I.M.T.*, vol. 18, p. 362.

the lawfulness of the policy of his country.[437] Even in case of doubt concerning the legality of orders from the viewpoint of international law, the soldier must obey.[438]

Another factor that defence counsel endeavoured to make use of when pleading in favour of the doctrine of *respondeat superior* is that of compulsion: the way they put it, the defendants were forced to obey orders, for, had they refused to do so, they would have been liable to the death penalty.[439] Merkel, counsel for the Gestapo, expressed it in the following way:

> 'It is true that cowardice is not a virtue; but it is equally true that heroism and martyrdom in the world of human beings are the exception. Should the Gestapo members form this exception?'[440]

As long as no super-State authority is in existence to safeguard soldiers who disobey orders for reasons of conscience, one cannot, in the opinion of the defence, demand from the soldier that he become a martyr as a result of such disobedience.[441]

I think that none of these last arguments is new. We have already discussed them, and after a close examination reached the conclusion that they are not so potent as to validate the doctrine of *respondeat superior*. It is perhaps worthwhile, though, to point out here the built-in contradiction that is perceptible in Exner's exposition in praise of this doctrine. At a certain point in his argumentation, Exner referred to the trials of the heroes of the anti-Hitler plot of 20 July 1944, which had taken place before a Nazi tribunal.[442] When it was pleaded, in the course of these trials, that participation in the attempted *coup d'état* had been due to obedience to orders, the Nazi tribunal rejected the plea with contempt.[443] And Exner hastened to justify this decision, saying:

> 'If ever a military order was issued which was outside the competence of the Armed Forces and was, therefore, not binding and did not exculpate, it was the order to murder the head of these very Armed Forces. But how an order

437. See Nuremberg trial, Final Plea for the High Command (by Laternser), *I.M.T.*, vol. 22, p. 46.
438. See Nuremberg trial, Final Plea for Defendant Jodl (by Exner), *I.M.T.*, vol. 19, p. 44; Final Plea for Defendant Doenitz (by Kranzbühler), *I.M.T.*, vol. 18, p. 362.
439. See Nuremberg trial, Final Plea for Defendant Jodl (by Exner), *I.M.T.*, vol. 19, p. 24; Final Plea for the Gestapo (by Merkel), *I.M.T.*, vol. 21, pp. 536–537. See also Nuremberg trial, Final Plea for the S.D. (by Gawlik), *I.M.T.*, vol. 21, p. 626.
440. Nuremberg trial, Final Plea for the Gestapo (by Merkel), *I.M.T.*, vol. 21, p. 537.
441. See Nuremberg trial, Final Plea for Defendant Jodl (by Exner), *I.M.T.*, vol. 19, p. 22.
442. *Ibid.*, p. 43.
443. *Ibid.*

> by some officer to murder the head of the state can be compared with the order of the head of the state to commit an act contrary to international law is incomprehensible to me'.[444]

When Exner regarded an order to murder the Head of State as an extraordinary one, he certainly hit the bull's eye. But, when he propounded that in this particular case the soldier is obliged to disobey the order and that obedience on his part will not automatically protect him from criminal prosecution, Exner himself sapped the doctrine of *respondeat superior.* Inadvertently, learned counsel here admitted that the allegation of '*Befehl ist Befehl*' is untenable. A soldier who has to inquire into the essence of orders prior to complying with them, and choose from their midst only certain orders to which obedience is permissible, is not a robot reacting mechanically to every superior command, but a percipient human being. Obedience to orders which is predicated on thought and analysis is not blind obedience.[445] Obedience to orders which constitutes a defence not in each and every case automatically and *a priori* but only in particular cases, be they the ordinary and recurrent cases or even the great majority of cases, is not in keeping with the conception underlying the doctrine of *respondeat superior.*[446]

Considering these critical remarks concerning the argumentation of the defence, we may conclude that, even if Article 8 had not entirely excluded the applicability of the doctrine of *respondeat superior,* the pleading should have fallen away on account of its innate flaws. When the provision of Article 8 is taken into consideration on top of that, it looks as if the defence were trying to pour water into a sieve.

(3) The *Führerprinzip*

Seeking to surmount the obstacle placed in its way by the provision of Article 8, the defence contended that the Tribunal ought to relieve the accused of responsibility in view of the fact that they had not obeyed ordinary orders but the orders of the *Führer,* which had a unique character within the authoritarian framework of the Third Reich and what was termed therein the *Führerprinzip* or leadership principle. To clarify the essence of this contention, we should say a few words about the *Führerprinzip.* The principle was

444. *Ibid.*
445. We have already observed *supra* (p. 53) that blind obedience is detrimental to the efficiency of the army. The illustrative case of obedience to an order concerning an attempt on the life of the Head of State bears instructive testimony to the validity of this proposition, and corresponds perfectly to the examples drawn by Stephen (see *supra,* p. 53).
446. See *supra,* note 129.

originally developed within the ranks of the Nazi party, and the International Military Tribunal defined it in the following way in its judgment:

> 'The procedure within the Party was governed in the most absolute way by the "leadership principle" (Führerprinzip).
>
> 'According to the principle, each Führer has the right to govern, administer or decree, subject to no control of any kind and at his complete discretion, subject only to the orders he received from above.
>
> 'This principle applied in the first instance to Hitler himself as the Leader of the Party, and in a lesser degree to all other party officials. All members of the Party swore an oath of "eternal allegiance" to the Leader'.[447]

From the Nazi party, the *Führerprinzip* penetrated and pervaded the whole Reich, and at Nuremberg the defendants argued that they had obeyed not a leader but 'the' Leader, the pinnacle of the pyramid and the omnipotent tyrant, the *Führer* of the Reich.

It is interesting to note that, in the very course of the Second World War, Levy predicted, with marvellous accuracy, that

> 'the Führerprinzip glorified by the Nazi and Fascist governments, and permeating the organization of their armies, may well cause the ghost of "superior orders" to be resuscitated in full vigor'.[448]

Kelsen, too, stated during that period:

> 'the number of persons who had the legal power of leading their country into war is in each of the Axis States very small. In Germany it is probably the Fuehrer alone'.[449]

In a leading speech dealing with legal issues, made on behalf of the whole defence at Nuremberg by Jahrreiss, counsel for the defendant Jodl, this statement of Kelsen was enthusiastically adduced in support,[450] and the theory based on the *Führerprinzip* was elaborately unfolded.[451] Jahrreiss explained that the *Führerprinzip* had been

> 'the organizational guiding principle in the development of the Reich constitution after 1933',[452]

447. Nuremberg trial, Judgment, *Cmd.* No. 6964, p. 5.
448. Levy, *op. cit.*, p. 1080.
449. Kelsen, *Peace*, p. 91; Kelsen, 'Responsibility', p. 546. Cf. Maugham, *op. cit.*, p. 82.
450. Nuremberg trial, Closing Speech for the Defence (by Jahrreiss), *I.M.T.*, vol. 17, p. 493.
451. *Ibid.*, pp. 482–494. Cf. Donnedieu de Vabres, 'Nuremberg', pp. 567, 571–572; Eustathiades, 'Ordres', p. 407; Schafer, *op. cit.*, p. 141.
452. Nuremberg trial, Closing Speech for the Defence (by Jahrreiss), *I.M.T.*, vol. 17, p. 482.

and laid stress upon the fact that

> 'the *Führer*'s orders became the central element of the German state edifice'.[453]

He described at great length the despotic-monocratic system of government in Nazi Germany, maintaining that the *Führer*'s orders had been the last word, so that it was absolutely impossible to raise objections to them or call them in question. He phrased his argument as follows:

> 'this development had given the *Führer*'s orders a special aura of sanctity...; there was no contradicting the *Führer*'s orders',[454]

adding,

> 'The functionaries had neither the right nor the duty to examine the orders of the monocrat to determine their legality. For them these orders could never be illegal at all'.[455]

Or in other words:

> 'an order by the *Führer* was binding—and indeed legally binding—on the person to whom it was given, even if the directive was contrary to international law'.[456]

On the basis of the extraordinary standing of the *Führer*'s orders in the Third Reich, Jahrreiss posed the following question, to which a negative reply seemed to him self-evident:

> 'Did they belong to the type of orders which were disallowed by the Charter of this Court as grounds for the exclusion of punishment?'[457]

The argument, in short, is that, when Article 8 of the London Charter precludes the possibility of considering 'the fact that the defendant acted pursuant to order' as a reason for discharge from responsibility, the term 'order' relates to ordinary orders but not to the exceptional orders issued by the *Führer* within the compass of the *Führerprinzip*.

In various formulations and in different presentations, whether in its entirety or in part, the contention predicated on the *Führerprinzip* was also reiterated in the pleadings of many other defence counsel, who emphasized that the exclusive and absolute responsibility for all the flagrant crimes committed by the accused at Nuremberg rested squarely on the devil incarnate, the *Führer* who had been vested with power, and not on those small fry in the

453. *Ibid.*, p. 483.
454. *Ibid.*, p. 484.
455. *Ibid.*, p. 489.
456. *Ibid.*, p. 491.
457. *Ibid.*, p. 484.

dictatorial pond who had merely obeyed his instructions.[458] In many respects, this line of argumentation can be traced to the vocabulary of the doctrine of *respondeat superior*; but it is unique in that it does not endeavour to apply to ordinary hierarchical relationships but only to the relationship between the leader and those who are led by him within the ambit of the *Führerprinzip*. The accent is put here not on the distress of the subordinate in general but on the plight and the anguish of the subordinate in Nazi Germany. As the idea was expressed by Laternser, counsel for the High Command:

> 'no one can deny that Hitler alone wielded the power of the Reich in his hands, and consequently also had the sole and total responsibility. The essence of every dictatorship ultimately lies in the fact that one man's will is almighty, that his will is decisive in all matters. In no other dictatorship was this principle developed so exclusively as in Hitler's dictatorship'.[459]

Merkel claimed that, on account of the 'devilish atmosphere' which had prevailed in the Reich, the small officials had been turned into 'tools without a will of their own'.[460] And Nelte asserted that the defendants had been

> 'merely mouthpieces or tools of an overwhelming will'.[461]

The flaw obviously inherent in this way of pleading is that it is founded on an unreal interpretation of Article 8, which in point of fact divests it of relevance to those very major war criminals whom the authors of the London Charter had in mind. No wonder, therefore, that one defence counsel—Steinbauer, representing Seyss-Inquart—proposed that, should the Tribunal not be willing to adopt the general attitude of the defence in this regard, at least it take the *Führerprinzip* into account when sentence was passed.[462]

458. See Nuremberg trial, Final Plea for Defendant Speer (by Flachsner), *I.M.T.*, vol. 19, p. 210; Final Plea for Defendant Ribbentrop (by Horn), *I.M.T.*, vol. 17, pp. 597–599; Final Plea for the High Command (by Laternser), *I.M.T.*, vol. 22, pp. 57, 83; Final Plea for the Gestapo (by Merkel), *I.M.T.*, vol. 21, pp. 536–537; Final Plea for Defendant Keitel (by Nelte), *I.M.T.*, vols. 17 (pp. 637–638), 18 (p. 6); Final Plea for Defendant Raeder (by Siemers), *I.M.T.*, vol. 18, pp. 426–427. Cf. Nuremberg trial, Final Plea for Defendant Frank (by Seidl), *I.M.T.*, vol. 18, p. 143; Final Plea for Defendant Rosenberg (by Thoma), *I.M.T.*, vol. 18, p. 103. Cf. also Appleman, *op. cit.*, p. 54; Calvocoressi, *op. cit.*, p. 76.

459. Nuremberg trial, Final Plea for the High Command (by Laternser), *I.M.T.*, vol. 22, p. 57.

460. Nuremberg trial, Final Plea for the Gestapo (by Merkel), *I.M.T.*, vol. 21, p. 537.

461. Nuremberg trial, Final Plea for Defendant Keitel (by Nelte), *I.M.T.*, vol. 18, p. 6.

462. Nuremberg trial, Final Plea for Defendant Seyss-Inquart (by Steinbauer), *I.M.T.*, vol. 19, p. 72.

C. *The Reply of the Prosecution to the Arguments of the Defence*

We have observed that most of the argumentation of the prosecution was based on the assumption that the manifest illegality principle is expressive of the accepted solution of the problem of obedience to orders in international law. We have also examined how the prosecution construed Article 8 of the Charter of the Tribunal and to what extent that construction differs from the interpretations put forward by the defence. But we ought to scrutinize now the response made by the prosecutors to the allegations of defence counsel in regard to compulsion, on the one hand, and the *Führerprinzip*, on the other.

To the contention that the accused had been forced to obey Hitler's orders, the prosecution retorted, through the French chief prosecutor who had replaced Menthon, Champetier de Ribes, that they should have refused to carry out these orders even at the cost of their lives.[463] Champetier de Ribes remarked that Hitler might have ruled their bodies but he had not governed their souls and their conscience, and if they had been afraid of the consequences of disobedience—well, then, cowardice does not constitute a reason for exemption from criminal responsibility.[464]

The gist of the reply of the prosecution to the pleading of the defence in the field of obedience to orders relates to the question of the *Führerprinzip*. First of all, let us turn to the closing speech of the Soviet chief prosecutor, Rudenko, who demonstrated how the Gordian knot of the arguments of the defence on this subject may be cut by one thrust of the sword of logic. Rudenko tackled the question presented by Jahrreiss in respect of the applicability of Article 8 to the particular orders of the *Führer*,[465] and made the following vehement and correct answer to it:

> 'it is quite incomprehensible what logical or other methods have led him to assert that the provisions of the Charter, specially drafted for the trial of major war criminals of fascist Germany, did not factually imply the very conditions themselves of the activities of these criminals. What orders then issued by whom and in what country are meant by the Charter of the Tribunal?'[466]

Indeed, it is difficult to contest the fact that the authors of the London Charter were aware of the exceptional conditions which had prevailed in Nazi Germany and paid heed to the *Führerprinzip*

463. Nuremberg trial, Closing Speech for the Prosecution (by Champetier de Ribes), *I.M.T.*, vol. 19, p. 534.
464. *Ibid.*
465. Nuremberg trial, Closing Speech for the Prosecution (by Rudenko), *I.M.T.*, vol. 19, p. 576.
466. *Ibid.*, p. 577.

also when they barred the defendants from relying upon the plea of obedience to orders. We have noted above[467] that in the course of the deliberations of the London Conference it was explicitly spelt out that Hitler's orders were subject to the stipulation of Article 8. It is a matter of sheer common sense, as Rudenko rightly pointed out, that those very criminals for whom the Charter was formulated should not be excluded from the range of its application. It is permissible to criticize the provision of Article 8; it may even be allowable to try to restrict its scope; but an attempt to render it devoid of any real significance is unacceptable.

Perhaps because of its somewhat formal colour, the Anglo-Saxon chief prosecutors, Jackson and Shawcross, were not satisfied with this rejoinder and did not wish to leave it as the sole answer to the argument of the defence on this subject. On their part, they preferred not to anchor their response to the provision of Article 8 and to the intention of the authors of the Charter. Thus, Jackson, even though he did not refrain from noting that the contention based on the *Führerprinzip* actually reflects an effort to evade the stipulation of Article 8,[468] shifted the centre of gravity in his reply to the following consideration:

> 'These men destroyed free government in Germany and now plead to be excused from responsibility because they became slaves. They are in the position of the fictional boy who murdered his father and mother and then pleaded for leniency because he was an orphan'.[469]

This line of thought may be regarded as a claim of estoppel against the defendants: it was they who fettered themselves and their fellow-men with the shackles of submission to the absolute authority of the *Führer*, and now, guilty of a cardinal sin, they cannot expect a reward. Shawcross, addressing himself to the allegation that the defendants had merely been powerless and non-volitional instruments in the hands of the *Führer*,[470] also stressed that the phantom of the *Führerprinzip* had been the creation of the accused themselves and it was their fault that the dictatorship behind which they sought shelter had been brought into existence in the first place.[471]

This counterclaim concerning the *Führerprinzip* is linked with the submission of the prosecution that the defendants were not just

467. See *supra*, p. 116.
468. Nuremberg trial, Closing Speech for the Prosecution (by Jackson), *I.M.T.*, vol. 19, p. 423.
469. *Ibid.*, p. 424.
470. Nuremberg trial, Closing Speech for the Prosecution (by Shawcross), *I.M.T.*, vol. 19, pp. 459, 465, 515.
471. *Ibid.*, pp. 466, 515.

inert pawns or marionettes moved by wires. On the contrary, it was they who pulled the strings and activated the Nazi monster. Jackson expressed it, in his closing speech, in the following way:

> 'I admit that Hitler was the chief villain. But ... we know that even the head of the state has the same limits to his senses and to the hours of his days as do lesser men. He must rely on others to be his eyes and ears as to most that goes on in a great empire. Other legs must run his errands; other hands must execute his plans. On whom did Hitler rely for such things more than upon these men in the dock? ... These men had access to Hitler and often could control the information that reached him and on which he must base his policy and his orders. They were the Praetorian Guard, and while they were under Caesar's orders, Caesar was always in their hands'.[472]

Shawcross had already spoken in similar vein in his opening speech:

> 'It may be said that ... these men were mere instruments of Hitler's will. But they were the instruments without which Hitler's will could not be carried out; and they were more than that ...
>
> '... They were the men whose skill and cunning, whose labor and activity made it possible for the German Reich to ... march against the peoples of the world'.[473]

Taylor, of the American prosecution, referring to the High Command, also pointed out that the leaders of the *Wehrmacht* were not just puppets,[474] and that Hitler was entirely dependent upon his generals, without whom he would have been helpless.[475] And Maxwell-Fyfe declared that

> 'Great captains are not automata to be weighed against a rubber stamp'.[476]

Both Jackson[477] and Shawcross[478] adduced, in their speeches, the illuminating testimony of the defendant Speer:

> 'I only wanted to say that even in an authoritarian system the leaders must accept a common responsibility, and that it is impossible for them to dodge

472. Nuremberg trial, Closing Speech for the Prosecution (by Jackson), *I.M.T.*, vol. 19, p. 430. See also Nuremberg trial, Opening Speech for the Prosecution (by Jackson), *I.M.T.*, vol. 2, pp. 151–152. Cf. Leventhal, Harris, Woolsey and Farr, *op. cit.*, p. 870 n. 58.
473. Nuremberg trial, Opening Speech for the Prosecution (by Shawcross), *I.M.T.*, vol. 3, pp. 143–144.
474. Nuremberg trial, Closing Speech for the Prosecution (by Taylor), *I.M.T.*, vol. 22, pp. 282–283.
475. *Ibid.*, pp. 283, 291. Cf. Nuremberg trial, Final Plea for the High Command (by Laternser), *I.M.T.*, vol. 22, p. 45.
476. Nuremberg trial, Closing Speech for the Prosecution (by Maxwell-Fyfe), *I.M.T.*, vol. 22, p. 236. Cf. Kilmuir (Maxwell-Fyfe), *op. cit.*, p. 17.
477. Nuremberg trial, Closing Speech for the Prosecution (by Jackson), *I.M.T.*, vol. 19, p. 423.
478. Nuremberg trial, Closing Speech for the Prosecution (by Shawcross), *I.M.T.*, vol. 19, p. 436.

that common responsibility after the catastrophe, for if the war had been won the leaders would also presumably have laid claim to common responsibility'.[479]

Here, too, the argument is laid on the foundation of estoppel. Had Nazi Germany been victorious in the war, the sundry Goerings, Ribbentrops and Keitels would have rushed to the head of the line, clamorously proclaiming their own decisive contribution to the cause and demanding a share in the laurels. Now that Germany has been utterly crushed and defeated, they withdraw into the shade, shrinking from responsibility and professing to have been impotent cogs in a vast machine. He who is not prepared to dissociate himself from the war effort when victory seems to be within easy grasp is not entitled to act like Pontius Pilate and wash his hands of accountability when disaster strikes.

D. *The Judgment*

The International Military Tribunal referred in its judgment to the 'doctrine of "superior orders"' on two different occasions, when reviewing the respective cases of the defendants Keitel and Jodl, commenting that it had been 'prohibited by Article 8 of the Charter as a defence'.[480] But the principal pronouncement of the Tribunal on the question of obedience to orders is to be found in the following passage, dealing in a general manner with Article 8:

> 'The provisions of this Article are in conformity with the law of all nations. That a soldier was ordered to kill or torture in violation of the international law of war has never been recognised as a defence to such acts of brutality, though, as the Charter here provides, the order may be urged in mitigation of the punishment. The true test, which is found in varying degrees in the criminal law of most nations, is not the existence of the order, but whether moral choice was in fact possible'.[481]

This impressive statement of the law, which resounded throughout the whole international legal world and was profusely quoted in

479. Nuremberg trial, Defendant Speer's Testimony, *I.M.T.*, vol. 16, p. 586. Even though the prosecution neglected to make use of it, attention should also be paid in this context to the interesting statement made by Ludinghausen, counsel for the defendant Neurath, as follows: 'The age of absolutism, where the will of the ruler alone determined the destiny and acts of a people, has definitely passed. In this age it may be said that one cannot imagine any avowed dictator or omnipotent despot who can rule without or against the will, or at least the tacit approval of the nation, at least its majority' (Nuremberg trial, Final Plea for Defendant Neurath (by Ludinghausen), *I.M.T.*, vol. 19, p. 221). If the nation, or its majority, may determine the fate of dictatorship, then *a fortiori* the ministers and the generals, the henchmen and the assistants of the dictator, may also control its destiny!

480. Nuremberg trial, Judgment, *Cmd.* No. 6964, pp. 92, 118. Cf. Spiropoulos, 'Principles', p. 193 n. 54; Woetzel, *op. cit.*, p. 119.

481. Nuremberg trial, Judgment, *Cmd.* No. 6964, p. 42.

subsequent cases as well as in the juristic literature,[482] has turned out to be the focal point of every serious discussion on the problem of obedience to orders up to the present day, and hence it merits a very close and thorough examination. Special stress should be laid upon the significance of the last sentence in the passage. Whereas in the first part of the statement the Tribunal contented itself with an expression of unequivocal support of Article 8, in the last sentence it added a contribution of its own to the subject of obedience to orders and established a test which cannot be found in the text of the Article, namely, the moral choice test. The trouble is that at this essential point the Tribunal pronounced itself in a way which, as one scholar terms it, is 'somewhat cryptic',[483] and it is not easy to fathom the full meaning of the sentence. In fact, there are several views concerning the availability of the moral choice test.

According to one view, the judgment applied the test to the question of mitigation of punishment only, in contradistinction to the question of discharge from responsibility.[484] In other words, if moral choice was possible to the defendant who was faced with an illegal order and he committed the offence nevertheless, severe

482. Among the cases see Eichmann trial (second instance), Judgment, *op. cit.*, p. 134; Einsatzgruppen case, Judgment, *N.M.T.*, vol. 4, p. 471; Farben case, Judgment, *N.M.T.*, vol. 8, p. 1176; High Command case, Judgment, *N.M.T.*, vol. 11, pp. 475–476; Roechling case, Judgment, *N.M.T.*, vol. 14, p. 1104. In the legal literature, see and cf. Appleman, *op. cit.*, p. 56; Benton, *op. cit.*, p. 23; Biddle, *op. cit.*, p. 12; Dix, 'The Judgments in the Nuremberg Trials of Economists', *German Views*, pp. 160–176 at p. 165; Donnedieu de Vabres, 'Nuremberg', p. 569; Eustathiades, 'Ordres', p. 403; Glaser, *Introduction*, p. 130; Glaser, 'L'Ordre', p. 327; Greenspan, *op. cit.*, pp. 493, 498; Guggenheim, *op. cit.*, vol. 2, p. 48 n. 1; Harris, *op. cit.*, p. 558; *History of U.N. W.C.C.*, p. 287; Keenan and Brown, *op. cit.*, p. 133; Levie, *op. cit.*, p. 464; Maugham, *op. cit.*, p. 45; Maunoir, *op. cit.*, pp. 230–231; Kilmuir (Maxwell-Fyfe), *op. cit.*, p. 16; Maxwell-Fyfe, 'Foreword' to *W.C.T.S.*, *op. cit.*, p. xx; Mignone, 'After Nuremberg, Tokyo', *Tex.L.R.*, vol. 25 (1946–1947), pp. 475–490 at p. 482; Parker, *op. cit.*, p. 551; Pompe, *op. cit.*, p. 216; Rochette, *op. cit.*, p. 135; Scelle, *op. cit.*, p. 984; Schafer, *op. cit.*, p. 141; Schick, 'Crimes against Peace', *J.C.L.C.*, vol. 38 (1947–1948), pp. 445–465 at p. 462; Schick, 'Nuremberg', p. 198; Schick, 'The Nuremberg Trial and the International Law of the Future', *A.J.I.L.*, vol. 41 (1947), pp. 770–794 at p. 793; Schwelb, 'The United Nations War Crimes Commission', *op. cit.*, p. 374; Schwarzenberger, *International Law*, vol. 1 (2nd ed., 1949), p. 323; Schwarzenberger, 'The Judgment of Nuremberg' (*T.L.R.*), *op. cit.*, p. 355; Schwarzenberger, 'The Judgment of Nuremberg' (*Y.B.W.A.*), *op. cit.*, p. 118; *S.G. Memorandum*, p. 42; Spiropoulos, 'Principles', p. 193; Starke, *op. cit.*, pp. 370–371; Stevens, *op. cit.*, p. xl; Taylor, *op. cit.*, p. 146.

483. Greenspan, *op. cit.*, p. 493.

484. See Benton, *op. cit.*, p. 23; Maugham, *op. cit.*, p. 45; Maunoir, *op. cit.*, pp. 230–231; Woetzel, *op. cit.*, p. 119. Cf. Birkett, *op. cit.*, p. 325; Graven, 'Code', pp. 374–375; Graven, 'Crimes', p. 582.

punishment ought to be meted out to him; on the other hand, if no such choice was open to the defendant when he committed the offence, there is room for leniency. Yet, even if the possibility of moral choice was excluded, this fact only constitutes a reason for alleviation of punishment and not an obstacle to criminal prosecution. The question of relief from responsibility is not at all relevant, according to this opinion, to the test formulated by the Tribunal.

I should like to make it perfectly plain at once that, to my mind, this conception, which injects an intrusive element into the text of the judgment, cannot be countenanced. The composition and the context of the Tribunal's statement indicate unmistakably that the moral choice test is commensurate with the subject of the assessment of criminal responsibility. The intention of the Tribunal becomes crystal-clear when the following official French text of the judgment is consulted:

> 'Le vrai critérium de la responsabilité pénale, celui qu'on trouve, sous une forme ou sous une autre, dans le droit criminel de la plupart des pays, n'est nullement en rapport avec l'ordre reçu. Il réside dans la liberté morale, dans la faculté de choisir, chez l'auteur de l'acte reproché'.[485]

This text, different in several respects from the English one, renders comprehension of the statement much easier[486] and completely solves the problem with which we are presented here. According to the French formulation, the Tribunal did not establish a mere test but rather a criterion of penal responsibility ('critérium de la responsabilité pénale'). Consequently, if the conditions of the test are fulfilled, if there is no possibility of moral choice—or moral liberty ('liberté morale') and the faculty of choice ('faculté de choisir') according to the French version—the defendant ought to be relieved of criminal responsibility and not just be subjected to a lenient punishment.[487]

485. Procès des Grands Criminels de Guerre devant le Tribunal Militaire International, Nuremberg, Jugement, vol. 1, p. 236.
486. It is noteworthy that in the course of the deliberations of the International Law Commission concerning the formulation of the Nuremberg Principles—in 1950—Sandström remarked that the French version of this passage appeared to him to be 'meaningless' (*I.L.C. Yearbook*, 1950, vol. 1, p. 48); and Scelle, who presided over the meeting, conceded that 'he too was not clear as to the meaning of the words' (*ibid.*). A year later, when the Commission discussed the Draft Code of Offences against the Peace and Security of Mankind, Alfaro 'observed that the French text of that passage of the Nürnberg judgment was much clearer than the English' (*I.L.C. Yearbook*, 1951, vol. 1, p. 241). My own opinion in this regard tallies with that of Alfaro.
487. Greenspan states: 'It is clear that the test of moral choice was applied to the question of criminal responsibility and not merely to that of punishment' (Greenspan, *op. cit.*, p. 493 n. 343); and then he proceeds to go into some detail in respect

If, however, the judgment enables the acquittal of an offender who acted pursuant to orders when the conditions of the moral choice test are satisfied, the question arises how it can conform to the provision of Article 8, which precludes any possibility of taking the fact of obedience to orders into account for defence purposes.

In my opinion, the explicit language of the judgment in the first portion of the statement as cited leaves no room for doubt that the Tribunal endorsed the stipulation of Article 8 and did not at all mean to renounce it or blunt its edge. The moral choice test was, therefore, not designed to establish that the fact of obedience to orders may play any role in defence. As the French text expressly declares, this test is nowise related ('n'est nullement en rapport') to the fact of obedience to orders. When, then, is the defendant entitled to be held not-guilty under this test? Obviously, when he ought to be acquitted anyway in accordance with the general principles of the law owing to the other circumstances of the case and without any consideration being given to the fact of obedience to orders.[488] This explanation of the Tribunal's statement is similar to the interpretation submitted above of Jackson's argumentation in his opening speech,[489] and it is in keeping with what we have said with regard to the doctrine of absolute liability.[490] The Tribunal did not wish to contest the rule that no defendant is entitled to be freed from responsibility on account of obedience to orders, but it desired to clarify as well that, on the other hand, no defendant is precluded from being acquitted just because he complied with orders. If a defendant who acted in pursuance of orders succeeds in building up a defence which is not dependent for its very existence upon the fact of obedience to orders, that fact cannot stand in his way and upset his defence. It emerges from the foregoing that the moral choice test in effect lies outside the bounds of the subject of obedience to orders, but that is precisely why the Tribunal found it necessary to make use of the test, thereby determining the perimeter of the subject.

Yet the majority of jurists do not subscribe to this interpretation of the Tribunal's statement. The generally accepted view is that, in formulating the moral choice test, the Tribunal did not leave the frontiers of the question of superior orders, but on the contrary

of this test: 'On the one hand it implies that a person who has a moral choice to carry out an illegal order is criminally responsible if he carries it out. On the other hand, it implies that a person without moral choice is free from responsibility' (*ibid.*, p. 493).

488. Apparently Scelle interprets the Tribunal's statement in similar vein (Scelle, *op. cit.*, pp. 984–985).

489. See *supra*, pp. 126–127.

490. See *supra*, p. 75.

entered into the very depths of it and pronounced when the fact of obedience to orders may be taken into consideration for defence purposes. From this standpoint, the moral choice test is the crucible in which the legal validity of the fact of obedience to orders in the sphere of discharge from responsibility is to be tried out. If this fact can contribute to establish lack of moral choice, it will be taken into account in that context; if it is incapable of doing that, the defence will not be permitted to benefit from it. To put it in different phrasing: the Tribunal expressed its willingness to consider the circumstance of obedience to orders as a factual element within the limits of a defence based on lack of moral choice, even though it denied this circumstance the status of a defence *per se*.[491]

This line of interpretation is admittedly very appealing, but I feel unable to accept it, for it has to be predicated on either one of two erroneous assumptions, as follows:

(a) The assumption that the Tribunal departed in its judgment from the strict provision of Article 8 and mollified it, when formulating the moral choice test.[492] This proposition does not square with the explicit enunciation of the Tribunal itself, and so must be rejected. It might have been preferable for the Tribunal to diverge from the track of Article 8, but there is a profound distinction between what is and what ought to be.

(b) The assumption that the moral choice test is compatible with the provision of Article 8, but that this Article, on its part, does not exclude the possibility of taking the fact of obedience to orders into account for defence purposes.[493] This approach is not

491. See Donnedieu de Vabres, 'La Théorie des Délits de Droit des Gens en Droit Pénal Interétatique', *op. cit.*, p. 161; Donnedieu de Vabres, 'Nuremberg', pp. 568–569; Eustathiades, 'Ordres', pp. 414–415, 421; *S.G. Memorandum*, p. 42; Q. Wright, 'The Outlawry of War and the Law of War', *op. cit.*, pp. 373–374. Cf. Graven, 'Code', p. 375 n. 85; Greenspan, *op. cit.*, pp. 493–494; Levontin, *op. cit.*, pp. 260–261; Rochette, *op. cit.*, p. 135.

492. It is interesting that this, in the main, is the attitude of a former judge in Nuremberg—Donnedieu de Vabres (see Donnedieu de Vabres, 'Nuremberg', p. 568. And cf. Donnedieu de Vabres, 'La Théorie des Délits de Droit des Gens en Droit Pénal Interétatique', *op. cit.*, p. 160; Donnedieu de Vabres, 'Le Procès de Nuremberg', *op. cit.*, p. 181). Eustathiades also subscribes to this view (Eustathiades, 'Ordres', pp. 414–415, 421). Maugham states, when discussing Article 8 of the London Charter, that 'the Judgment of the Tribunal had to be worded with care to avoid an appearance of complete disagreement on some of the ill-considered clauses in the Charter' (Maugham, *op. cit.*, p. 107). Greenspan dares to call a spade a spade, saying: 'If the tribunal's statement implies that a person who has no moral choice in carrying out an illegal order is free from guilt, then this implication is contrary... to Article 8 of the tribunal's charter' (Greenspan, *op. cit.*, p. 494).

493. We have seen *supra* (p. 118) that there are some who tend to construe Article 8 in such a way.

in keeping with the correct interpretation of Article 8.

A fortiori, one must reject the more extreme line of interpretation of the Tribunal's statement, according to which the judges, as it were, allowed that obedience to orders constitutes a defence *per se* when no moral choice is possible. In the judgment rendered in the Farben case, it is admittedly proclaimed that

> 'the IMT recognized that . . . an order is a complete defense where it is given under such circumstances as to afford the one receiving it of no other moral choice than to comply therewith'.[494]

But surely this is a far-fetched analysis which has no basis in the actual language used by the International Military Tribunal. Not the fact of obedience to orders, but the possibility of moral choice, guided the Tribunal, and the judgment spelt this out in terms.

There is, in my opinion, no escape from the conclusion that the moral choice test was meant to complement the provision of Article 8 and not to undermine its foundations, and that it does not permit the fact of obedience to orders to be considered for defence purposes.[495]

We have defined the relationship between the moral choice test and the question of obedience to orders, but our problems are not yet ended, for the expression 'moral choice' itself is not conspicuous for absolute lucidity. In what circumstances is a person deprived of the possibility of moral choice? When a person really acts under compulsion, that is, when he is physically coerced by over whelming force to behave in a certain way, he has no choice at all. In any other case, he is in fact confronted with a choice. Even if he acts at the point of the sword and out of fear of imminent death, there is still a choice open to him—commission of the act and life, or omission and death. Life or death is the result of the choice, but the choice is existent nonetheless. Yet in many cases it is impossible, from a moral viewpoint, to expect a person to choose death. From a moral viewpoint the person acts in such cases with no option: we resign ourselves in advance to his taking the course that will save his life. It is, consequently, possible to say that he has no moral choice. Not in every case of compulsion is a person divested of moral choice, for *per definitionem* it is the moral standpoint which here determines when a person has no choice but to submit to force. But, indubitably, in certain cases of compulsion at any rate, moral

494. Farben case, Judgment, *N.M.T.*, vol. 8, p. 1176. Cf. Greenspan, *op. cit.*, p. 498 n. 366; Maunoir, *op. cit.*, p. 277; *L.R.U.N.W.C.C.*, vol. 15 (Digest), p. 157. Cf. also Appleman, *op. cit.*, p. 56; Wechsler, *op. cit.*, pp. 18–19.

495. We shall see below, Part V, how the pronouncement of the International Military Tribunal on the subject of moral choice was construed during the debates of the International Law Commission and the Sixth (Legal) Committee of the General Assembly of the United Nations.

choice is eliminated, and there is no question that the test established by the International Military Tribunal relates to the subject of compulsion. If it is necessary to support this view by adducing authorities, this can easily be done.[496] True enough, the Attorney General in the Eichmann trial, in developing his case, reached the conclusion that moral choice is pertinent only to the question whether orders and actions are manifestly illegal and that it has nothing to do with the subject-matter of compulsion;[497] but this is definitely a misconception.[498] Insofar as there is room for any doubt, it relates to the question whether, apart from certain cases of compulsion, moral choice is also denied a person in other instances, namely, when mistake of fact or law is involved. In another form, we may query whether lack of moral choice is tantamount to lack of *mens rea*. And indeed, although this is not the prevalent view, it should be noted that several writers maintain that the moral choice test, as formulated by the International Military Tribunal, is relevant to the problem of mistake as well as to that of compulsion.[499] This is another occasion where the French version of the judgment may help us properly to understand the Tribunal's words. In this version, as we have seen, two terms—'moral liberty' and 'faculty of choice'—appear in lieu of the sole term 'moral choice' which is used in the English text. The question of 'moral liberty', I think, does not bear upon the issue of mistake: even when a person acts owing to a mistake, his liberty is not affected.[500] But perhaps it can be said that the problem of the 'faculty of choice' relates *inter alia* to the subject of mistake, for, when a person acts owing to a mistake,

496. Among the cases see Farben case, Judgment, *N.M.T.*, vol. 8, pp. 1176, 1179. In the legal literature, see Calvocoressi, *op. cit.*, p. 73; Dix, *op. cit.*, p. 165; Donnedieu de Vabres, 'Nuremberg', pp. 568–569; Eustathiades, 'Ordres', p. 415; Graven, 'Code', p. 375; Graven, 'Crimes', p. 582; Greenspan, *op. cit.*, pp. 493–494, 498; Kranzbühler, *op. cit.*, pp. 123–124; Levontin, *op. cit.*, pp. 259–260; Maunoir, *op. cit.*, pp. 231, 235, 239; Scelle, *op. cit.*, p. 984. Cf. Harris, *op. cit.*, p. 557; Pilloud, *Les Sanctions Pénales dans la Première Convention de Genève (Blessés et Malades) du 12 août 1949* (1952), p. 16; *Red Cross Commentary*, vol. 1, p. 365.

497. Eichmann trial (first instance), Minutes, *op. cit.*, Session No. 112, pp. Z1–Aa1.

498. The judgment of the Israel Supreme Court in the Eichmann trial states that 'it may well be' that by the expression 'moral choice' the International Military Tribunal meant 'the consideration of circumstances which placed the accused under the threat of having to pay with his life in the event of his failure to obey the criminal order', and thus 'the Tribunal recognised that a defence of "constraint" or "necessity" might be advanced' (Eichmann trial (second instance), Judgment, *op. cit.*, p. I34). But the Court explicitly points out that it does not intend to resolve the problem of the correct interpretation of this expression (*ibid.*).

499. See Maunoir, *op. cit.*, p. 239; Scelle, *op. cit.*, pp. 984–985; Starke, *op. cit.*, pp. 370–371. Cf. Dix, *op. cit.*, p. 165; Pilloud, *op. cit.*, p. 16; Wechsler, *op. cit.*, p. 19.

500. This is also Maunoir's opinion (Maunoir, *op. cit.*, p. 239).

his discretion is perverted and consequently his 'faculty of choice' is impaired.[501]

It is obvious, at all events, that if the test established in the judgment for the purpose of relieving a defendant of responsibility is limited to only one aspect of lack of *mens rea*—namely, that of compulsion—then it is incomplete, no matter what is the relationship between that test and the problem of obedience to orders.

So much for the subject of moral choice. Now we ought to ask the question whether the Tribunal endorsed the attitude of the majority of the prosecution and of several defence counsel that the provision of Article 8 should be construed in conformity with the manifest illegality principle and against the background of the basic presupposition, attributed to the authors of the London Charter, that, innately, the evil acts performed by the major war criminals were manifestly illegal. The answer to this question is that neither the manifest illegality principle, nor the personal knowledge principle, was discussed or confirmed in any part of the judgment dealing with discharge from responsibility. The Tribunal touched upon the problems underlying these principles only in the context of the evaluation of punishment, pronouncing in regard to the defendant Keitel:

> 'Superior orders, even to a soldier, cannot be considered in mitigation where crimes as shocking and extensive have been committed consciously, ruthlessly and without military excuse or justification'.[502]

Of course, those who share the view taken by most of the prosecutors and by some of the defence counsel with regard to the meaning of Article 8 may interpret the judgment in harmony with their line of thought. Thus, they may argue that the Tribunal's endorsement of the provision of Article 8, and its ruling that superior orders cannot serve for the purpose of discharge from responsibility, are derived by implication from the manifestly illegal character of the orders at issue in Nuremberg.[503] To prove that the Tribunal

501. See Scelle, *op. cit.*, pp. 984–985. Cf. Alfaro's observation during the debates of the International Law Commission on the Draft Code of Offences against the Peace and Security of Mankind (*I.L.C. Yearbook*, 1951, vol. 1, p. 246).
502. Nuremberg trial, Judgment, *Cmd.* No. 6964, p. 92. See also the statement of the Tribunal with respect to the defendant Jodl (*ibid.*, p. 118). Cf. Donnedieu de Vabres, 'Nuremberg', p. 571; Dunbar, *op. cit.*, p. 253; Lauterpacht – Oppenheim, *International Law*, vol. 2 (7th ed., 1952), p. 570 n. 2; Maunoir, *op. cit.*, pp. 231, 246; Flick case, Extracts from the Closing Statement for the Prosecution, *N.M.T.*, vol. 6, p. 1038; Hostage case, Extracts from Opening Statement of the Prosecution, *N.M.T.*, vol. 11, p. 840.
503. See Fenwick, *op. cit.*, (3rd ed., 1948), pp. 671–672. Cf. Graven, 'Crimes', p. 561; Lawrence, *op. cit.*, pp. 156–157; Morgan, *Assize*, p. 16; Morgan, 'Nuremberg', p. 333.

had in mind manifestly illegal orders, it is possible to lay stress upon its statement that the accused cannot rest their defence on orders relative to 'acts of brutality'—'to kill or torture'—for the unlawfulness of such acts and such orders is generally obvious to all concerned.[504] But such an ingenious interpretation is based more on a dialectical exegesis than on the phraseology actually used by the Tribunal, and it cannot be accepted.[505]

Finally, we are left with the contention based on the *Führerprinzip*. The following passage from the judgment is germane:

> 'Hitler could not make aggressive war by himself. He had to have the co-operation of statesmen, military leaders, diplomats and business men . . . They are not to be deemed innocent because Hitler made use of them, if they knew what they were doing. That they were assigned to their tasks by a dictator does not absolve them from responsibility for their acts. The relation of leader and follower does not preclude responsibility here any more than it does in the comparable tyranny of organised domestic crime'.[506]

In the first part of this passage, the Tribunal in fact adopted the argument put forward by Jackson and Shawcross that Hitler had not acted alone or in a vacuum, that he had needed the Nuremberg defendants and been dependent upon their goodwill. In the last portion of the passage, the judgment proclaims that the fact of the defendants having acted pursuant to the orders of the *Führer* of all other people does not change anything from the outlook of criminal responsibility: the *Führer*, in this respect, is just like any other arch-criminal.[507] Thus the attempt of defence counsel to circumvent the

504. See Biddle, *op. cit.*, p. 12.

505. At least one of the proponents of the manifest illegality principle admits that the International Military Tribunal's statement ought probably to be regarded as a departure from that principle (see Greenspan, *op. cit.*, p. 494).

506. Nuremberg trial, Judgment, *Cmd.* No. 6964, p. 44. See also Ministries case, Judgment, *N.M.T.*, vol. 14, p. 339; Roechling case, Judgment, *N.M.T.*, vol. 14, p. 1104. Cf. Biddle, *op. cit.*, p. 12; Calvocoressi, *op. cit.*, pp. 76–77; T. Gregory, *op. cit.*, p. 548; Parker, *op. cit.*, p. 551; Pompe, *op. cit.*, p. 217; Schafer, *op. cit.*, pp. 141–142.

The official French text of the last portion of this passage is again far from identical to the English version: 'S'ils furent, entre ses mains, des instruments, la conscience qu'ils en eurent empêche de les reconnaître comme innocents. Ils sont responsables de leurs actes, bien que nommés et commandés par un dictateur. En Droit international, aussi bien qu'en Droit interne, les rapports de chef à subordonné n'entraînent pas exemption de la peine' (Procès des Grands Criminels de Guerre devant le Tribunal Militaire International, Nuremberg, Jugement, vol. 1, pp. 237–238).

507. In an article subsequently written, the President of the International Military Tribunal—Judge Lawrence—expressed himself as follows: 'It makes no difference whether sovereign power is vested in a dictator or in a parliament; unless the orders of either are to be controlled by the law of nations there is no security for the nations of the world' (Lawrence, *op. cit.*, p. 156). See also the observation of another Nuremberg judge—Donnedieu de Vabres, 'Nuremberg', p. 572.

provision of Article 8, and to evade the statutory prohibition on utilizing the fact of obedience to orders for defence purposes, was undone.

In summation, let it be said that the judgment of the International Military Tribunal constitutes a powerful fulcrum and an important authority for the doctrine of absolute liability. The Tribunal toed the line of Article 8 of the London Charter, turning neither to the left nor to the right of it, and this is perhaps to be deplored. But at any rate the judgment repudiated the doctrine of *respondeat superior*, and in many respects it may be said that at Nuremberg the doom of this doctrine was sealed.

3. THE TOKYO TRIAL

On 19 January 1946, a Special Proclamation was issued at Tokyo by General MacArthur in his capacity as the Supreme Commander for the Allied Powers in the Far East, and annexed to it was the Charter of the International Military Tribunal for the Far East.[508] Article 6 of this Charter provides as follows:

> 'Neither the official position, at any time, of an accused, nor the fact that an accused acted pursuant to order of his government or of a superior shall, of itself, be sufficient to free such accused from responsibility for any crime with which he is charged, but such circumstances may be considered in mitigation of punishment if the Tribunal determines that justice so requires'.[509]

This Article combines the stipulations of Articles 7 and 8 of the Charter of the European International Military Tribunal, as formulated in London. Jurists, in general, hold the opinion that the provisions of the London and Tokyo Charters in regard to obedience to orders are coincident;[510] but in fact the authors of

508. The text of the Charter appears in *N.M.T.*, vol. 15 (Procedure, etc.), p. 1218. The International Military Tribunal for the Far East was established by General MacArthur in virtue of the provisions of the following documents: the Cairo Declaration of December 1943; the Declaration of Potsdam of July 1945; the Instrument of Surrender of Japan of September 1945; and the resolution of the Moscow Conference of December 1945. In its judgment, the Tokyo Tribunal elaborately examines these instruments. See Tokyo trial, Judgment of the International Military Tribunal for the Far East (mimeographed), pp. 2–6.
509. *N.M.T.*, vol. 15 (Procedure, etc.), p. 1219.
510. See Glaser, *Introduction*, pp. 129, 131 n. 3; Glaser, 'L'Ordre', pp. 325, 330 n. 132; Greenspan, *op. cit.*, p. 490; *History of U.N.W.C.C.*, p. 283; Lauterpacht – Oppenheim, *International Law*, vol. 2 (7th ed., 1952), p. 570 n. 2; Levie, *op. cit.*, p. 464 n. 125; Schick, 'War Criminals', p. 45; Spiropoulos, 'Code (1st Report)', p. 272. Cf. Dunbar, *op. cit.*, p. 249; Eustathiades, 'Ordres', pp. 399–400; Schwelb, 'The United Nations War Crimes Commission', *op. cit.*, p. 374 n. 8.

the Tokyo Charter departed in several respects from the original version of the London Charter. Every such departure must be strictly interpreted, for the very reason that the Far Eastern Charter is generally moulded in the cast of the European Charter. As Horwitz phrased it:

> 'The drafters of the Tokyo Charter took full advantage of the work of their predecessors in London, and to avoid substantial differences in carrying out relating programs, followed as closely as possible the Nuremberg Charter'.[511]

Consequently, we must ascribe the utmost significance to the main divergence in Article 6 of the Tokyo Charter from the course of Article 8 of the London Charter. The divergence is seen in this, that in London it was sweepingly pronounced that the fact of the defendant having acted pursuant to orders shall not bring about exemption of responsibility but in Tokyo it was merely stated that this fact shall not 'of itself be sufficient' to attain the same result. It follows that in Tokyo the fact of obedience to orders was not prevented from contributing, in conjunction with other facts, to discharge from responsibility and was rejected only as a defence *per se*. In effect, the authors of the Tokyo Charter shook off the spell of the Soviet conception regarding obedience to orders, one which left its mark, as we saw, on Article 8, and reverted to the position expressed by the first American drafts of the London Charter.[512] These drafts, it will be recalled, enabled the Tribunal to consider the fact of obedience to orders in defence, but not as an absolute defence or as a defence *per se*. In the wake of them, the authors of the Tokyo Charter prescribed a more flexible, and a more logical, rule than that enunciated in London. It is not the doctrine of absolute liability, but rather the principle which permits all the circumstances of the case to play their parts, that prevails here.[513]

The distinction existing between the provisions of the two Charters

511. Horwitz, 'The Tokyo Trial', *Int. Con.*, No. 465 (1950), pp. 473–584 at p. 486.
512. See *supra*, pp. 109–110, 114. The Tokyo Charter is particularly akin, in this respect, to the American draft of 30 June 1945, which, as mentioned above, was less lucidly formulated than the preceding drafts.
513. Writers usually dismiss Article 6 as self-explanatory and content themselves with remarking, without going into detail, that it excludes the defence of obedience to orders. See Horwitz, *op. cit.*, p. 534; Keenan and Brown, *op. cit.*, p. 130; Schafer, *op. cit.*, p. 141; Spiropoulos, 'Code (1st Report)', p. 272. Glaser, on the other hand, construes Article 6 in the same way that I do, namely, as excluding obedience to orders as a defence *per se*, while at the same time allowing it to be considered an element in the merits of the case (Glaser, *Introduction*, pp. 129, 131 n. 3; Glaser, 'L'Ordre', pp. 325, 330 n. 132). But Glaser maintains—as we have pointed out (*supra*, p. 118)—that Article 8 of the London Charter should also be interpreted in that manner, and he does not notice the textual distinction between the provisions of the two Charters in this regard.

on the subject of obedience to orders was overlooked by the International Military Tribunal sitting in Tokyo. This Tribunal, composed of eleven judges, tried twenty-five major Japanese war criminals and delivered its judgment at the end of 1948. The majority opinion quoted the ruling of the Nuremberg Tribunal on several issues, including the passage relating to the moral choice test, and pronounced as follows:

> 'With the foregoing opinions of the Nuremberg Tribunal and the reasoning by which they are reached this Tribunal is in complete accord... In view of the fact that in all material respects the Charters of this Tribunal and the Nuremberg Tribunal are identical, this Tribunal prefers to express its unqualified adherence to the relevant opinions of the Nuremberg Tribunal rather than by reasoning the matters anew in somewhat different language to open the door to controversy by way of conflicting interpretations of the two statements of opinions'.[514]

To be sure, the judgment did not accurately reflect the legal state of affairs, inasmuch as it proclaimed that 'in all material respects' the two Charters are identical in their provisions concerning the problem of obedience to orders. As a result of this misconception, the Tokyo Tribunal reached an erroneous conclusion to my mind, for it endorsed the moral choice test as formulated in Nuremberg, and hence submitted to the doctrine of absolute liability, failing to notice the place that it ought to have accorded to the fact of obedience to orders in the composition of the defence of the accused under the Tokyo Charter.

To wind up the discussion of the Tokyo trial, we ought to mention that in his dissenting opinion the Dutch judge—Roling—stated, in the context of the subject of crimes against peace, that

> 'No soldier who merely executed government policy should be regarded as a criminal, as guilty of the crime against peace. The duty of an army is to be loyal. Soldiers nor sailors, generals nor admirals should be charged with the crime of initiating or waging an aggressive war, in case they merely performed their military duty of fighting in a war waged by their government'.[515]

In the sequence, Roling explained that an army should not 'meddle in politics' for better or for worse and must obey the instructions of the political leadership to go to war.[516] Although he did not cope

514. Tokyo trial, Judgment of the International Military Tribunal for the Far East, *op. cit.*, p. 26. As for the position of the prosecution in Tokyo, see Keenan and Brown, *op. cit.*, pp. 134–135. Concerning the line taken by the defence, see Appleman, *op. cit.*, p. 249; Horwitz, *op. cit.*, p. 534.
515. Tokyo trial, Excerpts from the Dissenting Opinion of Judge Roling, Sohn, *Cases on United Nations Law* (1956), p. 931 at p. 941.
516. *Ibid.*

directly here with the problem of obedience to orders, and only pronounced judgment that a soldier taking part in an aggressive war commits no offence, his statement is couched in the terms of 'theirs not to reason why'. In fact, this is precisely the argument put forward by several defence counsel in the Nuremberg trial,[517] and it is an offshoot of the doctrine of *respondeat superior.* Once it is claimed that the army is bound blindly to obey the instructions of the political leadership to wage war, the question arises where we must draw the line of *ne plus ultra*. For, if the assumption is that the army consists of unintelligent robots, the soldier may be regarded as immune from responsibility even when he slaughters prisoners-of-war or leads helpless people to the gas chambers. If, on the other hand, the assumption is that a soldier is also an intelligent human being, it is not clear why he should be expected to lose his senses when commanded to fight in an aggressive war. Of course it is desirable that the army do not interfere in political matters. But when the military refuse to wage an aggressive war, the refusal must be regarded through the lens not of politics but of the law.

In this regard, the majority of the judges of Tokyo must be praised for declining to follow the trail blazed by Roling: when they adopted, erroneously, the test established in Nuremberg in the matter of obedience to orders, at least they raised their voice against the doctrine of *respondeat superior.*[518]

517. See *supra*, pp. 136ff.
518. Cf. Fenwick, *op. cit.*, (3rd ed., 1948), p. 671; *S.G. Memorandum*, p. 83.

CHAPTER 2

TRIALS BEFORE NATIONAL COURTS

1. HISTORICAL NOTE

Before we examine the judgments rendered by national courts in the trials of the Second World War criminals, it is perhaps opportune, for the sake of completeness, to call to mind two previous cases bearing upon the subject of obedience to orders in international law.

First, we shall take note of the Wirtz trial, which was conducted in 1865 in the United States.[519] Captain Wirtz served in the army of the Confederacy of the Southern States during the American Civil War, and held the post of commandant of the notorious prisoner-of-war camp at Andersonville, Georgia. At the conclusion of the war, he was brought to trial before a Military Commission in Washington for having maltreated scores of thousands of Federal prisoners, killing some of them, in contravention of the laws of war. One of the pleas of the defence was that the accused had merely obeyed superior orders. The Judge Advocate replied to this contention as follows:

> 'A superior officer cannot order a subordinate to do an illegal act, and if a subordinate obey such an order and disastrous consequences result, both the superior and the subordinate must answer for it'.[520]

The Commission rejected the plea of the defendant: he was convicted and sentenced to death.

Another case deserving of mention here is the Fryatt trial, which took place in 1916 in Germany.[521] Fryatt served in the course of

519. See Daniel, *op. cit.*, pp. 158–159; Dunbar, *op. cit.*, p. 241; Finch, 'Superior Orders', pp. 444–445; Janeczek, *op. cit.*, p. 69; Sack, 'Punishment', pp. 65–66; Sack, 'Superior Order', p. 13; Schick, 'War Criminals', p. 50; Schwarzenberger, 'Inductive Approach', p. 547; Schwarzenberger, *Lawlessness*, p. 63; Schwarzenberger, 'War Crimes', p. 72; Q. Wright, 'War Criminals', *op. cit.*, p. 278 n. 100. Cf. Cave, *op. cit.*, p. xxv; Myerson, *op. cit.*, p. 156; Scott, 'The Trial of the Kaiser', *op. cit.*, pp. 249–250. The Wirtz trial is discussed in detail by Chipman, *The Tragedy of Andersonville, Trial of Captain Henry Wirtz the Prison Keeper* (1911), *passim*.

520. Dunbar, *op. cit.*, p. 241; Finch, 'Superior Orders', p. 444; Janeczek, *op. cit.*, p. 69; Schwarzenberger, *Lawlessness*, p. 63; Schwarzenberger, 'War Crimes', p. 72. Cf. Daniel, *op. cit.*, pp. 158–159.

521. See Garner, *International Law*, vol. 1, pp. 407–413; Scott, 'The Execution of

the First World War as the captain of an unarmed British merchant vessel named the Brussels. During one of the sailings of the Brussels, in 1915, a German submarine signalled to her to stop and identify herself. Instead of obeying the signal, Fryatt turned his vessel's bows towards the submarine, went full speed ahead and tried to ram and sink it; it was all done in accordance with standing directives of the British Admiralty regarding procedure in such cases. The submarine escaped, but Fryatt saved the Brussels. During another voyage, a year later, the ship's luck deserted her: she fell into the hands of German men-of-war, and Fryatt was captured. In July 1916, the Germans brought Fryatt to trial for having committed a war crime, attempting to sink a submarine as a *franc tireur* without being a member of a combatant force. The court-martial convicted Fryatt and sentenced him to death, despite the fact that he had acted in compliance with the instructions of the Admiralty.

This judgment was subjected to very harsh criticism.[522] Garner, for instance, denounced it in hard words, as follows:

> 'When the case is stripped of the subtleties, technicalities, and sophistry with which German logic clothed it, the execution of Captain Fryatt was a plain act of judicial murder'.[523]

In the main, such censorious criticism stems from the basic stand of writers that the act performed by Fryatt did not violate any of the laws of war, and was perfectly legal. But even if, in the view of the German court-martial, Fryatt did commit a war crime, it is quite evident that this was a border-line case and that Fryatt did not, and could not, know of the unlawfulness of his act. When they convicted Fryatt, and sentenced him to death, the German judges consequently did not apply the test that was subsequently established—in respect of German war criminals—by the *Reichsgericht* in the Leipzig trials,[524] and did not inquire, when scrutinizing the act and the instruction of the Admiralty pertaining to it,

> 'if such an order is universally known to everybody, including also the accused, to be without any doubt whatever against the law'.[525]

Captain Fryatt', *A.J.I.L.*, vol. 10 (1916), pp. 865–877, *passim*. Cf. Bellot, 'Punishment', p. 55, note; Bellot, 'War Criminals', vol. 37, p. 21; Finch, 'Superior Orders', p. 442; Janeczek, *op. cit.*, p. 75; Myerson, *op. cit.*, pp. 158–159; Schwarzenberger, *Lawlessness*, p. 64 n. 2; Schwarzenberger, 'War Crimes', pp. 72–73 n. 7.

522. See Bellot, 'War Criminals', vol. 37, p. 21; Garner, *International Law*, vol. 1, p. 413; Myerson, *op. cit.*, pp. 158–159; Scott, 'The Execution of Captain Fryatt', *op. cit.*, p. 877. Cf. Jones, *op. cit.*, p. xxxix.

523. Garner, *International Law*, vol. 1, p. 413.

524. This point is particularly emphasized by Myerson, *op. cit.*, pp. 158–159. Janeczek maintains that the judgment rendered in the Dover Castle case constitutes 'a reversal of the German stand' in the Fryatt trial (Janeczek, *op. cit.*, p. 75).

525. To use the words of the Leipzig Court in the Llandovery Castle case (see

When foreign war criminals were concerned, German tribunals, therefore, found it appropriate to apply the doctrine of absolute liability.[526]

2. THE 'SUBSEQUENT PROCEEDINGS' AT NUREMBERG

A. *The Legal Basis of the Trials*

After the trial of the major Nazi war criminals by virtue of the London Agreement, twelve more trials of some 185 important Nazi criminals were conducted at Nuremberg in the years 1946–1949. These trials—known by the following names: the Einsatzgruppen case,[527] the Farben case,[528] the Flick case,[529] the High Command case,[530] the Hostage case,[531] the Justice case,[532] the Krupp case,[533] the Medical case,[534] the Milch case,[535] the Ministries case,[536] the Pohl case,[537] and the RuSHA case[538]—are called the 'Subsequent Proceedings', to distinguish them from the trial, first in time and first in importance, before the International Military Tribunal

supra, p. 15). Admittedly, the Leipzig Court itself departed, in the Stenger and Crusius case, from the rule established in the Llandovery Castle case, by convicting a defendant who was not found to be personally aware of the unlawfulness of the act performed by him in obedience to an order (see *supra*, pp. 18–19). But, as will be recalled, the Stenger and Crusius case involved an act that, according to all indications, had been manifestly illegal; this was not so in the Fryatt trial.

526. Apparently this doctrine also gained support in the trials of German war criminals conducted before French military tribunals during the First World War. See Garner, 'Articles', pp. 138–139; Garner, *International Law*, vol. 2, pp. 483–484, 487; Garner, 'Punishment', pp. 83–84, 87; Mérignhac, 'Sanction', p. 53; Sack, 'Punishment', p. 67; Sack, 'Superior Order', p. 14; Schwarzenberger, 'Inductive Approach', p. 546 n. 15; Schwarzenberger, *Lawlessness*, p. 64; Schwarzenberger, 'War Crimes', p. 72.
527. Einsatzgruppen case (Case No. 9, Military Tribunal II), *N.M.T.*, vol. 4, pp. 1–596.
528. Farben case (Case No. 6, Military Tribunal VI), *N.M.T.*, vols. 7–8.
529. Flick case (Case No. 5, Military Tribunal IV), *N.M.T.*, vol. 6.
530. High Command case (Case No. 12, Military Tribunal V), *N.M.T.*, vols. 10–11 (pp. 1–756).
531. Hostage case (Case No. 7, Military Tribunal V), *N.M.T.*, vol. 11 (pp. 757ff).
532. Justice case (Case No. 3, Military Tribunal III), *N.M.T.*, vol. 3.
533. Krupp case (Case No. 10, Military Tribunal III), *N.M.T.*, vol. 9.
534. Medical case (Case No. 1, Military Tribunal I), *N.M.T.*, vols. 1–2 (pp. 1–352).
535. Milch case (Case No. 2, Military Tribunal II), *N.M.T.*, vol. 2 (pp. 353ff).
536. Ministries case (Case No. 11, Military Tribunal IV), *N.M.T.*, vols. 12–14 (pp. 1–1096).
537. Pohl case (Case No. 4, Military Tribunal II), *N.M.T.*, vol. 5 (pp. 193ff).
538. RuSHA case (Case No. 8, Military Tribunal I), *N.M.T.*, vols. 4 (pp. 597ff)–5 (pp. 1–192).

in Nuremberg. The Subsequent Proceedings were held by the Military Government of the American Zone of Occupation of Germany, by means of American, that is, national, military tribunals, and what makes these trials singular in character is their legal basis: they were conducted under Law No. 10, promulgated on 20 December 1945 by the Control Council of the four Occupying Powers in Germany.[539] This Law prescribes in Article II(4)(b) as follows:

> 'The fact that any person acted pursuant to the order of his Government or of a superior does not free him from responsibility for a crime, but may be considered in mitigation'.[540]

Already at first sight, one notes the marked similarity between the text of this Article and that of Article 8 of the London Charter, and doubtless the provision of the Charter was borne in mind by the draftsmen of Law No. 10 when they formulated their own rule with regard to obedience to orders. Nevertheless, it is not difficult to point to a number of textual divergencies. The two principal ones are that, on the one hand, the proviso 'if the Tribunal determines that justice so requires', relating to the question of mitigation of punishment and appearing at the end of Article 8, was deleted from Article II(4)(b), and, on the other, the new words 'for a crime' were inserted into the latter Article, where the possibility of discharge from responsibility is excluded.[541] But these distinctions are not of the essence and cannot befog the transparent fact that, intrinsically, the provisions of the two Articles are equivalent. Indeed, writers in general identify the provisions,[542] and in the actual course of the Subsequent Proceedings counsel for the prosecution as well as for the defence pointed out that one corresponds to the other.[543] It is, therefore, interesting to note that,

539. The text of the Law is reproduced in *N.M.T.*, vol. 1, p. XVI. In the French Zone of Occupation of Germany, several trials of war criminals were also held (at Rastatt) by virtue of Law No. 10; the Roechling case is particularly notable (Roechling case, *N.M.T.*, vol. 14, pp. 1097–1143). In the British Zone of Occupation, on the other hand, trials of German war criminals were conducted not under this Law but under a special Royal Warrant. In the Soviet Zone, so far as is known, no trials under Law No. 10 took place either. See on this subject Taylor, *op. cit.*, pp. 136–137.

540. *N.M.T.*, vol. 1, p. XVII.

541. Cf. the text of Article 8, *supra*, p. 117.

542. See Dunbar, *op. cit.*, p. 249; Glaser, *Introduction*, p. 129; Glaser, 'L'Ordre', p. 326, Greenspan, *op. cit.*, pp. 490, 496; *History of U.N.W.C.C.*, p. 283; Knieriem, *op. cit.*, pp. 248, 545 n. 11; Lauterpacht – Oppenheim, *International Law*, vol. 2 (7th ed., 1952), p. 570 n. 2. Cf. Schwelb, 'The United Nations War Crimes Commission', *op. cit.*, p. 374 n. 8.

543. See Flick case, Extracts from the Closing Statement for the Prosecution,

in the Einsatzgruppen case, the judges reached the following conclusion, on the basis of the addition of the words 'for a crime' to Article II(4)(b):

> 'Law No. 10 does not invalidate the excuse of superior orders'.[544]

The explanation given in the judgment for this statement is that, when Article II(4)(b) rejects the possibility of discharge from responsibility on account of obedience to orders, it relates only to a 'crime', and not to every ordinary 'act'.[545]

I must confess that the meaning of these enigmatic words escapes me.[546] If the Tribunal wished to declare that the Article pertains not to ordinary offences, but merely to grave offences rated as crimes, then it should be noted that in any event all the provisions of Law No. 10, like those of the London Charter, concern crimes, namely, crimes against peace, war crimes and crimes against humanity.[547] The *materia* of Article II(4)(b) is consequently the same as that of the whole Law, and it is futile to attempt to divine in the use of the term crime in this particular Article a will on the part of the legislators to curtail its scope. On the other hand, if the Tribunal intended to state that the Article indeed relates to offences of all kinds—that is to say, unlawful acts—but to them only, and not to other acts—that is to say, lawful acts—we should put the question why the comment was made at all: anyway, when lawful acts are involved, there is no room for criminal prosecution, and hence there was no reason to exclude, in advance, an unnecessary defence against a non-existent indictment. The judgment in the Einsatzgruppen case itself proclaimed:

> 'Unless it is established that the deed in question is a crime, then naturally there needs to be no explanation for its commission'.[548]

How, then, does this observation conform to the conclusion that Law No. 10 does not deny the validity of the defence of obedience

N.M.T., vol. 6, p. 1038; Justice case, Opening Statement for the Prosecution, *N.M.T.*, vol. 3, p. 90; Ministries case, Closing Statement for the Prosecution, *N.M.T.*, vol. 14, p. 84; RuSHA case, Extract from the Closing Statement of the Prosecution, *N.M.T.*, vol. 5, p. 50; RuSHA case, Opening Statement for Defendant Greifelt (by Haensel), *N.M.T.*, vol. 4, p. 699.

544. Einsatzgruppen case, Judgment, *N.M.T.*, vol. 4, p. 485.
545. *Ibid.*, p. 486.
546. Parenthetically we may point out that Article 6 of the Tokyo Charter also precludes relieving the defendant of responsibility 'for any crime with which he is charged'. See *supra*, p. 156.
547. Law No. 10 is entitled: 'Punishment of Persons Guilty of War Crimes, Crimes against Peace and against Humanity' (*N.M.T.*, vol. 1, p. XVI).
548. Einsatzgruppen case, Judgment, *N.M.T.*, vol. 4, p. 486.

to orders? We must leave this riddle unanswered.[549]

In my opinion, the use of the words 'for a crime' in Article II(4)(b) neither adds to the substance of its provision nor detracts from it, and the Article ought to be construed in precisely the same way as Article 8 of the London Charter. As a result, we should regard Law No. 10 as excluding any possibility of taking the fact of obedience to orders into account in the context of any defence whatever (in contradistinction to assessment of punishment).

B. *The Arguments of the Defence*

In one form or another, the plea of obedience to orders was raised by the defence in each of the Subsequent Proceedings at Nuremberg.[550] In essence, it may be said that the crushing defeat suffered by the defence in the trial of the major war criminals, where the subject of obedience to orders is concerned, did not discourage defence counsel in the Subsequent Proceedings. Some of them tried to follow the trodden paths which ended, in the main Nuremberg trial, in an impasse; others sought new lines of approach; but most endeavoured to reach the desired goal of attaining the acquittal of the defendants on the basis of obedience to orders. The explicit provision of Article II (4)(b) did not halt this trend: several defence counsel simply determined to ignore it, or, alternatively, contest it; others contrived all sorts of ingenious ideas to remove this stumbling-block from their path.

Many defence counsel contended that the subordinate need not occupy himself too much with investigating the lawfulness of orders issued to him, for he is entitled to assume that they are without the least blemish of illegality,[551] and that their clients had not, and could not have, been aware of the unlawful character of the orders which they had obeyed.[552] Thus, in effect, they subscribed to the

549. With regard to the attitude of the Tribunal in this case towards the doctrine of *respondeat superior*, see below, Section D.

550. Cf. *N.M.T.*, Note, Pohl case, vol. 5, p. 786; Appleman, *op. cit.*, pp. 145, 167, 187, 311 n. 64.

551. See Pohl case, Closing Statement for Defendant Pohl (by Seidl), *N.M.T.*, vol. 5, p. 913.

552. See Flick case, Closing Statement for Defendant Flick (by Dix), *N.M.T.*, vol. 6, p. 1153; High Command case, Extracts from Closing Statement for Defendant Warlimont (by Leverkuehn), *N.M.T.*, vol. 11, p. 378; High Command case, Extracts from the Closing Brief for Defendant Roques (by Tipp), *N.M.T.*, vol. 11, p. 427; Medical case, Extract from the Final Plea for Defendant Brack (by Froeschmann), *N.M.T.*, vol. 1, p. 958; Medical case, Extracts from the Final Plea for Defendant Fischer (by Seidl), *N.M.T.*, vol. 1, pp. 961–963; Milch case, Closing Statement of the Defense (by Bergold), *N.M.T.*, vol. 2, pp. 746–747; Pohl case, Opening Statement for Defendant Pook (by Ratz), *N.M.T.*, vol. 5, p. 289; Pohl case, Closing Statement for Defendant Pohl (by Seidl), *N.M.T.*, vol. 5, pp. 916–917.

personal knowledge principle, as the rule that should be applied by the Tribunals in the Subsequent Proceedings. Particularly instructive in this regard is the argument put forward by Bergold, counsel for the defence in the Milch case. Bergold tried to exculpate the accused, a former Field-Marshal in the *Luftwaffe*, from the guilt of forcible employment of prisoners-of-war, and of civilians from Nazi-occupied territories, in the military industry of the Third Reich. With that purpose in mind, he submitted as follows:

> 'the defendant had the right to believe the information given to him by his superior office that employment of foreign manpower and of prisoners of war was admissible'.[553]

Here one must be careful in analyzing the plea of defence: Bergold did not claim that the defendant had used forced labour in pursuance of an order; his allegation was that Milch had acted on his own initiative after checking with superior authorities the legality of this course of action.[554] Thus Bergold, in point of fact, answered in the affirmative the question that we posed above,[555] whether a subordinate is entitled to rely on the expertness of his commander in matters of law, not only when the commander's words can be classified as a real order but even when they ought to be regarded as a mere statement of opinion. To the query of the Presiding Judge, whether ignorance of the law constitutes a defence,[556] Bergold responded:

> 'Everybody must inquire what the law is, but if his superior authorities give him certain information, he can rely on that'.[557]

When asked, further, whether a delinquent should also be relieved of responsibility in the case that he commits the offence in reliance on the erroneous opinion of his lawyer regarding the lawfulness of the act,[558] Bergold replied in the negative, saying:

> 'The client's lawyer is not sufficient. The authority must be a government official'.[559]

To my mind, this approach is wanting in logical consistency: if a soldier is entitled to rely on the legal opinion of his superiors, this

553. Milch case, Closing Statement of the Defense (by Bergold), *N.M.T.*, vol. 2, p. 747.
554. See *ibid.*, pp. 746–747.
555. See *supra*, p. 35.
556. Milch case, Intervention by Presiding Judge Toms, *N.M.T.*, vol. 2, p. 747.
557. Milch case, Closing Statement of the Defense (by Bergold), *N.M.T.*, vol. 2, p. 747.
558. Milch case, Intervention by Presiding Judge Toms, *N.M.T.*, vol. 2, p. 747.
559. Milch case, Closing Statement of the Defense (by Bergold), *N.M.T.*, vol. 2, p. 747.

must needs be an outcome of a hidden presumption, be it either a *praesumptio juris* or a *praesumptio juris et de jure*, that every superior is an expert in relation to his subordinates in the field of the laws of war. If such is the case, if the subordinate is allowed to rely on the legal expertness of his superior, *a fortiori* he must be permitted to rely on the advice of real specialists in questions of law—genuine experts, and not experts by dint of presumptions and suppositions.[560] And insofar as discharge from responsibility is acceptable on the strength of reliance on the legal erudition of another person, it flows from a recognition of the principle *ignorantia juris excusat.* Bergold could, perhaps, have formed a sensible line of defence, had he entrenched himself behind the parapet of mistake of law. But when he insisted that the hierarchical subordination factor, and no other, constituted the cornerstone in the construction of his defence, Bergold undermined the foundations of his own pleading.

It should further be noted that Bergold conceded that, when a commander opines murder, for instance, to be a lawful act, the subordinate cannot count on it, for the unlawfulness of this misdeed is obviously clear to one and all.[561] We may infer from this proposition that Bergold recognized the validity of the manifest illegality principle, as a secondary supplement to the personal knowledge principle. Another defence counsel—Haensel in the RuSHA case—went beyond this point and supported the manifest illegality principle in its own right, unlinked to the personal knowledge principle, saying:

> 'The command in itself... is... never a justification of obviously criminal actions'.[562]

We must now enquire how the defence reconciled its support for the personal knowledge and the manifest illegality principles with the express provision of Article II(4)(b). There are several answers to the question. One defence counsel—Seidl—developed, in both the Medical and the Pohl cases, the conception that the Tribunals should apply to the accused, not the stipulations of Law No. 10 or the principles of general international law, but the rules of the law which had been applicable to them at the time of the commission of the offences, that is to say, German national law.[563] And the rules

560. See *supra*, p. 36.
561. Milch case, Closing Statement of the Defense (by Bergold), *N.M.T.*, vol. 2, p. 748.
562. RuSHA case, Opening Statement for Defendant Greifelt (by Haensel), *N.M.T.*, vol. 4, p. 700.
563. Medical case, Extracts from the Final Plea for Defendant Fischer (by Seidl), *N.M.T.*, vol. 1, pp. 961–963, 968; Pohl case, Closing Statement for Defendant Pohl (by Seidl), *N.M.T.*, vol. 5, pp. 915–917.

of this law, as reflected in the Leipzig trials, tally with the personal knowledge and the manifest illegality principles.[564]

As this approach of total disrespect for the provisions of the law from which the authority of the Tribunals was derived did not appear to be very promising, Seidl tried his luck with an alternative argument. If Article II(4)(b) were applicable, said he, then it ought to be interpreted as denying to the fact of obedience to orders the status of a defence *per se* only, and not as entirely divesting this fact of all legal significance and relevance in the context of exemption from responsibility.[565] In Seidl's opinion:

> 'The provision merely states that the fact of such an order in itself does not exempt from responsibility for a crime but, by no means, does it preclude the possibility of this fact, together with other facts, being of importance in this question'.[566]

Had this statement been meant to give expression to the principles of general international law obtaining in the field of obedience to orders, one could well endorse it. I have suggested above that under general international law obedience to orders must be rejected as a defence *per se* but may be taken into account in conjunction with the other circumstances of the case within the ambit of another defence, namely, that based on lack of *mens rea*. Seidl, however, sought to describe and construe here not general principles but a special provision contained in a particular statutory Law. His statement ignored the fact that, notwithstanding the general principles and unlike the Tokyo Charter[567] but in line with the London Charter, Law No. 10 does not prescribe that obedience to orders 'of itself' is insufficient to relieve a defendant of responsibility. What Article II(4)(b) does set forth is that the fact of obedience to orders—not necessarily 'of itself'—does not free from responsibility, and that is all. This has to be regarded, in conformity with the interpretation given above to Article 8 of the London Charter, as an exclusion of any possibility of taking the fact of obedience to orders into consideration in any form of defence whatsoever for the purposes of acquittal.

Seidl's alternative argument is related to the following contention, put forward by another counsel—Dix—in the Flick case:

564. See *supra*, Part I, Chapter 2.
565. Medical case, Extracts from the Final Plea for Defendant Fischer (by Seidl), *N.M.T.*, vol. 1, p. 968; Pohl case, Closing Statement for Defendant Pohl (by Seidl), *N.M.T.*, vol. 5, p. 917.
566. Pohl case, Closing Statement for Defendant Pohl (by Seidl), *N.M.T.*, vol. 5, p. 917.
567. See *supra*, p. 156.

> 'This statute cannot mean and concern ... the act of a human being who acted free from guilt, because he neither was aware of the criminal nature, that is he was not conscious of its illegality, or because he had acted under physical compulsion'.[568]

This statement has to be understood in the sense that the provision of Article II(4)(b) is applicable only in the event that a pure plea of obedience to orders, not including the ingredients of mistake of law and compulsion, is raised, whereas, if the defendant may avail himself of the plea of compulsion or mistake, he ought to be relieved of responsibility. But, when Dix declared that Article II(4)(b) cannot concern the action of a person who acted free from guilt—having been impelled by mistake or compulsion—he ignored the conception underlying the doctrine of absolute liability, as reflected in the Article. Of course, neither the doctrine nor the Article seeks to preclude the discharge of an innocent man from responsibility. But the question is how we know that the man is really innocent. Law No. 10 lays down the rule that no one shall be relieved of responsibility on account of obedience to orders. Hence, if the defence of an accused, whether it be the defence of mistake or of compulsion, is contingent upon the factor of obedience to orders, the Law rejects it and proclaims that the accused is by no means innocent. On the other hand, if the defendant may anyway invoke an admissible defence of mistake or compulsion without any dependence upon the element of obedience to orders, the provision of the Law will not stand in his way, for the Law does not contest the fact that such a person is innocent. It transpires that the correct interpretation of Article II(4)(b) is entirely different from that submitted by Dix: the Article is applicable whenever the plea of obedience to orders is raised, no matter whether such plea is a pure one or is interlinked with another plea; the Article is inapplicable only in the case where a pure plea of mistake or compulsion is involved. This may not be just, but it is the Law nevertheless.

Another counsel for the defence who had a try at an argument with similar features was Ratz. He propounded, in the course of the Pohl case, that Article II(4)(b) is only concerned with shifting the *onus probandi* from the shoulders of the prosecution to the shoulders of the defence. In accordance with this assertion, the Article was only meant to provide that, if he is to extricate himself from the jaws of conviction, it is incumbent upon the accused to bear the burden of proof that he carried out an illegal order because of,

568. Flick case, Closing Statement for Defendant Flick (by Dix), *N.M.T.*, vol. 6, p. 1153.

for example, mistake of law. Ratz formulated it in the following way:

> 'it is thereby unquestionably not intended that the subordinate is automatically responsible in the eyes of criminal law; this would be contrary to all legal principles. Obviously only the burden of proof is thereby put on the subordinate; it is up to him to prove to what extent he is not responsible; for instance, that he was unable to recognize the order as unlawful and criminal'.[569]

This is admittedly an interesting and original contention, but, despite Ratz' absolute conviction of its veracity, it is untenable. In whatever way Article II(4)(b) is studied, one cannot find in it a trace of the idea of shifting the burden of proof from one side of the fence of litigation to the other. Ratz's attitude cannot, therefore, be of help to the defendant under Law No. 10, any more than the approach of Seidl or Dix.

Returning now to Dix's argument, we should bring out what has been kept in the background until now, namely, that it goes beyond the range of mistake of law, the subject of our discussion heretofore, and gets into another field of defence, that of compulsion. Indeed, the theme of compulsion deserves a place of honour in the whole line of defence in the Subsequent Proceedings. Actually, the defence attempted to utilize the buckler of compulsion in two different ways to parry the thrust of the prosecution.

The first way, followed by many counsel, was to advocate a defence based on compulsion—mainly, and more particularly, that of necessity—as a defence in itself, which spreads its canopy over the accused, and enables them to avoid the gathering storm-clouds of Article II(4)(b) and gain acquittal.[570] Within the context of this plea, the defence contended that the accused had acted perforce and without choice, bowing in submission to the awe-inspiring Nazi tyranny; and as they could not have been expected to die as martyrs for the sake of morality, they must be freed from responsibility.[571] The defence equally claimed that the accused had been no more than tiny cogs revolving passively in the huge machine of

569. Pohl case, Opening Statement for Defendant Pook (by Ratz), *N.M.T.*, vol. 5, p. 289.
570. Cf. *L.R.U.N.W.C.C.*, Notes, Krupp trial, vol. 10, p. 175.
571. See Farben case, Closing Statement for All Defendants on the Evidence on the Charges of Crimes against the Peace (by Metzler), *N.M.T.*, vol. 8, pp. 985–986; Flick case, Opening Statement for Defendant Flick (by Dix), *N.M.T.*, vol. 6, p. 115; Flick case, Closing Statement for Defendant Flick (by Dix), *N.M.T.*, vol. 6, pp. 1153–1154, 1156; High Command case, Extract from the Closing Brief for Defendant Kuechler (by Behling), *N.M.T.*, vol. 11, pp. 398–399; High Command case, Extract from the Closing Brief for Defendant Hoth (by Mueller-Torgow), *N.M.T.*, vol. 11, pp. 407–408; RuSHA case, Opening Statement for Defendant Greifelt (by Haensel), *N.M.T.*, vol. 4, p. 700.

the Third Reich.[572] But as for the element of obedience to orders, counsel who chose to follow this line of defence preferred to mention it in a still small voice, lest their plea be shattered against the bulwark of Article II(4)(b). Their principal aim was to neutralize the provision of that Article. As one of the defence counsel in the High Command case—Keller—phrased it:

> 'The prohibition to appeal to superior orders, as stipulated by the Control Council Law, does not exclude ... the claim of *necessity*'.[573]

The second line of approach taken by the defence was to accentuate the factor of compulsion while expounding the argument that an accused who had obeyed orders should not incur criminal responsibility.[574] An illustrative expression of this proposition was given by Gawlik in the Einsatzgruppen case:

> 'It has generally been recognized that it is unjust to punish a person who acted in compliance with an order. For, if he had refused to comply with the order, the subordinate would probably have been shot'.[575]

To the extent that the defence relied upon the element of compulsion only as a reason for relieving the recipient of illegal orders of responsibility, and not as a defence in itself, it simply gave currency to the doctrine of *respondeat superior* as explained by Renault and those proceeding in his wake.[576] And, indeed, this doctrine, in all its respects, gained a great deal of support on the part of defence counsel. Some of them reiterated the argument that strict discipline and blind obedience to orders constitute the mainstay of the military régime.[577] Others relied on the writings of

572. See RuSHA case, Opening Statement for Defendant Greifelt (by Haensel), *N.M.T.*, vol. 4, p. 700; RuSHA case, Extracts from the Closing Statement for Defendant Hofmann (by Schwarz), *N.M.T.*, vol. 5, p. 27.
573. High Command case, Extracts from the Closing Brief for Defendant Lehmann (by Keller), *N.M.T.*, vol. 11, p. 434. See also Farben case, Closing Statement for All Defendants on the Evidence on the Charges of Crimes against the Peace (by Metzler), *N.M.T.*, vol. 8, p. 985; Flick case, Closing Statement for Defendant Flick (by Dix), *N.M.T.*, vol. 6, pp. 1153–1154, 1156–1157; High Command case, Extract from the Closing Brief for Defendant Hoth (by Mueller-Torgow), *N.M.T.*, vol. 11, p. 407.
574. See Einsatzgruppen case, Extract from the Closing Statement for Defendant Naumann (by Gawlik), *N.M.T.*, vol. 4, pp. 332, 338; Einsatzgruppen case, Opening Statement for Defendant Blobel (by Heim), *N.M.T.*, vol. 4, pp. 86–87. Cf. *N.M.T.*, Introductory Note, Einsatzgruppen case, vol. 4, p. 222.
575. Einsatzgruppen case, Extract from the Closing Statement for Defendant Naumann (by Gawlik), *N.M.T.*, vol. 4, p. 332.
576. See *supra*, p. 51.
577. See Einsatzgruppen case, Extract from the Closing Statement for Defendant Naumann (by Gawlik), *N.M.T.*, vol. 4, pp. 334–335; Einsatzgruppen case, Final Statement by Defendant Naumann, *N.M.T.*, vol. 4, p. 394; High Command case, Extract from the Closing Brief for Defendant Hollidt (by Fritsch), *N.M.T.*,

learned scholars, primarily of Oppenheim, and enumerated those instruments, explored in the previous part of this study, which, in their view, demonstrated that obedience to orders constitutes an automatic and *a priori* defence *per se* against criminal prosecution.[578] Finally, there were those who voiced the doctrine of *respondeat superior* without making any attempt to base themselves on great names or detailed expositions.[579]

There is nothing new in the endorsement of the doctrine of *respondeat superior*, and we have already analyzed in previous chapters the authorities derived from the theory as well as the practice of international law, as put forward by defence counsel. It is of interest, though, that the propagation of this doctrine took place here before Tribunals supposed to apply Article II(4)(b), which utterly negates that very doctrine. Several defence counsel did not even endeavour to argue that their proposition was in conformity with the provision of Law No. 10, but demanded instead that the Tribunals disregard that provision as being diametrically opposed to the rules of positive international law, reflected, in their opinion, in the doctrine of *respondeat superior*.[580] Laternser maintained, in the Hostage case, that

> 'the Court is only bound by international law... The general international law, which... recognized the plea of superior orders as effective, may only be revised by general conventions or by an administration of law based upon

vol. 11, pp. 414–415. It is of interest that defence counsel who subscribed to the personal knowledge principle—rather than the doctrine of *respondeat superior*—also laid great stress upon the importance of discipline, and struck the chord of the gravity of the dilemma confronting the soldier who receives an order to perform an unlawful act. See and cf. Flick case, Closing Statement for Defendant Flick (by Dix), *N.M.T.*, vol. 6, p. 1154; High Command case, Extracts from Closing Statement for Defendant Warlimont (by Leverkuehn), *N.M.T.*, vol. 11, pp. 377–378; Medical case, Extracts from the Final Plea for Defendant Fischer (by Seidl), *N.M.T.*, vol. 1, p. 969; Pohl case, Closing Statement for Defendant Pohl (by Seidl), *N.M.T.*, vol. 5, pp. 917–918; RuSHA case, Opening Statement for Defendant Greifelt (by Haensel), *N.M.T.*, vol. 4, p. 700.

578. See Einsatzgruppen case, Opening Statement for Defendant Ohlendorf (by Aschenauer), *N.M.T.*, vol. 4, pp. 64–65; Einsatzgruppen case, Extract from the Closing Statement for Defendant Naumann (by Gawlik), *N.M.T.*, vol. 4, pp. 330–339; Hostage case, Opening Statement for Defendant List (by Laternser), *N.M.T.*, vol. 11, pp. 857–862; Hostage case, Extracts from Closing Statement for Defendant List (by Laternser), *N.M.T.*, vol. 11, pp. 1224–1225.

579. See and cf. Farben case, Closing Statement for All Defendants on Fundamental Issues of Law (by Wahl), *N.M.T.*, vol. 8, p. 902; Medical case, Final Plea for Defendant Brandt (by Servatius), *N.M.T.*, vol. 2, p. 127; Ministries case, Opening Statement for Defendant Stuckart (by Stackelberg), *N.M.T.*, vol. 12, p. 318.

580. See Einsatzgruppen case, Extract from the Closing Statement for Defendant Naumann (by Gawlik), *N.M.T.*, vol. 4, p. 329; Hostage case, Opening Statement for Defendant List (by Laternser), *N.M.T.*, vol. 11, p. 864.

general recognition, not, however, by unilateral acts of the victor nations which are directed against a conquered nation'.[581]

And Gawlik urged upon the Tribunal in the Einsatzgruppen case:

'The Charter and Control Council Law No. 10...can only be applied inasmuch as they coincide with the hitherto recognized rules of international law'.[582]

It can be readily perceived, however, that such a radical contention, like the one referred to above in respect of the need to apply German national law to the defendants, could not inspire those who formulated it with more than a flicker of hope of success.

To surmount the obstacle presented by Article II(4)(b), many defence counsel, either in their primary pleading, or in a secondary, or alternative, one, proposed to benefit from the *Führerprinzip* prevalent in Nazi Germany[583] which had already been unavailingly advanced by their colleagues in the trial of the major war criminals.[584] As will be recalled, it was argued in that trial that the statutory prohibition in the London Charter concerning the consideration of obedience to orders for the purposes of discharge from responsibility relates only to ordinary orders and not to the exceptional orders of the *Führer*. A parallel argument was invoked in the Subsequent Proceedings with regard to Law No. 10; as one of the defence counsel—Mueller-Torgow—put it in the High Command case:

'the provisions of Control Council Law No. 10 cannot include so-called "orders" from Hitler at all'.[585]

This artificial construction had already been rejected by the International Military Tribunal,[586] but the very effort to evade the application of Article II(4)(b) in the special case of obedience to

581. Hostage case, Opening Statement for Defendant List (by Laternser), *N.M.T.*, vol. 11, p. 864.
582. Einsatzgruppen case, Extract from the Closing Statement for Defendant Naumann (by Gawlik), *N.M.T.*, vol. 4, p. 329.
583. See *ibid.*, pp. 335–336; High Command case, Extracts from the Closing Brief for Defendant Lehmann (by Keller), *N.M.T.*, vol. 11, pp. 433–434; High Command case, Extract from the Closing Brief for Defendant Hoth (by Mueller-Torgow), *N.M.T.*, vol. 11, pp. 406–407; Medical case, Extract from the Final Plea for Defendant Brack (by Froeschmann), *N.M.T.*, vol. 1, pp. 959–960; Medical case, Extracts from the Final Plea for Defendant Fischer (by Seidl), *N.M.T.*, vol. 1, pp. 964–968. This contention was also submitted, and explained, by the defendants themselves in testifying in the Pohl case (*N.M.T.*, vol. 5, pp. 802–804).
584. See *supra*, pp. 140ff.
585. High Command case, Extract from the Closing Brief for Defendant Hoth (by Mueller-Torgow), *N.M.T.*, vol. 11, p. 407.
586. See *supra*, p. 155.

the *Führer*'s orders signifies, at least, a sober recognition of its validity and import in general.

We shall conclude our discussion of the defence arguments in the Subsequent Proceedings by pointing out that counsel did not struggle only for absolute discharge of their clients from responsibility, but also, as a minimal demand, for mitigation of their punishment in accordance with the possibility explicitly provided for by Article II(4)(b).[587]

C. *The Arguments of the Prosecution*

In correspondence with the attitude of most of the prosecutors in the trial of the major war criminals and in line with the approach of several defence counsel in that trial, as well as in the Subsequent Proceedings, the prosecution in these proceedings gave voice on more than one occasion to the manifest illegality principle or the personal knowledge principle, as the acceptable solution of the problem of obedience to orders under international law. Possibly, this phenomenon may be attributed to the fact that the helmsman of the prosecution in the Subsequent Proceedings was Taylor, whose previous assignment had been with the American prosecution in the main Nuremberg trial.[588]

The manifest illegality principle was demonstrably embraced by the prosecution in its closing statement, in the Einsatzgruppen case, which included the following passage:

> 'Normally, a subordinate is entitled to assume that orders issued to him by his superiors are lawful and do not require him to commit crimes in execution thereof; and we cannot hold the subordinates responsible to make careful inquiry or elaborate research into the background of the order to make sure that it is in fact lawful. But this general presumption for the benefit of subordinates has no application where, on its face, the order is palpably criminal'.[589]

In the continuation, the prosecution relied on the judgment rendered at Leipzig in the Llandovery Castle case, and observed that the principles set forth in that judgment were applicable to the case under discussion.[590] The question arises now whether one may detect in this proposition of the prosecution some sort of a reservation about Article II(4)(b), like the exception taken by the defence. To my mind, this can hardly be assumed, for in many

587. See and cf. *N.M.T.*, Introductory Note, Medical case, vol. 1, p. 957; Pohl case, Opening Statement for Defendant Pook (by Ratz), *N.M.T.*, vol. 5, p. 289; RuSHA case, Opening Statement for Defendant Griefelt (by Haensel), *N.M.T.*, vol. 4, pp. 699–700.
588. See *supra*, note 405.
589. Einsatzgruppen case, Closing Statement of the Prosecution, *N.M.T.*, vol. 4, p. 376.
590. *Ibid.*

instances the prosecution, in the Subsequent Proceedings in general, and in the Einsatzgruppen case in particular, recurrently and patently associated itself with the provision of that Article.[591] The only construction of the arguments of the prosecution which makes them compatible with one another is that which, in keeping with the interpretation given above[592] to the line of thought of the prosecution in the trial of the major war criminals, regards the endorsement of the manifest illegality principle as an historical explanation of Article II(4)(b). In other words, the prosecution bowed to the provision contained in the Article but at the same time confined its applicability to those specific acts enumerated in Law No. 10, which, as it were, had been looked upon by the legislators as *a priori* unlawful. Pursuant to this view, the Article does not, in the opinion of the prosecution as cited, reflect the general rule of international law (that is, the rule which allows the subordinate to assume in advance, without any close and careful scrutiny in fact, that the orders of his superior are perfectly legal and furnishes the subordinate with a defence accordingly), but rather the exception to the rule (which denies that defence to the subordinate when manifestly illegal orders are involved). And indeed, the prosecution in the Einsatzgruppen case expressly stated that the orders there in issue were manifestly illegal and that the provision of Article II(4)(b) ought to be applied *literatim* to the defendants.[593]

The personal knowledge principle gained support, on the part of the prosecution, in several cases.[594] As was expressed in the closing statement in the Flick case:

> 'The military profession puts a high premium on discipline and obedience and usually does not permit subordinates to question the orders of their superiors. But it is well established under military law... that a subordinate is not bound and in fact is bound not to obey an order which he knows directs the commission of a criminal act'.[595]

591. See *ibid.*, pp. 376–377; Einsatzgruppen case, Opening Statement of the Prosecution, *N.M.T.*, vol. 4, p. 53; Flick case, Extracts from the Closing Statement for the Prosecution, *N.M.T.*, vol. 6, p. 1038; Hostage case, Extracts from Opening Statement of the Prosecution, *N.M.T.*, vol. 11, pp. 839–840; Justice case, Opening Statement of the Prosecution, *N.M.T.*, vol. 3, p. 90; Ministries case, Closing Statement for the Prosecution, *N.M.T.*, vol. 14, p. 84; RuSHA case, Extracts from the Closing Statement of the Prosecution, *N.M.T.*, vol. 5, p. 50.
592. See *supra*, p. 129.
593. Einsatzgruppen case, Closing Statement of the Prosecution, *N.M.T.*, vol. 4, pp. 376–377.
594. See and cf. Farben case, Closing Statement for the Prosecution, *N.M.T.*, vol. 8, p. 1045; Flick case, Extracts from the Closing Statement for the Prosecution, *N.M.T.*, vol. 6, p. 1038; High Command case, Extracts from the Closing Statement of the Prosecution, *N.M.T.*, vol. 11, p. 370.
595. Flick case, Extracts from the Closing Statement for the Prosecution, *N.M.T.*, vol. 6, p. 1038.

Here again it may be assumed that the prosecution meant to say that Article II(4)(b) had been formulated the way it had because the legislators held that those charged with the crimes listed in Law No. 10 must have been aware of the unlawfulness of their acts.

Even so, such an historical explanation of Article II(4)(b), predicated on either the personal knowledge principle or the manifest illegality principle, is groundless, just as there is no foundation for the similar exposition proposed with regard to Article 8 of the London Charter. If these were really the intentions of the authors of Law No. 10, they most certainly succeeded in concealing and disguising them in a manner that defies comprehension. We cannot, therefore, accept the attitude of the prosecution towards this question.

We shall now proceed to examine the reply of the prosecution to the general plea of compulsion, upon which the defence, as we have observed, laid stress in a variety of ways. First, we should point out the unconditional and incisive repudiation by the prosecution of the conception which looks upon the soldier as some kind of a puppet forced to comply with the instructions of whoever is pulling the strings. Thus, in its closing statement in the High Command case, the prosecution maintained that

> 'This argument of military immunity, which would reduce military men to a sort of sub-human status as men incapable of exercising moral judgment on their behalf—no more answerable to the laws of God and man than animals and small children—has, fortunately, found no acceptance in international penal law'.[596]

Secondly, it is worth mentioning that the prosecution warned against the confusion of the defence of compulsion with that of obedience to orders; or as it expressed this idea in the Farben case:

> 'The defense of necessity or compulsion is closely related to, but by no means identical with, the so-called defense of "superior orders"'.[597]

It is implied in the contention of the prosecution that, even though it vehemently rejected the defence of obedience to orders—at least insofar as concerns orders that are known, personally or universally, to be unlawful—it did not disavow the defence founded on compulsion.[598] In the Ministries case, the prosecution conceded that, especially in trials of war criminals, it is not easy to distinguish between the questions of compulsion and obedience to orders, which

596. High Command case, Extract from the Closing Statement of the Prosecution, *N.M.T.*, vol. 10, p. 336.
597. Farben case, Closing Statement for the Prosecution, *N.M.T.*, vol. 8, p. 1044.
598. With regard to the defence of compulsion, see particularly Flick case, Extracts from the Closing Statement for the Prosecution, *N.M.T.*, vol. 6, pp. 1038–1040. Cf. Eustathiades, 'Ordres', p. 418.

are frequently tackled together in the cases.[599] But it emphasized that the defence of compulsion is subject to definite limitations and any departure from them is apt, in effect, to transform obedience to orders, as well, into a defence, which is improper and anyhow against the letter and the spirit of Article II(4)(b).[600] In the cases under discussion in the Subsequent Proceedings, claimed the prosecution, there was no factual basis for the application of the defence of compulsion, as the accused had had discretion and they had acted out of volition and voluntarily.[601] As the prosecution phrased it in the Farben case in respect of the defence of necessity:

> 'We believe that this defense, assuming its legal validity, is based upon demonstrably false factual assumptions as far as these defendants are concerned, and that the evidence in this case completely cuts the ground from under such a plea'.[602]

We are faced here not with a denial of the legal principle in issue, but rather with a legal admission and a factual rebuttal.

The prosecution also argued against the possibility, expressly provided for in Article II(4)(b), of mitigating the punishment of the defendants in the Subsequent Proceedings, for they had acted with willing hearts, with callous souls and with open eyes, not going against the grain, or groping in the dark, or blundering by inadvertence.[603]

D. *The Judgments*

The Tribunals in the Subsequent Proceedings did their best to display that the provisions of general international law guided their footsteps, so that the defendants were accorded a just trial and their responsibility was established in keeping with objective criteria applicable to victors and vanquished alike. The leading principle

599. Ministries case, Closing Statement for the Prosecution, *N.M.T.*, vol. 14, p. 85.
600. *Ibid.*, p. 88.
601. See Farben case, Closing Statement for the Prosecution, *N.M.T.*, vol. 8, pp. 1044–1047; Flick case, Extracts from the Closing Statement for the Prosecution, *N.M.T.*, vol. 6, pp. 1038–1040; Hostage case, Extracts from Closing Statement of the Prosecution, *N.M.T.*, vol. 11, p. 1160; Ministries case, Closing Statement for the Prosecution, *N.M.T.*, vol. 14, pp. 87–88.
602. Farben case, Closing Statement for the Prosecution, *N.M.T.*, vol. 8, p. 1044.
603. See Einsatzgruppen case, Closing Statement of the Prosecution, *N.M.T.*, vol. 4, pp. 377–378; High Command case, Extracts from the Closing Statement of the Prosecution, *N.M.T.*, vol. 11, p. 372; Medical case, Extracts from the Closing Statement of the Prosecution, *N.M.T.*, vol. 1, p. 958. Cf. Farben case, Closing Statement for the Prosecution, *N.M.T.*, vol. 8, pp. 1044–1045; Flick case, Extracts from the Closing Statement for the Prosecution, *N.M.T.*, vol. 6, p. 1038; Hostage case, Extracts from Opening Statement of the Prosecution, *N.M.T.*, vol. 11, p. 840.

was formulated by the Tribunal in the Ministries case as follows:

> 'Both care and caution must be exercised not to prescribe or apply a yardstick to these defendants which cannot and should not be applied to others, irrespective of whether they are nationals of the victor or of the vanquished'.[604]

In the light of this basic tenet, the judgments weighed the doctrine of *respondeat superior* which had been espoused by several defence counsel and found it wanting in international law.[605] In the Hostage case, for instance, the Tribunal rejected the theory advocated by Oppenheim, ruling that it had never been the prevailing view among scholars,[606] and pronounced:

> 'International Law has never approved the defensive plea of superior order as a mandatory bar to the prosecution of war criminals'.[607]

The judgments granted that discipline is indispensable to every military system, and that the first duty of the soldier is to obey orders.[608] In the Hostage case, it was also underscored that the soldier is driven upon the horns of a dilemma, for he is liable to punishment whether he consents to obey the order or refuses to do so.[609] Yet, first of all, as the Tribunal in the Einsatzgruppen case proclaimed in a noted passage that is suggestive of Stephen's influence,[610] the very interests of the efficiency of the army demand that discipline shall not be blind:

> 'It is a fallacy of wide-spread consumption that a soldier is required to do everything his superior officer orders him to do. A very simple illustration will show to what absurd extreme such a theory could be carried. If every military person were required, regardless of the nature of the command, to obey unconditionally, a sergeant could order the corporal to shoot the lieutenant, the lieutenant could order the sergeant to shoot the captain, the captain could order the lieutenant to shoot the colonel, and in each instance the executioner would be absolved of blame. The mere statement of such a proposition is its own commentary'.[611]

Consequently, pronounced this judgment, one ought to draw a

604. Ministries case, Judgment, *N.M.T.*, vol. 14, p. 317.
605. See Einsatzgruppen case, Judgment, *N.M.T.*, vol. 4, pp. 470–471; High Command case, Judgment, *N.M.T.*, vol. 11, pp. 508–509, 582; Hostage case, Judgment, *N.M.T.*, vol. 11, pp. 1236–1238; Justice case, Judgment, *N.M.T.*, vol. 3, p. 1011; Medical case, Judgment, *N.M.T.*, vol. 2, p. 227.
606. Hostage case, Judgment, *N.M.T.*, vol. 11, p. 1237. Cf. Dunbar, *op. cit.*, p. 252; Greenspan, *op. cit.*, p. 440 n. 108.
607. Hostage case, Judgment, *N.M.T.*, vol. 11, p. 1238.
608. See Einsatzgruppen case, Judgment, *N.M.T.*, vol. 4, p. 470; High Command case, Judgment, *N.M.T.*, vol. 11, p. 510; Hostage case, Judgment, *N.M.T.*, vol. 11, p. 1236.
609. Hostage case, Judgment, *N.M.T.*, vol. 11, pp. 1236–1237. Cf. Dunbar, *op. cit.*, p. 252.
610. See *supra*, p. 53.
611. Einsatzgruppen case, Judgment, *N.M.T.*, vol. 4, p. 470.

painstaking distinction between lawful orders, which are directly related to the military duties of the soldier, and criminal orders, which exceed these bounds, like an order issued to a soldier to steal for his commander.[612] Military discipline pertains only to orders that belong to the first category, and it does not, nay, it cannot, oblige compliance with criminal orders.[613]

Secondly, the Tribunals did not lose sight of the other side of the coin of military discipline, namely, the interests of the supremacy of the law.[614] The judgment in the High Command case observed that the outcome of an escalating transfer of responsibility would be global immunity and concentration of accountability on the shoulders of the tyrant—Hitler—alone,[615] and it concluded:

> 'To recognize such a contention would be to recognize an absurdity'.[616]

It is impermissible, declared the Tribunal, that

> 'the dictator, absolute though he may be, shall be the scapegoat on whom the sins of all his governmental and military subordinates are wished; and..., when he is driven into a bunker and presumably destroyed, all the sins and guilt of his subordinates shall be considered to have been destroyed with him'.[617]

The Tribunal in the Einsatzgruppen case rejected also the assertion that superior orders affect soldiers with paralysis of all independent will-power and transform them into robots which react automatically to the instructions of their engineers:

> 'The obedience of a soldier is not the obedience of an automaton. A soldier is a reasoning agent. He does not respond, and is not expected to respond, like a piece of machinery'.[618]

Nevertheless, the Tribunal did not deny the possibility of discharge from responsibility on the basis of obedience to orders, under circumstances that actually partake of compulsion, and laid down the rule that there is no room for conviction when the defendants acted pursuant to orders associated with a threat which is 'imminent, real and inevitable'.[619] The Tribunal stated:

612. *Ibid.*, pp. 470, 484.
613. *Ibid.*, p. 470; Hostage case, Judgment, *N.M.T.*, vol. 11, p. 1236.
614. See e.g. Hostage case, Judgment, *N.M.T.*, vol. 11, p. 1237.
615. High Command case, Judgment, *N.M.T.*, vol. 11, pp. 507–508.
616. *Ibid.*, p. 508. Cf. Eustathiades, 'Ordres', p. 398.
617. High Command case, Judgment, *N.M.T.*, vol. 11, pp. 508–509.
618. Einsatzgruppen case, Judgment, *N.M.T.*, vol. 4, p. 470. Cf. Dunbar, *op. cit.*, p. 254; Glaser, 'L'Ordre', p. 328; *History of U.N.W.C.C.*, p. 288; Kafr Kassem case (first instance), *op. cit.*, p. 219.
619. Einsatzgruppen case, Judgment, *N.M.T.*, vol. 4, p. 480. See *supra*, p. 80.

> 'The test to be applied is whether the subordinate acted under coercion or whether he himself approved of the principle involved in the order. If the second proposition be true, the plea of superior orders fails'.[620]

With regard to the case in issue, the Tribunal found, as we have noted above,[621] that the defendants in the dock, the commanders of the Einsatzgruppen, had willingly and approvingly carried out the orders that they had received, and therefore it convicted them all.[622] But, even had the Tribunal maintained that these criminals submitted to orders under duress, and even had it taken the position that acquittal is allowable in cases of duress where death is inflicted, in my opinion it still ought to have held the defendants criminally responsible in the light of the following criterion established by it:

> 'If one claims duress in the execution of an illegal order it must be shown that the harm caused by obeying the illegal order is not disproportionally greater than the harm which would result from not obeying the illegal order'.[623]

When the scales of the balance hold the life of the individual offender as against the lives of the thousands and myriads annihilated by the extermination gangs, how can it be said that the danger which looms for the subordinate who refuses to obey an order is of the same order of magnitude as the calamity that is liable to befall if the order is carried out? The Tribunal, admittedly, said that

> 'No court will punish a man who, with a loaded pistol at his head, is compelled to pull a lethal lever',

and furthermore noted that, for acquittal purposes, the peril to the life of the offender need not be as imminent as in the illustration of the loaded pistol aimed at his head.[624] But it seems that the Tribunal forgot for a moment that a slight motion and one pull of the lever mean death to many scores of innocent people in the gas chambers. No amount of compulsion directed against the individual is capable of relieving him of criminal responsibility if he pulled the lever and thereby brought about wholesale massacre.

Whether acquittal of the commanders of the Einsatzgruppen was conceivable under certain conditions on account of compulsion, or was entirely out of the question, it is quite evident that the Tribunal recognized in principle the possibility of exemption from

620. Einsatzgruppen case, Judgment, *N.M.T.*, vol. 4, p. 480. Cf. Eichmann trial (second instance), Judgment, *op. cit.*, pp. 134–135.
621. See *supra*, p. 80.
622. Einsatzgruppen case, Judgment, *N.M.T.*, vol. 4, pp. 480ff, 587–589.
623. *Ibid.*, p. 471. Cf. Eustathiades, 'Ordres', p. 416 n. 63; Levie, *op. cit.*, p. 465; *L.R.U.N.W.C.C.*, vol. 15 (Digest), p. 158.
624. Einsatzgruppen case, Judgment, *N.M.T.*, vol. 4, p. 480. Cf. Eustathiades, 'Ordres', p. 416 n. 63; Maunoir, *op. cit.*, p. 293; *L.R.U.N.W.C.C.*, Notes, Krupp trial, vol. 10, p. 175; *L.R.U.N.W.C.C.*, vol. 15 (Digest), pp. 156, 174.

responsibility on the basis of obedience to orders in circumstances of compulsion. This approach is, of course, incompatible with the provision of Article II(4)(b) of Law No. 10, which excludes any possibility of taking the fact of obedience to orders into account for the purpose of relief from responsibility. But one may, perhaps, ask the question whether the Tribunal did not rush its fences, and whether it is not implied in the judgment that there is substance in the doctrine of *respondeat superior*. More especially in view of the fact that, as we shall presently see, the Tribunal conceded the factor of ignorance of the law as a reason for putting forward the plea of obedience to orders: after all, compulsion and mistake of law are the main elements of the doctrine of *respondeat superior*. Yet the answer to our question is certainly negative. The distinctive feature of the doctrine is that, in the opinion of its proponents, obedience to orders creates an absolute, *a priori* defence *per se*. Mistake of law and compulsion constitute a part of the rationalization of the doctrine—according to Renault and those following him—but its touchstone is an automatic discharge from responsibility whenever obedience to orders is involved, without there being any need to prove the existence of compulsion or mistake in the concrete case. The judgment in the Einsatzgruppen case clearly rejected the attitude of automatic acquittal owing to obedience to orders. What the Tribunal ruled is that in certain instances, and in them only, when the defence is able to establish the existence of mistake of law or compulsion, and on condition that it is indeed able to do that, the accused may avail themselves of the defence of obedience to orders. In accordance with this conception, obedience to orders does indeed constitute a defence *per se* but by no means sets up an *a priori* defence. We have already pointed out[625] that there is no sense in regarding obedience to orders as even a defence *per se*, and that the real defence is, or ought to be, that of compulsion or mistake.[626] In this respect the judgment in the Einsatzgruppen case is unfortunately at fault. But the significance of the fault must not be exaggerated, and we must not leap erroneously to the conclusion that the Tribunal crossed the Rubicon into the realm of the doctrine of *respondeat superior*.

Whereas the judgment in the Einsatzgruppen case coped with

625. See *supra*, p. 82.

626. The editors of the Law Reports of the United Nations War Crimes Commission, followed by Eustathiades, noted that the real defence, according to the judgment delivered in the Einsatzgruppen case, is—or ought to be—compulsion, rather than obedience to orders (see *L.R.U.N.W.C.C.*, Notes, Krupp trial, vol. 10, pp. 174–175; *L.R.U.N.W.C.C.*, vol. 15 (Digest), p. 156; and also Eustathiades, 'Ordres', p. 416 n. 63). But they did not observe that, in the corresponding case, the real defence should be mistake of law, and not obedience to orders.

the factor of compulsion within the make-up of the defence of obedience to orders, several other judgments recognized the defence founded on compulsion as a defence in itself which does not hinge on the fact of obedience to orders as a condition precedent. In the Ministries case, the Tribunal addressed itself to the plea of the defendants that they had acted against their will, and rejected it for factual reasons, holding that the circumstances of the case did not justify their acquittal on account of coercion or duress.[627] The Tribunal in the High Command case stated that the defendants in the dock, who had received manifestly illegal orders, had indeed been placed in a difficult position, but not more than that, and hence did not deserve to benefit from the defence of coercion or necessity.[628] With regard to the defendant Kuechler, the Tribunal proclaimed:

> 'the fact that he was caught "between the devil and the deep blue sea", or that it would have endangered him as a disobedient commander if he had not carried out the order, is not a defense to . . . the crime charged'.[629]

Nonetheless, the Tribunal expressly added that, in appropriate circumstances, which did not exist in the case at issue, it is possible by means of the defence of coercion or necessity to protect defendants who had been placed in jeopardy.[630]

The most important and best known recognition of the defence based on compulsion was accorded in the judgments delivered in the industrialists' trials: the Flick, Farben and Krupp cases. All these three judgments fully endorsed, as a matter of law, the independent defence of necessity in case of a 'clear and present danger'.[631] As a matter of fact, in two of the trials, the Flick and Farben cases, this defence even availed the accused in certain instances;[632] but in the Krupp case the Tribunal concluded that there was no factual justification for its application to the specific accused standing trial before it.[633]

627. Ministries case, Judgment, *N.M.T.*, vol. 14, p. 339.
628. High Command case, Judgment, *N.M.T.*, vol. 11, p. 509.
629. *Ibid.*, p. 567.
630. *Ibid.*, p. 509. Cf. Eustathiades, 'Ordres', p. 419 n. 75; Greenspan, *op. cit.*, pp. 497–498; Levie, *op. cit.*, p. 464 n. 126; *L.R.U.N.W.C.C.*, vol. 15 (Digest), pp. 171–172.
631. Farben case, Judgment, *N.M.T.*, vol. 8, pp. 1174–1179; Flick case, Judgment, *N.M.T.*, vol. 6, pp. 1200–1201; Krupp case, Judgment, *N.M.T.*, vol. 9, pp. 1435–1439. Cf. Eustathiades, 'Ordres', pp. 417–419; Greenspan, *op. cit.*, pp. 496–497; Taylor, *op. cit.*, pp. 187, 193, 199; *L.R.U.N.W.C.C.*, Notes, Krupp trial, vol. 10, p. 175; *L.R.U.N.W.C.C.*, vol. 15 (Digest), pp. 156, 171.
632. Farben case, Judgment, *N.M.T.*, vol. 8, pp. 1192–1195; Flick case, Judgment, *N.M.T.*, vol. 6, p. 1201. Cf. Greenspan, *op. cit.*, p. 497; Kranzbühler, *op. cit.*, p. 123; Taylor, *op. cit.*, pp. 187, 199.
633. Krupp case, Judgment, *N.M.T.*, vol. 9, p. 1439. Cf. Taylor, *op. cit.*, p. 193.

The judgment in the Flick case found it incumbent explicitly to indicate, when recognizing the defence of necessity, that it did not ignore the provision of Article II(4)(b) of Law No. 10, saying that the Article had not been intended 'to be employed to deprive a defendant of the defense of necessity'.[634] If this statement relates to an offender who is relying for his defence on the element of compulsion without at all resorting to the plea of obedience to orders, it is self-evident: unquestionably Article II(4)(b) neither deals with the subject of necessity nor is designed to exclude the defence of necessity as such. On the other hand, if the statement relates to a war criminal who, in the construction of a defence based even on necessity, resorts to the plea of obedience to orders, it should be recalled that the Article, as formulated, does exclude any possibility of taking the fact of obedience to orders into consideration for defence purposes. Inasmuch, therefore, as the defence of necessity is predicated on obedience to orders, Article II(4)(b) thwarts this defence by removing its foundation. Thus the Article may indirectly deprive a person of the defence of necessity.

In the Farben case, the Tribunal probably noticed that, when the factor of obedience to orders is essential to the composing of the defence based on compulsion, Article II(4)(b) may not be disregarded offhand. Hence it set aside the statutory provision, and preferred to follow in the footsteps of judicial precedents. In particular, the judgment rendered here relied on the famous enunciation of the International Military Tribunal with regard to moral choice, which it interpreted, as we have already seen,[635] as a validation of a defence *per se* of obedience to orders in circumstances of lack of moral choice.[636] Clearly, if the fact of obedience to orders may constitute a defence *per se*, it may *a fortiori* serve as an element in another defence, to wit, that of necessity, when no moral choice is possible. The Tribunal in the Farben case relied furthermore on the previous rulings in the Flick and Roechling cases,[637] and declared:

> 'From a consideration of the IMT, Flick, and Roechling judgments, we deduce that an order of a superior officer... will not justify the defense of necessity unless, in its operation, it is of a character to deprive the one to whom it is directed of a moral choice as to his course of action'.[638]

634. Flick case, Judgment, *N.M.T.*, vol. 6, p. 1200.
635. See *supra*, p. 152.
636. Farben case, Judgment, *N.M.T.*, vol. 8, p. 1176.
637. See Roechling case, Judgment, *N.M.T.*, vol. 14, pp. 1104–1105. This judgment, as will be recalled, was delivered by a French Court under Law No. 10. See *supra*, note 539.
638. Farben case, Judgment, *N.M.T.*, vol. 8, p. 1179. Cf. Eustathiades, 'Ordres', p. 417 n. 68.

We have pointed out above[639] that an interpretation of the pronouncement of the International Military Tribunal in a way that would imply that the fact of obedience to orders is in itself a defence, be it even in circumstances of lack of moral choice, is groundless. Likewise, I am of opinion that one cannot deduce from that pronouncement a permission to take the fact of obedience to orders into account for the purpose of establishing any defence whatever, the defence of necessity not excluded.

One of the judges who sat on the bench in the Farben case—Judge Herbert—noted in a dissenting opinion that the majority judgment did not conform to the ruling in the trial of the major war criminals and was obviously incompatible with the stipulation of Article II(4)(b).[640] The trouble is that Herbert went too far in the opposite direction, and entirely denied the possibility of any kind of reliance on the factor of compulsion.[641] Thus he opined that a recognition of the defence of necessity was

> 'utterly inconsistent with the provisions of Control Council Law No. 10 which indicate quite clearly that governmental compulsion is merely a matter to be considered in mitigation and does not establish a defense to the fact of guilt'.[642]

In fact, however, Article II(4)(b) does not mention the subject of compulsion at all, nor does it explicitly or implicitly rule out the defence of necessity. All that it does is deny the possibility of taking the fact of obedience to orders into account within the bounds of this, or any other, defence. Herbert made another inaccurate statement when he observed that

> 'The IMT judgment embraces no doctrinal defense of necessity by governmental coercion. That decision, it seems to me, constitutes complete negation of any such theory'.[643]

This statement disregards the moral choice test, in which the International Military Tribunal in effect admitted the validity of a defence based on compulsion, provided that it is not dependent upon the fact of obedience to orders. Consequently, just as we cannot accept the opinion of the majority in the Farben case on this subject, we cannot endorse the opinion of the minority either.

And now from the sphere of compulsion to that of mistake of law. In several judgments rendered in the Subsequent Proceedings,

639. See *supra*, p. 152.
640. Farben case, Dissenting Opinion of Judge Herbert, *N.M.T.*, vol. 8, pp. 1309–1310.
641. *Ibid.*
642. *Ibid.*, p. 1309.
643. *Ibid.*, p. 1310.

the pennant of the personal knowledge principle was boldly unfurled. Thus, for example, it was said in the High Command case that the soldier is not a lawyer and that he cannot be expected to screen every order that he receives and determine the law by himself when complicated and controversial legal points are involved.[644] According to this judgment, the subordinate is entitled to assume that the legality of the orders issued to him has already been examined by his superiors and that the orders are indeed in conformity with the rules of international law.[645] The view of the Tribunal in respect of a soldier complying with an order was that

> 'He cannot be held criminally responsible for a mere error in judgment as to disputable legal questions'.[646]

In another judgment, delivered in the Einsatzgruppen case, it was proclaimed in no uncertain terms:

> 'To plead superior orders one must show an excusable ignorance of their illegality'.[647]

In the Medical case, the Tribunal rejected the defence of obedience to orders raised by the accused Fischer, explaining that he had acted in complete knowledge that the act which he had been ordered to perform, and had performed, was fundamentally criminal.[648] And in the Hostage case, the Tribunal adduced in support the judgment rendered at Leipzig in the Llandovery Castle case,[649] and stated:

> 'We are of the view... that if the illegality of the order was not known to the inferior, and he could not reasonably have been expected to know of its illegality, no wrongful intent necessary to the commission of a crime exists and the inferior will be protected'.[650]

As a supplement to the personal knowledge principle, the Tribunals in the Subsequent Proceedings used the manifest illegality

644. High Command case, Judgment, *N.M.T.*, vol. 11, pp. 510–511. Cf. Dunbar, *op. cit.*, p. 254; Eustathiades, 'Ordres', p. 413 n. 53; Maunoir, *op. cit.*, pp. 249, 256–257; *L.R.U.N.W.C.C.*, vol. 15 (Digest), p. 183.
645. High Command case, Judgment, *N.M.T.*, vol. 11, p. 511. Cf. Dunbar, *op. cit.*, p. 254; Eustathiades, 'Ordres', p. 413 n. 53; Greenspan, *op. cit.*, p. 492; Kranzbühler, *op. cit.*, p. 122; Maunoir, *op. cit.*, pp. 249, 256–257.
646. High Command case, Judgment, *N.M.T.*, vol. 11, p. 511. Cf. Eustathiades, 'Ordres', p. 413 n. 53; Greenspan, *op. cit.*, pp. 492–493; Kranzbühler, *op. cit.*, p. 122; *L.R.U.N.W.C.C.*, vol. 15 (Digest), p. 183.
647. Einsatzgruppen case, Judgment, *N.M.T.*, vol. 4, p. 473. Cf. Eustathiades, 'Ordres', p. 416 n. 63; *L.R.U.N.W.C.C.*, Notes, Krupp trial, vol. 10, p. 174; *L.R.U.N.W.C.C.*, vol. 15 (Digest), p. 156.
648. Medical case, Judgment, *N.M.T.*, vol. 2, p. 296.
649. Hostage case, Judgment, *N.M.T.*, vol. 11, p. 1236. See also Einsatzgruppen case, Judgment, *N.M.T.*, vol. 4, pp. 483–484.
650. Hostage case, Judgment, *N.M.T.*, vol. 11, p. 1236. Cf. Maunoir, *op. cit.*, p. 256.

principle. Thus the judgment in the High Command case held that, when a manifestly illegal order is involved, the subordinate is no longer entitled to rely on his superior and must refuse to obey the order, lest punishment be meted out to him.[651] And in the Einsatzgruppen case the Tribunal ruled:

> 'If the nature of the ordered act is manifestly beyond the scope of the superior's authority, the subordinate may not plead ignorance to the criminality of the order'.[652]

In various judgments it was stressed that, if murder or any other heinous crime is committed, the offender cannot evade criminal responsibility just because he acted in obedience to orders.[653]

Is it possible to construe the attitude of the Tribunals in this regard along the lines of the foregoing interpretation[654] of the approach of the prosecution, both in the trial of the major war criminals and in the Subsequent Proceedings, as a mere historical explanation of Article II(4)(b)? Can it be stated that the Tribunals recognized the twin principles of personal knowledge and manifest illegality as the accepted principles in general international law, but nevertheless conceded that, within the concrete ambit of the Subsequent Proceedings, it was not permissible or necessary to examine the extent of the personal awareness of each defendant of the unlawfulness of the orders carried out by him, because all the offences for which these defendants were brought to trial had been *a priori* manifestly illegal? To this question we ought to reply, first of all, that the Tribunals did not content themselves with any supposition existing in this field *a priori*, and painstakingly checked whether the defendants, actually and according to the circumstances of the case, knew, or should have known, that they were acting pursuant to unlawful orders.[655]

Admittedly the truth of the matter is that, although the judgments loudly trumpeted the principles of personal knowledge and manifest illegality, they almost invariably reached the conclusion that the defendants had knowingly obeyed unlawful orders and hence were not entitled to unburden themselves of responsibility for their actions. Yet there is one exception to this rule, which is in striking contradiction to Article II (4)(b) and renders the historical explanation meaningless. We have in mind the High Command case. In the judgment delivered there,

651. High Command case, Judgment, *N.M.T.*, vol. 11, p. 512. Cf. Eustathiades, 'Ordres', p. 413.
652. Einsatzgruppen case, Judgment, *N.M.T.*, vol. 4, p. 471.
653. See *ibid.*, p. 486; Hostage case, Judgment, *N.M.T.*, vol. 11, p. 1236.
654. See *supra*, pp. 129, 175–176.
655. See e.g. the passage dealing with the defendant Fischer in the judgment rendered in the Medical case (*N.M.T.*, vol. 2, p. 296).

it was indeed established, in most instances, that the orders relied upon by the defendants had been unlawful even in the eyes of a soldier of elementary intelligence, who does not excel in legal erudition, that is, they had been manifestly illegal orders, and therefore the defendants were not able to benefit from them.[656] In regard to certain orders, however, concerning the use of prisoners-of-war in the construction of fortifications in non-dangerous areas, the Tribunal determined that, in view of the uncertainty of the provisions of international law as to this matter, such orders cannot be regarded as manifestly illegal, so that the defendants had the right to rely on their superiors and should not incur responsibility for these acts.[657] Thus the Tribunal gave voice here to the principles of manifest illegality and personal knowledge not only in a theoretical but in a most practical and operative way. We are confronted with a clear and express departure from the stipulation of Law No. 10 that the fact of obedience to orders ought not to be considered for purposes of discharge from responsibility. It is true that, in another part of the judgment, the Tribunal pronounced that

> 'It is not necessary to support the provision of Control Council Law No. 10, Article II, paragraphs 4 (a) and (b), by reason, for we are bound by it as one of the basic authorities under which we function as a juridical tribunal'.[658]

And the Tribunal did not leave it at that, but even added with spirited advocacy that, if one is nevertheless seeking reason for this clause, such reason is not lacking.[659] What the Tribunal practised, however, is more important than what it preached, and in fact its decision in respect of the orders to use prisoners-of-war in the construction of fortifications is inconsistent with the stringent language of Law No. 10.

Now that we have observed the tendency of numerous judgments in the Subsequent Proceedings to mollify the rigid provision of Article II(4)(b) and not to accept it in letter as well as in spirit, it is fitting to mention that in one case, at least, the Article was applied as it stands. This is the RuSHA case, in which the Tribunal held that the plea of obedience to orders may be considered only with a view to mitigation of punishment and not for defence purposes.[660] In this it faithfully

656. High Command case, Judgment, *N.M.T.*, vol. 11, pp. 509, 512, 567. Cf. Dunbar, *op. cit.*, p. 254.
657. High Command case, Judgment, *N.M.T.*, vol. 11, p. 534. Cf. Lauterpacht – Oppenheim, *International Law*, vol. 2 (7th ed., 1952), p. 570 n. 2, *L.R.U.N.W.C.C.*, Notes, High Command trial, vol. 12, p. 98; *L.R.U.N.W.C.C.*, vol. 15 (Digest), p. 159 n. 1.
658. High Command case, Judgment, *N.M.T.*, vol. 11, p. 508.
659. *Ibid.*
660. RuSHA case, Judgment, *N.M.T.*, vol. 5, pp. 153–154.

expressed the doctrine of absolute liability, as reflected by the Article.

Naturally, even those judgments that evinced, in principle, a willingness to take the factor of obedience to orders into account within the compass of total discharge from responsibility, thereby repudiating the doctrine of absolute liability, did not abstain from a consideration of this factor as well when evaluating the punishment of the defendants who had been convicted. In this particular context, they chose to follow the provision of Law No. 10 verbatim.[661] Especially outstanding, from the viewpoint of alleviation of punishment, is the case of the defendant Dehner, whose sentence—only seven years' imprisonment—was the lightest passed upon all those arraigned and convicted in the Hostage case.[662] The Tribunal accounted for its verdict as follows:

> 'There is much that can be said... in mitigation of the punishment to be assessed from the standpoint of the defendant. Superior orders existed'.[663]

It stands to reason that the other relatively light sentences inflicted in this judgment were the outcome of the Tribunal's recognition that the defendants had acted at the beck and call of their superiors.[664] In the High Command case, the fact of obedience to orders also figured among the extenuating circumstances when the punishment of certain defendants, including the one who headed the roster of accused in this trial, namely Leeb, was assessed.[665]

We shall conclude our discussion of the Subsequent Proceedings by taking note of the Tribunals' rejection of the defence plea based on the *Führerprinzip*. First, they reiterated the statement originally put forward by the prosecution in the trial of the major war criminals,[666] and followed by the International Military Tribunal in its judgment,[667] that Hitler could not have acted alone, and that he had needed the defendants, as well as depended upon them, for the accomplishment of his schemes.[668] The judgments further proclaimed that the defendants had not been mere robots, operated

661. See High Command case, Judgment, *N.M.T.*, vol. 11, p. 563; Hostage case, Judgment, *N.M.T.*, vol. 11, p. 1238.
662. Hostage case, Judgment, *N.M.T.*, vol. 11, p. 1319.
663. *Ibid.*, p. 1299. Cf. Dunbar, *op. cit.*, p. 258.
664. See *L.R.U.N.W.C.C.*, Notes, Hostages trial, vol. 8, p. 90.
665. With regard to the defendant Leeb, see High Command case, Judgment, *N.M.T.*, vol. 11, p. 563. And see also *ibid.*, pp. 565 and 582, in regard to the defendants Kuechler and Hoth respectively.
666. See *supra*, p. 146.
667. See *supra*, p. 155.
668. See Einsatzgruppen case, Judgment, *N.M.T.*, vol. 4, pp. 507–508; High Command case, Judgment, *N.M.T.*, vol. 11, p. 486; Milch case, Judgment, *N.M.T.*, vol. 2, p. 794. Cf. Justice case, Judgment, *N.M.T.*, vol. 3, pp. 1010ff.

by the *Führer* at his whim, and acting without thought, aim or reflection: they had aided and abetted Hitler willingly, knowingly and with malice aforethought.[669] In the Einsatzgruppen case, the Tribunal declared:

> 'That Hitler was a man of extraordinary capacities cannot be doubted, but his capabilities for harm would have been *nil* had he not had willing, enthusiastic collaborators like the defendants...
>
> 'Hitler struck the match, but the fire would have died a quick death had it not been for his fellow arsonists, big and little, who continued to supply the fuel'.[670]

The judgments in the Subsequent Proceedings also subscribed to the estoppel argument, initially submitted by the prosecution against the major war criminals.[671] The Tribunal in the Milch case expressed it in the following way:

> 'If they abjectly place all the power in the hands of one man, with no right reserved to check or limit or repudiate, they must accept the bitter with the sweet'.[672]

In the sequel, the Tribunal in fact echoed the conception formulated in the instructive testimony of the defendant Speer before the International Military Tribunal,[673] and held that, had the die been cast in a different way, had Germany been victorious in the war, Milch would almost certainly have been hailing and praising all of the acts and orders of the *Führer*, boasting that it was he who carried out several of the orders, and probably even claiming co-authorship in some of them.[674] Now that his world has collapsed, Hitler is dead and Germany defeated, will he be allowed to take refuge behind the shadow of the *Führer* and contend that responsibility for the despicable acts committed by the Nazi monster devolves upon the head only, while the arms are innocent?[675]

Thus the plea failed that the *Führer*'s orders were of an exceptional nature, justifying a departure from the provision of Article II(4)(b). In view, however, of the fact that the Tribunals in the Subsequent Proceedings, as we have seen, anyway refused to toe the line of this provision, either in the field of compulsion or in that of mistake of law, it cannot be said that the defence laboured in vain.

669. See particularly Pohl case, Concurring Opinion by Judge Musmanno, *N.M.T.*, vol. 5, p. 1160.
670. Einsatzgruppen case, Judgment, *N.M.T.*, vol. 4, pp. 507–508.
671. See *supra*, p. 145.
672. Milch case, Judgment, *N.M.T.*, vol. 2, p. 794.
673. See *supra*, pp. 146–147.
674. Milch case, Judgment, *N.M.T.*, vol. 2, p. 795.
675. *Ibid.*, pp. 794–795.

In this section, we shall deal with trials of war criminals that were held before national courts after the Second World War, besides the Subsequent Proceedings at Nuremberg discussed in the previous section. Mainly, though not exclusively, our analysis will be based on those cases of which account is given in the Law Reports of Trials of War Criminals, selected and prepared by the United Nations War Crimes Commission.[676] We must remember, however, that these cases are merely a drop in the ocean. The Commission epitomized only 89 cases, including those of the Subsequent Proceedings, out of 1911 submitted to it for report;[677] and even the larger of these two figures cannot be regarded as exhaustive, when one keeps in mind the plethora of war crimes trials that took place throughout the world after the war.[678]

A. *The Arguments of the Defence*

In war crimes trials galore conducted before national courts after the Second World War, the defence put forward the plea of obedience to orders as a reason for relieving the accused of responsibility.[679] A typical expression was given to this argument by counsel

676. *L.R.U.N.W.C.C.*, vols. 1–15.
677. *L.R.U.N.W.C.C.*, vol. 15 (Digest), p. xvi.
678. See Eustathiades, 'Les Sujets du Droit International et la Responsabilité Internationale, Nouvelles Tendances', *R.A.D.I.*, vol. 84 (1953), pp. 401–614 at p. 473 n. 1.
679. See Almelo trial, *L.R.U.N.W.C.C.*, vol. 1, pp. 37–39; Awochi trial, *L.R.U.N.W.C.C.*, vol. 13, p. 123; Bauer trial, *L.R.U.N.W.C.C.*, vol. 8, p. 16; Belsen trial, *L.R.U.N.W.C.C.*, vol. 2, pp. 77–79, 95; *W.C.T.S.*, vol. 2, pp. xxxii, 506–508, 512, 562–563; Bruns trial, *L.R.U.N.W.C.C.*, vol. 3, pp. 18–19; Buck trial, *L.R.U.N.W.C.C.*, vol. 5, p. 42; Buhler trial, *L.R.U.N.W.C.C.*, vol. 14, p. 38; Bury and Hafner trial, *L.R.U.N.W.C.C.*, vol. 3, p. 64; Dachau trial, *L.R.U.N.W.C.C.*, vol. 11, p. 8; Dostler trial, *L.R.U.N.W.C.C.*, vol. 1, pp. 27–28, 31; Double Tenth trial, *W.C.T.S.*, vol. 8, pp. 237, 240–243; Eichmann trial (first instance), Minutes, *op. cit.*, Session No. 75, pp. S1–T1; Session No. 114, pp. T2–W1; Eichmann trial (second instance) (Criminal Appeal 336/61, Eichmann v. Attorney General), Minutes (mimeographed, English), Session No. 1, pp. E1, F1; Session No. 2, pp. H1–I1; Falkenhorst trial, *L.R.U.N.W.C.C.*, vol. 11, p. 25; *W.C.T.S.*, vol. 6, pp. 195–196; Flesch trial, *L.R.U.N.W.C.C.*, vol. 6, pp. 117, 120; Goeth trial, *L.R.U.N.W.C.C.*, vol. 7, pp. 9–10; Golkel trial, *L.R.U.N.W.C.C.*, vol. 5, pp. 49–50; Gozawa trial, *W.C.T.S.*, vol. 3, pp. 88, 225; Greiser trial, *L.R.U.N.W.C.C.*, vol. 13, pp. 102–103, 114; Hadamar trial, *L.R.U.N.W.C.C.*, vol. 1, p. 54; *W.C.T.S.*, vol. 4, p. 233; Hans trial, *L.R.U.N.W.C.C.*, vol. 5, p. 86; Hoess trial, *L.R.U.N.W.C.C.*, vol. 7, p. 17; Holzer trial—Notes, Sawada trial, *L.R.U.N.W.C.C.*, vol. 5, pp. 15–16; Jaluit Atoll case, *L.R.U.N.W.C.C.*, vol. 1, p. 74; Kharkov trial, *People's Verdict*, pp. 65, 71, 77, 82, 117–120; Maelzer trial, *L.R.U.N.W.C.C.*, vol. 11, p. 53; Manstein trial, *A.D.*, 1949, pp. 510, 524; Peleus trial, L.R.U.N.W.C.C., vol. 1, pp. 4, 9–10; W.C.T.S., vol. 1, pp. 44, 96, 100–101, 103, 107–115; Rauter trial, *L.R.U.N.W.C.C.*, vol. 14, p. 107; Renoth trial, *L.R.U.N.W.C.C.*, vol. 11,

for the defence in the Eichmann trial, Servatius, who, in the first instance of the case, while advocating the doctrine of *respondeat superior*, pointed out the practical results that would be implied by the rejection of this doctrine:

> 'The basic principle of every State is loyalty to the leadership and confidence in it. The deed is dumb and obedience is blind. These are the virtues on which alone a State can build its foundations. Do such virtues merit reward? This depends upon the success of the policy. If it failed, the order would be considered a crime in the eyes of the victor. Then the one who had obeyed would be unfortunate and would be called upon to pay for his loyalty. The gallows or a decoration—that is the question. To fail, is heinous crime. To succeed, is sanctified action'.[680]

One must not think, however, that, whenever the defence invoked the plea of obedience to orders, it embraced the doctrine of *respondeat superior.* In numerous cases, defence counsel expressed support for the personal knowledge principle or the manifest illegality principle,[681] either because in their opinion these principles accurately reflect international law or else because they sought to apply the provisions of German national law as enunciated in the Leipzig trials.[682] An illustrative case, in which the personal knowledge principle was endorsed by the defence, is the Peleus trial, which will be discussed at length below. Here one of the counsel—Pabst—submitted in his closing speech as follows:

> 'Regarding the culpability of a soldier, one must distinguish between the cases in which the subordinate knew the illegality of the order, and those in

p. 77; Rohde trial, *L.R.U.N.W.C.C.*, vol. 5, p. 58; Sakai trial, *L.R.U.N.W.C.C.*, vol. 14, p. 2; Sawada trial, *L.R.U.N.W.C.C.*, vol. 5, p. 13; Scuttled U-Boats case, *L.R.U.N.W.C.C.*, vol. 1, pp. 60–63; Stalag Luft III case, *L.R.U.N.W.C.C.*, vol. 11, pp. 46, 50; Szabados trial, *L.R.U.N.W.C.C.*, vol. 9, pp. 60–61; Thiele and Steinert trial, *L.R.U.N.W.C.C.*, vol. 3, p. 58; R. Wagner trial, *L.R.U.N.W.C.C.*, vol. 3, pp. 38, 54; Yamamoto trial, *L.R.U.N.W.C.C.*, vol. 3, p. 77; Zuehlke trial, *L.R.U.N.W.C.C.*, vol. 14, pp. 141, 147. See also Mackenzen and Maelzer trial, *L.R.U.N.W.C.C.*, vol. 8, pp. 2–3, 7. Cf. Appleman, *op. cit.*, p. 311 n. 64; Glaser, 'L'Ordre', pp. 327–328.

680. Eichmann trial (first instance), Minutes, *op. cit.*, Session No. 114, p. V2. The translation is corrected. Cf. Eichmann trial (first instance), Judgment, *op. cit.*, s. 216.
681. See Buhler trial, *L.R.U.N.W.C.C.*, vol. 14, p. 38; Flesch trial, *L.R.U.N.W.C.C.*, vol. 6, p. 120; Golkel trial, *L.R.U.N.W.C.C.*, vol. 5, p. 50; Gozawa trial, *W.C.T.S.*, vol. 3, pp. 88, 225; Peleus trial, *L.R.U.N.W.C.C.*, vol. 1, p. 9; *W.C.T.S.*, vol. 1, pp. 109–112; Rohde trial, *L.R.U.N.W.C.C.*, vol. 5, p. 58; Stalag Luft III case, *L.R.U.N.W.C.C.*, vol. 11, pp. 46, 48, 50. Cf. Almelo trial, *L.R.U.N.W.C.C.*, vol. 1, pp. 37, 39, 45; Belsen trial, *W.C.T.S.*, vol. 2, pp. 562–563.
682. A reference to German law was made in the following cases—Peleus trial, *L.R.U.N.W.C.C.*, vol. 1, p. 9; *W.C.T.S.*, vol. 1, p. 109; Rohde trial, *L.R.U.N.W.C.C.*, vol. 5, p. 58; Stalag Luft III case, *L.R.U.N.W.C.C.*, vol. 11, pp. 46, 48.

which he did not know it. Only in the former case can one speak of the responsibility of the subordinate obeying'.[683]

The element of compulsion was emphasized by defence counsel on many occasions, at times as an independent defence, alongside the defence of obedience to orders,[684] at other times as one of the components contributing to the composition of the defence of obedience to orders,[685] and at still others as the genuine defence under the guise of obedience to orders.[686] In this last respect, the following statement of H. Smith on behalf of the defence in the Belsen trial is of particular interest:

> 'What is called the defence of "superior orders" is rather a misleading phrase, because the real nature of the defence is that of freedom of the realm, coercion'.[687]

The defence also advanced the plea of obedience to orders combined with the factor of mistake of fact.[688] A characteristic example of this argumentation may be found in the Scuttled U-Boats case.[689] Here a German naval officer was brought to trial before a British Military Court at Hamburg, in 1946, for having scuttled two German submarines of a modern type after the surrender of the German armed forces in the theatre in which he served and in

683. Peleus trial, Closing Speech for Defendants Hoffmann *et al.* (by Pabst), *W.C.T.S.*, vol. 1, p. 110. Cf. Peleus trial, *L.R.U.N.W.C.C.*, vol. 1, p. 9.
684. See Bruns trial, *L.R.U.N.W.C.C.*, vol. 3, p. 19; Eichmann trial (second instance), Minutes, *op. cit.*, Session No. 2, p. J1; Hadamar trial, *L.R.U.N.W.C.C.*, vol. 1, p. 54; Holzer trial—Notes, Sawada trial, *L.R.U.N.W.C.C.*, vol. 5, pp. 15–16; Stalag Luft III case, *L.R.U.N.W.C.C.*, vol. 11, p. 47; Zuehlke trial, *L.R.U.N.W.C.C.*, vol. 14, p. 141. See also Klinge trial, *L.R.U.N.W.C.C.*, vol. 3, p. 14; Rauter trial, *L.R.U.N.W.C.C.*, vol. 14, p. 133. Cf. *L.R.U.N.W.C.C.*, Notes, Krupp trial, vol. 10, p. 174; *L.R.U.N.W.C.C.*, vol. 15 (Digest), pp. 155–156; Eustathiades, 'Ordres', p. 416.
685. See Double Tenth trial, *W.C.T.S.*, vol. 8, p. 237; Eichmann trial (first instance), Minutes, *op. cit.*, Session No. 75, p. T1; Session No. 114, pp. V1, W1; Eichmann trial (second instance), Minutes, *op. cit.*, Session No. 2, p. I1; Falkenhorst trial, *W.C.T.S.*, vol. 6, pp. xxxv, 196; Peleus trial, *W.C.T.S.*, vol. 1, pp. 103, 109, 112, 115. See also Belsen trial, *L.R.U.N.W.C.C.*, vol. 2, p. 79; Bruns trial, *L.R.U.N.W.C.C.*, vol. 3, p. 18; Kharkov trial, *People's Verdict*, pp. 65, 71, 118–120. Cf. *L.R.U.N.W.C.C.*, Notes, Krupp trial, vol. 10, p. 174; *L.R.U.N.W.C.C.*, Notes, Sawada trial, vol. 5, p. 13; *L.R.U.N.W.C.C.*, vol. 15 (Digest), pp. 156–157.
686. See Belsen trial, *W.C.T.S.*, vol. 2, pp. 506, 508. See also Almelo trial, *L.R.U.N.W.C.C.*, vol. 1, pp. 37, 39.
687. Belsen trial, Legal Argument for the Defence (by Smith), *W.C.T.S.*, vol. 2, p. 508.
688. See Almelo trial, *L.R.U.N.W.C.C.*, vol. 1, p. 39; Buck trial, *L.R.U.N.W.C.C.*, vol. 5, pp. 43–44; Scuttled U-Boats case, *L.R.U.N.W.C.C.*, vol. 1, pp. 60–62; Stalag Luft III case, *L.R.U.N.W.C.C.*, vol. 11, p. 50. See also Klinge trial, *L.R.U.N.W.C.C.*, vol. 3, p. 14.
689. Scuttled U-Boats case, *L.R.U.N.W.C.C.*, vol. 1, p. 55.

violation of the terms of the surrender. It emerged at the trial that the German Admiralty, at a certain stage, ordered that all submarines be scuttled before they fell into the hands of the victorious Allies, but that the order was cancelled immediately after issue and prior to the commission of the offence by the accused. The defence claimed that the accused had acted pursuant to the Admiralty's order, without being aware of the fact of its revocation and furthermore without any knowledge of the terms of the surrender which made his act illegal.[690] The mistake of the defendant in regard to the state of facts was, therefore, double:

(a) He erroneously believed that he was acting in compliance with a valid order, for he did not know of the countermand.

(b) He erroneously thought that he was acting lawfully, for he was unaware of the fact—namely, the terms of surrender—which infected the order, even had it been in force, with illegality and rendered his act a war crime.

Another plea raised by defence counsel was that the accused had transgressed the provisions of international law in obedience to orders which had misled them to conceive of the acts in question as lawful reprisals.[691] We have already noted that this line of defence ought to be viewed through the lens of either mistake of law or mistake of fact, or of both of them together.[692]

It should be kept in mind that the principal distinction between the trials surveyed in this section and those dwelt upon in previous chapters is that here, in most cases, the defence did not have to overcome the hurdle of a statutory stipulation, like that of Article 8 of the London Charter, endorsing the doctrine of absolute liability and excluding the possibility of taking the fact of obedience to orders into account for defence purposes. Consequently, in the trials which are the subject of our present examination, the defence had a wider scope of action, for it was not precluded in advance from availing itself of the plea of obedience to orders as a relevant factual factor within the ambit of the defence of mistake (of law or of fact) or of compulsion. Yet, evidently, insofar as the defence paid no heed to the fact that mistake and compulsion are the core of the matter, whereas the issuance of the orders is of secondary importance—inasmuch as it attempted to make use of the plea of obedience to orders as a defence *per se*—its contentions were logically and legally untenable and therefore deserved to come to naught.

690. *Ibid.*, pp. 60, 62.
691. See Dostler trial, *L.R.U.N.W.C.C.*, vol. 1, pp. 28, 31; Falkenhorst trial, *L.R.U.N.W.C.C.*, vol. 11, p. 26; *W.C.T.S.*, vol. 6, p. 195. See also Mackenzen and Maelzer trial, *L.R.U.N.W.C.C.*, vol. 8, p. 2. Cf. Dunbar, *op. cit.*, p. 250.
692. See *supra*, pp. 84ff.

The foregoing is related to the contribution of the fact of obedience to orders to the total discharge of the accused from responsibility. For the sake of completeness, however, we ought to mention that in several cases the defence tried to benefit from this fact as a reason for mitigation of punishment only, without seeking refuge in it from criminal conviction itself.[693]

B. *The Arguments of the Prosecution*

As might be expected, the prosecution in the war crimes trials utterly rejected the plea that the fact of obedience to orders should, or could, relieve the defendants of responsibility for their misdeeds.[694] It is noteworthy, though, that it did not necessarily tend to move in the direction of the doctrine of absolute liability. In many a trial, including the Eichmann trial, it explicitly maintained that the personal knowledge principle, or the manifest illegality principle, ought to serve as the guiding light for the judges.[695] In this, the prosecutors, in fact, continued along the course which their colleagues had been drawn to since the trial of the major war criminals at Nuremberg.

C. *The Judgments*

(*1*) The Trials in General

In almost all the cases in which the plea of obedience to orders was submitted by war criminals, it was rejected by the Courts in their judgments and by the Judge Advocates in their summing-up[696]

693. See Klinge trial, *L.R.U.N.W.C.C.*, vol. 3, p. 14; W. Wagner trial—Notes, Sawada trial, *L.R.U.N.W.C.C.*, vol. 5, p. 17.

694. See e.g. Almelo trial, *L.R.U.N.W.C.C.*, vol. 1, p. 40; Belsen trial, *L.R.U.N.W.C.C.*, vol. 2, pp. 107–108; *W.C.T.S.*, vol. 2, pp. 589–591; Dostler trial, *L.R.U.N.W.C.C.*, vol. 1, pp. 28, 33; Double Tenth trial, *W.C.T.S.*, vol. 8, p. 258; Eichmann trial (first instance), Minutes, *op. cit.*, Session No. 5, p. B2; Session No. 112, pp. Y1–Cc1; Eichmann trial (second instance), Minutes, *op. cit.*, Session No. 2, pp. T1—U1; Session No. 5, pp. E1–F1; Falkenhorst trial, *W.C.T.S.*, vol. 6, p. 216; Hadamar trial, *W.C.T.S.*, vol. 4, pp. 209, 243–244; Jaluit Atoll case, *L.R.U.N.W.C.C.*, vol. 1, pp. 75–76; Kharkov trial, *People's Verdict*, pp. 114–115; Peleus trial, *L.R.U.N.W.C.C.*, vol. 1, pp. 10–11; *W.C.T.S.*, vol. 1, pp. 118–119; Renoth trial, *L.R.U.N.W.C.C.*, vol. 11, pp. 77–78; Zuehlke trial, *L.R.U.N.W.C.C.*, vol. 14, p. 147.

695. See and cf. Almelo trial, *L.R.U.N.W.C.C.*, vol. 1, pp. 39–40; Belsen trial, *L.R.U.N.W.C.C.*, vol. 2, p. 107; *W.C.T.S.*, vol. 2, pp. 589–590; Double Tenth trial, *W.C.T.S.*, vol. 8, p. 258; Eichmann trial (first instance), Minutes, *op. cit.*, Session No. 112, pp. Y1–Cc1; Eichmann trial (second instance), Minutes, *op. cit.*, Session No. 2, p. T1; Session No. 5, p. E1; Falkenhorst trial, *W.C.T.S.*, vol. 6, p. 216; Jaluit Atoll case, *L.R.U.N.W.C.C.*, vol. 1, p. 75; Kharkov trial, *People's Verdict*, pp. 114–115.

696. A reference to the summing-up of Judge Advocates will be made only when Military Courts operating on the lines of the British system are concerned. To

as a reason for an *a priori* discharge of the defendants from criminal responsibility.[697] And this all but uniform rule applies also to those trials conducted and terminated prior to the delivery of the judgment of the International Military Tribunal at Nuremberg.[698] In reality, only in one case among those published in the Law Reports of the United Nations War Crimes Commission was the

clarify the position held by Judge Advocates in such Courts, it may be advantageous to quote the following explanatory note of Lord Wright: 'In the case of the British Courts the Judge Advocate, who sits to help the Tribunal on questions of law and who sums up, provides in his address an analysis of the facts and the law which goes to explain the judgment' (Lord Wright, 'Foreword' to *L.R.U.N.W.C.C.*, vol. 1, p. x). See full details regarding the position of the Judge Advocate in British Military Courts—*L.R.U.N.W.C.C.*, vol. 1, Annex I, pp. 106–107; in Canadian Military Courts—*ibid.*, vol. 4, Annex, pp. 126–127; and in Australian Military Courts—*ibid.*, vol. 5, Annex, p. 99. The function of the Judge Advocate in American Military Tribunals is entirely different: under the judicial system of the armed forces in the United States, he serves as a prosecutor. See *ibid.*, vol. 1, Annex 2, p. 116; vol. 3, Annex 3, p. 108.

697. See Almelo trial, *L.R.U.N.W.C.C.*, vol. 1, pp. 40–41, 44; Awochi trial, *L.R.U.N.W.C.C.*, vol. 13, p. 123; Bauer trial, *L.R.U.N.W.C.C.*, vol. 8, pp. 16, 20; Belsen trial, *L.R.U.N.W.C.C.*, vol. 2, pp. 117–118; *W.C.T.S.*, vol. 2, pp. 631–632; Bruns trial, *L.R.U.N.W.C.C.*, vol. 3, p. 18; Buck trial, *L.R.U.N.W.C.C.*, vol. 5, p. 43; Buhler trial, *L.R.U.N.W.C.C.*, vol. 14, p. 38; Bury and Hafner trial, *L.R.U.N.W.C.C.*, vol. 3, p. 64; Dachau trial, *L.R.U.N.W.C.C.*, vol. 11, p. 8; Dostler trial, *L.R.U.N.W.C.C.*, vol. 1, p. 31; Double Tenth trial, *W.C.T.S.*, vol. 8, p. 276; Eichmann trial (first instance), Judgment, *op. cit.*, ss. 180, 216, 218–222, 225, 228, 231, 238–241; Eichmann trial (second instance), Judgment, *op. cit.*, pp. I2–I3, I30–I35, III1–III2, III6, III12–III13; Falkenhorst trial, *L.R.U.N.W.C.C.*, vol. 11, p. 25; *W.C.T.S.*, vol. 6, p. 226; Flesch trial, *L.R.U.N.W.C.C.*, vol. 6, pp. 117, 120; Goeth trial, *L.R.U.N.W.C.C.*, vol. 7, p. 10; Golkel trial, *L.R.U.N.W.C.C.*, vol. 5, p. 51; Gozawa trial, *W.C.T.S.*, vol. 3, pp. 227–228; Greiser trial, *L.R.U.N.W.C.C.*, vol. 13, pp. 114–116; Hadamar trial, *L.R.U.N.W.C.C.*, vol. 1, p. 54; Hans trial, *L.R.U.N.W.C.C.*, vol. 5, pp. 88, 92–93; Hoess trial, *L.R.U.N.W.C.C.*, vol. 7, p. 18; Holzer trial—Notes, Sawada trial, *L.R.U.N.W.C.C.*, vol. 5, p. 15; Jaluit Atoll case, *L.R.U.N.W.C.C.*, vol. 1, p. 76; Kharkov trial, *People's Verdict*, p. 124; Mackenzen and Maelzer trial, *L.R.U.N.W.C.C.*, vol. 8, p. 7; Maelzer trial, *L.R.U.N.W.C.C.*, vol. 11, p. 53; Manstein trial, *A.D.*, 1949, pp. 524–525; Motomura trial, *L.R.U.N.W.C.C.*, vol. 13, pp. 144–145; Ohashi trial, *L.R.U.N.W.C.C.*, vol. 5, p. 31; Peleus trial, *L.R.U.N.W.C.C.*, vol. 1, p. 12; *W.C.T.S.*, vol. 1, pp. 128–130; Rauter trial, *L.R.U.N.W.C.C.*, vol. 14, pp. 132–133; Renoth trial, *L.R.U.N.W.C.C.*, vol. 11, p. 78; Roechling case, *N.M.T.*, vol. 14, pp. 1103–1104; Rohde trial, *L.R.U.N.W.C.C.*, vol. 5, p. 58; Sakai trial, *L.R.U.N.W.C.C.*, vol. 14, p. 5; Sawada trial, *L.R.U.N.W.C.C.*, vol. 5, p. 7; Stalag Luft III case, *L.R.U.N.W.C.C.*, vol. 11, pp. 46–47, 51; Szabados trial, *L.R.U.N.W.C.C.*, vol. 9, p. 61; Thiele and Steinert trial, *L.R.U.N.W.C.C.*, vol. 3, p. 58; Yamamoto trial, *L.R.U.N.W.C.C.*, vol. 3, p. 79; Zuehlke trial, *L.R.U.N.W.C.C.*, vol. 14, pp. 147–150. Cf. *L.R.U.N.W.C.C.*, vol. 15 (Digest), pp. 155, 158–159; Appleman, *op. cit.*, p. 312 n. 67; Brand, *op. cit.*, p. 416; Dunbar, *op. cit.*, pp. 250–251; Eustathiades, 'Ordres', pp. 404, 414; Glaser, *Introduction*, p. 130; Glaser, 'L'Ordre', p. 328; Guggenheim, *op. cit.*, vol. 2, pp. 47–48 n. 3; *History of U.N.W.C.C.*, p. 287; Lauterpacht – Oppenheim, *International Law*, vol. 2 (7th ed., 1952), p. 571; Levie, *op. cit.*, p. 463; Spaight, *op. cit.*, (3rd ed., 1947), p. 57; Woetzel, *op. cit.*, p. 243.

698. This point is particularly emphasized by Green, 'Book Review (on *L.R.U.N.W.C.C.*, vol. 1)', *op. cit.*, p. 106.

use of the defence of obedience to orders successful in bringing about an automatic acquittal of the accused. This is the trial of Wagner, *Gauleiter* and civil governor of Alsace at the time of the Nazi occupation, and his assistants, who were brought to trial in 1946 before a French Military Tribunal at Strasbourg.[699] Wagner claimed that he had complied with the instructions of the *Führer*, whereas the rest of the defendants contended that they had acted in pursuance of Wagner's orders.[700] The Tribunal established the fact that none of the accused save one really perpetrated his crimes in submission to superior orders; all these, including Wagner, were, therefore, found guilty and sentenced to death.[701] But in respect of one of the defendants, named Luger, who had been charged with complicity in murder—having functioned as a public prosecutor in a Nazi trial, or rather mistrial, in which innocent men were sentenced to death—the Tribunal reached the conclusion that he had indeed obeyed Wagner's orders and consequently decided to acquit him.[702] This is a unique case, and it seems to be an anomalous phenomenon and an historical anachronism, which does not fall into line with all the other post-Second World War cases.[703]

Yet, again, the repudiation of obedience to orders as an automatic defence does not necessarily mean acquiescence in the doctrine of absolute liability. Very illuminating in this regard is the judgment rendered in 1948 by a Dutch Court at Amsterdam in the case of the German warden Zuehlke, who was brought to trial for maltreatment of Jewish and other prisoners.[704] When the prosecution in this case tried to rely on Article 8 of the London Charter to reject the defendant's plea of having complied with superior orders, the Court pronounced that the Article had been formulated as it had been only because it was designed to apply exclusively to major war criminals.[705] The judgment further proclaimed, with regard to the provision of the Article:

699. R. Wagner trial, *L.R.U.N.W.C.C.*, vol. 3, p. 23.
700. *Ibid.*, pp. 38, 54. Eustathiades rightly points out this case as a classical illustration of shifting the responsibility upwards from one hierarchical rung to another (Eustathiades, 'Ordres', p. 397).
701. R. Wagner trial, *L.R.U.N.W.C.C.*, vol. 3, pp. 41–42, 54. An appeal by these defendants to a higher court was dismissed (*ibid.*, pp. 47, 49).
702. *Ibid.*, pp. 42, 54. See particularly *L.R.U.N.W.C.C.*, Notes, Sawada trial, vol. 5, pp. 16–17. Cf. *L.R.U.N.W.C.C.*, vol. 15 (Digest), p. 158 nn. 2, 4; Appleman, *op. cit.*, p. 311 n. 65; Eustathiades, 'Ordres', p. 397 n. 8.
703. Knieriem indeed reports two other French judgments, in which defendants who had committed war crimes pursuant to orders were acquitted (Knieriem, *op. cit.*, p. 253); but he himself admits that these cases 'constitute a rare exception' (*ibid.*).
704. Zuehlke trial, *L.R.U.N.W.C.C.*, vol. 14, p. 139.
705. *Ibid.*, pp. 147–148.

'This provision ... has no direct application in the present case, but could apply indirectly if it were to be regarded as a rule concerning a special instance of an express general rule of international criminal law.

'It is the opinion of the Court that this is not so, and it cannot be understood why the exonerating effect of an official order ... should not be valid in the sphere of international criminal law'.[706]

These are strong words, but the Court nevertheless ruled that the fact that the defendant had carried out superior orders did not justify his acquittal.[707] It emerges that the Court by no means subscribed to automatic discharge from responsibility as a result of obedience to orders and did not intend to be the protagonist of the doctrine of *respondeat superior.* It only wished to establish that there is no substance in the opposite doctrine of absolute liability, as reflected in Article 8, and that in certain circumstances the fact of obedience to orders may bring about acquittal. There is, however, a certain ambiguity in the laconic explanation given in the sequence of the judgment to this conclusion: on the one hand, the Court held that an order to commit actions forbidden by international law should not be obeyed and that mistake of law in this regard does not exculpate; on the other, it adduced in support the German rule on the subject of obedience to orders, as applied in the Leipzig trials, and declared that the defendant ought to be convicted, for he had been aware of the illegality of his actions.[708] Now, if mistake of law is no cause for acquittal, why was conviction here predicated on the fact of lack of mistake and how is it consistent with the rule laid down in Leipzig? If I understand the judgment correctly, the Court desired to give expression to the manifest illegality principle as the binding rule under international law. The defendant had obeyed orders that were apparently regarded by the Court as manifestly illegal; the judgment explicitly stated that he must have known that ill-treatment of prisoners does not belong to the sphere of military submission to orders and instructions.[709] In these conditions, of manifest illegality, mistake of law was rejected as a defence. But, in different circumstances, had the illegality not been obvious on the face of it, the defendant might have been able to benefit from such a mistake and be relieved of responsibility.

The Special Court of Cassation affirmed the judgment of the lower Court.[710] It also denied that Article 8 of the London Charter reflects

706. *Ibid.*, p. 147.
707. *Ibid.*, p. 148.
708. *Ibid.*
709. *Ibid.*
710. *Ibid.*

the rule of international law in respect of ordinary offenders and held that it applies, and can apply, only to the major war criminals.[711] The conviction of the defendant was mainly based, in the second instance, on the test provided by German military law and underlying the judgments rendered in Leipzig: the defendant, while carrying out orders, knew full well of the unlawfulness of his acts and hence ought to incur responsibility.[712] Thus, in point of fact, the Court of Cassation subscribed to the personal knowledge principle.

The judgments in the two instances in the Zuehlke trial are not the only ones pointing in the direction of the personal knowledge principle or the manifest illegality principle; these twin principles gained enthusiastic support from Courts and Judge Advocates in many important cases.[713] Particularly noteworthy is the summing-up of the Judge Advocate in the Buck trial, conducted before a British Military Court at Wuppertal in 1946, in which he

> 'expressed the view that an accused would be guilty if he committed a war crime in pursuance of an order, first if the order was *obviously unlawful*, secondly if the accused *knew that the order was unlawful*, or thirdly if he *ought to have known it to be unlawful had he considered the circumstances in which it was given*'.[714]

It is peculiar, however, that the Judge Advocate found it necessary to classify under three distinct heads the cases in which offenders acting in compliance with orders should be convicted. Actually, it would have been sufficient to enumerate just the two last categories, namely, when the defendant is aware of the unlawfulness of the order and when he ought to have been aware of it. The first category,

711. *Ibid.*, pp. 148–149. Cf. Eustathiades, 'Ordres', pp. 401–402.
712. Zuehlke trial, *L.R.U.N.W.C.C.*, vol. 14, pp. 149–150.
713. See Almelo trial, *L.R.U.N.W.C.C.*, vol. 1, p. 44; Belsen trial, *L.R.U.N.W.C.C.*, vol. 2, pp. 117–118; *W.C.T.S.*, vol. 2, pp. 631–632; Buck trial, *L.R.U.N.W.C.C.*, vol. 5, pp. 43–44; Eichmann trial (first instance), Judgment, *op. cit.*, ss. 218–219, 221–222; Eichmann trial (second instance), Judgment, *op. cit.*, pp. I32–I33, III1; Falkenhorst trial, *L.R.U.N.W.C.C.*, vol. 11, p. 25; *W.C.T.S.*, vol. 6, p. 226; Flesch trial, *L.R.U.N.W.C.C.*, vol. 6, pp. 117, 120; Golkel trial, *L.R.U.N.W.C.C.*, vol. 5, p. 51; Hans trial, *L.R.U.N.W.C.C.*, vol. 5, p. 92; Holzer trial—Notes, Sawada trial, *L.R.U.N.W.C.C.*, vol. 5, p. 15; Motomura trial, *L.R.U.N.W.C.C.*, vol. 13, pp. 144–145; Ohashi trial, *L.R.U.N.W.C.C.*, vol. 5, p. 31; Peleus trial, *L.R.U.N.W.C.C.*, vol. 1, pp. 12, 19; *W.C.T.S.*, vol. 1, p. 129; Rauter trial, *L.R.U.N.W.C.C.*, vol. 14, pp. 132–133; Rohde trial, *L.R.U.N.W.C.C.*, vol. 5, p. 58; Stalag Luft III case, *L.R.U.N.W.C.C.*, vol. 11, pp. 46–47. See also Buhler trial, *L.R.U.N.W.C.C.*, vol. 14, p. 38. Cf. *L.R.U.N.W.C.C.*, vol. 15 (Digest), pp. 157–158; *L.R.U.N.W.C.C.*, Notes, Sawada trial, vol. 5, p. 16; Eustathiades, 'Ordres', pp. 404–405, 411–412; Glaser, *Introduction*, p. 130; Glaser, 'L'Ordre', p. 328; Greenspan, *op. cit.*, p. 441; Kelsen, *Principles*, p. 137 n. 27.
714. Buck trial, *L.R.U.N.W.C.C.*, vol. 5, p. 43. See also Golkel trial, *L.R.U.N.W.C.C.*, vol. 5, p. 51. Cf. Eustathiades, 'Ordres'. p. 411 n. 47.

of manifestly illegal orders, is in fact fully covered by the two others and has no right to independent existence, for, when a manifestly illegal order is involved, the defendant either knows or ought to know of the illegality. Ultimately, the triple classification, by its very redundancy, merely adds force to the argument that the manifest illegality principle should be regarded as an auxiliary device to ascertain the personal knowledge of the accused, and no more.

The best-known case of the application of the personal knowledge principle and the manifest illegality principle after the Second World War is the Peleus trial,[715] which took place in 1945 before a British[716] Military Court at Hamburg. The facts in this trial are amazingly similar to those in the Llandovery Castle case.[717] The Peleus was a Greek ship in British service, sunk by a German submarine commanded by the first defendant, Eck. Most of the members of the crew of the Peleus succeeded in reaching two rafts or grasping at the wreckage which floated around. The German submarine promptly surfaced and at Eck's order opened fire on the survivors, of whom the great majority were hit and drowned. Eck and four of his subordinates who had fired on the survivors were brought to trial. Eck's defence was that the criminal act had been necessary to eliminate all traces of the sinking of the Peleus and enable the submarine to slip away from the area without fear of being intercepted by Allied planes.[718] Eck did not contend that he had acted in obedience to orders or try to rely on such a plea,[719] but the defence of the four other accused mainly centred around the fact that they had complied with Eck's command.[720] All five were convicted.[721] With regard to the defence of obedience to orders, the Judge Advocate made the following impressive statement:

> 'It is quite obvious that no sailor and no soldier can carry with him a library of International Law, or have immediate access to a professor in that subject who can tell him whether or not a particular command is a lawful one. If this were a case which involved the careful consideration of questions of International Law as to whether or not the command to fire at helpless survivors struggling in the water was lawful, you might well think it would

715. Peleus trial, *L.R.U.N.W.C.C.*, vol. 1, p. 1; *W.C.T.S.*, vol. 1, *passim.*
716. Among the members of the Court there were, however, Greek officers. See Peleus trial, *L.R.U.N.W.C.C.*, vol. 1, p. 1.
717. See *supra*, pp. 14ff.
718. Peleus trial, *L.R.U.N.W.C.C.*, vol. 1, pp. 4–5, 15; *W.C.T.S.*, vol. 1, p. xxxiv.
719. See Peleus trial, *L.R.U.N.W.C.C.*, vol. 1, pp. 4, 15; *W.C.T.S.*, vol. 1, pp. xli–xlii, 128. See also Peleus trial, *W.C.T.S.*, vol. 1, Appendix XX, p. 228; Mohle trial, *L.R.U.N.W.C.C.*, vol. 9, p. 81.
720. Peleus trial, *L.R.U.N.W.C.C.*, vol. 1, pp. 4, 9–10; *W.C.T.S.*, vol. 1, pp. xliii–xlv, 44, 96, 100–101, 103, 107–115.
721. Peleus trial, *L.R.U.N.W.C.C.*, vol. 1, p. 12; *W.C.T.S.*, vol. 1, p. 139.

not be fair to hold any of the subordinate accused in this case responsible for what they are alleged to have done; but is it not fairly obvious to you that if in fact the carrying out of Eck's command involved the killing of these helpless survivors, it was not a lawful command, and that it must have been obvious to the most rudimentary intelligence that it was not a lawful command, and that those who did that shooting are not to be excused for doing it upon the ground of superior orders?'[722]

It clearly emerges from this passage that, when an offender complies with superior orders out of unawareness of the law, he ought to be relieved of responsibility. The Judge Advocate underscored that a soldier cannot be expected to be a scholar in international law; but when a manifestly illegal order is involved, when the law is not wrapped in mystery and the soldier does not have to indulge in homiletical interpretations, the contention that the soldier did not know the law will not be put up with: knowledge of the law is imputed to him in such a case, being implicit in the nature of things.[723] Criminal responsibility is, therefore, contingent on the personal knowledge of the accused.

Of course, when they raised the banner of the personal knowledge or manifest illegality principle, the Courts overstepped the boundaries fixed by the doctrine of absolute liability as reflected in Article 8 of the London Charter and in Article II(4)(b) of Control Council Law No. 10. Yet, strange as it may seem, the editors of the Law Reports of the United Nations War Crimes Commission deliberately ignored the incompatibility between the views of these Courts and the provisions of the Articles mentioned. They recapitulated in the following way the gist of the judgments supporting the two principles in question:

'The true test in practice is whether an order, *illegal* under international law, on which an accused has acted was or must be presumed to have been known to him to be so illegal, or was obviously so illegal . . . or should have been recognised by him as being so illegal. The *general upshot* of a large number of decisions, and of the advice of Judge Advocates to British or Commonwealth courts, is that, if the order comes within one or more of these categories, then the accused cannot rely upon the plea of superior orders'.[724]

So far so good. But in the sequence it appears that there is a hitch in this summation:

722. Peleus trial, *L.R.U.N.W.C.C.*, vol. 1, p. 12; *W.C.T.S.*, vol. 1, p. 129. Cf. Dunbar, *op. cit.*, p. 255; Eustathiades, 'Ordres', p. 412; Schafer, *op. cit.*, p. 143; Kafr Kassem case (first instance), *op. cit.*, pp. 219–220; Kafr Kassem case (second instance), *op. cit.*, pp. 411–412. Cf. also Buck trial, *L.R.U.N.W.C.C.*, vol. 5, p. 44.

723. Dunbar quotes the address of the Judge Advocate in the Peleus trial and states: 'Thus, knowledge of the unlawful nature of an order may often be inferred' (Dunbar, *op. cit.*, p. 255).

724. *L.R.U.N.W.C.C.*, vol. 15 (Digest), p. 158. Cf. Kelsen, *Principles*, p. 137 n. 27.

'As to the effectiveness of the plea when put forward in circumstances which, in accordance with the rules just laid down, make it permissible to plead superior orders, the general attitude of the courts and the rule expressed in numerous municipal and international law enactments, including the Charter of the International Military Tribunal and Law No. 10, has been that, while obedience to superior orders does not constitute a defence upon which an accused can rely with certainty of being completely protected thereby, it may at the discretion of the court be treated as a factor which justifies mitigation of punishment'.[725]

This is a not particularly successful attempt to reconcile the irreconcilable. Thus, the editors of the Law Reports tried to create the impression that the Courts advocating the espousal of the personal knowledge principle or the manifest illegality principle in fact restricted the applicability of the principles to the sphere of the assessment of punishment and did not contest the rule expressed in various enactments that obedience to orders constitutes no defence. To qualify this broad—and odd—statement slightly, they referred to the fact of obedience to orders as not constituting a defence upon which the accused may rely 'with certainty of being completely protected thereby'. The trouble is that, even with this qualification, the statement misrepresents the tenor of the judgments and the enactments. The London Charter and Law No. 10 are not at all ready to recognize obedience to orders as a defence, either as a certain defence or as one available in emergency. On the other hand, the Courts which subscribed to the personal knowledge and manifest illegality principles made it abundantly clear that, under specified conditions, that is, in case of a permissible mistake of law, the accused who obeyed orders may rely with certainty on a full defence. How wide of the mark the Law Reports' summing-up is may be deduced from the address of the Judge Advocate in the Peleus trial, where, as we have just observed, it is unequivocally stated that, had that case not involved orders whose illegality was obvious to the most rudimentary intelligence, it would have been perfectly legitimate to free the defendants from responsibility for their acts. In the address of the Judge Advocate in the Buck trial cited above, it was also emphasized, lucidly and expressly, that personal knowledge of the illegality, or, alternatively, manifest illegality, is a condition precedent to criminal conviction. According to the ruling in these as well as in other trials, the very conviction, and not merely the evaluation of the punishment, is thrown into the scale.

Evidently, only some of the Courts admitted the validity of the principles of personal knowledge and manifest illegality, whereas others endorsed the rule laid down in the London Charter. The fallacy in the summing-up of the editors of the Law Reports lies in

725. *L.R.U.N.W.C.C.*, vol. 15 (Digest), pp. 158–159. See also *ibid.*, p. 184.

the vain attempt to lump together the notions of two distinct schools of thought into one coherent concept, and demonstrate that even the proponents of the twin principles feel bound by the provision of Article 8 of the London Charter. Doubtless the summing-up in this vein is derived from the perfectly good intention to find a common denominator, universally accepted, in the knotty problem of obedience to orders. But good intentions, as is well known, do not necessarily pave the road to heaven. The summing-up is especially fraught with danger because it is invested with an aura of respectability, coming as it does straight from the horse's mouth, from the editors of the very Law Reports that are the main source of our information regarding the war crimes trials, and there is a natural tendency in the literature to reproduce it without first reconsidering the matter.[726] The editors would have done a much greater service had they made a clear distinction between the different schools of thought that are discerned in the cases dealing with the subject of obedience to orders, and had they illuminated the points of conflict between them. Then they might have detected the error made by those Courts, advocating the personal knowledge and manifest illegality principles, which looked upon obedience to orders as a defence *per se* under certain conditions—namely, when the accused is unaware, and need not be aware, of the unlawfulness of the order—and failed to take note that in such cases obedience to orders constitutes only a factual facet of another defence, to wit, that of mistake of law.

And from mistake of law to mistake of fact. We have observed that defence counsel in the war crimes trials put forward, *inter alia*, a combined plea of obedience to orders and mistake of fact. And indeed in some cases, Courts and Judge Advocates held that a defendant who had obeyed an unlawful order on account of mistake of fact should not incur responsibility for his act.[727] Of particular interest in this regard is the Scuttled U-Boats case, of which the facts have been given above.[728] As will be recalled, the defendant here claimed that when he scuttled the submarines he mistakenly thought that he was acting in compliance with an order, and was not aware of the terms of surrender which had rendered his act a war crime. The Judge Advocate expressly stated in his summing-up that, if the judges really believed this allegation of the defendant,

726. See e.g. Brand, *op. cit.*, p. 416. Cf. Eustathiades, 'Ordres', pp. 413–414.
727. See Almelo trial, *L.R.U.N.W.C.C.*, vol. 1, pp. 40–41, 44–45; Hans trial, *L.R.U.N.W.C.C.*, vol. 5, pp. 86, 88–93; Rath and Thiel trial, *L.R.U.N.W.C.C.*, vol. 15 (Digest), p. 184 n. 4; Scuttled U-Boats case, *L.R.U.N.W.C.C.*, vol. 1, pp. 69–70; Stalag Luft III case, *L.R.U.N.W.C.C.*, vol. 11, p. 51. See also Buck trial, *L.R.U.N.W.C.C.*, vol. 5, p. 44. Cf. *L.R.U.N.W.C.C.*, vol. 15 (Digest), p. 184; Maunoir, *op. cit.*, p. 239.
728. See *supra*, pp. 192–193.

they ought to acquit him on the basis of his dual mistake in respect of the state of facts.[729] The Court apparently did not believe the story, for the accused was found guilty of the charge;[730] but we ought to be careful in analyzing the important legal direction of the Judge Advocate. If there were a solid factual foundation to the defendant's plea and he had been acquitted, his salvation would not have come from the defence of obedience to orders, for actually no order existed at the time of the commission of the offence. The defence that would have availed him in that case would have been one of mistake of fact, as an aspect of the broader defence of lack of *mens rea*.[731] It ought to be kept in mind, though, that the effect of the defence of mistake of fact is that no criminal responsibility can be imposed on an accused to any greater extent than he would have had to incur for his act had the real state of affairs been such as he mistakenly believed to exist.[732] The question, therefore, is on what basis would the defendant here have been entitled to exemption from responsibility had the real state of affairs been such as he mistakenly believed to exist? The answer is, the basis of mistake of law. The defendant believed not only that he was carrying out an order, but that he was doing it in such circumstances—namely, circumstances in which the terms of the surrender, as it were, did not exist—as rendered the order entirely lawful. Had he believed that he were indeed carrying out an order, but in circumstances that did not remove the stain of unlawfulness, there would have been no legal foundation for acquittal. In such a case, the position of the defendant would not have been more advantageous than that of any offender obeying an illegal order which exists in the world of reality and not only in his imagination. If the defendant had a peg to hang his defence on, it was the mistaken belief in facts that transformed the imaginary order from an unlawful to a lawful one.

Another interesting case is the Hans trial,[733] which was heard in 1947 before Norwegian Courts. Hans had been the leader of a *Sonderkommando* which had executed hundreds of Norwegians, and charges were laid against him on account of those executions which he had carried out pursuant to orders of his superior without previous trial of the victims. Hans contended that in all cases his superior had informed him that the executions were in accordance with the

729. Scuttled U-Boats case, *L.R.U.N.W.C.C.*, vol. 1, pp. 69–70.
730. *Ibid.*, p. 65.
731. That is also how this defence is labelled by the editors of the Law Reports of the United Nations War Crimes Commission. See *ibid.*, p. 69.
732. Cf. the text of Section 12 of the Israel Criminal Code Ordinance, 1936, *supra*, note 267.
733. Hans trial, *L.R.U.N.W.C.C.*, vol. 5, p. 82.

sentence of a court.[734] In the first instance, Hans was acquitted on several of the counts of the indictment, for the Court was convinced that in these cases he had indeed not known that the executions had been carried out without previous legal proceedings.[735] On the other counts, however, he was convicted by a majority of the judges, who were of opinion that in those cases he ought to have been aware of the actual situation.[736] The minority, on the other hand, maintained that he should be acquitted even on the latter counts, because it had not been proved that he had really known that the executions he had carried out were not preceded by trials.[737] Hans appealed to the Norwegian Supreme Court, and here the minority opinion in the lower Court prevailed and the conviction was quashed.[738] In this trial, therefore, a defendant who had committed crimes in obedience to orders was successfully relieved of responsibility thanks to the defence of a mistake of fact.

Despite the recognition of both mistake of law and mistake of fact as legitimate defences from which the subordinate who acts pursuant to orders is entitled to benefit, in no case did the Courts accept the plea put forward by defence counsel that the accused ought to be acquitted on the ground that he committed criminal acts in obedience to orders that misrepresented the acts as lawful measures of reprisal.[739]

Another plea that did not avail the defendants was that based on a combination of obedience to orders and compulsion.[740] Nevertheless, there is no reason to think that, in the trials of the ordinary war criminals, the knell was sounded for the defence of compulsion. The most radical opinion expressed against this defence was enunciated in the following way by the Judge Advocate in the Fauerstein

734. *Ibid.*, p. 86.
735. *Ibid.*
736. *Ibid.*, pp. 86–88.
737. *Ibid.*, pp. 88–89.
738. *Ibid.*, pp. 89–92.
739. See Dostler trial, *L.R.U.N.W.C.C.*, vol. 1, p. 31; Mackenzen and Maelzer trial, *L.R.U.N.W.C.C.*, vol. 8, pp. 7–8. See also Falkenhorst trial, *L.R.U.N.W.C.C.*, vol. 11, p. 26.
740. See Bruns trial, *L.R.U.N.W.C.C.*, vol. 3, pp. 18–20; Eichmann trial (first instance), Judgment, *op. cit.*, ss. 222, 225, 228, 231, 238–241; Eichmann trial (second instance), Judgment, *op. cit.*, pp. I2–I3, I34–I35, III1, III13; Fauerstein trial, *L.R.U.N.W.C.C.*, vol. 15 (Digest), p. 173; Hadamar trial, *L.R.U.N.W.C.C.*, vol. 1, p. 54; Holzer trial—Notes, Sawada trial, *L.R.U.N.W.C.C.*, vol. 5, p. 16; *L.R.U.N.W.C.C.*, vol. 15 (Digest), p. 173; Rauter trial, *L.R.U.N.W.C.C.*, vol. 14, p. 133; Roechling case, *N.M.T.*, vol. 14, pp. 1104–1105; Stalag Luft III case, *L.R.U.N.W.C.C.*, vol. 11, p. 47; Zuehlke trial, *L.R.U.N.W.C.C.*, vol. 14, p. 150. See also Almelo trial, *L.R.U.N.W.C.C.*, vol. 1, pp. 44–45. Cf. *L.R.U.N.W.C.C.*, Notes, Falkenhorst trial, vol. 11, p. 25.

trial, which was conducted in 1948 before a British Military Court at Hamburg:

> 'There is, further, a defence which to some extent is akin to that of superior orders, and that is the defence... of "duress and coercion"... Now that defence of "duress and coercion" is not a defence in law. You are not entitled, even if you wished to save your own life, to take the life of another'.[741]

According to this view, the remedy in the case of compulsion lies in the power of the Court to reduce the punishment.[742] But while the statement of the Judge Advocate allows compulsion no standing as a defence, it relates to a very grave act, the infliction of death, and ignores the numerous possibilities of committing lighter offences under the spur of necessity or duress. What is the rule in case of compulsion to commit a war crime of an inferior degree? The Judge Advocate in the Holzer trial, which took place in 1946 before a Canadian Military Court in Germany, distinguished between ordinary offences and grave crimes, saying:

> 'There is no doubt on the authorities that compulsion is a defence when the crime is not of a heinous character. But the killing of an innocent person can never be justified'.[743]

And it can also be gathered from the pronouncements of other Courts that in certain cases and under specified conditions, which were not fulfilled insofar as the accused in the dock were concerned, the defence based on compulsion can absolve from guilt an offender who acted in pursuance of superior orders.[744]

Finally, it is noteworthy that in many of the trials it was established that in appropriate circumstances, especially those of mistake of law and compulsion, the fact of obedience to orders may serve as a cause for leniency in punishment.[745] And it should be carefully

741. Fauerstein trial, *L.R.U.N.W.C.C.*, vol. 15 (Digest), p. 173. Cf. Eustathiades, 'Ordres', pp. 417–418 n. 69.
742. Fauerstein trial, *L.R.U.N.W.C.C.*, vol. 15 (Digest), p. 173. Cf. Eustathiades, 'Ordres', p. 418 n. 69.
743. Holzer trial—Notes, Sawada trial, *L.R.U.N.W.C.C.*, vol. 5, p. 16; *L.R.U.N.W.C.C.*, vol. 15 (Digest), p. 173.
744. See Rauter trial, *L.R.U.N.W.C.C.*, vol. 14, p. 133. See also Roechling case, *N.M.T.*, vol. 14, pp. 1104–1105; Stalag Luft III case, *L.R.U.N.W.C.C.*, vol. 11, p. 47. Cf. *L.R.U.N.W.C.C.*, vol. 15 (Digest), p. 174; Eustathiades, 'Ordres', pp. 415, 419, 421; Glaser, *Introduction*, p. 130; Glaser, 'L'Ordre', p. 328.
745. See Bauer trial, *L.R.U.N.W.C.C.*, vol. 8, pp. 16, 20–21; Fauerstein trial, *L.R.U.N.W.C.C.*, vol. 15 (Digest), p. 173; Gozawa trial, *L.R.U.N.W.C.C.*, vol. 15 (Digest), p. 159; *W.C.T.S.*, vol. 3, pp. 230–231; Jaluit Atoll case, *L.R.U.N.W.C.C.*, vol. 1, p. 76; Notes, Sawada trial, *L.R.U.N.W.C.C.*, vol. 5, pp. 18–19; *L.R.U.N.W.C.C.*, vol. 15 (Digest), p. 159 n. 1; Manstein trial, *A.D.*, 1949, p. 525; Melchior and Hirschelman trial—Notes, Sawada trial, *L.R.U.N.W.C.C.*, vol. 5, p. 17; Neuber trial—Notes, Sawada trial, *L.R.U.N.W.C.C.*, vol. 5, pp. 17–18; Sawada trial, *L.R.U.N.W.C.C.*, vol. 5, pp. 7–8, 13. See also W. Wagner trial—

observed that not in every case of obedience to orders is the defendant entitled to extenuation of his sentence: the scales of punishment are tipped not automatically but by the circumstances of the concrete case.[746]

(2) The Eichmann Trial

Writing, as I do, in the State of Israel, on the subject of obedience to superior orders, I feel that it is incumbent upon me to devote a special section to a full discussion of the judgments delivered in the two instances in the trial of Adolf Eichmann. The principal defence of the accused was that 'all he did, was in accordance with orders from his superiors',[747] and hence he did not have to incur responsibility for his part in the implementation of the so-called 'final solution of the Jewish question'.[748] The District Court of Jerusalem, in the first instance, and the Supreme Court of Israel, in appeal, were at one in their opinion that the defence of obedience to orders could not avail the accused,[749] and he was convicted and sentenced to death. But there are differences of shade in the judges' approach, and it is desirable to point out in detail the reasons that underlay the rejection of this defence.

As for the judgment of the District Court, it should be noted, in the first place, that it cut even the factual basis from under the plea of obedience to orders. The Court proclaimed:

> 'We reject absolutely the accused's version that he was nothing more than a "small cog" in the extermination machine. We find that in the RSHA, which was the central authority dealing with the final solution of the Jewish question, the accused was at the head of those engaged in carrying out the final solution. In fulfilling this task, the accused acted in accordance with general directives from his superiors, but there still remained to him wide powers of discretion which extended also to the planning of operations on his own initiative. He was not a puppet in the hands of others; his place was amongst those who pulled the strings'.[750]

The Court, however, did not content itself with a factual rejection of the defence of the accused, and in the sequel of its judgment it

Notes, Sawada trial, *L.R.U.N.W.C.C.*, vol. 5, p. 17. Cf. *L.R.U.N.W.C.C.*, vol. 15 (Digest), pp. 155, 158–159, 174, 184, 187; Brand, *op. cit.*, p. 416; Eustathiades, 'Ordres', pp. 398, 413, 414 n. 60, 418 n. 69; Lauterpacht – Oppenheim, *International Law*, vol. 2 (7th ed., 1952), pp. 570 n. 2, 571; Levie, *op. cit.*, p. 463; Maunoir, *op. cit.*, pp. 259–260; Spaight, *op. cit.*, (3rd ed., 1947), p. 60.

746. See particularly Bruns trial, *L.R.U.N.W.C.C.*, vol. 3, p. 18; Klinge trial, *L.R.U.N.W.C.C.*, vol. 3, p. 6.
747. Eichmann trial (first instance), Judgment, *op. cit.*, s. 216.
748. For references to the arguments of counsel for the defence (Servatius) in this regard, see *supra*, note 680. See also *supra*, p. 191.
749. See *supra*, note 697.
750. Eichmann trial (first instance), Judgment, *op. cit.*, s. 180.

emphasized that, according to the Israeli statute under which Eichmann was indicted, the Nazis and Nazi Collaborators (Punishment) Law, 5710–1950,[751] the plea of obedience to orders could not relieve him of responsibility for his crimes.[752]

The Nazis and Nazi Collaborators (Punishment) Law provides as follows in Section 8:

> 'Sections 16, 17, 18 and 19 of the Criminal Code shall not apply to offences under this Law'.[753]

It should be clarified here that, of these Sections of the Criminal Code Ordinance, 1936, whose application is excluded, Section 17 allows the defence of constraint,[754] Section 18 permits the defence of necessity,[755] and Section 19(b) validates the defence of obedience to superior orders when orders that are not manifestly unlawful are concerned.[756] All these three defences are, therefore, denied to offenders who are brought to trial by virtue of the Nazis and Nazi Collaborators (Punishment) Law. But Section 11 of that Law stipulates that

> 'In determining the punishment of a person convicted of an offence under this Law, the court may take into account, as grounds for mitigating the punishment, the following circumstances:
>
> '(a) that the person committed the offence under conditions which, but for section 8, would have exempted him from criminal responsibility or constituted a reason for pardoning the offence, and that he did his best to reduce the gravity of the consequences of the offence'.[757]

The District Court pronounced that the orders obeyed by Eichmann were manifestly illegal.[758] Even though the manifest illegality test is objective in character—and the Court expressly stated so[759]—the judgment, to make assurance doubly sure, quoted the instructive testimony of the defendant, in which he had openly admitted that the illegality of the orders which he had obeyed did not escape him:

> 'Your Honour, President of the Court, since you call upon me to say and give a clear answer, I must declare that I see in this murder, in the extermination of Jews, one of the gravest crimes in the history of humanity'.[760]

751. Laws of the State of Israel, vol. 4 (5710–1949/50), p. 154.
752. Eichmann trial (first instance), Judgment, *op. cit.*, s. 218.
753. Laws of the State of Israel, vol. 4 (5710–1949/50), p. 156.
754. See *supra*, note 241.
755. See *supra*, note 242.
756. See *supra*, p. 9.
757. Laws of the State of Israel, vol. 4 (5710–1949/50), p. 157.
758. Eichmann trial (first instance), Judgment, *op. cit.*, ss. 221–222.
759. *Ibid.*, s. 221. See *supra*, note 62.
760. Eichmann trial (first instance), Judgment, *op. cit.*, s. 221. This testimony appears in the Eichmann trial (first instance), Minutes, *op. cit.*, Session No. 95, p. V1. In the transcript of both the English and the Hebrew renderings, however,

To the question whether that was the way in which he had regarded the matter at the time of the perpetration of the crimes, Eichmann replied:

> 'I already at that time realised that this solution by the use of force was something unlawful, something terrible, but to my regret, I was obliged to deal with it in matters of transportation, because of my oath of loyalty, from which I was not released'.[761]

It is indicated in the judgment that, since Eichmann obeyed manifestly illegal orders, even had it not been for the special provision of Section 8 of the Nazis and Nazi Collaborators (Punishment) Law—that is, even had the general legal rule obtaining in Israel, as expressed in Section 19(b) of the Criminal Code Ordinance, applied to this case—the fact of obedience to orders would not have availed the defendant as a shield against criminal responsibility; hence the possibility of mitigating his punishment in accordance with Section 11 was also eliminated.[762]

Did Eichmann act out of compulsion? The Court described the defence plea as follows:

> 'the accused tried to convince us that only obedience to orders motivated and guided him in all his activities, that only blind obedience, "cadaver-like" obedience (*Kadavergehorsam*), is the thing which silenced his conscience. That is why he presented himself as an insignificant official, with no opinion of his own in all matters with which he had to deal, and as lacking in all initiative in his work'.[763]

As we noted at the outset, the judgment—in the light of all the facts assembled—uncompromisingly rejected the defence of the 'small cog', and held that Eichmann belonged to those who had made the big wheels turn. The Court added here that, inasmuch as the defendant had received orders, he had not acted perforce; his key position and hideous part in the implementation of the 'final solution' had been a result not of '"cadaver-like" obedience', or even ordinary human obedience, but of a whole-hearted inner conviction.[764]

When the approach of the District Court to the question of obedience to orders is summarized, it is patent that the judgment relied almost exclusively on the foundations of Israel national law. The

the key words 'I see' were translated as 'I saw' (see Hebrew minutes of this session, pp. 35–36). The English version of the testimony which appears in the Minutes is also slightly different in various other, secondary, respects from that reproduced in the judgment.

761. Eichmann trial (first instance), Judgment, *op. cit.*, s. 221. This statement appears, in a different translation, in the Eichmann trial (first instance), Minutes, *op. cit.*, Session No. 95, p. W1.
762. Eichmann trial (first instance), Judgment, *op. cit.*, s. 222.
763. *Ibid.*, s. 228.
764. *Ibid.*, ss. 228, 231, 238–241.

Court did indeed point out that the Nazis and Nazi Collaborators (Punishment) Law, in suppressing the plea of obedience to orders as a reason for exemption from responsibility, follows the London Charter and Control Council Law No. 10.[765] It was also stressed in the judgment that

> 'in civilised countries, the rejection of the defence of "superior orders" as exempting completely from criminal responsibility has now become general'.[766]

In the same way, the judgment adduced in support the Resolution of the General Assembly of the United Nations in respect of the Affirmation of the Nuremberg Principles.[767] The Court, however, apparently thought that, with this, it had discharged its duty: it did not seek to fathom international law on the subject, nor did it attempt to examine the authorities or to explore the theories in the international field. It is typical that, while the judgment quoted *in extenso* from the pronouncements of the Israel Military Courts of both instances in the Kafr Kassem case, regarding obedience to orders,[768] it did not dwell at all upon the enunciations of the International Military Tribunal in the Nuremberg trial on the same subject.

In this last respect, the approach of the Supreme Court, in the first part of its judgment, was completely different. After having surveyed the argumentation of counsel for the appellant (Servatius) concerning obedience to orders,[769] the Court observed that its principal object in the matter was to clarify the meaning and significance of the plea of obedience to orders from the particular viewpoint of international law.[770] The Court found it advisable, first of all, to draw a methodical distinction between the subjects of acts of State and of obedience to superior orders in international law.[771] It noted the dilemma generated by an unlawful order from a theoretical—that is, the legal system's—outlook, as well as from a practical—that is, the soldier's—outlook, as a result of the conflict of interests between military discipline and the supremacy of the law, and the sanctions threatening the soldier on all sides.[772] Before it started to enquire into the international rule, the Court repeated briefly that the defence of the appellant ought to have been rejected in accordance with the general criminal law obtaining in Israel,

765. *Ibid.*, s. 218.
766. *Ibid.*, s. 220.
767. *Ibid.* With regard to the Resolution of the General Assembly, see below, Part V, Chapter 2.
768. Eichmann trial (first instance), Judgment, *op. cit.*, s. 219.
769. Eichmann trial (second instance), Judgment, *op. cit.*, p. I2.
770. *Ibid.*, p. I30.
771. *Ibid.*
772. *Ibid.*, p. I31.

even irrespective of the express provision of Section 8 of the Nazis and Nazi Collaborators (Punishment) Law, because Eichmann had obeyed manifestly illegal orders and in view of the fact that he 'was fully conscious at the time that he was a party to the perpetration of the most grave and horrible crimes'.[773] But the main question that the Court felt itself bound to answer was whether the attitude taken by the Israeli legislature in excluding the defence of obedience to orders from the scope of application of the Nazis and Nazi Collaborators (Punishment) Law is in conformity with international law.[774] This, in fact, is the focal point of the judgment.

The conclusion reached by the Court was that this statutory provision does fall into line with the principles of international law, for an examination of the authorities reveals that the doctrine of *respondeat superior* has never secured a place in that law.[775] What, however, is the reason for the strict provision embodied in Section 8 of the Israeli statute which precludes the possibility of relying on the fact of obedience to orders for the purposes of discharge from responsibility, even in cases of mistake of law (when the order is not manifestly illegal), of duress and necessity? The Court scrutinized the stipulation of Article 8 of the London Charter corresponding to that Section in spirit if not in letter, and gave the following dual reply to the question:

(a) The principle of the supremacy of the law requires that the Nazi criminals will not be able to reduce the plea of obedience to orders to absurdity by resorting to the *Führerprinzip* so as to shift the responsibility for all their misdeeds to one person, and one person only: Hitler.[776]

(b) 'The very commission of the crimes in question necessarily points to the existence of criminal consciousness[777] in the perpetrator'.[778]

The first part of this reply is self-explanatory. As for the second part, the intention of the Court, if I understand it correctly, was to say that the nature of the crimes dealt with by the London Charter as well as by the Nazis and Nazi Collaborators (Punishment) Law

773. *Ibid.*, p. 132.
774. *Ibid.*
775. *Ibid.*, pp. 132–134.
776. *Ibid.*, pp. 133–134.
777. The term used here in the semi-official English translation is 'criminal intent', but this is not a precise rendering of the original Hebrew. I have used the term 'criminal consciousness', though a literal translation would apparently be '*mens rea*'. The latter term has been discarded here, because to my mind it is not borne out in its full sense by the context of the Court's pronouncement. See the Hebrew text of the judgment, p. 140.
778. Eichmann trial (second instance), Judgment, *op. cit.*, p. 134.

is such that criminal consciousness may be imputed to offenders brought to trial by virtue thereof. In essence, the approach of the Court is parallel to the above-expounded proposition of the prosecution in the main Nuremberg trial and in the Subsequent Proceedings,[779] according to which the provisions of Article 8 of the London Charter and Article II(4)(b) of Law No. 10 were phrased in their rigorous form on account of their application to acts that were known in advance to be manifestly illegal. The apparent inference is that the Court held that, if the Nazis and Nazi Collaborators (Punishment) Law thought it right to deny to defendants brought to trial thereunder the use of the plea of obedience to orders as a cause for discharge from responsibility, this was not due to the fact that the authors of the Law wished to dispute the validity of the manifest illegality principle obtaining in Israel as a general rule. On the contrary: they conceded the general applicability of the principle, but whereas in ordinary cases the Court is vested with the power to determine when a certain act, performed pursuant to superior orders, is manifestly illegal, the legislators themselves pondered the acts enumerated in this particular Law and reached the conclusion that they are manifestly illegal. For that reason, and for that very reason only, they excluded in this case, *a priori*, the applicability of the plea of obedience to orders for purposes of acquittal, and relieved the Court of its power to examine anew the question of manifest illegality with regard to every individual defendant.

Of course, it is not within the scope of this study, devoted as it is to international law, to inquire to what extent these were really the considerations of the Israeli legislators when they rejected the plea of obedience to orders in the context of absolving Nazis and Nazi collaborators from responsibility.[780] The important thing, however, is that the Supreme Court handed down its ruling in this regard while dealing with the question of obedience to orders from the standpoint of international law. Hence, if the above interpretation of its statement is correct, it follows that the Court indirectly added its voice to the chorus of the proponents of the manifest illegality principle as the generally acceptable criterion for establishing criminal responsibility under international law in case of compliance with orders. This conclusion is strengthened by the fact that at a certain point the judgment, adopting the enunciation of the Military Court of Appeal in the Kafr Kassem case,[781] referred to the manifest

779. See *supra*, pp. 129, 175 176.
780. But we may as well repeat here what has been emphasized above (*supra*, p. 130), namely, that the corresponding construction of Article 8 of the London Charter has no historical foundation.
781. See *supra*, p. 9.

illegality principle as 'the "golden mean" solution'.[782]

The subject of compulsion was tackled by the Court separately. It did not express any authoritative opinion on the question whether international law recognizes the defence of compulsion in circumstances of obedience to orders.[783] But, from the viewpoint of Israel national law, it ruled that Eichmann would not have been able successfully to set up the defence of constraint or necessity even had it been open to him under the Nazis and Nazi Collaborators (Punishment) Law, since the conditions necessary for such a defence had not been fulfilled in his case.[784]

So far, the first part of the judgment of the Court of Appeal. In an inconspicuous place in it, there is a reference to the third part of the judgment, according to which the Court intended there to demonstrate that

> 'within the framework of the order to carry out the Final Solution, the Appellant acted independently, and even exceeded the tasks assigned to him through the service channels of the official chain of command'.[785]

From here the conclusion might be drawn that, as far as the subject of obedience to orders is concerned, the third part is designed merely to serve as a sort of an annex to the first, for its task is to cope with just one narrow facet of the subject, all the more so in view of the fact that the whole matter has already been elaborately discussed in the first part. But, lo and behold, the Court not only recapitulates again, at the outset of the third part, the contentions of counsel for the appellant in respect of obedience to orders,[786] although it has already done that in the first part,[787] but it proceeds to pronounce as follows:

> 'We could easily, and in a very few words, dismiss all these contentions by saying: . . . an order from above does not exculpate the offender, when the illegality is blatant and visible to the eyes of the perpetrator; and as to the fear of the death penalty that prompted Eichmann to obey, ostensibly against his will, the orders he received, that contention would not, in view of the provisions of Sections 8 and 11 of the Law (Nazis and Nazi Collaborators (Punishment) Law 1950), be tenable save in so far as the degree of punishment is concerned.
>
> 'But we shall not take this facile and convenient path'.[788]

In the continuation of the discussion, the Court examines closely and minutely the circumstances of the case, and finds that

782. Eichmann trial (second instance), Judgment, *op. cit.*, p. I32. Translation corrected.
783. *Ibid.*, p. I34.
784. *Ibid.*, pp. I34–I35.
785. *Ibid.*, p. I31.
786. *Ibid.*, p. III1.
787. See *supra*, note 769.
788. Eichmann trial (second instance), Judgment, *op. cit.*, pp. III1–III2.

> 'As a matter of fact, the Appellant did not at all receive orders "from above"; it was he who was the high and mighty one, he who was the commander in all that pertains to Jewish Affairs'.[789]

And, in similar vein

> 'He (the Appellant) was not coerced into doing what he did'.[790]

One must be affected by more than a scintilla of doubt whether the different parts of the judgment constitute a coherent unity or whether each part does not rather seek to wrestle alone, uncorrelated with the other, against the problem of obedience to orders. It seems that we are faced here with two independent answers to the question, tagged artificially together. After all, whereas the first part rejects Servatius' arguments at length for legal reasons, the third declares that this is a 'facile and convenient path' that will not be taken by the Court, and instead it predicates conviction on the sole basis of the facts of the case. Granted, in the judgment of the District Court, the contentions of the defence were also rejected, as we have seen, for both legal and factual reasons, but in that instance there was a convergence, and not a divergence, of explanations, and the intrinsic unity of the opinion of the Court was not impaired.

Nevertheless it should be noted, on the substance of the brief reference to the legal side of the matter of obedience to orders in the quotation from the third part of the judgment in appeal, that, even there, the Court reiterates its unconditional support of the manifest illegality principle as the proper solution of the problem under discussion.[791]

789. *Ibid.*, p. III12.
790. *Ibid.*, p. III13.
791. It is strange, though, that Sections 8 and 11 of the Nazis and Nazi Collaborators (Punishment) Law are expressly mentioned in the passage, as quoted, only in the context of the question of compulsion.

A summing-up of the cases from the standpoint of obedience to superior orders is not an easy undertaking. There are innumerable decisions that blow hot and cold and point in many directions. There is only one solid element in this fluid judicial front, and that is the conclusive repudiation of the doctrine of *respondeat superior* in almost all the judgments. This doctrine may, unquestionably, be regarded as now *passé*. The trouble is that it is not at all evident from the cases which is the course to be followed by positive international law in the field of obedience to orders. Furthermore, what cannot be found in the collection of the cases, as a whole, cannot be found either in any one given decision among them. In my opinion, no one specific case of those examined is satisfying from every point of view as an answer to the problem. Neither the judgment of the International Military Tribunal at Nuremberg, hobbled as it was by the tether of Article 8 of the London Charter, nor other less renowned opinions overcome all the obstacles and resolve all the questions.

Yet, if I may be allowed to attempt to trace a pattern of sorts in the manifold variety of the cases, I believe that, by and large, it can be said that there is a certain trend in the decisions of the courts:

(1) not to deny any standing to the fact of obedience to orders when the criminal responsibility of the defendant is being established;

(2) not to take the fact of obedience to orders into consideration when establishing responsibility in cases other than those of mistake of law or fact and compulsion.

Obviously, this is only a trend and not crystallized in any clear-cut form. One cannot argue, on the basis of it, that the judgments confirm the validity of the *mens rea* principle, proposed at the conclusion of our discussion of the theory of international law,[792] or of any other principle. It should be noted, though, that the *mens rea* principle does indeed conform to the trend, and even sustains it and is sustained by it. All that needs correction or clarification from the standpoint of that principle is that obedience to orders never constitutes a defence *per se*, but only a factual element. It is just a circumstance that may be taken into account for purposes of discharge from responsibility, within the scope of a defence based on compulsion or mistake, namely, on lack of *mens rea*.

792. See *supra*, pp. 88–90.

PART V: INTERNATIONAL LEGISLATION SINCE 1946

THE trials of the war criminals at the close of the Second World War accentuated the need for a generally accepted and agreed provision—embodied in a valid international instrument—on the subject of obedience to superior orders. In this part of the study we shall follow the attempts made during the late 'forties and the early 'fifties to formulate such a provision; but let it be said at once that none of these attempts has yet been crowned with success. There is still no binding provision in respect of obedience to orders in any general international agreement in force.

CHAPTER I

DOUBTS AND VACILLATIONS

1. THE GENOCIDE CONVENTION, 1948

In the course of the formulation of the Genocide Convention,[793] the question arose whether it should contain a clause expressly excluding the possibility of considering the fact of obedience to orders for defence purposes. In the Draft Convention that was prepared and submitted by the Secretariat of the United Nations Organization on 26 June 1947, the following Article was included (Article V):

> 'Command of the law or superior orders shall not justify genocide'.[794]

This Article is somewhat similar in its form to the first Soviet draft (dated June 1945) of Article 8 of the Charter of the International Military Tribunal,[795] and hence it may be assumed that it also reflects the doctrine of absolute liability. From the discussions in UN bodies regarding the Genocide Convention, which are to be presently examined, it also transpires that the Secretariat proposal was generally regarded as a self-evident expression of the doctrine in question.

In an Ad Hoc Committee on Genocide, which was established by the Economic and Social Council and which in April–May 1948 debated the text of the Draft Convention,[796] one of the seven members,

793. This famous term was coined by Lemkin, who explained in his book *Axis Rule in Occupied Europe* (1944), p. 79, that he had affixed the Greek word *genos* (meaning race or tribe) to the Latin radical *cide* (meaning killing).

794. Draft Convention on the Crime of Genocide (E/447), pp. 8, 36. Cf. Dunbar, *op. cit.*, p. 260; N. Robinson, *The Genocide Convention, a Commentary* (1960), pp. 19–20, 125; Spiropoulos, 'Code (1st Report)', pp. 270, 272. See also the text of Article 5, as initially proposed by the United Nations Secretariat, on 6 June 1947: 'Genocide cannot be excused under the plea of the application of the law or instructions of a superior authority' (Draft Convention for the Prevention and Punishment of Genocide (A/AC. 10/42), p. 4). In a revised draft of the Secretariat—dated 12 June—another phrasing was suggested for Article 5, more in line with that of the final draft: 'Command of the law or of a superior authority shall not justify genocide' (Draft Convention for the Prevention and Punishment of Genocide (A/AC.10/42/Rev.1), p. 4).

795. See *supra*, p. 113.

796. See Ad Hoc Committee on Genocide—Report (May 1948), (ECOSOC,

the Soviet representative Morozov, proposed incorporating a provision identical in its wording to that phrased by the Secretariat.[797] The proposal was supported by the Polish representative, Rudzinski,[798] but the majority of the Committee objected to it. The objectors were led by the Chairman of the Committee, the American Maktos.[799] It should, however, be remarked that Maktos did not explicitly reject the doctrine underlying the proposed Article, and certainly did not proceed to support the opposite doctrine of *respondeat superior.* It is true that he emphasized the grave dilemma which confronts a soldier who receives an unlawful order, but he explained that his disapproval was mainly based on unwillingness to involve the Convention in a complicated problem, as well as on acquiescence in the application—in the absence of any provision to the contrary—of the principles of general international law relating to obedience to orders, whatever they may be, in the field of genocide.[800] It is noteworthy that in its written comments, a few months previously, on the Draft Convention formulated by the Secretariat, the Government of the United States found no fault with the idea that a stipulation relating to obedience to orders be included in the Convention, and only suggested that the phrasing of Article V be modified to read:

> 'Command of the law or superior orders shall be no defence for the crimes set out in this Convention, but may be considered in mitigation of punishment'.[801]

Since this text excludes the fact of obedience to orders as a defence, but does not explain whether what is meant is that this fact shall not be taken into account for defence purposes at all, or that it shall only not constitute a defence *per se*,[802] it is not sufficiently clear whether the Americans sought to modify the substance, or merely the style, of the Article. Even, however, if the intention of the United

O.R., 3rd year, 7th Session, Supp. 6) (E/794), p. 1. On the developments that preceded the establishment of this Committee, see N. Robinson, *op. cit.*, pp. 20–23.

797. See Ad Hoc Committee on Genocide—Report, *op. cit.*, p. 9; Summary Records (E/AC.25/SR.18), pp. 4, 6–7. Cf. Sibert, *op. cit.*, vol. 1, p. 441.
798. See Ad Hoc Committee on Genocide—Report, *op. cit.*, p. 9; Summary Records, *op. cit.*, p. 5. Cf. Sibert, *op. cit.*, vol. 1, p. 441.
799. See Ad Hoc Committee on Genocide—Summary Records, *op. cit.*, pp. 4–5, 8.
800. See *ibid.*, pp. 4–5 (as corrected in E/AC.25/SR.18/Corr.2).
801. Communication Received from the United States of America (30 September 1947), (G.A., O.R., 2nd Session, 6th Committee, Annex 3a) (A/401 and Addenda), p. 239.
802. Cf. the text of the American proposals of April–June 1945 to the Charter of the International Military Tribunal (*supra*, pp. 109–110, 114). There the fact of obedience to orders was expressly excluded as an 'absolute defense' or a 'defense *per se*'.

States as expressed in its proposal had been to raise objection to the formulation of the Article in the mould of the doctrine of absolute liability, it is not evident why the American representative in the Ad Hoc Committee chose completely to discard the Article and made no effort to introduce amendments in it. By doing that, he, in fact, opened the door to the champions of the doctrine of *respondeat superior*.

Following Maktos, both the Chinese representative in the Committee, Lin Mousheng, and the Venezuelan representative, Pérez-Perozo, declared against the Article in question; but they also contended that the Article was not consistent with the provisions of national law in certain States.[803] Pérez-Perozo went as far as to make the following statement with regard to the principle from which the Article is derived:

> 'that principle is a danger to the stability of the institutions of the State. The Charter of the Military Tribunal of Nürnberg admitted that principle having in mind the crimes of war; but to accept it in time of peace is to invite the armed forces to disobedience, when they are in themselves a non-political body, bound to obedience and non-deliberative'.[804]

This contention in effect reflects the familiar line of thought that an army must serve without reasoning why and obey orders blindly. We have already encountered this argumentation several times, and we have seen that it rests on a quicksand. Let it only be added here that the very attempt to distinguish between peacetime and war time exposes the fallacy in this contention: if there is a time when the interests of the supremacy of the law are prepared to give in a little to the demands of military discipline, it is war time, for there are eventualities in which a nation fighting for survival may find itself in dire straits unless the grip of discipline is clenched. But in peacetime there is no justification for sacrificing the supremacy of the law on the altar of military discipline. It may be presumed that Pérez-Perozo was led to make his statement in the light of the unfortunate experience of his own country, and the whole Latin American subcontinent, with soldiers who, instead of obeying the instructions of their Government, rise in arms against it time and again and take the reins of power into their own hands. The trouble is that precisely the blind obedience of soldiers and non-commissioned officers to the commands of their superiors in times of rebellion is the basis of the disobedience of mutinous colonels and generals. The ritual of military discipline is a double-edged sword.

A different kind of objection to the Soviet-sponsored Article was

803. See Ad Hoc Committee on Genocide—Report, *op. cit.*, p. 9; Summary Records, *op. cit.*, p. 6.
804. Ad Hoc Committee on Genocide—Report, *op. cit.*, p. 9.

raised by the Lebanese representative, Azkoul, who claimed that it was superfluous.[805] He stated that criminal intent is one of the component elements in the crime of genocide, so that, if this crime is committed only in compliance with orders, and without any will or intent to carry it out, the defendant is not guilty *per definitionem*; on the other hand, if the crime is committed of volition and with intention, the defendant is guilty even if he acted pursuant to superior orders; in any case, *cadit quaestio*.[806] Actually, from Azkoul's viewpoint, the fact of obedience to orders does not play any decisive role when criminal responsibility is established: responsibility is incurred in accordance with the exclusive criteria of will and intent to accomplish the criminal act.

For all these reasons, the majority of the members of the Committee decided to vote down the Soviet proposal. Only two members cast their vote in favour, four voted against, and one abstained.[807]

As a result, the Draft Convention, which came up for discussion by the Sixth (Legal) Committee of the General Assembly of the United Nations in the third session of 1948,[808] did not contain any provision on the subject of obedience to orders. The Soviet Union, however, did not abandon its efforts, and submitted an amendment that would add the controversial Article to the Draft.[809] The amendment was supported by a number of delegates, but again a majority objected. Some of the objectors repeated the argument that the proposed Article would conflict with the provisions of national law relating to obedience to orders.[810] Others underlined once more the well-known dilemma faced by the soldier who receives an unlawful order.[811] Another contention that was restated was that the army

805. See *ibid.*, as well as Ad Hoc Committee on Genocide—Summary Records, *op. cit.*, p. 6.
806. See as in note 805.
807. See Ad Hoc Committee on Genocide—Report, *op. cit.*, p. 9; Summary Records, *op. cit.*, p. 9. Cf. Dunbar, *op. cit.*, p. 260; N. Robinson, *op. cit.*, p. 72; Sibert, *op. cit.*, vol. 1, p. 441; Spiropoulos, 'Code (1st Report)', pp. 270, 272.
808. As for the chain of events that brought the Draft Convention before the Sixth Committee of the General Assembly, see N. Robinson, *op. cit.*, p. 25.
809. The amendment was proposed on 9 October 1948, in document A/C.6/215/Rev.1, p. 3. The Soviet delegate, Morozov, introduced his amendment in the Committee's meeting of 5 November—G.A., O.R., 3rd Session, Part I, 6th Committee, p. 302. Cf. N. Robinson, *op. cit.*, p. 72; Sibert, *op. cit.*, vol. 1, p. 441.
810. See the statements made by the following delegates: the Belgian, Kaeckenbeeck—G.A., O.R., 3rd Session, *op. cit.*, p. 302; the Venezuelan, Pérez-Perozo—*ibid.*, p. 306; the Greek, Spiropoulos—*ibid.*, p. 307; the Dominican, Messina—*ibid.*, p. 308; and the Peruvian, Maurtua—*ibid.*, p. 309. Cf. Dunbar, *op. cit.*, p. 261; N. Robinson, *op. cit.*, p. 72; Spiropoulos, 'Code (1st Report)', p. 272.
811. See the statements made by the following delegates: the Venezuelan, Pérez-Perozo—G.A., O.R., 3rd Session, *op. cit.*, p. 306; the American, Maktos—*ibid.*,

is a non-political body, bound to obey orders blindly,[812] and that the amendment undermines military discipline.[813] All these assertions indicate, or are apt to indicate, the influence of the doctrine of *respondeat superior*, and, had they alone mirrored the motives of opposition to the Article in controversy, it could have amounted to a victory of that doctrine over the rival doctrine of absolute liability. But, in the main, opposition sprang from other reasons that have nothing in common with the doctrine of *respondeat superior*. Thus, many delegates maintained that the proposed Article was too rigid, and that its rejection would enable the competent court to pass judgment in accordance with the rules of general international law and on the basis of the specific circumstances of every case; in particular, it would enable the court to rest its decision on the fact of the existence or non-existence of criminal intent on the part of the subordinate.[814] There were those who held the view, furthermore, that the time was simply not ripe for a discussion on the subject of obedience to orders, as the International Law Commission had been instructed by the General Assembly to study that matter.[815] And others warned against the inclusion of a controversial Article in the Convention, lest it create a serious obstacle to its ratification by all nations.[816]

The advocates of the Soviet amendment, on the other hand, pointed out that the rules of international law are superior to those of national law,[817] and cautioned that, if the amendment were not

p. 307; and the Cuban, Dihigo—*ibid.*, p. 308. Cf. Sibert, *op. cit.*, vol. 1, pp. 441–442.

812. See the statement made by the Venezuelan delegate, Pérez-Perozo—G.A., O.R., 3rd Session, *op. cit.*, p. 306.

813. See the statements made by the following delegates: the Venezuelan, Pérez-Perozo—*ibid.*; the Dominican, Messina—*ibid.*, p. 308; and the Iranian, Abdoh—*ibid.*, p. 310. Cf. Graven, 'Crimes', p. 581; Sibert, *op. cit.*, vol. 1, p. 441.

814. See the statements made by the following delegates: the Venezuelan, Pérez-Perozo—G.A., O.R., 3rd Session, *op. cit.*, p. 306; the Greek, Spiropoulos—*ibid.*, p. 307; the American, Maktos—*ibid.*; the Cuban, Dihigo—*ibid.*, p. 308; the Iranian, Abdoh—*ibid.*, p. 311; and the Ecuadorian, Corea—*ibid.*, p. 314. Cf. N. Robinson, *op. cit.*, pp. 72–73; Sibert, *op. cit.*, vol. 1, p. 442.

815. See the statements made by the following delegates: the American, Maktos—G.A., O.R., 3rd Session, *op. cit.*, pp. 307, 314; the Dutch, Beus—*ibid.*, p. 314; and the Brazilian, Amado—*ibid.* Cf. N. Robinson, *op. cit.*, p. 73 n. 11.

816. See the statements made by the following delegates: the Venezuelan, Pérez-Perozo—G.A., O.R., 3rd Session, *op. cit.*, p. 306; the Belgian, Kaecken beeck—*ibid.*, p. 309; the Iranian, Abdoh—*ibid.*, p. 310; the Dane, Federspiel—*ibid.*, p. 311; and the Filipino, Inglés—*ibid.*, p. 312. Cf. N. Robinson, *op. cit.*, pp. 72, 73 n. 11.

817. See the statements made by the following delegates: the Egyptian, Raafat—G.A., O.R., 3rd Session, *op. cit.*, p. 307; the Czech, Zourek—*ibid.*, pp. 308–309; and the Yugoslav, Bartos—*ibid.*, p. 310.

adopted, the Convention would not be effective, since most offenders might go scot-free.[818] They also denied the allegation that the amendment was too rigid and that it left no room for an examination of the merits of the case, for in their opinion it would enable the competent court to take into account the criminal intent of the specific offender in each case.[819]

This last point deserves special consideration. We shall quote here from two noteworthy observations on both sides of the fence: one by the Polish delegate, Lachs, who supported the amendment; and the other by the Greek delegate, Spiropoulos, who objected to it. Lachs stated:

> 'If the USSR amendment suppressed the justification of superior orders, it did not suppress certain other elements in the criminal act, such as coercion and the impossibility of refusing to act, which could play an important part in determining the responsibility of the accused'.[820]

Spiropoulos referred to the judgment in the trial of the major war criminals at Nuremberg, and said:

> 'It was clear... that the Tribunal, in order to decide whether or not the accused was responsible for the crimes of which he was accused, had attempted to determine whether or not he had full freedom of action, in other words, whether he had had any possibility of disobeying the orders he had received.
>
> 'The delegation of Greece considered it preferable not to adopt the Soviet Union amendment and to leave the judge free to decide, in each individual case, whether the element of intention was present or not'.[821]

The common denominator between the views of Lachs and Spiropoulos in respect of the question of obedience to orders is plain, both agreeing that such obedience does not constitute a defence *per se*. If there was disagreement between them relating to the Soviet amendment, it was due to the fact that Spiropoulos held that the court is entitled to consider all the circumstances of the case, including the fact of obedience to orders, when weighing the defence of the accused founded on compulsion or lack of intent (and that is, to my mind, the principle obtaining under general international law); whereas Lachs sought to exclude the fact of obedience to orders from among the circumstances that may be reckoned with for defence purposes, but he emphasized that the accused is not precluded from putting forward the defence of compulsion on the basis of the other facts of

818. See the statements made by the following delegates: the Czech, Zourek—*ibid.*, p. 308; the French, Chaumont—*ibid.*, pp. 309–310; the Yugoslav, Bartos—*ibid.*, p. 310; the Pole, Lachs—*ibid.*, pp. 311–312; the Guatemalan, Camey-Herrera—*ibid.*, p. 312; and the Soviet, Morozov—*ibid.*, p. 313.
819. See the statements made by the following delegates: the Czech, Zourek—*ibid.*, p. 308; the Pole, Lachs—*ibid.*, p. 311; and the Soviet, Morozov—*ibid.*, p. 313.
820. *Ibid.*, p. 311.
821. *Ibid.*, p. 307.

the case (and that is the rule laid down by the doctrine of absolute liability, as reflected in the London Charter and in the Nuremberg judgment).

One might have expected that those delegates, like Spiropoulos, who opposed the doctrine of *respondeat superior* but were also dissatisfied with the strict wording of the Soviet amendment and with the doctrine of absolute liability underlying it, would endeavour to amend the amendment and not utterly discard it. But, instead, they sided with the adherents of the doctrine of *respondeat superior* and brought about the defeat of the proposed Article. The reasons adduced for this negative attitude, which do not relate to the essence of the matter—namely, that the time was not ripe for the adoption of the amendment and the whole Convention was imperilled by the controversy on this point—perhaps denote the cause of it, to wit, the wish not to be entangled in a complicated problem.

Ultimately, the Soviet amendment was defeated in a vote, receiving only fifteen votes, whereas twenty-eight States voted against and six abstained.[822] Thus, the Convention on the Prevention and Punishment of the Crime of Genocide, which was finally approved by the Plenary of the General Assembly on 9 December 1948 and came into force on 12 January 1951, does not contain any provision on the question of obedience to orders.[823]

2. THE RED CROSS CONVENTIONS, 1949

In December 1948, a few months prior to the assembling of the Diplomatic Conference at Geneva in which the four Red Cross Conventions for the Protection of War Victims were formulated and signed, the International Red Cross Committee had established a commission of experts, consisting of four members—Lauterpacht and Phillimore from Britain, Graven from Switzerland, and Mouton from the Netherlands—with a view to studying the problems involved in sanctions against violations of the Conventions and drafting the necessary provisions.[824] On the recommendation of the

822. *Ibid.*, p. 313. Cf. Dunbar, *op. cit.*, pp. 260–261; Kunz, 'The United Nations Convention on Genocide', *A.J.I.L.*, vol. 43 (1949), pp. 738–746 at p. 743; N. Robinson, *op. cit.*, p. 72; Sibert, *op. cit.*, vol. 1, p. 442; Spiropoulos, 'Code (1st Report)', pp. 270, 272; Eichmann trial (second instance), Minutes, *op. cit.*, Session No. 2, pp. H1–I1 (Servatius).

823. The text of the Convention appears in *Kitvei Amana* (Israel Treaty Series), vol. 1, No. 5, p. 66.

824. See *Red Cross Commentary*, vol. 1, p. 358. See also Glaser, *Introduction*, p. 128; Glaser, 'L'Ordre', p. 324; Graven, 'Code', p. 376; Graven, 'Crimes', p. 583; Levie, *op. cit.*, p. 465; Maunoir, *op. cit.*, p. 232; Pilloud, *op. cit.*, p. 9. Cf. Eustathiades 'Ordres', p. 421 n. 84.

experts, the Committee submitted a proposal to the Diplomatic Conference to include in each of the four Red Cross Conventions four Articles, the third of which prescribes as follows:

> 'The fact that the accused acted in obedience to the orders of a superior or in pursuance of a law or regulation shall not constitute a valid defence, if the prosecution can show that in view of the circumstances the accused had reasonable grounds to assume that he was committing a breach of this Convention. In such a case the punishment may nevertheless be mitigated or remitted, if the circumstances justify.
>
> '...[825]

Under this stipulation, the defence of obedience to orders is excluded in the absence of mistake, of law and perhaps of fact as well, on the part of the defendant. The converse follows, that the defence of obedience to orders is not excluded—that is, it is permitted—in case of mistake. The commission of experts was apparently unimpressed by the stress laid in the Nuremberg judgment, through the moral choice test, on the defence of compulsion, and rendered the problem of mistake the focal point.[826] Nevertheless, it is questionable whether the commission adopted the opinion of one of its members, Lauterpacht—as expressed by him in Oppenheim's treatise[827]—that compulsion is not an admissible defence in war crimes trials. After all, the commission explicitly stated that, even in the absence of mistake, punishment of the offender may be entirely remitted when the circumstances of the case justify it.[828] And when one has in mind such circumstances, the state of compulsion instantly comes to the fore.

I shall add here that, in my view, the commission did not formulate this provision with complete accuracy, for the implication is that obedience to orders constitutes a defence *per se* in appropriate circumstances. Actually, the defence that ought to obtain, in accordance with the criterion set by the commission, is that of mistake, whereas obedience to orders should only serve as a factual element.

As it turned out, the Diplomatic Conference decided not to include the proposed Article in the Conventions that it drafted.[829] The reasons for this decision were as follows: (a) the apprehension that, owing to the lack of general agreement on the subject of obedience

825. *Red Cross Commentary*, vol. 1, p. 359 n. 1.
826. See in particular Pilloud, *op. cit.*, p. 16. Cf. Maunoir, *op. cit.*, p. 235.
827. See *supra*, p. 79.
828. It is appropriate to quote here the last sentence of the above citation in its French version: 'Toutefois, si les circonstances le justifient, la peine pourra être atténuée ou même exclue' (Pilloud, *op. cit.*, p. 10 n. 1). This sentence is particularly underlined by Eustathiades, 'Ordres', p. 421 n. 84.
829. See *Red Cross Commentary*, vol. 1, p. 365. See also Draper, *The Red Cross Conventions* (1958), p. 22 n. 69; Glaser, *Introduction*, pp. 128–129; Glaser, 'L'Ordre', p. 324; Graven, 'Code', p. 376; Graven, 'Crimes', p. 583; Levie, *op. cit.*, p. 465; Maunoir, *op. cit.*, p. 233; Pilloud, *op. cit.*, p. 16.

to orders, this Article might hinder the ratification of the Conventions; (b) the desire to leave the determination of the question to the competent court that would settle it on the basis of national law; (c) the knowledge that the rules of international law relating to obedience to orders were anyway being examined by the competent bodies of the United Nations.[830] In summary, the wind that blew in the Geneva Conference was not different from that prevailing in the Sixth Committee of the General Assembly at the time of the drafting of the Genocide Convention. In both cases, when the authors of the Conventions encountered the kernel of a problem, they preferred to get rid of it rather than spend time and energy on baring its pith.

The only clause relating, indirectly, to the subject of obedience to orders which was incorporated in the four Red Cross Conventions for the Protection of War Victims, signed at Geneva on 12 August 1949, stipulates as follows:

> 'The High Contracting Parties undertake to enact any legislation necessary to provide effective penal sanctions for persons committing, or ordering to be committed, any of the grave breaches of the present Convention defined in the following Article'.[831]

It is evident, as Draper states, that:

> 'Although the Article equates the legal responsibility of those who order with those who commit grave breaches, it does not deal with the vexed question of the responsibility for committing grave breaches pursuant to the orders of a superior'.[832]

The problem that is dealt with in this study is, therefore, not resolved in the Geneva Conventions.

830. See Graven, 'Code', p. 376; Graven, 'Crimes', pp. 583–584.
831. See Article 49 of the Convention for the Amelioration of the Condition of the Wounded and Sick in Armed Forces in the Field, *Kitvei Amana* (Israel Treaty Series), vol. 1, No. 30, p. 387 at p. 409; Article 50 of the Convention for the Amelioration of the Condition of Wounded, Sick and Shipwrecked Members of Armed Forces at Sea, *ibid.*, p. 423 at p. 442; Article 129 of the Convention relative to the Treatment of Prisoners of War, *ibid.*, p. 453 at p. 518; Article 146 of the Convention relative to the Protection of Civilian Persons in Time of War, *ibid.*, p. 559 at p. 621.

Cf. also the following provision, contained in the Peace Treaties of 10 February 1947—'... shall take all necessary steps to ensure the apprehension and surrender for trial of: (a) Persons accused of having committed, ordered or abetted war crimes and crimes against peace or humanity'. This is Article 45(1) of the Peace Treaty with Italy (*A.J.I.L.*, vol. 42 (1948), Supp., p. 47 at p. 61); Article 5(1) of the Peace Treaty with Bulgaria (*ibid.*, p. 179 at p. 180); Article 9(1) of the Peace Treaty with Finland (*ibid.*, p. 203 at p. 205); Article 6(1) of the Peace Treaty with Hungary (*ibid.*, p. 225 at p. 228); and Article 6(1) of the Peace Treaty with Rumania (*ibid.*, p. 252 at p. 254).
832. Draper, *op. cit.*, p. 21. Cf. Glaser, 'L'Ordre', p. 324 n. 116. But see Pella's observation on this matter (Pella, 'Le Code des Crimes contre la Paix et la Sécurité de l'Humanité (Observations et Réflexions)', *op. cit.*, vol. 32, p. 357).

CHAPTER 2

THE WORK OF THE INTERNATIONAL LAW COMMISSION

1. HISTORICAL BACKGROUND

In the course of the Nuremberg trial, the chief prosecutors declared that the sword of the law, hanging over the heads of the defendants, is double-edged, and that, while it is pointed for the present at the Nazi war criminals, it may be directed in the future at the victors now so serenely dispensing justice; and the prosecutors did not withhold a warning that, insofar as the Charter of the International Military Tribunal creates new law, it establishes a precedent for the future: the same measure that is being meted out today by the victors to the vanquished may be their own fate tomorrow.[833] In a Report submitted by him to the President of the United States on 7 October 1946, one week after the judgment in the Nuremberg trial had been delivered, the American chief prosecutor, Jackson, quoted Cardozo's well-known statement that 'the power of the precedent is the power of the beaten path', and pronounced:

> 'No one can hereafter deny or fail to know that the principles on which the Nazi leaders are adjudged to forfeit their lives constitute law—and law with a sanction'.[834]

In an oral report presented to the General Assembly by the Secretary-General of the United Nations on 24 October of the same year, it was suggested that the principles which had been employed in the Nuremberg trials, and under which the Nazi war criminals were sentenced, should be made a permanent part of the body of international law.[835] A more concrete proposal was included in another report, transmitted to the President of the United States several

833. See Nuremberg trial, Opening Speech for the Prosecution (by Jackson), *I.M.T.*, vol. 2, pp. 101, 154; Opening Speech for the Prosecution (by Shawcross), *I.M.T.*, vol. 3, p. 106.

834. R. Jackson, 'Report to the President (1946)', *International Conference*, pp. 433–440 at p. 437.

835. Supplementary Report of the Secretary-General on the Work of the Organization, G.A., O.R., 1st Session, Part II, Plenary, p. 693 at pp. 699–700. Cf. *S.G. Memorandum*, p. 11; Spiropoulos, 'Principles', p. 188 n. 35.

weeks later, on 8 November, by Biddle, the American judge who had been on the bench at Nuremberg. He recommended that

> 'the United Nations as a whole reaffirm the principles of the Nürnberg Charter in the context of a general codification of offences against the peace and security of mankind'.[836]

In his reply to Biddle, President Truman welcomed the recommendation, and expressed the hope that the United Nations would carry it out.[837] A draft Resolution on the lines of the recommendation was submitted by the American delegation to the first session of the General Assembly as early as 15 November,[838] and on 11 December the Plenary unanimously adopted Resolution No. 95(I), according to which the General Assembly

> '*Affirms* the principles of international law recognized by the Charter of the Nürnberg Tribunal and the judgment of the Tribunal;
>
> '*Directs* the Committee on the codification of international law... to treat as a matter of primary importance plans for the formulation, in the context of a general codification of offences against the peace and security of mankind, or of an International Criminal Code, of the principles recognized in the Charter of the Nürnberg Tribunal and in the judgment of the Tribunal'.[839]

The Committee on the Progressive Development of International Law and its Codification held the view that this Resolution of the General Assembly did not call upon it to undertake the actual formulation of the Nuremberg Principles, but rather to study methods and devise plans in that regard, and that it would be better to entrust the formulation itself to the International Law Commission whose establishment it decided to recommend to the General Assembly.[840] As a result, the General Assembly, during its second session on 21 November 1947, passed the following Resolution No. 177(II):

836. See *S.G. Memorandum*, p. 11; Spiropoulos, 'Code (1st Report)', p. 255; Spiropoulos, 'Principles', p. 188 n. 35. Cf. Biddle, *op. cit.*, p. 6.
837. See *S.G. Memorandum*, p. 11; Spiropoulos, 'Code (1st Report)', p. 256; Spiropoulos, 'Principles', p. 188 n. 35. Cf. Biddle, *op. cit.*, p. 6.
838. Draft Resolution relating to the Codification of the Principles of International Law Recognized by the Charter of the Nürnberg Tribunal (A/C.6/69). Cf. *S.G. Memorandum*, p. 12; Spiropoulos, 'Code (1st Report)', p. 256; Spiropoulos, 'Principles', p. 188 n. 35.
839. Resolution 95(I), 'Affirmation of the Principles of International Law Recognized by the Charter of the Nürnberg Tribunal', Resolutions Adopted by the General Assembly, 1st Session, Part II (A/64/Add.1), p. 188.
840. Report of the Committee on the Progressive Development of International Law and its Codification on the Plans for the Formulation of the Principles of the Nuremberg Charter and Judgment, 17 June 1947 (A/AC.10/52), pp. 1–2. Cf. Liang, 'The General Assembly and the Progressive Development and Codification of International Law', *A.J.I.L.*, vol. 42 (1948), pp. 66–97 at pp. 91–93; Schick, 'Crimes against Peace', *op. cit.*, p. 465; *S.G. Memorandum*, pp. 15–19; Spiropoulos, 'Code (1st Report)', p. 256; Spiropoulos, 'Principles', p. 188.

> '*Decides* to entrust the formulation of the principles of international law recognized in the Charter of the Nürnberg Tribunal and in the judgment of the Tribunal to the International Law Commission . . . ; and
>
> '*Directs* the Commission to
>
> '(a) Formulate the principles of international law recognized in the Charter of the Nürnberg Tribunal, and in the judgment of the Tribunal, and
>
> '(b) Prepare a draft code of offences against the peace and security of mankind, indicating clearly the place to be accorded to the principles mentioned in sub-paragraph (a) above'.[841]

The International Law Commission was established on the same day, by Resolution 174(II).[842]

2. THE NUREMBERG PRINCIPLES

In its first session, in 1949, the International Law Commission considered the precise scope of the task assigned to it with respect to the formulation of the Nuremberg Principles. The question arose whether, under General Assembly Resolution 177(II), it was incumbent upon the Commission to ascertain to what extent these Principles constitute a part of international law; and the conclusion of the Commission was that, since the Principles had already been affirmed by the General Assembly in Resolution 95(I), it was not its task to express any opinion on this question, but it had to concern itself only with the mere formulation of the Principles.[843] As a starting-point for its work, the Commission appointed three of its members—François, Sandström and Spiropoulos—as a sub-committee, and instructed them to draw up a working paper containing a formulation of the Principles.[844] The resultant working paper included the following draft Principle (No. 8):

841. Resolution 177(II), 'Formulation of the Principles Recognized in the Charter of the Nürnberg Tribunal and in the Judgment of the Tribunal', Resolutions Adopted by the General Assembly, 2nd Session (A/519), pp. 111–112.
842. Resolution 174(II), 'Establishment of an International Law Commission', *ibid.*, p. 105.
843. See Report of the I.L.C., 1st Session, *I.L.C. Yearbook*, 1949, pp. 277–290 at p. 282. See also Report of the I.L.C., 2nd Session, *I.L.C. Yearbook*, 1950, vol. 2, pp. 364–385 at p. 374; Spiropoulos, 'Principles', p. 189. Cf. Eagleton, 'First Session of the International Law Commission', *A.J.I.L.*, vol. 43 (1949), pp. 758–762 at p. 761; Eagleton, 'The Second Session of the International Law Commission', *A.J.I.L.*, vol. 45 (1951), pp. 148–151 at p. 148; Liang, 'Notes', pp. 515, 517; Parry, 'Some Considerations upon the Content of a Draft Code of Offences against the Peace and Security of Mankind', *I.L.Q.*, vol. 3 (1950), pp. 208–227 at pp. 208–209; Sohn, 'Formulation of the Nuremberg Principles by the International Law Commission', *A.B.A.J.*, vol. 36 (1950), p. 505.
844. See *I.L.C. Yearbook*, 1949, p. 134; Report of the I.L.C., 1st Session, *op. cit.*, p. 282. Cf. Spiropoulos, 'Principles', p. 189.

'The fact that an individual acts pursuant to order of his Government or of a superior does not free him from responsibility. It may, however, be considered in mitigation of punishment, if justice so requires'.[845]

At first glance, one can observe that, subject to merely stylistic changes, this draft reproduced the provision of Article 8 of the London Charter, and the fact was expressly pointed out by Spiropoulos, spokesman of the sub-committee, when the working paper was presented to the Commission.[846] At the request of the Commission, the sub-committee redrafted the Principles that it had proposed, but the text of the Principle relating to obedience to orders (now fourth in sequence) was not modified save for the substitution of the words 'an individual' in the first line by the words 'a person'.[847] The Commission did not discuss the new draft, as it reached the conclusion that, in accordance with General Assembly Resolution 177(II), the question of the formulation of the Nuremberg Principles was so closely connected with the question of the preparation of a Draft Code of Offences against the Peace and Security of Mankind that it would be advisable to advance further in the work on the Code before attempting a final formulation of the Principles.[848] Consequently, the Commission appointed Spiropoulos as a Special Rapporteur on both subjects, and requested him to submit a report, that would serve as a basis for the final formulation of the Nuremberg Principles, simultaneously with a working paper on the Draft Code.[849]

In a report presented by him in April 1950,[850] Spiropoulos proposed that the Commission adopt the following Principle on the subject of obedience to orders (Principle IV):

'The fact that a person acted pursuant to order of his Government or of a superior does not free him from responsibility under international law. It may, however, be considered in mitigation of punishment, if justice so requires'.[851]

It is evident that this text, just like the proposal of the sub-committee, was identical, in all material respects, with the provision of Article 8 of the Charter of the International Military Tribunal; and Spiropoulos himself emphasized that in his report.[852]

845. *I.L.C. Yearbook*, 1949, p. 183 n. 9. Cf. Spiropoulos, 'Principles', p. 190.
846. *I.L.C. Yearbook*, 1949, p. 183.
847. *Ibid.*, p. 227 n. 8. Cf. Spiropoulos, 'Principles', p. 190.
848. See Report of the I.L.C., 1st Session, *op. cit.*, pp. 282–283.
849. See *ibid.*, p. 283. Cf. Report of the I.L.C., 2nd Session, *op. cit.*, p. 374; Spiropoulos, 'Principles', p. 191.
850. References throughout the present study to this report by Spiropoulos are made under the abbreviation: Spiropoulos, 'Principles'.
851. Spiropoulos, 'Principles', pp. 192, 195.
852. *Ibid.*, p. 192. Cf. Glaser, *Introduction*, p. 130 n. 3; Glaser, 'L'Ordre', p. 330 n. 132.

When the report came up for discussion before the International Law Commission, at its second session in 1950, Principle IV was subjected to a cross-fire of criticism.[853] The fusillade started with the following statement by Yepes:

> 'So far as he personally was concerned, he could not subscribe to principles that were contrary to all legal concepts. Was it possible to say that an official who received a formal order from his superior could avoid carrying out that order? Such an official was in reality faced with a *force majeure* from which there was no escape and he could not possibly avoid obeying the order. One of the essential principles of law was free will'.[854]

In the sequel of his statement, Yepes conceded that high-ranking officials are indeed vested with freedom of choice whether or not to obey superior orders; but he stressed that this was not the case where soldiers and officers of lower grades are concerned.[855] The latter, in his opinion, are in danger of losing their lives if they disobey orders, whereas

> 'a man must be morally free to make his choice if he was to be held responsible'.[856]

It should be noted, with regard to these observations, that Yepes gave expression here to the view, which we have already encountered and rebutted several times, that, whenever an act is carried out pursuant to superior orders (by those in lower ranks), it is performed under compulsion. It is interesting, however, that Yepes made use of the pronouncement of the Nuremberg Tribunal relating to moral choice, that very pronouncement according to which an accused who carried out orders should be acquitted only on condition that the defence of compulsion—that is, of lack of moral choice—is available to him, without any dependence upon the fact of submission to orders. In other words, while Yepes blew the horn of the doctrine of *respondeat superior*, he played a tune from the score of the doctrine of absolute liability.

Yepes' objections to the Principle proposed by Spiropoulos were 'partly agreed' by the Chairman of the Commission, Scelle, who put forward the idea of incorporating in the Principle a proviso that would authorize the acquittal of the defendant on the basis of obedience to orders, if justice so required.[857] It will be recalled that the

Cf. also a statement made by the Brazilian delegate, Amado, in the Sixth Committee of the General Assembly (G.A., O.R., 5th Session, 6th Committee, p. 133).

853. See *I.L.C. Yearbook*, 1950, vol. 1, pp. 42ff.
854. *Ibid.*, p. 42. Cf. Maunoir, *op. cit.*, p. 234.
855. *I.L.C. Yearbook*, 1950, vol. 1, p. 42.
856. *Ibid.* Cf. Maunoir, *op. cit.*, p. 234.
857. *I.L.C. Yearbook*, 1950, vol. 1, pp. 42–43. Cf. Eustathiades, 'Ordres', p. 400 n. 17a.

first American drafts in April–June 1945—on the eve of the London Conference—of Article 8 of the Charter of the International Military Tribunal were formulated in such a way;[858] and Scelle's proposal ought to be construed, as these drafts have been construed above, in the sense that it excludes obedience to orders as a defence *per se*, but permits taking this fact into account among the other circumstances of the case for the purpose of acquitting the defendant. And the circumstances which are relevant here are those that together establish, in one form or another, lack of *mens rea*. Scelle made it clear that this was what he had in mind, by saying:

> 'Mr. Yepes had stated that the essential principle of all law lay in the free choice of the individual. If he was not acting freely he might not have *mens rea*. That condition might also be lacking if he were subject to *force majeure*—i.e., if he were confronted by an event which prevented him from taking a decision and he had to obey an order'.[859]

Although Scelle and Yepes shared the opinion that the doctrine of absolute liability reflected in the Principle drafted by Spiropoulos was not satisfactory, there is in fact an hiatus between the conception of Scelle, who articulated what we have termed the *mens rea* principle, and the attitude of Yepes, who advocated the doctrine of *respondeat superior*. Nevertheless, Yepes was ready to content himself with Scelle's proposal and forsake the doctrine of *respondeat superior*, for at a later stage he officially suggested amending the Principle in question by inserting the words: 'or he may be acquitted' before the final proviso: 'if justice so requires'.[860] This addition would have empowered the court to take the fact of obedience to orders into consideration for the purposes of exemption from responsibility, if justice so required, but on no account would it have transformed obedience to orders into an *a priori* defence.

At the last moment, Yepes withdrew his amendment in favour of another that had been introduced in the meantime by Brierly, when he found out that most of the members of the Commission did not see any distinction between the two.[861] Brierly's proposal was that the Commission adopt the words of the International Military Tribunal and add to the Principle under discussion, at the end of the first sentence, the following stipulation:

> 'provided a moral choice was in fact possible to him'.[862]

Cf. also the statement made by the Brazilian delegate, Amado, in the Sixth Committee of the General Assembly (*op. cit.*, p. 133).

858. See *supra*, pp. 109–110.
859. *I.L.C. Yearbook*, 1950, vol. 1, p. 42.
860. *Ibid.*, p. 45.
861. *Ibid.*, p. 47.
862. *Ibid.*, pp. 43, 46. Cf. Maunoir, *op. cit.*, p. 235.

This proposal was put forward on the basis of, and in response to, the criticism of Yepes, all of whose darts, aimed at Spiropoulos' draft, were centred on the point of compulsion. We have already remarked[863] that not in every case of compulsion is a person divested of moral choice, for by this test it is the moral standpoint which determines when a person has no choice. This particular apparently escaped the attention of Cordova, who opposed Brierly's proposal on the ground that, if a soldier receives an order to torture a prisoner-of-war, for example, he

> 'must act rightly even if it meant losing his life'.[864]

When a prisoner-of-war is tortured, even under compulsion, there is no room, morally speaking, for equanimity, and one cannot refer to lack of moral choice. Cordova's objection, therefore, fails to expose any inherent weakness in the Brierly amendment. The vulnerable spot in the amendment is revealed in a completely different aspect of it: whereas it is obvious that in appropriate cases of compulsion the amendment permits discharge from responsibility, it is not at all clear whether it also relates to additional facets of lack of *mens rea*. Scelle, admittedly, as we have seen, sought to broaden the purview of the discussion so as to embrace the whole province of *mens rea*, but the rest of the Commission's members did not follow suit. None of them even addressed himself directly to the problem involved in the commission of an offence owing to a combination of obedience to orders and mistake of law or fact.[865] If the Brierly amendment is taken only as a solution of the questions that arose in the course of the Commission's deliberations, there is no reason to apply it to the subject of mistake. We have seen, as it is, that the moral choice test in the Nuremberg judgment is sometimes understood to be applicable to the whole field of *mens rea*, but generally it is confined within the bounds of the defence of compulsion.[866]

Brierly constructed his amendment in such a way that the possibility of moral choice constitutes a condition of the exclusion of obedience to orders as an element that brings about the discharge of the defendant from responsibility. Hence, if the condition is not

863. See *supra*, p. 152.
864. *I.L.C. Yearbook*, 1950, vol. 1, p. 43.
865. Contrariwise, Alfaro, for instance, stated in the course of the discussions: 'even the most ignorant person in the civilized world could judge whether an act was criminal or not' (*ibid.*, p. 45). If this is the case, the defence of mistake of law is groundless.
866. See *supra*, pp. 153–154. It is noteworthy that the French version of the Brierly amendment reads: 'si elle a eu moralement la faculté de choisir'. As we have observed (*ibid.*), the term 'faculty of choice (faculté de choisir)' may relate also to the subject of mistake.

fulfilled, that is, if no moral choice is possible, the fact of obedience to orders should not be excluded, namely, it should be taken into account, as a factor in the exemption from responsibility. Here, however, a certain logical difficulty faces us: from the formulation of the amended Principle it appears as if one should first consider whether moral choice was possible, and only later, insofar as it transpires that no such choice was possible, may the fact of obedience to orders be taken into account for the purpose of acquitting the defendant. But the moment we reach the conclusion that no moral choice was possible, what do we need the further plea of obedience to orders for? In any event, the defendant should be acquitted forthwith in such a case. If the plea of obedience to orders is to be invoked at all, there is sense in it only while the possibility of moral choice is being weighed, and not subsequent to such consideration and the resultant verdict. The Brierly amendment, therefore, must, in my opinion, be interpreted as permission to take the fact of obedience to orders into account—in conjunction with the other circumstances of the case—right at the first stage, to wit, during the determination of the possibility of moral choice.

Brierly explained that the amendment that he was proposing was based on the Nuremberg judgment,[867] and presumably he meant that not only its wording but also its essence and substance were derived from the pronouncement of the Tribunal. If that is so, it indicates that Brierly would not accept my suggested interpretation of the moral choice test in the judgment,[868] according to which the fact of obedience to orders cannot by any means be considered for the purposes of discharge from responsibility, either as a defence *per se* or within the compass of another defence, and the defendant cannot be acquitted on the ground of this test unless the other circumstances of the case, without any relation to the fact of obedience to orders, justify it. Instead of drawing a line that would separate and differentiate between the defence of lack of moral choice and the fact of obedience to orders, Brierly amalgamated them. It follows that he construed the Nuremberg judgment—in keeping with the view endorsed by the majority of jurists,[869] which I do not share—as denying to the fact of obedience to orders the status of a defence *per se*, but, in conformity with the principles of general international law as expounded above, allowing that it should be taken into account as a factual element within the bounds of the defence of lack of moral choice.

As usual, however, this line of thought is not universal. In the

867. *I.L.C. Yearbook*, 1950, vol. 1, p. 46.
868. See *supra*, p. 150.
869. See *supra*, pp. 150–151.

course of the debates of the International Law Commission, el-Khoury interpreted the Brierly amendment as follows:

> 'Mr. Brierly sub-divided the question. There was first of all superior order. Secondly, there was the moral choice open to the person committing the act... The true criterion of criminal responsibility had nothing to do with orders received, but lay in moral liberty and the possibility of choice on the part of the person committing the act alleged. The judgment could be interpreted in this sense'.[870]

With the last portion of the passage, stating that this is the proper way to construe the Nuremberg judgment, I wholeheartedly concur, all the more so in view of the fact that el-Khoury here reiterated the French version of the judgment almost literally;[871] but I fail to comprehend how that same explanation is ascribed, in the first part of the passage, to the Brierly amendment as well. The opinion that under the amendment it is permissible to take the fact of obedience to orders into consideration within the ambit of the defence of lack of moral choice was expressed by Brierly himself, who observed:

> 'The Nürnberg Tribunal had applied the principle recognized by all systems of criminal law and by all courts that the perpetrator of an act was not responsible for it and should be acquitted if he did not possess moral freedom not to perpetrate it, that was to say, if he had no choice. Many circumstances might deprive a person of moral freedom or choice. The person might be mad, might act under compulsion, or in pursuance of an order which he could not disobey. In many cases the order of a superior completely deprived the person of moral freedom'.[872]

It is worthwhile, however, to point out that Brierly did not construct his statement in a satisfactory form. He seems to have enumerated three distinct categories of lack of moral choice: (a) insanity; (b) compulsion; (c) obedience to orders. We shall disregard, for the purpose of this discussion, the first category, which is of no interest at all to us within the scope of this study. As for the two other categories, they are not on an equal footing. Compulsion may, under certain conditions, constitute a legitimate defence. Obedience to orders can never constitute a defence *per se*, and that was, undoubtedly, laid down by the Nuremberg judgment; it can only serve as a factual element that may, or may not, be taken into account in the context of a legitimate defence, like compulsion, resting on the infrastructure of lack of moral choice. One must, consequently, beware of equal treatment of obedience to orders and compulsion, at least when the standard of the Nuremberg judgment is brandished aloft.

Now that we have seen how Brierly harmonized his amendment

870. *I.L.C. Yearbook*, 1950, vol. 1, p. 46.
871. See *supra*, p. 149.
872. *I.L.C. Yearbook*, 1950, vol. 1, p. 288.

with the Nuremberg judgment, we ought to inquire into the relationship between the amendment and the provision of Article 8 of the London Charter. One of the proponents of the amendment in the Commission, Hudson, suggested the following answer to this query:

> 'Mr. Brierly's proposal was based on the judgment, which mitigated the severity of the Charter'.[873]

As pointed out above, the explicit wording of the judgment demonstrates that the Tribunal had no intention whatever to depart from the stipulation of Article 8 or to take the edge off it; though we have noticed that the view that this is precisely what the Tribunal did is not uncommon.[874] But, in any case, that opinion was not subscribed to by Brierly himself, as he stated that

> 'it was not correct to say that the Nürnberg Tribunal had modified the provisions of the Charter. The Tribunal had merely extracted from the provisions of the Charter conclusions universally accepted in criminal law'.[875]

Brierly's contention that in his amendment he only gave expression to the London Charter and to the Nuremberg judgment as they were was contested by the chief opponent of the amendment in the Commission, the Special Rapporteur Spiropoulos, who argued as follows:

> 'He had been greatly puzzled as to the sense of the passage quoted by Mr. Brierly.[876] For a while he had interpreted the passage as Mr. Brierly interpreted it. But a thorough study of the text of the judgment had brought to light two passages[877] ... Those passages were quite categorical. They stated that article 8 of the Charter prohibited the doctrine of superior orders being used as a defence. That meant that Principle IV must not be given a different sense from article 8 of the Charter. Mr. Pella, ... with whom he had had a long conversation, had reached the same conclusion ... what was involved was degree of responsibility and not absolute defence'.[878]

If I understand this statement correctly, Spiropoulos' proposition was that the moral choice test in the Nuremberg judgment relates merely to the question of mitigation of punishment, and not to that of full discharge from responsibility. I have already submitted above[879] that such a construction of the ruling of the International

873. *Ibid.*, p. 46.
874. See *supra*, p. 151 and note 492.
875. *I.L.C. Yearbook*, 1950, vol. 1, p. 288.
876. The passage concerned is the excerpt from the judgment of the International Military Tribunal at Nuremberg, which relates to the moral choice test. See *supra*, p. 147.
877. These are the two passages appearing in that part of the Nuremberg judgment which deals with the defendants Keitel and Jodl. See *supra*, p. 147.
878. *I.L.C. Yearbook*, 1950, vol. 1, p. 46. Already in his report, Spiropoulos had said of the moral choice test in the Nuremberg judgment that it pertains to the question of the 'degree of responsibility' (Spiropoulos, 'Principles', p. 193).
879. See *supra*, p. 149.

Military Tribunal is untenable. Spiropoulos himself, as he admitted in the beginning of the statement quoted, had initially comprehended the judgment in an entirely different way and had regarded the moral choice test as relevant to the problem of exemption from responsibility and not only to that of assessment of punishment. A good illustration of the previous state of his mind may be found in his observation, as delegate for Greece, in the course of the debate in the Sixth Committee of the General Assembly on the subject of genocide.[880] The two passages in the judgment that brought about his conversion do indeed reject obedience to orders as a defence, but they are not linked to the moral choice test. Admittedly, Brierly misinterpreted the enunciation of the Nuremberg Tribunal with regard to moral choice. But, in my opinion, his mistake was that he did not perceive that the Tribunal had excluded the possibility of considering the fact of obedience to orders—within the purview of the moral choice test—for defence purposes. When Brierly regarded the Tribunal's pronouncement as pertaining to the root of the problem of criminal responsibility, and not to the question of alleviation of punishment, I believe that he did hit the target. Even Pella, consultation with whom Spiropoulos had adduced in support, did not show any tendency to construe the judgment in line with Spiropoulos' interpretation when he presented a memorandum of his own to the International Law Commission.[881] Moreover, in a memorandum that he submitted to another body of the United Nations on the subject of the establishment of an International Criminal Court, Pella proposed to include the following Article (No. 58) as a part of the Statute of the Court:

> '(1) Neither the command of the law nor instructions of the legitimate authority may be treated as exonerating circumstances.
>
> '(2) If justice so requires, the Court may reduce the penalty by applying the principle of attenuating circumstances. The Court may entirely exonerate a defendant from all liability in cases of *force majeure* or irresistible coercion'.[882]

And in his explanatory note, Pella based the final portion of this Article, dealing with absolute discharge from responsibility, on the statement of the Nuremberg Tribunal in respect of moral choice.[883]

Parenthetically, we might as well note here that Spiropoulos' opposition to the Brierly amendment was only predicated on the ground of the construction of the London Charter and the Nuremberg

880. See *supra*, p. 222.
881. See Pella, 'Mémorandum' (A/CN.4/39), *I.L.C. Yearbook*, 1950, vol. 2, pp. 278–362 at p. 326.
882. Pella, 'Memorandum concerning the Establishment of an International Criminal Court', 17 July 1951 (A/AC.48/3), p. 121.
883. *Ibid.*, p. 122.

judgment, because for himself, irrespective of the Nuremberg precedent, Spiropoulos was also of opinion that obedience to orders should play a part in the imposition of criminal responsibility, and not only in the evaluation of the punishment.[884]

At first, several members of the International Law Commission sounded as if they were convinced by Spiropoulos' argument that the Brierly amendment was out of place in the Nuremberg Principles.[885] But ultimately the view prevailed that there was no reason to interpret the moral choice test in the Nuremberg judgment as pertaining only to the question of alleviation of punishment.[886] By a majority of six to three the Commission decided to adopt the Brierly amendment.[887]

Towards the close of the Commission's session, it was resolved further to amend Principle IV by deleting the sentence that deals with mitigation of punishment, for the members held the view that it was no longer necessary to mention this possibility expressly after total acquittal of the defendant had been allowed on the basis of lack of moral choice.[888] In its Report to the UN General Assembly, the Commission explained that the question of leniency in punishment should be determined by the competent court.[889] The Commission also, at the last moment, substituted the verb 'free', that had been used by Spiropoulos in his proposal in the pattern of the wording of Article 8 of the London Charter, by the verb 'relieve'.[890] Principle IV consequently reads, in its final form, as follows:

> 'The fact that a person acted pursuant to order of his Government or of a superior does not relieve him from responsibility under international law, provided a moral choice was in fact possible to him'.[891]

In its Report to the General Assembly, the Commission added the

884. We shall see that clearly below, when we get to the discussion of Spiropoulos' proposal regarding the Draft Code of Offences against the Peace and Security of Mankind, prepared at the same time. Spiropoulos himself emphasized the fact in the course of the exchange of views in the Commission on the Brierly amendment. See *I.L.C. Yearbook*, 1950, vol. 1, p. 47.
885. See *ibid.*, pp. 43–45.
886. See e.g. Hudson's observation, *ibid.*, p. 46.
887. *Ibid.*, p. 47. Cf. Maunoir, *op. cit.*, p. 235.
888. *I.L.C. Yearbook*, 1950, vol. 1, p. 288. It is interesting that this deletion was overlooked by Sohn in his note 'International Criminal Law', *A.B.A.J.*, vol. 36 (1950), pp. 683–684 at p. 683.
889. Report of the I.L.C., 2nd Session, *op. cit.*, p. 375. Lauterpacht severely criticized this explanatory note and maintained that the Commission's decision to delete the stipulation in respect of mitigation of punishment had been based on 'a misconception of the nature of the judicial function' (Lauterpacht – Oppenheim, *International Law*, vol. 2 (7th ed., 1952), p. 568 n. 1).
890. *I.L.C. Yearbook*, 1950, vol. 1, p. 288.
891. Report of the I.L.C., 2nd Session, *op. cit.*, p. 375.

following explanatory note to the Principle that it formulated:

> 'This text is based on the principle contained in Article 8 of the Charter of the Nürnberg Tribunal as interpreted in the judgment. The idea expressed in Principle IV is that superior orders are not a defence provided a moral choice was possible to the accused'.[892]

Thus, the Commission made it clear that it did not intend to abandon Article 8 of the Charter of the International Military Tribunal, but only construed it in the same way that it thought the judgment did. But this explanatory note is faulty and incorrectly drafted. Faulty, because actually the Commission did depart from the provision of Article 8[893] as well as from the judgment. Incorrectly drafted, because it is implied in the note that obedience to orders constitutes a defence *per se* in appropriate circumstances, namely, when no moral choice is possible. In point of fact, the defence that obtains, according to Principle IV, is the defence of lack of moral choice. The Principle as formulated rejects the fact of obedience to orders as a defence *per se*, but permits the taking of it into consideration within the scope of the defence of lack of moral choice.

When the Commission's Report came to be examined by the Sixth Committee of the General Assembly at its fifth session, opinions of delegates in respect of the formulation of Principle IV were sharply divided. Nevertheless, it should be stressed that only one delegate ventured to dispute the essence of the Principle and explicitly to propound that obedience to orders creates on occasion an automatic defence. This was the Dutch delegate, Roling, who had previously been a member of the International Military Tribunal for the Far East, and who had given some expression, in his dissenting opinion, to the conception of blind discipline.[894] In the Sixth Committee, Roling observed:

> 'an "order... of a superior", although properly excluded as a defence in article 8 of the charter of Nürnberg, should not be ruled out for people who did not belong to the small group of leaders to whom the provisions of the charter applied'.[895]

He particularly stressed that, from the viewpoint of criminal responsibility, one cannot compare the positions of the private and the general who act in compliance with superior orders.[896] In these arguments Roling was isolated in the Sixth Committee. For the rest

892. *Ibid.*
893. Cf. Liang, 'Notes', p. 521.
894. See *supra*, pp. 158–159.
895. G.A., O.R., 5th Session, 6th Committee, p. 137. Cf. Spiropoulos, 'Code (2nd Report)', p. 52.
896. G.A., O.R., 5th Session, *op. cit.*, p. 137.

of the delegates the bone of contention lay in the Brierly amendment, as adopted by the International Law Commission. There were those who justified the amendment and upheld it,[897] among them even Spiropoulos, representing Greece.[898] On the other hand, there were those who criticized the amendment and preferred a reversion to the original text of Article 8 of the London Charter.[899] And several contended that the term 'moral choice' is ambiguous and equivocal.[900]

It should be noted that one of the opponents of the Brierly amendment, the Polish delegate Lachs, based his objection on the following ground:

> 'the formula on moral choice . . . omitted any mention of the self-imposed duty of self-sacrifice which is necessary when the choice is between the life of one individual and the life of hundreds or thousands of human beings'.[901]

This is, in fact, the argument that had already been presented by Cordova against the Brierly amendment during the deliberations of the International Law Commission; and, as we have remarked, there is no substance in the argument, for it is not in every case of compulsion that a person is deprived of moral choice: it is the moral standpoint that determines when a person has no choice.

Whereas Lachs voiced the apprehension that every case of compulsion falls within the range of the Brierly amendment, Amado, the Brazilian delegate, apparently held the view that the amendment did not apply at all to the subject-matter of compulsion, for he maintained:

> 'The fact that an order had been given could relieve the executant from responsibility only when such responsibility existed. Where there was absolute

897. See the statements made by the following delegates: the Brazilian, Amado—G.A., O.R., 5th Session, *op. cit.*, p. 133; the Iranian, Abdoh—*ibid.*, p. 160; and the Belgian, Glabbeke—*ibid.*, p. 163. Cf. Spiropoulos, 'Code (2nd Report)', pp. 52–53. It is noteworthy that the Belgian delegate supported Principle IV, as formulated by the Commission, although he interpreted the moral choice test in the Nuremberg judgment as relating only to the question of mitigation of punishment (G.A., O.R., 5th Session, *op. cit.*, p. 163).
898. G.A., O.R., 5th Session, *op. cit.*, p. 154. Cf. Spiropoulos 'Code (2nd Report)', p. 52.
899. See the statements made by the following delegates: the Chinese, Hsu—G.A., O.R., 5th Session, *op. cit.*, p. 164; the Israeli, Robinson—*ibid.*, p. 175; the Pole, Lachs—*ibid.*, p. 178; and the Czech, Gottlieb—*ibid.*, p. 188. Cf. Spiropoulos, 'Code (2nd Report)', p. 53.
900. See the statements made by the following delegates: the Dutch, Roling—G.A., O.R., 5th Session, *op. cit.*, p. 138; the British, Fitzmaurice—*ibid.*, p. 144; the Yugoslav, Bartos—*ibid.*, p. 150; and the Czech, Gottlieb—*ibid.*, p. 188. Cf. Spiropoulos, 'Code (2nd Report)', p. 52. Cf. also Liang, 'Notes', p. 521; Pompe, *op. cit.*, p. 333.
901. G.A., O.R., 5th Session, *op. cit.*, p. 178. Cf. Spiropoulos, 'Code (2nd Report)', p. 53.

compulsion, people could not be relieved from responsibility because they had none'.[902]

To what, then, did the amendment apply? Amado opined that Principle IV corresponds to the provision that the commission of experts of the Red Cross had proposed to insert in the Geneva Conventions of 1949; and we have already seen that this provision disposes of the problem of obedience to orders mainly on the foundation of the defence of mistake.[903] But to my mind Amado's proposition will not hold water. Unlike the proposal of the commission of experts, Principle IV applies, and was designed to apply, particularly, and perhaps exclusively, in certain cases of compulsion; and there is ample proof for that in the discussions of the International Law Commission.[904] Whatever doubt there is belongs to the question whether Principle IV is also applicable to the subject of mistake.[905]

Ultimately, the General Assembly declined to affirm the formulation of the Nuremberg Principles as drafted by the Commission. Instead, it invited the Governments of Member-States in the Organization to furnish their observations on the text of the Principles, and requested the Commission, in preparing the Draft Code of Offences against the Peace and Security of Mankind, to take into account both the observations that would be received from the Governments and the comments already made during the fifth session of the General Assembly by delegations.[906]

In pursuance of this Resolution, several Governments furnished their observations on Principle IV.[907] Thus the Lebanese Government assailed the omission from the text of the sentence dealing with

902. G.A., O.R., 5th Session, *op. cit.*, p. 133.
903. See *ibid.* and *supra*, p. 224.
904. It is odd that a member of the Commission like Amado, of all people, should err in this regard.
905. It is interesting here to quote Pilloud's observation relating to Article 4 of the Draft Code of Offences against the Peace and Security of Mankind of 1951 (an Article which—as we shall see below— is identical, in all material respects, with Principle IV): 'Les conclusions de la Commission du Droit international se rapprochent des propositions du Comité international de la Croix-Rouge ... La Commission du Droit international a préféré la notion de la possibilité du choix morale, notion plus vaste puisqu'elle couvre non seulement les cas où l'inculpé a commis une erreur de droit, mais aussi ceux dans lesquels il a agi sous une contrainte morale et physique' (Pilloud, *op. cit.*, p. 16. Cf. Maunoir, *op. cit.*, p. 235).
906. Resolution 488(V), 'Formulation of the Nürnberg Principles', 12 December 1950, Resolutions Adopted by the General Assembly, 5th Session (A/1775), p. 77.
907. Observations of Governments of Member States of the United Nations relating to the Formulation of the Nürnberg Principles Prepared by the International Law Commission, 19 April 1951 (A/CN.4/45 and addenda), *I.L.C. Yearbook*, 1951, vol. 2, pp. 104–109.

mitigation of punishment;[908] and the Norwegian Government made the following suggestion:

> 'the words "provided a moral choice was in fact possible to him" ought to be deleted. If this reservation is intended to cover cases of duress affecting the wrongdoer's free volition to such an extent that the act cannot be held against him under criminal law, the words seem superfluous... If, on the other hand, the coercion exercised did not have the character above described, the generally recognized principles of criminal law would not seem to afford sufficient grounds for acquittal'.[909]

The Norwegian observation is entirely justified inasmuch as it indicates that the real defence is that of compulsion and not of obedience to orders. But it is rather strange to contend that the proviso relating to moral choice is superfluous if it corresponds to the generally recognized principles of law. The contention of superfluity would have been more consistent had it applied to the whole Article on the subject of obedience to orders, and not only to the moral choice proviso. For if there is no sense in a transformation of general principles of law into *lex scripta*, then not only the moral choice proviso, but also the nucleus of the provision, excluding obedience to orders as a defence *per se*, is redundant. Insofar as it is regarded as necessary to commit to paper the general rule regarding obedience to orders, so as to remove doubts and avoid disputes and controversies in the future, this should be done with the whole rule, provisos and reservations included, and not only with selected parts of it. On the assumption that the moral choice proviso is in conformity with the general principles of law, it is difficult to find any reason for its deletion from the text of Principle IV.

3. THE DRAFT CODE OF OFFENCES AGAINST THE PEACE AND SECURITY OF MANKIND

As we have seen, General Assembly Resolution 177(II) assigned to the International Law Commission the task to prepare, in conjunction with the formulation of the Nuremberg Principles, a Draft Code of Offences against the Peace and Security of Mankind. We have also observed that at its first session, in 1949, the Commission appointed Spiropoulos as a Special Rapporteur on this subject—as well as on the linked subject of the Nuremberg Principles—to prepare a working paper on the Draft Code.[910] In the paper that Spiropoulos submitted to the Commission in April 1950, the following

908. *Ibid.*, p. 107.
909. *Ibid.*, p. 105.
910. See *supra*, p. 229, as well as Spiropoulos, 'Code (1st Report)', p. 257.

provision was suggested as Basis of Discussion No. 3:

> '[The fact that a person acted under command of the law or pursuant to superior order may be taken into consideration either as a defence or in mitigation of punishment if justice so requires]'.[911]

Spiropoulos was afraid that any solution of the problem of obedience to orders might be controversial, and perhaps even endanger the adoption of the Draft Code as a whole,[912] and hence he decided to place the provision between brackets. Alternatively, he proposed that the Commission follow the precedent of the Genocide Convention and refrain from incorporating in the Code any stipulation whatever on the matter of compliance with orders.[913]

Spiropoulos' proposal bears a resemblance to the first American drafts of April–June 1945—on the eve of the London Conference—of Article 8 of the Charter of the International Military Tribunal.[914] Like them, it allows of taking the fact of obedience to orders into consideration for the purpose of acquitting the defendant, when justice so requires. But we have observed that the drafts excluded obedience to orders as a defence *per se*, and permitted the taking of it into account only as a factual aspect of another defence. Spiropoulos, on the other hand, phrased his proposal in a different form, so that it seems to imply that in certain circumstances, that is, when justice so requires, the fact of submission to orders may constitute a defence *per se*. The question arises whether this was indeed what he meant or only an outcome of an imperfect or incautious drafting.

Spiropoulos regarded his proposal as a clear-cut departure from the rule that had been enunciated in the Charter and in the judgment of the International Military Tribunal and was contemporaneously formulated by him within the compass of the Nuremberg Principles.[915] In an explanatory note he stated:

> 'Though it is not agreeable to depart, a few years only after the Nürnberg trial from a rule established by the Nürnberg Charter,[916] we do not hesitate to suggest a solution which would not exclude superior order as a defence'.[917]

There is no doubt that Spiropoulos wanted to discard the un-

911. Spiropoulos, 'Code (1st Report)', p. 278.
912. *Ibid.*, p. 272.
913. *Ibid.* With regard to the Genocide Convention, see *supra*, p. 223.
914. See *supra*, pp. 109–110. Spiropoulos himself cited one of the American drafts in his report (Spiropoulos, 'Code (1st Report)', p. 271).
915. See *supra*, pp. 229, 236–237.
916. It should be noted that even though, in this passage, Spiropoulos did not mention the Nuremberg Tribunal, but only the Charter, in a previous paragraph he stated: 'The rule of article 8 of the Charter, according to which superior order is no defence, was applied in the same way by the Nürnberg Tribunal' (Spiropoulos, 'Code (1st Report)', p. 272).
917. *Ibid.*

compromising rule expressed in the Nuremberg trial and to authorize the consideration of the factor of obedience to orders for defence purposes. But why did he see fit to establish that the fact of obedience to orders may constitute a defence *per se*? In another passage, when he sought dogmatically to analyze the effect of obedience to orders, he stated:

> 'Actually, this was the main argument of the defendants in the war crime trials. They alleged that if they had not obeyed they would have been shot or otherwise punished'.[918]

And if that was the reason for the new rule that he formulated, it seems that the remedy he found is not commensurate with the affliction that he wished to cure. The problem that troubled him was, as implied in the last quotation, that of compulsion, under which soldiers obey unlawful orders. But, to solve this problem, there was no need to ascribe to the fact of obedience to orders the standing of a defence *per se*. It would have sufficed to provide that, contrary to what had been laid down in the London Charter and in the Nuremberg judgment, this fact may be taken into account, as an admissible circumstance, within the ambit of the defence of compulsion.

It is not inconceivable that Spiropoulos was simply not careful enough in the formulation of his draft, and that he did not realize that he was attaching to the fact of submission to orders a label which it does not merit, that of a defence *per se*. This view is borne out when one examines his oral observations in the course of the deliberations of the International Law Commission. When his proposal came up for discussion by the Commission at its second session, in 1950, the decision had already been taken to incorporate the Brierly amendment in the phrasing of Nuremberg Principle No. IV. In the light of this development, Hudson expressed the opinion that it would be better if the Special Rapporteur redrafted Basis of Discussion No. 3 to bring it into line with the terms used by the Commission in that Principle.[919] It will be recalled that Principle IV, as amended at Brierly's suggestion, excludes the fact of obedience to orders as a defence *per se*, but permits of its being taken into consideration as a circumstantial element within the bounds of the defence of lack of moral choice. Spiropoulos' reaction to Hudson's proposal is, therefore, most illuminating:

> 'Mr. Spiropoulos accepted Mr. Hudson's suggestion that Basis of Discussion No. 3 should be worded in accordance with the exact terms of the Nürnberg

918. *Ibid.*
919. *I.L.C. Yearbook*, 1950, vol. 1, p. 154.

> Principles as formulated by the Commission, although he considered the two texts substantially the same'.[920]

The last words here are particularly significant: the draft prepared by Spiropoulos is substantially identical, in the opinion of its author, with Nuremberg Principle No. IV. If that is the case, then inasmuch as this draft, unlike the Principle in question, recognizes obedience to orders as a defence *per se*, this may not be indicative of the actual intention of the author.

Spiropoulos' Basis of Discussion was transmitted to a Drafting Sub-Committee, whose members were he himself, Hudson and Alfaro, and there it underwent certain changes to read (Article III):

> 'The fact that a person acted under the orders of a Government or a superior does not relieve him from responsibility for committing a crime under international law, provided a moral choice was in fact possible to him; but this fact may be considered in mitigation of punishment'.[921]

This is an almost literal repetition of the text of Principle IV, as it then stood, that is, before the Commission decided, on the eve of the closure of the session, to delete from it the stipulation relating to alleviation of punishment.[922]

Without discussing this new draft, the Commission referred it to the Special Rapporteur, who was requested to continue his work and submit a further report on the subject of the Draft Code at the next session.[923] In this second report of April 1951, Spiropoulos took into account the critical views expressed during the debates of the Sixth Committee of the General Assembly concerning Nuremberg Principle No. IV, and proposed to supersede the Sub-Committee's draft by the following provision (Article II):

> 'The fact that a person charged with a crime defined in this code acted under the orders of a government or a superior may be taken into consideration either as a defence or in mitigation of punishment if justice so requires'.[924]

Thus, Spiropoulos refrained from using here the moral choice proviso, which had been the main target of the attack in the Sixth Committee, and reverted, in substance, to the draft that he had proposed as a Basis of Discussion in the preceding year.[925]

920. *Ibid.*, p. 155.
921. *Ibid.*, p. 258, note.
922. See *supra*, p. 237.
923. See Report of the I.L.C., 2nd Session, *op. cit.*, p. 380. Cf. Spiropoulos, 'Code (2nd Report)', p. 44.
924. Spiropoulos, 'Code (2nd Report)', p. 60.
925. In his explanatory note Spiropoulos maintained that 'The above text corresponds to article 8 of the charter of the International Military Tribunal' (*ibid.*). The use of the verb 'correspond' in this sentence is not especially apt, and that was also commented upon by members of the International Law Commission

When this new-but-familiar proposal came before the Commission, gusts of amendment and revision began to blow around it. The beginning was modest: François suggested that the qualifying term 'only' be inserted before the final condition: 'if justice so requires', and with Spiropoulos' consent the amendment was adopted.[926] At a later stage, Hudson, supported by Brierly in the chair, proposed to delete the words: 'either... or in mitigation of punishment', for, as he looked upon it,

> 'the court could always decide to reduce the penalty, but... it was not for the Commission to introduce that idea into the code'.[927]

This time the amendment encountered opposition, but ultimately the view of its advocates prevailed and it was carried by a majority vote.[928] Now Hudson advised replacing the whole modified last portion of the Article, which at this juncture read: 'may be taken into consideration as a defence only if justice so requires', by the following sentence:

> 'does not relieve him from responsibility if a moral choice was in fact possible to him'.[929]

The purpose of the proposal was obvious: to make the text of the Article conform to the language used by the Commission when it had formulated Nuremberg Principle No. IV. The members of the Commission were, of course, well aware of the criticism to which the moral choice proviso had been subjected in the Sixth Committee of the General Assembly, but most of them were not convinced by the strictures, and saw no reason to depart, within the phrasing of the Draft Code, from a term that they had coined in Principle IV.[930] By a majority of nine votes to two, the Commission decided to revert to the use of the moral choice proviso, by adopting Hudson's amendment.[931]

Accordingly, Article 4 of the Draft Code of Offences against the Peace and Security of Mankind, as formulated by the Commission in 1951, provides:

(*I.L.C. Yearbook*, 1951, vol. 1, p. 80). In fact what Spiropoulos had in mind here was a formal correspondence (in the subject of the discussion) between Article 8 and his proposal, and not a material correspondence (in the content); and this is clarified by the statements that he made during the debates of the Commission (*ibid.*, pp. 60, 80).

926. *I.L.C. Yearbook*, 1951, vol. 1, p. 80.
927. *Ibid.*, p. 240.
928. *Ibid.*
929. *Ibid.*, pp. 240–241.
930. See *ibid.*, pp. 240–242, 245–246.
931. See *ibid.*, p. 241.

> 'The fact that a person charged with an offence defined in this Code acted pursuant to order of his government or of a superior does not relieve him from responsibility, provided a moral choice was in fact possible to him'.[932]

This Article reproduces, in all material respects, the provision of Nuremberg Principle No. IV, and it must be construed in the same way: it excludes obedience to orders as a defence *per se*, and allows consideration of that fact within the structure of the defence of lack of moral choice.[933] The text of the Article—and of the Principle—is consequently much preferable to that proposed by Spiropoulos in his drafts, which imply that in certain circumstances the fact of obedience to orders constitutes a defence *per se*.

In its Report to the General Assembly, the Commission expounded its decision as follows:

> 'The observations on Principle IV, made in the General Assembly during its fifth session, have been carefully studied; no substantial modification, however, has been made in the drafting of this article, which is based on a clear enunciation by the Nürnberg Tribunal. The article lays down the principle that the accused is responsible only if, in the circumstances, it was possible for him to act contrary to superior orders'.[934]

With regard to this explanation, it should be remarked, first of all, that, although the moral choice proviso was terminologically derived from the judgment of the International Military Tribunal, its employment by the Commission, in my opinion, does not conform to the conception of the Tribunal in respect of obedience to orders, which is based on the doctrine of absolute liability; hence the enunciation of the Tribunal does not support the substance of the decision of the Commission. It should further be remarked, not without surprise, that the last part of the explanation deals with the possibility of action as a condition of responsibility and ignores the moral standpoint. On a strict interpretation, one may say that action is possible in every case in which a person is not physically forced—by external power—to act in an opposite way; a threat, even one of

932. Report of the I.L.C., 3rd Session, *I.L.C. Yearbook*, 1951, vol. 2, pp. 123–144 at p. 137. This final text contains several stylistic modifications—in comparison with the original proposal of Spiropoulos and Hudson's amendment—that have not been dwelt upon in detail, but their principal aim was to unify as far as possible the terminology of Article 4 and that of Nuremberg Principle No. IV.

933. Not all scholars display caution when analyzing the provision of Article 4. Young, for instance, states: 'Article 4 provides that superior orders are no defense, provided that a moral choice was in fact possible' (Young, 'The 1951 Session of the International Law Commission', *A.B.A.J.*, vol. 37 (1951), pp. 850–851, 854 at pp. 851, 854). It would follow that, in the absence of a possibility of moral choice, obedience to orders does constitute a defence under Article 4. This, however, is not the case.

934. Report of the I.L.C., 3rd Session, *op. cit.*, p. 137.

death, does not exclude the possibility of action.[935] It follows that the explanatory note does not reflect all the cases in which Article 4 actually justifies discharge from responsibility. It may, of course, be argued that one should not construe the term 'possible' so meticulously, and that, when a person is confronted with a threat of death, he is in effect deprived of the possibility of action contrary to the threat. But, in that case, we reach the converse conclusion of opening the gates of exemption from responsibility to many offenders, in a way not envisaged by the text of Article 4. That is so because the explanation disregards the moral limitations that curtail the scope of action on the part of a person who is subjected to compulsion, and it implies that in every instance of obedience to orders out of compulsion, even when orders relating to mass murders are concerned, the defendant is not accountable for his act. It is very odd that the Commission found it necessary to furnish an 'explanation' that, instead of enabling us to gain further insight into Article 4, clouds the issues and veils them in doubt.

The question of the Draft Code was included in the provisional agenda of the General Assembly at its sixth session, in 1951, but the General Committee decided to recommend to the Plenary that the item be omitted from the final agenda and discussion be postponed to the next session, so that Governments of Member-States might be able to study the proposals of the International Law Commission in the meantime.[936] After this recommendation had been approved by the Plenary,[937] the Secretary-General addressed a circular letter to the Governments of Member-States, in which he drew their attention to the Draft Code and invited them to transmit their comments.[938] Again the question of the Draft Code was included in the provisional agenda of the General Assembly at its seventh session, in 1952, but once more the General Committee recommended omitting the item from the final agenda.[939] The recommendation was approved by the Plenary on the understanding that the matter would continue to be considered by the International Law Commission.[940] In view of this development, the Commission decided at

935. See *supra*, p. 152.

936. See G.A., O.R., 6th Session, General Committee (A/BUR/SR.75), p. 3; Report of the General Committee, 10 November 1951 (A/1950), para. 4.

937. See G.A., O.R., 6th Session, Plenary (A/PV.342), p. 96. Cf. Report of the I.L.C., 5th Session, *I.L.C. Yearbook*, 1953, vol. 2, pp. 200–269 at p. 231; Report of the I.L.C., 6th Session, *I.L.C. Yearbook*, 1954, vol. 2, pp. 140–173 at p. 149.

938. See Report of the I.L.C., 5th Session, *op. cit.*, p. 231; Report of the I.L.C., 6th Session, *op. cit.*, p. 149.

939. See G.A., O.R., 7th Session, General Committee (A/BUR/SR.79), p. 2; Report of the General Committee, 16 October 1952 (A/2225/Rev. 1), para. 5.

940. See G.A., O.R., 7th Session, Plenary (A/PV.382), p. 71. Cf. Report of the I.L.C., 5th Session, *op. cit.*, p. 231; Report of the I.L.C., 6th Session, *op. cit.*, p. 149.

its fifth session, in 1953, to instruct the Special Rapporteur, Spiropoulos, to undertake a further study of the subject and submit a new report.[941]

In his third report, of April 1954, Spiropoulos examined the comments that had been received from Governments in response to the request of the Secretary-General after the sixth session of the General Assembly.[942] In these observations, the Governments of the United Kingdom, Yugoslavia and Egypt reiterated the arguments against the use of the moral choice proviso in Article 4 of the Draft Code; but each of them had its own reasons: whereas the Yugoslav Government wished to revert to the text of Article 8 of the London Charter, the Governments of the United Kingdom and Egypt upheld the principle allowing the fact of obedience to orders to be taken into account for the purposes of relieving the defendant of responsibility, but they deplored the vagueness of the term 'moral choice'.[943] To overcome this difficulty, the British proposed to redraft Article 4 so that it would contain 'some of the phraseology' of the final sentence in the above-cited explanatory note of the Commission in its Report to the General Assembly.[944] I have already expressed criticism of that particular sentence in the explanatory note, which in no way makes it clear when action is possible[945] and disregards the moral limitations that curtail the use of the element of compulsion as an admissible defence. In my opinion, instead of improving the formulation of Article 4, the British proposal only impairs it. The same is true, in fact, with regard to the Egyptian proposal, which, in a more concrete way, brought out an alternative formulation to the moral choice proviso, as follows:

> 'provided that, in the existing circumstances, the possibility of acting contrary to such an order was open to him'.[946]

Assuming that the possibility of action contrary to the order does not exist in case of a threat of death, one cannot ignore the nature of the order and its consequences when the responsibility of the offender is evaluated.

941. See Report of the I.L.C., 5th Session, *op. cit.*, p. 231. Cf. Report of the I.L.C., 6th Session, *op. cit.*, p. 149.
942. Spiropoulos, 'Code (3rd Report)', *passim.*
943. See *ibid.*, pp. 28–29.
944. See Comment on the Draft Code of Offences against the Peace and Security of Mankind by the United Kingdom Government, 3 September 1952 (A/2162/Add.1), Sohn, *Cases on United Nations Law* (1956), pp. 990–998 at p. 997. Cf. Spiropoulos, 'Code (3rd Report)', p. 29.
945. The British conceded that the meaning of the term 'possible' in the sentence in question is not sufficiently clear (see and cf. *ibid.*).
946. See Spiropoulos, 'Code (3rd Report)', p. 28. Cf. Maunoir, *op. cit.*, p. 236.

A more constructive suggestion came from the Netherlands Government, which recommended inserting in the Article, after the words: 'does not relieve him from responsibility', the following condition:

> 'in case he could be aware of the criminal character of the act'.[947]

From a stylistic point of view, this addition is a little cumbersome; but at least it constitutes a new contribution to the discussions of the International Law Commission on the subject of obedience to orders, inasmuch as it sheds light on the aspect of mistake of law which had been neglected by the Commission.

In his proposals, Spiropoulos did not make allowance for the Netherlands recommendation, with all that it entails. The comments of the United Kingdom and Egypt were the ones that influenced his way of thinking, and in the same spirit as they he redrafted Article 4 to read:

> 'The fact that a person charged with an offence defined in this Code acted pursuant to order of his government or of a superior does not relieve him from responsibility in international law if, in the circumstances at the time, it was possible for him not to comply with such order'.[948]

This new formulation is faulty, just as are the British and Egyptian proposals, in that it omits the moral criterion, uses the obscure test of the possibility of action, and, as it seems, permits discharge from responsibility of persons accused of atrocities. It should be remarked, moreover, in the context of the problem raised by the Netherlands proposal, that, if the moral choice proviso could perhaps still be interpreted liberally to apply to the subject of mistake also, and not only to that of compulsion,[949] the new proviso is indubitably restricted to the exclusive bounds of compulsion.[950] Spiropoulos' draft cannot, therefore, be regarded as an improvement of the Draft Code.

When the new report of Spiropoulos came up for discussion by the Commission, Zourek said that he would prefer the wording of Article 4 to be identical with that of Article 8 of the London Charter.[951] Although Zourek did not particularly press in that direction, two of his colleagues rushed to the defence of the Special Rapporteur. Amado observed that allowance must be made for human weakness, and that not always can a person be expected to resist an order to perform an unlawful act.[952] Salamanca added his support for

947. See and cf. *ibid.*
948. Spiropoulos, 'Code (3rd Report)', p. 30.
949. See *supra*, note 905.
950. See Maunoir, *op. cit.*, p. 236.
951. *I.L.C. Yearbook*, 1954, vol. 1, p. 138.
952. *Ibid.*

Spiropoulos' proposal but explained himself in an original way:

> 'because it would not be reasonable to expect officials to be fully aware of the rules of international law'.[953]

In other words, Salamanca regarded the draft prepared by Spiropoulos as strengthened by the need to take into consideration the factor of mistake of law. This very reasoning, however, cuts the ground from under the proposed draft, which clearly, one might almost say explicitly, ignores the problem of mistake. How Salamanca could lump together Spiropoulos' draft and the subject of mistake of law evades comprehension.

After only a few minutes of debate on the new draft of Article 4, the Commission without objection, eight voting in favour and five abstaining, adopted the proposal of the Special Rapporteur.[954] The meeting at which this decision had been taken was not attended by Lauterpacht, and at a subsequent one he sought to turn back the legislative wheels.[955] Objecting vehemently to the Commission's decision, he stated:

> 'The second half of the sentence constituted a dangerously retrograde step. The defence was admissible in time of war, but not in time of peace. The draft code was, in fact, concerned primarily with peacetime conditions. Under the formulation as adopted the accused might escape punishment for the reason that "it was not possible for him" not to comply with the order for fear of losing his post, or forfeiting a chance of promotion, or displeasing his superiors, or incurring the odium of disobeying a decision of his party, and the like'.[956]

Nevertheless, after he had failed to obtain the required majority of two-thirds of the members of the Commission for reconsideration of a decision on another point, Lauterpacht withdrew his proposal to discuss Article 4 again.[957]

Even though, for reasons just spelt out, I share the opinion that the draft proposed by Spiropoulos and accepted by the Commission constitutes 'a dangerously retrograde step', I do not share Lauterpacht's objection to that draft. All the queries posed by Lauterpacht relate to the construction of the term 'possible' appearing in the Article. But the difficulty inherent in this term, as indicated above, is different: on the one hand, one may say that action contrary to an unlawful order is always possible in the absence of physical violence; as Johnson correctly defined it:

953. *Ibid.*
954. *Ibid.*
955. *Ibid.*, p. 151.
956. *Ibid.* Cf. *ibid.*, p. 195.
957. *Ibid.*, p. 152.

'it must always have been *possible* for the accused "not to comply with" the order—at the price, if need be, of a martyr's death'.[958]

And, on the other hand, the possibility of action cannot serve as a criterion without any moral limitations. But there is no reason, to my mind, to think, or to apprehend, that a court, interpreting the accepted draft in a sensible way, would establish that fear of losing a job, or unwillingness to forfeit a chance of promotion, deprives a person of the possibility of action. Lauterpacht's statement from the floor of the International Law Commission is nonetheless of the greatest import, not so much as illuminating the new Article 4 as indicating a significant change that occurred in the attitude of Lauterpacht himself. In holding that the defence based on compulsion is admissible in time of war, he appears to have altered his view again in respect of the availability of this defence to war criminals. His statement in the Commission is in conformity with his original approach to the subject as expressed in the article that he published in 1944, but it is incompatible with his later opinion as propounded in Oppenheim's treatise.[959]

In its final shape, Article 4 of the new Draft Code of Offences against the Peace and Security of Mankind, as formulated by the International Law Commission in 1954, provides:

'The fact that a person charged with an offence defined in this Code acted pursuant to an order of his Government or of a superior does not relieve him of responsibility in international law if, in the circumstances at the time, it was possible for him not to comply with that order'.[960]

In its Report to the General Assembly, the Commission explained the new stipulation in the following way:

'Since some Governments had criticized the expression "moral choice", the Commission decided to replace it by the wording of the new text'.[961]

The Commission refrained from dwelling upon the distinctions between the two drafts, and left the explanation at that.

The discussion on the Draft Code of 1954 has been postponed by the General Assembly of the United Nations *sine die*, owing to the impossibility of reaching a common denominator in the matter of the definition of the term 'aggression' appearing in the Draft.[962] The

958. Johnson, 'The Draft Code of Offences against the Peace and Security of Mankind', *I.C.L.Q.*, vol. 4 (1955), pp. 445–468 at p. 464.
959. See *supra*, pp. 78–79.
960. Report of the I.L.C., 6th Session, *op. cit.*, pp. 150, 152.
961. *Ibid.*, p. 151.
962. See Resolution 897(IX), 'Draft Code of Offences against the Peace and Security of Mankind', 4 December 1954, Resolutions Adopted by the General Assembly, 9th Session (A/2890), p. 50; Resolution 1186(XII), 'Draft Code of Offences against the Peace and Security of Mankind', 11 December 1957, Resolutions Adopted by the General Assembly, 12th Session (A/3805), pp. 51–52.

whole subject is consequently blanketed in a fog of unreality. Yet I think that it would not be out of place, after all the critical remarks made in this study with regard to the formulations of the International Law Commission, to suggest an alternative phrasing which might, I submit, answer the purpose:

> The fact that a defendant acted in obedience to superior orders shall not constitute a defence *per se*, but may be considered—in conjunction with other circumstances—within the scope of an admissible defence based on lack of *mens rea*.

CONCLUSIONS

I cannot help but conclude my study of the subject of obedience to superior orders in international law with some incertitude. Though, theoretically and logically, the solution of the problems raised by this subject seems to be clear and simple—that is, the fact of obedience to orders should be excluded as a defence *per se*, but permitted to be taken into account, among the other circumstances of the case, for the purpose of establishing a defence based on lack of *mens rea*—yet in practice, in the spheres of the cases and of international legislation, international law seems still to be haunted by the spectre of obedience to orders.

One thing, however, is not open to doubt: the doctrine of *respondeat superior* has proved to be a chimera and the number of those who preach it is lessening. On the other hand, there is an ever-rising trend not to fetter the principles of international law in this regard by the shackles of the opposite doctrine of absolute liability. If international law continues to develop in that direction, one may hope that in the not too distant future the cascading flow of the demands of life will sweep away dogmatic barriers and clear the path for pragmatic solutions.

SUBJECT INDEX

NAME INDEX

The manufacturer's authorised representative in the EU for product safety is Oxford University Press España S.A. of El Parque Empresarial San Fernando de Henares, Avenida de Castilla, 2 - 28830 Madrid (www.oup.es/en or product.safety@oup.com). OUP España S.A. also acts as importer into Spain of products made by the manufacturer.
Printed and bound by CPI Group (UK) Ltd, Croydon, CR0 4YY
12/09/2026
02215905-0005